CHOREOGRAPHY
BY GEORGE BALANCHINE

CHOREOGRAPHY
by
GEORGE BALANCHINE

A Catalogue of Works

THE EAKINS PRESS FOUNDATION
NEW YORK

Lyre by Pavel Tchelitchew from *Orpheus and Eurydice*, 1936
Epigraphs from an interview with Balanchine, 1978
Portrait by Tanaquil Le Clercq, 1952

Copyright © 1983
THE EAKINS PRESS FOUNDATION

☞

Library of Congress Catalog Card Number 82-83072
International Standard Book Number 0-87130-050-8

The eye of man hath not heard,
the ear of man hath not seen,
man's hand is not able to taste,
his tongue to conceive,
nor his heart to report,
what my dream was.

WILLIAM SHAKESPEARE

Eye hath not seen, nor ear heard,
neither have entered into the heart of man,
the things which God hath prepared
for them that love him.

SAINT PAUL

CONTENTS

A *printed listing of the works of George Balanchine may be set along-side the Köchel catalogue of Mozart: the works of choreographer and composer share many qualities.*

Balanchine has been extremely prolific. For over fifty years his invention has been uninterrupted. There has been hardly a season since he was a boy of eighteen when he has not brought out something new in the nature of dancing.

A catalogue is not a visualization, yet even a list demonstrates the extraordinary variety and inclusiveness of Balanchine's musical support and his unprecedented use of musical literature since the seventeenth century. A trained musician, he has been able to have always at his fingertips the quality of structure and sonority that fills his needs at a certain moment of development or necessity.

If he is to be compared with anyone in his time in the frame of his own talents, visual or plastic or musical, these must be Picasso and Stravinsky. Painting and musical composition, however, have had their universal acceptance for more than five hundred years, while classic academic dance, which issued from court-shows in the seventeenth century and court theaters in the nineteenth, has only in our own century begun to compete on an equal level of popularity with the repertories of opera and orchestra.

He has specialized in pièces d'occasion, creating musical celebrations. Certain events summon or suggest appropriate answers. He has operated on the order of public official as well as very private experimenter. He has been profligate in stage production when patronage was available, and parsimonious when decoration would have been superfluous or patronage was absent.

Balanchine issued from a school which inherited an imperial tradition. He left Russia at a time when the Soviet Union froze taste and attempted to stabilize artistic expression as a lowest common denominator. Entering the Diaghilev company in London at the age of twenty, he was plunged into an ambience of extreme artistic license for which he had prepared himself by student experiments even before leaving Leningrad. When Diaghilev died, five years later, Balanchine attempted to continue the formula of elegant improvisation with whatever means were at hand. Russia was closed, the Soviet schools were no longer a source for recruitment, and the efforts of European impresarios proved haphazard and without institutional stability.

Balanchine decided to come to the United States as if the decision was almost a foregone conclusion, although there were other possibilities which might have been attractive had he not already had the experience of the Diaghilev years. When he came to America late in 1933 he founded a school which would commence teaching American dancers, toward forming an eventual American company. The School of American Ballet was conceived to be a national service school like the Imperial School in St. Petersburg, which held parity with the military and naval academies.

The first company Balanchine organized was called the American Ballet. Balanchine's present company, founded in 1948, bears the name of the town that is its home, New York City, the cultural capital of the nation. The name of the school has remained the same. It is now a national service institution with students from forty states and more than a dozen nations. The city built Balanchine the theater he required. National foundations, recognizing their importance, gave his school and the New York City Ballet the support they needed.

His imperial ambitions as a servant of social democracy seem to have been fulfilled according to a logical schedule and a simple history. Reading the catalogue of his work, however, one may deduce some of the difficulties in the path, and along the way. The conditions of theatrical production, the size of companies, the presence or absence of patronage or money, the requirements of seasonal circumstance, all determine the state of repertory at a given moment. Just as certain ballets were abandoned and the effort ploughed under, so certain expenditures in nerve and work have served to braid sinew toward further strength. Many ballets are no longer performed, yet parallels and portions can be recognized as resurrected in subsequent dances.

The present adoption of classic dance throughout the country continues to appear a mystery to those who have come to its performances relatively lately. In one form or another, however, formal stage dance has been available to be seen in America for more than six decades. But now, in large measure due to Balanchine's insistence on a rigorous profile and authoritarian practice, classic ballet is less confused with other forms of dance, and its training has advanced toward high professional criteria and performance. It is granted the status of peak virtuosity — as hard to attain and as quick to be recognized as the violin, the piano or the Olympic categories.

One aspect of 'modernism' has been its effort to annihilate history, to create an art without precedent, to renovate sensibility, to canonize the New. We have had more than a half-century of newness, and suddenly it has aged. The classic ballet, born in the seventeenth century, combines historical legitimacy with contemporary manner. Its gestures are courtly, yet respond in accent, celerity and syncopation to the colloquial cadence of the day. Balanchine has defined the 'modern' direction of classic ballet.

Our century has licensed extremes of chaos and violence on the grandest scale known to man. The reflections in literature, music and the plastic arts of two world wars scarred the whole structure of the imaginative process. The fragmentary, the night-marish, the mad, exploited to their capacity of excess, have become mechanical, repetitive, dead-end.

The essence of ballet, on the other hand, is order. What one sees in Balanchine's ballets are structures of naked order, executed by celebrants who have no other aim than to show an aspect of order in their own persons, testifying to an impersonal purity and a personal interest.

There has undoubtedly occurred what must be called an unfocussed but active revival of religious interest in the West, seeking unfamiliar access to an absolute. It is not too much to consider a well-performed ballet a rite, executed and followed with intense devotion, that shares in some sort of moral figuration. The response of the audience to good dancing is a release of body and breath, a thanksgiving that is selfless,

13

generous, complete, and leaves the spectator corroborated in the hope that, despite the world and its horrors, here somehow is a paradigm of perfection.

The consideration of last things, millennial factors, the approach of another century, wars and the rumor of war, surround us. We have a sense that the times we live in are extremely frail, that frailty is the single cohering net that connects. Nothing is more frail or transient than a ballet. Every action is evanescent, and after its enactment it is gone for good, or until a next time, when the same conditions obtain. Human bodies are frail. The design the dancers thread is also frail, and to a degree entirely imaginary. It can be learned, but never completely documented.

The whole operation of a ballet company is a microcosm of a civil condition. The frailty of its operation is that of any artistic or cultural institution in a civilization that prefers to spend its bounty on armament and consumer goods. However, a ballet company, existing in the interstices of the community, almost vaunts its hardy frailty. In an infinitesimal way, each good performance clears a small area of menace, and for the moment reminds us of the possible which, if it is not perfection, approaches it.

In this process of asserting the importance of the classic dance, Balanchine acts as a public servant of order. He is a maker and teacher. The twentieth century has specialized in the metrics of time and space. Nobody before has ever danced as fast as a Balanchine dancer; no one has ever had such markedly separate structures of steps to dance. No dancers before have been obliged to analyze with their feet the kinds of musical composition that Balanchine has set for them. Only a dancer dancing can say for him, what he says to them.

LINCOLN KIRSTEIN

'I believe that if some Michelangelo were alive today—so it occurred to me, looking at the frescoes in the Sistine Chapel— the only thing that his genius would admit and recognize is choreography. And this is now coming to life again . . . . The only form of theatre art that makes its cornerstone the problems of beauty and nothing more is the ballet, just as the only goal that Michelangelo pursued was the beauty of the perceived.'

IGOR STRAVINSKY (1911)

On the basis of the ballets listed in this catalogue of works it is possible to read the above words as a prophecy, fulfilled in the choreography created by George Balanchine. In 1911, Balanchine was seven years old. His first formal choreography was made in 1920, nine years later. *Apollo*, to Stravinsky's music in 1928, became a catalytic moment that in addition to commencing a partnership and creating a masterpiece marked a new development and direction for classic dance in the twentieth century. Balanchine's choreography renews and perpetuates ideals of human skill and civilization that find their origin in the sources of Euterpe and Terpsichore. He joins in one unbroken line, through dance, the very earliest and very latest in human art.

Choreography by George Balanchine is a first chronological listing, giving first-performance details, note of major revisions, a record of stagings, and other information in a condensed form for each work Balanchine has created since his student days through June, 1982. Research has included archival study as well as correspondence and interviews with associates and dancers in the United States, Canada, Mexico, South America, England, Denmark, France, Germany, Austria, Monaco, Spain, Italy, and the Soviet Union. Balanchine's own participation in the effort has been invaluable.

Unlike the works of a musical composer, whose creations have the permanence of written form, or those of a painter or sculptor, works of dance are perpetuated through a tradition of staging that relies essentially not on notation, words, or even images preserved on film, but on one dancer teaching another. Dance is living art. While certain works

15

survive and are perpetuated in repertory or in stagings at different times by different companies, even when remounted by the choreographer himself they often evolve, develop, and undergo revision, in detail if not in essentials.

The entries in *Choreography by George Balanchine* are based on records of premieres; ensuing performances by dancers who have danced roles throughout the life of a ballet, often in sustained repertory, cannot be documented within the scope of the book. Nor can the book reflect the essential contributions of the administrative and technical staffs whose continued dedication over the years has provided the structure upon which a ballet company depends for its existence. Credit cannot be given here to individual patrons whose generosity has made continuity of production possible. Photographic illustration is beyond the intention of the *Catalogue*.

Basic to Balanchine's accomplishment is the School of American Ballet; a special volume commemorating its fiftieth anniversary will give recognition to those teachers and directors who have nurtured generations of students. They have become the dancers for whom his choreography is designed.

Within the table of *Contents* headings designate and divide the choreographer's production, reflecting his principal locations, associations and milieu: Russia, Europe with Diaghilev, Europe after Diaghilev, the United States and early companies, followed by the formation of Ballet Society, culminating in the New York City Ballet.

The schematic *Chronology* is designed to provide the reader with a comprehensive overview and context of works year by year, giving the names of composers, relating the geographical location and Balanchine's company associations, and noting important events related to the progress of his undertakings. It is intended as a chronology of work, providing neither biography nor critical assessment.

The *Chronology* cannot suggest Balanchine's larger responsibilities, which have made the mounting of ballets possible. The choreographing and production of new works involves conception, selection and often commissioning of music, direction and approval of scenic and costume design, rehearsals and changes up to the moment of premiere, and adjustment and revision after. Balanchine's supervision and main-tenance of the repertory of the New York City Ballet has been accompanied by his organization and administration of the Company and the School: Although not commented upon in the *Chronology* or *Catalogue*, these factors play a constant and essential role in the creation of the listed works.

A *Chronological Title List* of numbered entries precedes the *Catalogue*. Entry numbers, rather than page numbers, are the primary reference indicators of the book and are used in the *Indexes*. Titles are given in the language of the premiere performance, with the exception of works first performed in Russia, which are given their most common Western title. Later or variant names of works appear in parentheses following the title; when a work enters the repertory of a later company under a different (or translated) name, that is given as title, with the original name following in parentheses. Subtitles of works are retained when given in printed programs, and are supplied to identify works other than ballets. The *Chronological Title List* is supplemented by an alphabetical listing of *Titles by Category*, given as one of the indexes; the categories are Ballet, Ballet for Opera, Opera, Opera-Ballet, Staged Choral Works, Operetta, Concert Works, Musical Theater, Theater, Circus, Film, and Television.

Each catalogue entry presents information under the subheadings MUSIC, PRODUCTION, PREMIERE, and CAST, and where appropriate, a NOTE, REVISIONS, STAGINGS, TELEVISION, and at the end, cross references in italics. Due to difficulty of access, and often fragmentary nature, notated scores and films of ballets have not been listed.

Subsequent mountings of a ballet that has entered the repertory of more than one of the companies directed by Balanchine, or entered the repertory of a company directed by him after having first been performed by another company, are given separate entries. Full information is included in the first entry; the later mountings appear in chronological sequence, with the principal entry number starred in the italic cross references, which also link different works choreographed to the same music. This serves to indicate the repeated and varying use of certain scores, and the importance of works that have remained in the repertory of different companies with which Balanchine has been associated, as for instance *Apollo*, which has entries in 1928 [84, Diaghilev's Ballets Russes], 1937 [176, American Ballet], 1941 [198, American Ballet Caravan], and 1951 [284, New York City Ballet]. For works which continued from the Ballet Society repertory directly into that of the New York City Ballet, no second entry is given.

Student performances are included only in cases where they are unique (such as *Circus Polka*, 1945 [230]), not when they are precedent to professional performances (such as *Serenade*, 1934 [141]).

Ballets choreographed for operas are principally short divertissements that appear as interludes, and have been given abbreviated entries, including all available information on the dance passages but not providing production information for the opera; full entries are given only for operas directed or staged by Balanchine.

Each work is treated as it appeared at the time of its creation and premiere, as a creative venture with an identity and existence of its own apart from its reception or survival. The long life in repertory of such well-known or key ballets as *Apollo, Serenade* and *Ballet Imperial* (*Tschaikovsky Piano Concerto No. 2*) is suggested by their several entries and detailed treatment; however, the entry gives no indication of how many performances the ballet received or whether it continues in repertory. The length of an entry is no indication of a ballet's significance or importance: *Kammermusik No. 2* [408], for example, receives a very short entry, while *House of Flowers* [305], because of its large cast and elaborate production, has a long entry.

Each entry begins with the subheading MUSIC, giving composer, title, date, and note of commission when applicable. The variation in duration of performance is extreme, from a few minutes to a full evening. For certain ballets, such as *Agon* [316] and *The Four Temperaments* [236], Balanchine commissioned scores; for others, such as *Jewels* [358], he is responsible not only for the selection of music but its sequence; and in other instances, such as *Union Jack* [401], he has commissioned the orchestration of existing music. For the purposes of his conceptions, he has also combined selections made from a number of works of the same composer, as in *A Midsummer Night's Dream* [340]. Readers unfamiliar with any specific work can form some idea of length by studying the MUSIC entry, together with other entry information.

Information concerning scenic design, costumes, décor, lighting, and executors is given under the subheading PRODUCTION. Listings under PREMIERE provide the date of the first performance, the name of the performing company, the theater or place of performance, and the names of the conductor and principal soloists.

Listings of CAST follow the original printed program. In addition to providing the names of principal dancers they frequently indicate roles, scenes, or the movements of the music, suggesting the structure of the work. When the cast listing does not refer to form or content, principal dancers and soloists are distinguished from supporting dancers and corps de ballet by the use of semicolons. Dancers' names have in most instances been standardized to the form most commonly used (for example, Geva rather than Gevergeyeva); in cases where the name given in the program is a variant, there is a bracketed reference (as in the case of Sylvia Giselle [Gisella Caccialanza]). The names of roles are given throughout in English. When a synopsis of action is given under CAST, it is taken from the printed program or musical score.

The NOTES within the entries are intended to provide minimal but essential information not given under other subheadings. Although the primary subject matter and content of all Balanchine ballets may be described as dance itself, for those ballets that feature a subject, locale or plot, in actuality or by suggestion, annotation has been provided. Further description of many of the works may be found in sources provided in the *Bibliography*.

Under REVISIONS, principal alterations of works are detailed. Major remountings within the repertory of companies directed by Balanchine are given under NEW PRODUCTIONS. When a work has had a completely new interpretation, but retains the same music and title, there is a listing of OTHER VERSIONS.

The names of professional companies which have staged each work appear under STAGINGS, with the year of first performance. Ballets requested (and even set), but never performed, are not included. Restagings and revivals have not been included. When a company changes its name or merges with another company, repertory often carries over and no new first performance date is given; the exception is the New York City Ballet and its predecessor companies (excluding Ballet Society). Guest performances and performances by temporary companies are generally not included. Company names are often simplified; the *Key to Companies Staging Balanchine Works*, preceding the *General Index*, provides information on the company name at the time of staging and subsequently, as well as clarification of geographic location, dates of existence, or note of disbanding.

Television versions of ballets are listed under the subheading TELEVISION, with date and broadcasting channel; geographic locations are given for foreign and little-known American channels, with the names of such major program series as The Bell Telephone Hour and Dance in America. Full information on televised and filmed rehearsals and performances, including casts, production information, critical comments, and bibliographies of reviews, forms part of the project archive.

Following the *Catalogue* are *Source Notes*, which give sources of published and archival information, and especially information obtained from individuals, used to clarify or correct programs and to construct entries for works for which programs do not exist or have not been located. A number of persons closely associated with Balanchine who have generously provided valuable information are credited in the *Source Notes*.

The *Company Itineraries* provide context for Balanchine's work. Information on seasons and tours has been limited to American companies directed by him beginning in 1934. While his earlier travels after leaving Russia, and then with Diaghilev's Ballets Russes and after are partially indicated in the *Chronology*, the earlier and less well known periods of his career remain open to further study.

Festivals Directed by Balanchine lists the works of each performance (including works by choreographers other than Balanchine) for five principal festivals conceived by him and produced under his direction: the Stravinsky Festival, 1937; the Stravinsky Festival, 1972; the Ravel Festival, 1976; the Tschaikovsky Festival, 1981; and the Stravinsky Centennial Celebration, 1982.

Roles Performed by Balanchine is a list of all known roles performed from the choreographer's student days until the present.

The *Bibliography* includes all writings known to have been published by Balanchine, arranged chronologically, and a selection of books relating to him, arranged alphabetically. While not complete, the list has been chosen to provide an initial guide for further study. For the general reader, five titles can be described as principal reference works: *Balanchine's Complete Stories of the Great Ballets* (with Francis Mason; Doubleday, 1977); *The New York City Ballet*, by Anatole Chujoy (Knopf, 1953); *Thirty Years: Lincoln Kirstein's The New York City Ballet* (Knopf, 1978); *Repertory in Review: Forty Years of the New York City Ballet*, by Nancy Reynolds (Dial, 1977); and *Balanchine: A Biography*, by Bernard Taper (Macmillan, 1974).

The *General Index* provides reference by entry number to all names and titles of works in the *Catalogue*. Supplementary indexes list *Titles by Category* and provide a *Key to Companies Staging Balanchine Works*.

★

Choreography by George Balanchine—a work of scholarship—should also be understood to be a book of a million dreams come true. Each entry signifies a separate creation, a work of art with a life of its own. The procession of ballets traces a steady, inspired journey, a pilgrimage holding its course from continent to continent, maintaining its direction and identity in the face of opposition, establishing in its progress centers of creativity, overcoming circumstance by the magic of vision and faith in form, through training and utilizing successive generations of dancers. Absorbing into classic discipline the irrepressible vitality of the vernacular, proving the universality of native character, persisting in every medium of theatrical production open to ballet, a moral imagination found recognition and support. All this seriousness dares joy, tragedy, exuberance, delight, renewed in every performance.

George Balanchine is a cultural avatar whose work and standards have affirmed in the United States the nation's own best dreams and ideals. The compilers of the book, like the myriad uncounted members of audiences, offer thanks for the gift and heritage given us. This printed list is testament and tribute.

Leslie George Katz
Nancy Lassalle
Harvey Simmonds

CHRONOLOGY OF WORK

1904-1924
Russia

1904   Georgi Melitonovich Balanchivadze is born in St. Petersburg on January 22.

1913   Enters ballet section of Imperial Theater School, St. Petersburg.

1915   While still a student, first appears on stage at Maryinsky Theater; dances in school performances, and acts in plays.

1917   Schooling interrupted by Revolution for more than a year.

1918   Resumes studies at Petrograd Theater (Ballet) School. – Performs in repertory maintained at State Theater of Opera and Ballet (formerly Maryinsky); performs with fellow students for workers' clubs, army units and educational institutions.

1919   Creates first choreography, for Ballet School concerts [1-3]. – Studies piano and other instruments at Petrograd Conservatory of Music, directed by Alexander Glazounov. – Begins to compose music.

1921   Graduates with honors from Petrograd Theater (Ballet) School [4-5]. – Enters ballet company of State Theater of Opera and Ballet. – Sees and is influenced by performances of Kasyan Goleizovsky's Chamber Ballet. – Obtains score of Stravinsky's *Pulcinella* [35].

1922   Choreographs works for Petrograd Theater School graduation performances and continues to perform with State Theater of Opera and Ballet [6-13]. – With Pëtr Gusev, Vladimir Dimitriev, Yuri Slonimsky, and others, organizes company called Young Ballet, performing in Petrograd, nearby resorts and Moscow. – Fëdor Lopukhov, artistic director of State Theater of Opera and Ballet, invites Young Ballet to participate in his independent production, *Dance Symphony*.

1923   Creates works for official debut of Young Ballet. – Performs as pianist and dancer in cabarets, cinemas and at Svobodny Theater, and works with FEKS company (The Fabricators of Eccentricities, Inc.). – Is named ballet master of Maly Opera Theater in Petrograd. [14-29]

1924   Choreographs works for what will be final performances of Young Ballet [30-35]. – With Dimitriev forms troupe of dancers, singers and musicians to tour Germany. – Departs from Russia as head of troupe which, as Principal Dancers of the Russian State Ballet, performs in Berlin and tours Rhineland towns. – At end of tour, company decides not to return to Soviet Union and goes to London. – Performs at popular music hall; seen by Anton Dolin and Boris Kochno. – In Paris, group auditions for Serge Diaghilev. – Diaghilev engages dancers, who join his Ballets Russes in London, and changes name Georgi Balanchivadze to Georges Balanchine.

1925-1929
Europe, with Serge Diaghilev

1925   Goes to Monte Carlo, where Ballets Russes is based. – Assigned by Diaghilev to choreograph ballets for productions of Opéra de Monte-Carlo [38-42, 44-47, 49], which employs dancers from Ballets Russes between touring seasons. – For Opéra, choreographs world premiere of *L'Enfant et les Sortilèges* (Ravel) [48]. – As first assignment for Ballets Russes, revises Léonide Massine's choreography of *Le Chant du Rossignol* (Stravinsky) [52], given premiere in Paris. – For London premiere choreographs *Barabau* (Rieti) [53], his first original ballet for Diaghilev. – While creating new works, rehearses Ballets Russes repertory and dances with company, which performs in Barcelona, London, Paris, Antwerp, and Berlin.

1926   Choreographs for Opéra de Monte-Carlo [54-60], and for Diaghilev creates *La Pastorale* (Auric) [62] and *Jack in the Box* (Satie) [63]. – Goes to Rome to work with Lord Berners on *The Triumph of Neptune* [64], which has its premiere in London. – Revises divertissement from *The Sleeping Beauty* (Tschaikovsky) [65], among many changes he makes to repertory pieces of Ballets Russes as *maître de ballet*. – Company presents seasons in Paris and London, and on tour in Berlin, Ostend and Le Touquet.

1927   Provides choreography for productions of Opéra de Monte-Carlo [66-71], and for Ballets Russes choreographs *La Chatte* (Sauguet) [72]. – For Nikita Balieff's traveling Russian cabaret choreographs *Grotesque Espagnol* (Albéniz) and *Sarcasm* (Prokofiev) [73, 74], his first works to be seen in America. – Ballets Russes gives seasons in Paris and London, and tours in France, Italy, Germany, Austria, Switzerland, and Spain.

1928   Creates dances for Opéra de Monte-Carlo productions [76-82]. – For South American tour of Anna Pavlova's company, choreographs *Aleko* (Rachmaninoff) and *Polka Grotesque* (music unknown) [83]. – For Ballets Russes, creates *Apollon Musagète* [84], his first original ballet to Stravinsky's music, which receives premiere in Paris. – First performance of *The Gods Go A-Begging* (Handel) [85] given in London. – Ballets Russes gives seasons in Paris and London, tours Great Britain, and performs in Antwerp, Liège, Brussels, Lausanne, and Ostend.

1929   Sets ballets for Opéra de Monte-Carlo [86-90, 92], and for Diaghilev choreographs *Le Bal* (Rieti) [93]. – Ballets Russes performs in Berlin, Cologne and London. – Choreographs Cole Porter's song 'What Is This Thing Called Love?' for 1929 Cochran Revue in London [91]. – For Ballets Russes premiere in Paris, creates *Le Fils Prodigue* (Prokofiev) [94], last ballet to be commissioned and presented by Diaghilev. – Performs with Ballets Russes in Ostend and Vichy. – In London, choreographs dance sequence to music by Moussorgsky for *Dark Red Roses* [97], first feature-length talking movie made in England. – Diaghilev dies in Venice August 19, and his Ballets Russes ceases to exist. – For small group formed by Dolin in London, Balanchine choreographs *Pas de Deux* (da Costa) [95]. – In Paris, at invitation of Jacques Rouché, director of Paris Opéra, conceives and begins to choreograph ballet to *Les Créatures de Prométhée* (Beethoven) [96], which, due to illness, is completed by Serge Lifar.

1930-1933
Paris, London, Copenhagen, Monte Carlo

1930   In Paris, creates *Aubade* (Poulenc) [98] for company formed by Vera Nemtchinova. – In London, choreographs seven numbers (music by Berners, Sauguet and others) for *Charles B. Cochran's 1930 Revue* [99]. – In Copenhagen as guest ballet master of Royal Danish Ballet for five months, stages and rechoreographs six ballets by Fokine and

Massine [101-106]; presents two all-Balanchine programs for several performances.

1931   Returning to London, gathers small company sometimes billed as '16 Delightful Balanchine Girls 16' to perform numbers he stages for Sir Oswald Stoll's Variety Shows [107], to music by Liszt, Glinka, Mendelssohn, Rimsky-Korsakov, and others. – At same time, stages dances for *Charles B. Cochran's 1931 Revue* [108]. – In Paris, makes ballets for production of Offenbach's comic opera *Orphée aux Enfers* [109], with group of dancers called Les Ballets Russes de Georges Balanchine. – René Blum invites Balanchine to become ballet master of new company to be based in Monte Carlo.

1932   While organizing and rehearsing first season of Ballets Russes de Monte-Carlo, choreographs ballets for eighteen opera productions of the Opéra de Monte-Carlo [111-128]. – For the new company creates four ballets, *Cotillon* (Chabrier), *La Concurrence* (Auric), *Le Bourgeois Gentilhomme* (Richard Strauss), and *Suites de Dance* (Glinka) [129-132]. – Disagreements over policy with Blum's partner, Colonel Vasily de Basil, lead to departure from company.

1933   In Paris, forms Les Ballets 1933 with Kochno. – For brief seasons in Paris and London, creates completely new repertory of six works [134-139]; four are to be included in repertories of his future companies: *Mozartiana* (his first major work to Tschaikovsky), *Les Songes* (Milhaud), *Les Sept Péchés Capitaux* (*The Seven Deadly Sins*, Weill/Brecht), and *L'Errante* (Schubert). – The others are *Fastes* (Sauguet) and *Les Valses de Beethoven*. – Les Ballets 1933 disbands. – Lincoln Kirstein meets Balanchine in London and invites him to the United States to establish a ballet school and company. – He accepts, canceling second engagement with Royal Danish Ballet. – On October 17, Balanchine arrives in New York with Dimitriev.

1934-1945
America, with Lincoln Kirstein

1934   School of American Ballet opens at 637 Madison Avenue in New York City on January 2, with Balanchine, Dimitriev and Kirstein as officers, Balanchine, Pierre Vladimiroff and Dorothie Littlefield as faculty, and Edward M. M. Warburg as first patron. – In March, Balanchine begins choreographing *Serenade* (Tschaikovsky) for students, who first perform it with stagings of *Mozartiana* and *Dreams* (a revision of *Les Songes*) at Woodland, the Warburg estate near White Plains. – In Hartford, Connecticut, non-professional Producing Company of the School of American Ballet, predecessor of American Ballet, presents programs that include *Mozartiana* and three new ballets: *Serenade*, *Alma Mater* (Swift), and *Transcendence* (Liszt). – Balanchine, Kirstein and Warburg establish American Ballet, with dancers from the School.

1935 In New York City, American Ballet has first professional season, with official premieres of *Serenade*, *Alma Mater*, *Reminiscence* (Godard), and *Transcendence*, and American premieres of *Errante* and *Dreams* [141-146]. – After performances in Philadelphia, New York and White Plains, company begins projected United States tour in Greenwich, Connecticut, which ends one week later in Scranton, Pennsylvania. – Edward Johnson, general manager of Metropolitan Opera, engages Balanchine as ballet master, and American Ballet (to be called American Ballet Ensemble) as resident ballet company. – Choreographs ballets for seven opera productions [150-156], and in first of several programs combining independent ballets with opera, presents *Reminiscence* with Humperdinck's *Hansel and Gretel*.

1936 For Metropolitan Opera season, sets ballets for seven operas [158-161, 163, 167, 168]. – With William Dollar, choreographs *Concerto* [165]; creates the ballet *The Bat* (Johann Strauss the Younger) [169]. – Directs and choreographs the opera *Orpheus and Eurydice* (Gluck) [170] in a production designed by Pavel Tchelitchew. – Stages first ballets for a Broadway musical, six pieces for *Ziegfeld Follies: 1936 Edition* (Duke) [162]. – Creates *Serenata: Magic* (Mozart) [164] for Hartford Festival. For Broadway, choreographs *Slaughter on Tenth Avenue* and other ballets for *On Your Toes* (Rodgers and Hart) [166].

1937 Choreographs opera ballets [171, 173, 174, 179], and stages and choreographs *Le Coq d'Or* (Rimsky-Korsakov) [172], for Metropolitan Opera. – Prepares his first Stravinsky Festival, presented at Metropolitan Opera House for two evenings by American Ballet: Revives *Apollon Musagète* for its first performance in America, creates

27

The Card Party, his and Kirstein's first commission to Stravinsky, and choreographs *Le Baiser de la Fée* [176-178]. – Sets dances for *Babes in Arms* (Rodgers and Hart) [175]. – Engaged by Samuel Goldwyn for first Hollywood assignment, creates dances with members of American Ballet for *Goldwyn Follies* (Gershwin) [185]. – Choreographs opera ballets for winter/spring Metropolitan Opera season [179-181].

1938　Metropolitan Opera terminates engagement of American Ballet after spring season. – Dancers continue to work with Balanchine in musical comedy and with Ballet Caravan, a touring company founded by Kirstein in 1936. – For Broadway, choreographs *I Married an Angel* and *The Boys from Syracuse* (Rodgers and Hart), and *Great Lady* (Loewe) [182-184]. – Plans for Balanchine company to be sponsored by Broadway producers Dwight Deere Wiman and J. H. Del Bondio lead to rehearsals, but not to production.

1939　Balanchine becomes a United States citizen. – In Hollywood, directs dances for film version of *On Your Toes* [186], and later directs dances for film *I Was an Adventuress* [191].

1940　In New York, stages *Le Baiser de la Fée, Poker Game (The Card Party)*, and *Serenade* for Ballet Russe de Monte Carlo. – Choreographs dances for Broadway musicals *Keep Off the Grass* (McHugh) and *Louisiana Purchase* (Berlin), and stages entire production of *Cabin in the Sky* (Duke) [187, 188, 190]. – School of American Ballet is incorporated as non-profit institution with Kirstein as President and Director, and Balanchine as Chairman of Faculty.

1941　For de Basil's current company, Original Ballet Russe, choreographs *Balustrade* (to Stravinsky's Violin Concerto) [192], first ballet created in America for company not his own. – With Kirstein, establishes American Ballet Caravan, formed with dancers from American Ballet, Ballet Caravan and School of American Ballet, for five-month good-will tour of Latin America arranged by Nelson A. Rockefeller, Coordinator of Inter-American Affairs. – Choreographs new ballets for tour: *Ballet Imperial* (Tschaikovsky) and *Concerto Barocco* (Bach; first conceived for School of American Ballet students); *Divertimento* (Rossini–Britten) and *Fantasia Brasileira* (Mignone) are choreographed in South America during tour [194-196, 200]. – Also stages *Serenata (Serenade), Alma Errante (Errante)*,

Apolo Musageta (*Apollon Musagète*), and *El Murciélago* (*The Bat*)
[**193, 197-199**]. – Tour opens in Rio de Janeiro, and continues in
Argentina, Chile, Peru, Colombia, and Venezuela. – Company is
disbanded at end of engagement. – In New York, stages dances for
Broadway musical *The Lady Comes Across* (Duke/Latouche) [**201**].

1942　Choreographs *The Ballet of the Elephants* [**202**] to Stravinsky's *Circus Polka*, written at Balanchine's request for Ringling Brothers and Barnum & Bailey Circus, Madison Square Garden, with cast of fifty elephants and fifty women. – In Argentina as guest director of ballet of Teatro Colón in Buenos Aires, creates choreography for opera *Mârouf* (Rabaud) [**204**], stages *Apollon Musagète* in new production designed by Tchelitchew, and choreographs *Concierto de Mozart* [**205**]. – In New York, for recently formed New Opera Company, choreographs *Rosalinda* (*Die Fledermaus*, Johann Strauss the Younger) [**206**], choreographs for opera productions [**207-211**], and stages *Ballet Imperial*, using members of former American Ballet Caravan. – In Hollywood, choreographs Harold Arlen and Johnny Mercer's 'That Old Black Magic' for film *Star Spangled Rhythm* [**213**].

1943　In first association with Ballet Theatre, founded in 1939, stages *Apollo* and *The Wanderer* (*Errante*), and assists David Lichine in revising Fokine's last ballet, *Helen of Troy* (Offenbach) [**214**]. – With Leopold Stokowski and Robert Edmond Jones, collaborates on production of *The Crucifixion of Christ* [**215**], a modern miracle play set to Bach's *St. Matthew Passion*, using students from School of American Ballet. – Stages dances for New Opera Company production of *The Merry Widow* (Lehár) [**216**], and for Broadway musical comedy *What's Up* (Loewe) [**217**]. – Plans resident company in New York to give performances on Sunday evenings, but project does not materialize. – Stages *Concerto Barocco* for American Concert Ballet, company formed by members of former American Ballet Caravan.

1944　Choreographs ballet sequences for Broadway musical comedy *Dream with Music* (Warnick) [**218**]. – In Los Angeles, stages dances for operetta *Song of Norway* [**219**] to music by Edvard Grieg, using ensemble from Ballet Russe de Monte Carlo. – Begins two-year association with that company as resident choreographer; first original work for company is *Danses Concertantes* (Stravinsky) [**220**];

stages new version of *Le Bourgeois Gentilhomme* (Richard Strauss) [**221**]. – To honor his twenty-fifth year as choreographer, Chicago Public Library mounts exhibition. – Choreographs *Waltz Academy* (Rieti) [**222**], first original work for Ballet Theatre.

1945 Devises movement sequences for role of Ariel in Broadway production of Shakespeare's *The Tempest* [**224**], directed by Margaret Webster. – *Dance Index*, the magazine founded by Kirstein in 1942, devotes February-March issue to a study of Balanchine's work, including his own 'Notes on Choreography.' – Ballet Russe de Monte Carlo celebrates Balanchine's twenty-fifth year as choreographer with two full evenings of his work; for the occasion he creates *Pas de Deux* (Tschaikovsky) [**225**], and stages *Ballet Imperial* and *Mozartiana*. – In Mexico City, with former American Ballet Caravan members and advanced students of School of American Ballet, choreographs ballets for productions of the Ópera Nacional, Palacio de Bellas Artes [**226-228**], and stages ballets, including *Concerto Barocco* and *Apollo*. – Choreographs dances for Broadway musical *Mr. Strauss Goes to Boston* (Johann Strauss the Younger–Stolz) [**229**]. – Choreographs *Circus Polka* (Stravinsky), *Élégie* (Stravinsky) and *Symphonie Concertante* (Mozart) [**230, 245, 241**] for Carnegie Hall performance with students of School of American Ballet for *Adventure in Ballet*, Kirstein's first enterprise in ballet following his return from wartime service.

1946-1948
Ballet Society

1946 For Ballet Russe de Monte Carlo, choreographs *The Night Shadow* (Rieti) [**232**], stages *Le Baiser de la Fée*, and collaborates with Alexandra Danilova in a version of *Raymonda* (Glazounov) [**233**] after Petipa. – In Hollywood, begins choreography for film titled *The Life and Loves of Pavlova*, canceled after two months. – Stages traditional Maryinsky Act II death scene for Ballet Theatre revival of *Giselle* (Adam) [**234**]. – With Kirstein, organizes Ballet Society, Inc., a subscription-supported company to advance lyric theater. – For first performance, at Central High School of Needle Trades, Balanchine rechoreographs *L'Enfant et les Sortilèges* (Ravel) [**235**] for

American premiere, and creates *The Four Temperaments* (Hindemith) [236] to score he commissioned from composer in 1940. – Balanchine and Kirstein commission *Orpheus* from Stravinsky; Balanchine goes to Hollywood to work with composer.

1947   For second series of Ballet Society performances, at Hunter College Playhouse, choreographs *Renard* (Stravinsky) [237] and *Divertimento* (Haieff) [238]. – Stages dances for Broadway production of operetta *The Chocolate Soldier* (Oscar Straus) [239]. – During six months as guest ballet master of Paris Opéra, mounts *Serenade*, *Le Baiser de la Fée* and *Apollon Musagète*, and to recently rediscovered Bizet First Symphony creates *Le Palais de Cristal* [240], retitled *Symphony in C* for American premiere in 1948. – In Hollywood, continues work on *Orpheus* with Stravinsky. – During first series of Ballet Society performances at City Center of Music and Drama in New York, presents *Symphonie Concertante* (Mozart) [241]. – Choreographs *Theme and Variations* (Tschaikovsky) [242] for Ballet Theatre.

1948-1964
New York City Ballet: City Center

1948   Choreographs *The Triumph of Bacchus and Ariadne* (Rieti) [243] for second series of Ballet Society performances at City Center. – Ballet Society gives American premiere of *Symphony in C* [244]. – Ballet Society presents *Élégie* (Stravinsky) [245] and the Stravinsky–Balanchine–Noguchi *Orpheus* [246] at City Center of Music and Drama, in what prove to be its final performances. – Following the premiere of *Orpheus*, Morton Baum, Chairman of Executive Committee of City Center, invites Kirstein and Balanchine to found permanent company, to be called New York City Ballet, with residency at City Center; Ballet Society, Inc., continues as sponsor for special projects. – In addition to presenting independent repertory, Company is to provide opera ballets for New York City Opera productions; ballet evenings are to be Mondays and Tuesdays. – In Monte Carlo, for Grand Ballet du Marquis de Cuevas, stages *Night Shadow* and *Concerto Barocco*, and choreographs *Pas de Trois Classique* (Minkus) [247], given its premiere in London. – While preparing inaugural season of New York City Ballet,

Balanchine choreographs dances for Broadway musical *Where's Charley?* (Loesser) [249] and ballets for New York City Opera [248, 251-253, 255, 256]. – New York City Ballet and *Where's Charley?* open October 11. – For first performance, New York City Ballet presents *Concerto Barocco*, *Orpheus* and *Symphony in C*; second performance consists of *Serenade*, *The Four Temperaments* and *Orpheus*. – Directs movements for actors in Broadway production of Giraudoux's play *The Madwoman of Chaillot* [257].

1949 New York City Ballet presents first independent season, and provides New York City Opera ballets [258, 260]. – Company is to give regular repertory seasons each year at City Center, and later at New York State Theater (detailed in *Company Itineraries*, page 297). – For Ballet Theatre, adapts Petipa's choreography for *Princess Aurora* [259] and *Don Quixote* and *Swan Lake (Black Swan) Pas de Deux* [262], and stages *Theme and Variations* and *Apollo*. – Balanchine's first original production for television, *Cinderella* [261], to music by Tschaikovsky, is telecast by CBS. – Stages Fokine's choreography of *La Mort du Cygne* (Saint-Saëns) [263] for performance at Holland Festival in Amsterdam. – For New York City Ballet, choreographs Stravinsky's *Firebird* [264] and *Bourrée Fantasque* (Chabrier) [265].

1950 Revives Prokofiev's *Prodigal Son* [267] for New York City Ballet, and appears several times in role of the Father. – Choreographs *Pas de Deux Romantique* (Weber) [268], and with Jerome Robbins creates *Jones Beach* (Andriessen) [269]. – In London, stages *Ballet Imperial* for Sadler's Wells Ballet at invitation of Ninette de Valois. – New York City Ballet presents six-week season at Royal Opera House, Covent Garden, London, and makes three-week tour of England in first of frequent foreign tours (detailed in *Company Itineraries*, page 297). – Choreographs Haydn's *Trumpet Concerto* [270] for touring company of Sadler's Wells Ballet. – For New York City Ballet, stages *The Fairy's Kiss* (*Le Baiser de la Fée*) (Stravinsky) and choreographs *Mazurka from 'A Life for the Tsar'* (Glinka) and *Sylvia: Pas de Deux* (Delibes) [271-273].

1951 Engaged by Samuel Goldwyn to choreograph dances for film *Hans Christian Andersen*, but schedule conflicts with New York City Ballet season prevent participation. – Is principal choreographer for *Music and Dance* [274], presented by National Orchestral Society at

Carnegie Hall, performed by members of New York City Ballet and students from School of American Ballet. – For New York City Ballet, stages *The Card Game* (Stravinsky) and *Pas de Trois* (Minkus), and choreographs Ravel's *La Valse* and Mendelssohn's *Capriccio Brillant* [275-277, 279]. – Designs pavane to music by David Diamond for Dwight Deere Wiman's Broadway production of Shakespeare's *Romeo and Juliet* [278]. – New York City Ballet presents first American season outside New York at Civic Opera House, Chicago. – Stages dances for Broadway musical comedy *Courtin' Time* (Lawrence/Walker) [280]. – New York City Ballet dances *La Valse* on first color television program, broadcast by CBS. – For New York City Ballet, choreographs *À la Françaix* (Françaix) and *Tyl Ulenspiegel* (Richard Strauss), stages *Apollon Musagète* under title *Apollo, Leader of the Muses*, and presents his own version of Act II of the Petipa/Ivanov *Swan Lake* [282-285].

1952   For New York City Ballet, choreographs *Caracole* [286] to Mozart's Divertimento No. 15, and *Bayou* (Thomson) [287]. – In Milan, stages *Ballet Imperial* for ballet company of La Scala. – New York City Ballet forms exchange program with San Francisco Ballet, which stages *Serenade*. – For New York City Ballet, choreographs *Scotch Symphony* (Mendelssohn), *Metamorphoses* (Hindemith), *Harlequinade Pas de Deux* (Drigo), and *Concertino* (Françaix) [288-290, 292]. – As Christmas program for television, stages abridged treatment of *Coppélia* (Delibes), titled *One, Yuletide Square* [291].

1953   Choreographs *Valse Fantaisie* (Glinka) [293] for New York City Ballet. – Company performs in Washington, D.C., on eve of inauguration of President Dwight D. Eisenhower. – Publication of Anatole Chujoy's book *The New York City Ballet* (Knopf). – Choreographs *The Countess Becomes the Maid* [294] to music by Johann Strauss the Younger for telecast on Kate Smith Hour. – Directs American premiere of Stravinsky's opera *The Rake's Progress* [295] for Metropolitan Opera. – Arranges *Cotillion Promenade* [296] for five hundred couples at Negro Debutante Ball, 369th Armory, in Harlem, New York City. – Stages opera ballets for La Scala in Milan, and in Florence [297-300]. – New York City Ballet performs in Colorado and California on first of continuing tours throughout United States (detailed in *Company Itineraries*, page 297).

33

1954   Appears on cover of *Time* magazine. – Choreographs *Opus 34* (Schoenberg) [301] while preparing *The Nutcracker* (Tschaikovsky) [302], New York City Ballet's first full-length ballet and most elaborate production, using children from School of American Ballet. – Publication of Balanchine's *Complete Stories of the Great Ballets*, edited by Francis Mason (Doubleday). – Choreographs *Western Symphony* (Kay) [303]; *Ivesiana* [304] is given premiere four months after death of composer Charles Ives. – Stages dances for Broadway musical *House of Flowers* (Arlen) [305], but withdraws prior to New York opening.

1955   For New York City Ballet, choreographs *Roma* (Bizet) [306] and *Pas de Trois* (Glinka) [307]. – Stages ballet masque for American Shakespeare Festival production of *The Tempest* [308] in Stratford, Connecticut. – Choreographs *Pas de Dix* (Glazounov) [309] and *Jeux d'Enfants* (Bizet) [310] for New York City Ballet.

1956   Stage director of NBC Opera Theatre color telecast of *The Magic Flute* (Mozart) [311]. – School of American Ballet moves to new classrooms at 2291 Broadway. – For New York City Ballet, choreographs *Allegro Brillante* (Tschaikovsky) [312]. – Choreographs *A Musical Joke* (Mozart) [313] and *Divertimento No. 15* (Mozart) [314] for bicentennial Mozart Festival produced by American Shakespeare Festival in Stratford, Connecticut. – Stages *Apollon Musagète* and *Serenade* for Royal Danish Ballet during absence of five months from United States and New York City Ballet.

1957   Company goes to Montreal for first formal filming of ballets from repertory, made for Canadian Broadcasting Company: *Pas de Dix* and *Serenade* are among initial works made into kinescopes for telecasts; others are filmed during subsequent visits. – Conceives and choreographs *Square Dance* (Vivaldi–Corelli) [315] for New York City Ballet. – Working closely with Stravinsky, creates *Agon* [316] to third commission from Stravinsky by Balanchine and Kirstein.

1958   Immediately following *Agon*, presents *Gounod Symphony* [317] and *Stars and Stripes* (Sousa-Kay) [318]. – New York City Ballet makes five-month tour of Japan, Australia and Philippines, sponsored by United States Department of State and American National Theatre and Academy (ANTA). – Choreographs dance passages for American Shakespeare Festival productions of *A Midsummer Night's*

Dream [319] and *The Winter's Tale* [320]. – Choreographs *Waltz-Scherzo* (Tschaikovsky) [321] and restages *The Seven Deadly Sins* (Weill/Brecht) [322] for New York City Ballet. – Designs production of *The Nutcracker* especially for CBS Christmas telecast; performs role of Drosselmeyer.

1959 Choreographs *Native Dancers* (Rieti) [323] for New York City Ballet. – Company performs *Stars and Stripes* at inauguration celebration of Governor Rockefeller in Albany. – In Paris, stages *Gounod Symphony* for Opéra Ballet. – Choreographs *Part II* of *Episodes* [324] to music by Webern; at his invitation, *Part I* is choreographed by Martha Graham. – Invited by Kirstein, Imperial Gagaku troupe of dancers and singers from Japan performs on regular programs of New York City Ballet. – For American Shakespeare Festival, stages dances for productions of *Romeo and Juliet* [325] and *The Merry Wives of Windsor* [326]. – Under W. McNeil Lowry, Director of the Program in Humanities and the Arts, the Ford Foundation awards grant to Ballet Society enabling School of American Ballet to survey American ballet instruction and to establish first national scholarship fund. – Through Department of State, Balanchine arranges to give his ballets to state-supported national companies in Europe; first companies to benefit are La Scala, Netherlands Ballet and Royal Swedish Ballet.

1960 For New York City Ballet, revives and restages *Night Shadow* (later called *La Sonnambula*, Rieti), creates *Panamerica* (Latin American composers), stages *Theme and Variations* (Tschaikovsky), and choreographs *Pas de Deux* (Tschaikovsky) [328-331]; creates *The Figure in the Carpet* (Handel) [332] in honor of Fourth International Congress of Iranian Art and Archeology. – Gives first of continuing School of American Ballet seminars for regional teachers, a four-day program. – *Theme and Variations* performed by American Ballet Theatre during first visit by an American ballet company to Russia. – *Symphony in C* and *The Four Temperaments* performed in People's Republic of China by Royal Swedish Ballet. – New York City Ballet performs series of Saturday matinees for underprivileged New York City children, sponsored by Ballet Society. – Balanchine presides at Ballet Society national convocation of ballet company directors. – For Company, choreographs *Variations from Don Sebastian* (later called *Donizetti Variations*), *Monumentum pro Gesualdo* (Stravinsky), *Liebeslieder Walzer* (Brahms), and *Ragtime (I)* (Stravinsky) [333-336].

1961   For New York City Ballet, choreographs *Modern Jazz: Variants* (Schuller) [337], and *Electronics* (Gassmann-Sala) [338] to electronic tape. – Atlanta Civic Ballet presents *Serenade*, first result of Balanchine's offer to make works available to United States regional companies able to stage them. – Assists in efforts to form company that becomes Pennsylvania Ballet. – For New York City Ballet, choreographs *Valses et Variations* (*Raymonda Variations*, Glazounov) [339].

1962   Choreographs *A Midsummer Night's Dream* (Mendelssohn) [340], his first wholly original full-length ballet. – Under auspices of New York State Council on the Arts, New York City Ballet makes first of continuing tours to upstate New York; also gives lecture-demonstrations in twelve cities. – In Germany, stages and choreographs *Eugen Onegin* (Tschaikovsky) [341] for Hamburg State Opera, at invitation of its director, Rolf Liebermann. – Working with Stravinsky, choreographs *Noah and the Flood* [342], composed for television. – Returns to Hamburg with dancers of New York City Ballet to participate with Stravinsky in celebrations of composer's eightieth birthday; *Agon*, *Orpheus* and *Apollo* are performed. – Participates in planning Saratoga Performing Arts Center at Saratoga Springs, New York. – Company performs in Germany and Austria, and Balanchine makes first return to Russia, as Company makes its initial tour of Soviet Union, visiting Moscow, Leningrad, Kiev, Tbilisi, and Baku.

1963   Publication of Bernard Taper's biography *Balanchine* (Macmillan). – In Washington, D. C., New York City Ballet dances *Stars and Stripes* at Second Anniversary Inaugural Celebration of Kennedy administration. – For Company, choreographs *Bugaku* (Mayuzumi) [343] and *Movements for Piano and Orchestra* (Stravinsky) [344]. – New York City Ballet begins lecture-demonstrations in New York City schools. – Directs and choreographs Gluck's *Orpheus und Eurydike* [345] for Hamburg State Opera. – For Company, choreographs *Meditation* (Tschaikovsky) [346]. – Stages *Concerto Barocco*, *Scotch Symphony*, *The Four Temperaments*, and *Bourrée Fantasque* for Paris Opéra Ballet. – Ford Foundation makes first of a series of grants

to support New York City Ballet, and first of two grants to School
of American Ballet.

1964-1982
New York City Ballet: New York State Theater

1964   Last performance of New York City Ballet at City Center; choreographs *Tarantella* (Gottschalk-Kay) [347]. – Company participates in gala opening of New York State Theater at Lincoln Center for the Performing Arts, designed by Philip Johnson in consultation with Balanchine and Kirstein. – *Clarinade* (Gould) [348] is first work choreographed for Company in new permanent home. – Establishes costume shop for New York City Ballet under direction of Barbara Karinska. – Founds James A. Doolittle–George Balanchine Ballet of Los Angeles, intended to become permanent West Coast company closely associated with New York City Ballet; company will disband after two years. – For large-scale stage of New York State Theater, restages *The Nutcracker* with new scenery and costumes; mounts *Ballet Imperial* (*Tschaikovsky Piano Concerto No. 2*) [349] for its first New York City Ballet production.

1965   For New York City Ballet, choreographs *Pas de Deux and Divertissement* (Delibes) [350] and *Harlequinade* (Drigo) [351]; creates full-length ballet *Don Quixote* (Nabokov) [352] and performs title role at preview performance. – First annual School of American Ballet Workshop performance.

1966   New York City Ballet has first subscription season; subscription plan significantly enlarges audience attending on regular basis. – Choreographs *Variations* (Stravinsky) [353] and *Brahms–Schoenberg Quartet* [354]. – For *A Festival of Stravinsky: His Heritage and His Legacy*, directed by Lucas Foss at Philharmonic Hall, choreographs *Élégie* [355] and *Ragtime (II)* [356]. – New York City Ballet's production of *A Midsummer Night's Dream* becomes first feature-length ballet film made in United States; filming is under Balanchine's direction and supervision. – First New York City Ballet season at new permanent summer home, Saratoga Performing Arts Center, Saratoga Springs, New York, where it is to give seasons each July. – In Stockholm, supervises final rehearsals for Royal Swedish Ballet all-Balanchine evening.

1967   For New York City Ballet, choreographs *Trois Valses Romantiques* (Chabrier), the full-length, plotless *Jewels* (Fauré, Stravinsky, Tschaikovsky), and *Glinkiana* [357-359].

1968   For New York City Ballet, creates *Metastaseis & Pithoprakta* (Xenakis) [360], and restages *Slaughter on Tenth Avenue* [361], originally created for *On Your Toes* in 1936. – Produces and directs stage movements for Company performance of *Requiem Canticles* (Stravinsky) [362], presented once, in memory of Martin Luther King, Jr. – For Ed Sullivan Show on television, choreographs *Diana and Actaeon Pas de Deux* (Pugni) [363]. – Choreographs *La Source* (Delibes) [364] for New York City Ballet.

1969   For Hamburg State Opera, stages and choreographs first production outside Russia of Glinka's opera *Ruslan und Ludmilla* [365]. – Agrees to allow his ballets to be staged by West Berlin Ballet Ensemble, to work with young choreographers there, and to encourage exchanges between Berlin and New York City Ballet. – For New York City Ballet, stages second section of *Glinkiana*, *Valse Fantaisie* [366], as separate ballet. – Between New York and Saratoga seasons, New York City Ballet participates in Diaghilev Festival held in Monte Carlo to commemorate fortieth anniversary of last season of Ballets Russes and sixtieth anniversary of founding of that company, performing *Apollo* and *Prodigal Son*. – School of American Ballet moves to its own specially designed quarters in Juilliard School of Music building at Lincoln Center for the Performing Arts. – In Switzerland, stages four-act production of Ivanov/Petipa *Le Lac des Cygnes* (Tschaikovsky) [367] for Ballet du Grand Théâtre of Geneva. – In West Berlin, rehearses Berlin Opera Ballet in *Episodes*, *Symphony in C* and *Apollon Musagète* in preparation for its first all-Balanchine evening. – Becomes artistic advisor of ballet school and company of Grand Théâtre, Geneva, which presents its first all-Balanchine evening. – Kirstein becomes Chairman of the Board and Balanchine a Vice President of Dance Theatre of Harlem, the black classical ballet company and school newly founded by former New York City Ballet principal Arthur Mitchell. – National Endowment for the Arts makes first of a series of grants to New York City Ballet.

1970   For New York City Ballet, creates *Who Cares?* (Gershwin) [368] and choreographs full *Tschaikovsky Suite No. 3* [369], incorporating choreography of the 1947 *Theme and Variations* as fourth movement. – Receives Handel Medallion, New York City's highest cultural award. – New York State Council on the Arts makes first of a series of grants for New York City Ballet production and administration costs.

1971 Dance Theatre of Harlem appears with New York City Ballet in single performance of *Concerto for Jazz Band and Orchestra* (Liebermann) [370], choreographed by Balanchine and Mitchell. – Choreographs *PAMTGG* [371] to music based on radio and television airline commercial. – Ballet du Grand Théâtre in Geneva presents performances of *Divertimento No. 15*, *Episodes*, *Theme and Variations*, and *Who Cares?*, with guest artists from New York City Ballet.

1972 Under auspices of New York State Council on the Arts, Governor Rockefeller presents New York State Award to Balanchine honoring his unique contribution to development of dance and dance audiences in New York. – Conceives and directs eight-day festival to celebrate the music of Stravinsky, who had died in 1971, honoring ninetieth anniversary of composer's birth. – Thirty-one ballets to Stravinsky compositions are presented, twenty-two of which are newly created by seven choreographers. – Ten new ballets and stagings are by Balanchine: *Sonata*, *Symphony in Three Movements*, *Violin Concerto*, *Danses Concertantes* (revised from first presentation in 1944), *Divertimento from 'Le Baiser de la Fée,'* *Scherzo à la Russe*, *Duo Concertant*, *Pulcinella*, *Choral Variations on Bach's 'Vom Himmel Hoch,'* and a staging of *Symphony of Psalms* [372-381]. – In *Pulcinella*, choreographed in collaboration with Robbins, Balanchine and Robbins dance as masked beggars. – In Munich, New York City Ballet represents United States in cultural presentations at Olympic Games. – Company makes second Russian tour, followed by first engagement in Poland.

1973 *Tschaikovsky Concerto No. 2* [382, originally created in 1941 as *Ballet Imperial*] is given first performance by New York City Ballet in revised form. – In West Berlin, stages Act II *Polovtsian Dances* (based on Fokine's choreography) for Berlin Opera production of Borodin's *Prince Igor* [383]. – In Paris, rehearses ballet sequences for Paris Opéra production of Gluck's *Orfeo ed Euridice*, and *Symphony in C* for

Paris Opéra Ballet. – Choreographs *Cortège Hongrois* [384] for Melissa Hayden on her retirement from New York City Ballet. – Goes to Berlin with eighty-one members of New York City Ballet for RM Productions filming of fifteen Balanchine ballets. – Publication of Kirstein's *The New York City Ballet* (Knopf) marks Company's twenty-fifth anniversary year.

1974   For Company, creates *Variations pour une Porte et un Soupir* (Henry) [386] to *musique concrète* recorded on tape. – For Saratoga Springs premiere, Balanchine and Danilova recreate full-length production of *Coppélia* (Delibes) [387] from Petipa choreography. – Stages polonaise for Metropolitan Opera production of *Boris Godunov* (Moussorgsky) [388].

1975   Conceives and supervises New York City Ballet Ravel Festival in honor of the composer and France. – During two-week period, twenty ballets are presented to Ravel's music; sixteen are new works by four choreographers, eight by Balanchine. – These are *Sonatine*, *L'Enfant et les Sortilèges* (his third version of the opera-ballet), *Shéhérazade*, *Le Tombeau de Couperin*, *Pavane*, *Tzigane*, *Gaspard de la Nuit*, and *Rapsodie Espagnole* [389-396]. – France awards Balanchine Order of the Légion d'Honneur. – Choreographs *Walpurgisnacht Ballet* in Paris Opéra production of *Faust* (Gounod) [397]. – In Saratoga Springs, *The Steadfast Tin Soldier* (Bizet) [398] receives premiere during Company's summer season. – In Chicago, choreographs dance sequences for Chicago Lyric Opera production of *Orfeo ed Euridice* (Gluck) [399].

1976   *Chaconne* [400], based on choreography for 1963 Hamburg State Opera production of Gluck's *Orfeo ed Euridice*, is presented by New York City Ballet as independent ballet. – Creates *Union Jack* [401] to British military, music-hall and folk music arranged by Hershy Kay as New York City Ballet tribute to United States Bicentennial. – In Paris, as part of French salute to Bicentennial, New York City Ballet gives series of performances featuring ballets from Stravinsky repertory. – Choreographs dances for School of American Ballet students in Juilliard American Opera Center production of *Le Roi Malgré Lui* (Chabrier) [403]. – Revival of *The Seven Deadly Sins* is rehearsed by New York City Ballet, but canceled due to musicians' strike.

40

1977   Publication of Nancy Reynolds' *Repertory in Review: Forty Years of the New York City Ballet* (Dial). – Choreographs *Étude for Piano* (Scriabin) [405] for first Spoleto Festival U. S. A. in Charleston, South Carolina. – Creates *Vienna Waltzes* (Johann Strauss the Younger, Lehár, Richard Strauss) [406] for New York City Ballet. – Balanchine and members of Company travel to Nashville, Tennessee, to film under his direction first of series of four programs devoted to his ballets for Dance in America on public television. – In Montreal, under his supervision, Canadian Broadcasting System films *Bugaku* and *Chaconne*.

1978   Creates for Company *Ballo della Regina* (Verdi) [407] and *Kammermusik No. 2* (Hindemith) [408]. – *Coppélia* is televised as New York City Ballet's first appearance on Live from Lincoln Center series. – School of American Ballet becomes first professional dance academy to receive a major grant from National Endowment for the Arts and, in 1980, first to receive a Challenge Grant. – Supervises production of *Tricolore* (Auric) [409], which, with *Stars and Stripes* and *Union Jack*, forms an 'Entente Cordiale.' – In appreciation of his contribution to Royal Danish Ballet, is named Knight of the Order of Dannebrog, First Class. – First annual Kennedy Center Honors are presented by President Jimmy Carter to Marian Anderson, Fred Astaire, George Balanchine, Richard Rodgers, and Arthur Rubinstein.

1979   Choreographs *Le Bourgeois Gentilhomme* (Richard Strauss) [410] as first Balanchine ballet presented by New York City Opera together with an opera performance, and assists with pantomime scenes in *Dido and Aeneas* (Purcell) [411]. – In London, rehearses Royal Ballet production of *Liebeslieder Walzer*. – New York City Ballet, in cooperation with Board of Education, presents first annual Young People's Matinee at New York State Theater for New York City public-school children.

1980   For New York City Ballet, choreographs Fauré's *Ballade* [412] and stages *Walpurgisnacht Ballet* (Gounod) [413] to music from *Faust*, earlier choreographed for Paris Opéra. – *Le Bourgeois Gentilhomme* (Richard Strauss) [414] enters New York City Ballet repertory. – Creates for Company *Robert Schumann's 'Davidsbündlertänze'* [415]. – Receives first National Gold Medal Award of National Society of

Arts and Letters. – New York City Ballet performs in festivals honoring Stravinsky Centennial in Berlin and Paris.

1981   For special production designed for television, using New York City Ballet dancers, creates fourth realization of Ravel's *L'Enfant et les Sortilèges* [416]. – Organizes and presents two-week Tschaikovsky Festival for New York City Ballet. – Included are twelve new works by six choreographers, of which Balanchine choreographs two and sections of two others. – These are *Mozartiana, Hungarian Gypsy Airs, Garland Dance* from *The Sleeping Beauty* for *Tempo di Valse*, and *Adagio Lamentoso* from *Symphony No. 6—Pathétique* [417-420].

1982   Plans acoustical improvements for New York State Theater. – To celebrate one-hundredth anniversary of Stravinsky's birth, conceives and supervises Stravinsky Centennial Celebration by New York City Ballet. – Between June 10 and June 18, twenty-five ballets and staged choral works set to Stravinsky's music by six choreographers are performed. — Of ten new works, Balanchine choreographs *Tango* and *Élégie*, and costages *Noah and the Flood* and *Perséphone* [421-424]. – Following official closing of Centennial Celebration rechoreographs, as solo for a ballerina, Stravinsky's *Variations for Orchestra* [425].

CHRONOLOGICAL TITLE LIST

1920

1 La Nuit (Romance)
2 Schön Rosmarin
3 [Concert Works]

1921

4 Poème
5 [Foxtrots]

1922

6 Waltz
7 Waltz and Adagio
8 Romanza
9 Waltz
10 Valse Triste
11 Matelotte
12 Orientalia
13 Hungarian Gypsy Dance

1923

14 Valse Caprice
15 Columbine's Veil
  (Der Schleier der Pierrette)
16 La Mort du Cygne
17 Adagio
18 Spanish Dance
19 Marche Funèbre
20 Waltz
21 Extase
22 Pas de Deux
23 Polka
24 Le Coq d'Or
25 Enigma
26 Caesar and Cleopatra
27 Eugene the Unfortunate
  (The Broken Brow)

28 Chorus Reading
29 [Cabaret Entertainment]
30 Étude
31 Oriental Dance
32 Elegy

1924

33 Pas de Deux
34 Invitation to the Dance
35 Le Bœuf sur le Toit and Pulcinella

1925

36 Pizzicato Polka
37 Valse Caprice
38 Carmen
39 Thaïs
40 Manon
41 Le Hulla
42 Le Démon
43 Hopac
44 Fay-Yen-Fah
45 Faust
46 Hérodiade
47 Un Début
48 L'Enfant et les Sortilèges
49 La Damnation de Faust
50 Étude
51 Polka Mélancolique
52 Le Chant du Rossignol
53 Barabau

1926

54 Boris Godunov
55 Judith
56 L'Hirondelle (La Rondine)
57 Lakmé

58 Les Contes d'Hoffmann
59 Jeanne d'Arc
60 Hamlet
61 Romeo and Juliet
62 La Pastorale
63 Jack in the Box
64 The Triumph of Neptune

1927

65 Aurora's Wedding:
    Ariadne and Her Brothers
66 Samson et Dalila
67 La Traviata
68 Turandot
69 La Damnation de Faust
70 Ivan le Terrible
71 Obéron
72 La Chatte
73 Grotesque Espagnol
74 Sarcasm
75 Swan Lake

1928

76 Mireille
77 Les Maîtres Chanteurs (Die
    Meistersinger von Nürnberg)
78 Venise
79 Sior Todéro Brontolon
80 Un Bal Masqué
    (Un Ballo in Maschera)
81 Don Juan (Don Giovanni)
82 La Fille d'Abdoubarahah
83 Aleko and Polka Grotesque
84 Apollon Musagète
85 The Gods Go A-Begging

1929

86 Roméo et Juliette

87 La Gioconda
88 Rigoletto
89 La Femme Nue
90 Martha
91 Wake Up and Dream!
92 La Croisade des Dames
    (Die Verschworenen)
93 Le Bal
94 Le Fils Prodigue
95 Pas de Deux (Moods)
96 Les Créatures de Prométhée
97 Dark Red Roses

1930

98   Aubade
99   Charles B. Cochran's 1930 Revue
100 [Duet and Trio]
101 Den Trekantede Hat
     (Le Tricorne)
102 Schéhérazade
103 Legetøjsbutiken
     (La Boutique Fantasque)
104 Fyrst Igor (Prince Igor)
105 Rosendrømmen
     (Le Spectre de la Rose)

1931

106 Josef-Legende
     (La Légende de Joseph)
107 Dances for Sir Oswald Stoll's
     Variety Shows
108 Charles B. Cochran's 1931 Revue
109 Orphée aux Enfers

1932

110 Les Amours du Poète
111 Tannhäuser
112 Les Contes d'Hoffmann

113 *Le Prophète*
114 *Une Nuit à Venise*
115 *Lakmé*
116 *Samson et Dalila*
117 *Faust*
118 *Patrie*
119 *Hérodiade*
120 *Turandot*
121 *Rigoletto*
122 *Manon*
123 *La Traviata*
124 *Roméo et Juliette*
125 *Fay-Yen-Fah*
126 *Aïda*
127 *Carmen*
128 *La Périchole*
129 *Cotillon*
130 *La Concurrence*
131 *Le Bourgeois Gentilhomme*
132 *Suites de Danse*
133 *Numéro les Canotiers*

1933

134 *Mozartiana*
135 *Les Songes*
136 *Les Sept Péchés Capitaux*
137 *Fastes*
138 *L'Errante*
139 *Les Valses de Beethoven*
140 *Dans l'Élysée*

1935

141 *Serenade*
142 *Alma Mater*
143 *Errante*
144 *Reminiscence*
145 *Dreams*

146 *Transcendence*
147 *[Solo]*
148 *Jeanne d'Arc*
149 *Mozartiana*
150 *La Traviata*
151 *Faust*
152 *Aïda*
153 *Lakmé*
154 *Tannhäuser*
155 *Carmen*
156 *Rigoletto*
157 *[Pas de Deux]*

1936

158 *Mignon*
159 *Manon*
160 *La Juive*
161 *La Rondine*
162 *Ziegfeld Follies: 1936 Edition*
163 *Die Meistersinger von Nürnberg*
164 *Serenata: 'Magic'*
165 *Concerto (Classic Ballet)*
166 *On Your Toes*
167 *The Bartered Bride*
168 *Lucia di Lammermoor*
169 *The Bat*
170 *Orpheus and Eurydice*
    (Orfeo ed Euridice)
171 *Samson et Dalila*

1937

172 *Le Coq d'Or*
173 *Caponsacchi*
174 *La Gioconda*
175 *Babes in Arms*
176 *Apollon Musagète*
177 *The Card Party*

45

46

47

287 *Bayou*
288 *Scotch Symphony*
289 *Metamorphoses*
290 *Harlequinade Pas de Deux*
291 *One, Yuletide Square*
292 *Concertino*

1953

293 *Valse Fantaisie*
294 *The Countess Becomes*
     the Maid
295 *The Rake's Progress*
296 *[Cotillion Promenade]*
297 *La Favorita*
298 *Boris Godunov*
299 *Adriana Lecouvreur*
300 *Amahl and the Night Visitors*

1954

301 *Opus 34*
302 *The Nutcracker*
303 *Western Symphony*
304 *Ivesiana*
305 *House of Flowers*

1955

306 *Roma*
307 *Pas de Trois*
308 *The Tempest*
309 *Pas de Dix*
310 *Jeux d'Enfants*

1956

311 *The Magic Flute*
312 *Allegro Brillante*
313 *A Musical Joke*
314 *Divertimento No. 15*

1957

315 *Square Dance*
316 *Agon*

1958

317 *Gounod Symphony*
318 *Stars and Stripes*
319 *A Midsummer Night's Dream*
320 *The Winter's Tale*
321 *Waltz-Scherzo*
322 *The Seven Deadly Sins*

1959

323 *Native Dancers*
324 *Episodes*
325 *Romeo and Juliet*
326 *The Merry Wives of Windsor*
327 *The Warrior*

1960

328 *Night Shadow*
329 *Panamerica*
330 *Theme and Variations*
331 *Pas de Deux*
     (Tschaikovsky Pas de Deux)
332 *The Figure in the Carpet*
333 *Variations from Don Sebastian*
     (Donizetti Variations)
334 *Monumentum pro Gesualdo*
335 *Liebeslieder Walzer*
336 *Ragtime (I)*

1961

337 *Modern Jazz: Variants*
338 *Electronics*
339 *Valses et Variations*
     (Raymonda Variations)

48

CATALOGUE

1920

1 LA NUIT (later called ROMANCE)

MUSIC: By Anton Rubinstein (Romance in E-flat, Op. 44, no. 1, for voice and piano, danced to piano and violin).

PREMIERE: 1920?, concert at Petrograd Theater (Ballet) School.

CAST: Olga Mungalova (or possibly Lydia Ivanova), George Balanchine.

NOTE: Balanchine remembers this as the first work he choreographed, although the date of its premiere has not been established. Mikhail Mikhailov, a contemporary of Balanchine's at the official ballet school in St. Petersburg/Petrograd, suggests in *My Life in Ballet* that it may have been created as early as 1917-18. Mungalova's unpublished memoirs describe her performance of this dance with Balanchine at the ballet school in the summer of 1920. She danced it with Pëtr Gusev at the school graduation performance of 1920 or 1921. As *Romance*, the ballet was presented on June 1, 1923, at the first performance of the Young Ballet, the company created by Balanchine, Gusev, Vladimir Dimitriev, Boris Erbshtein, and Yuri Slonimsky; it was also in the repertory of the Principal Dancers of the Russian State Ballet, the small troupe led by Balanchine and Dimitriev on tour in Germany during the summer of 1924. The work was performed for many years in the Soviet Union after Balanchine's departure.

2 SCHÖN ROSMARIN

MUSIC: By Fritz Kreisler (from *Alt Wiener Tanzweisen*, 1911).

PREMIERE: April 4, 1920, Petrograd Theater (Ballet) School graduation performance, State Theater of Opera and Ballet (formerly Maryinsky).

CAST: O. Barysheva, D. Kirsanov.

NOTE: Also performed by the Principal Dancers of the Russian State Ballet in 1924 on their summer tour of Germany and in London that October at the Empire Theatre.

See 22

3 [CONCERT WORKS]

As a young man, Balanchine frequently created, as he says, 'informal little things,' performed once or twice and then forgotten. Among these were compositions to music by Nicolai Medtner and to excerpts from *Salome* by Richard Strauss. He also remembers making 'something new' to Chopin (or to the 'Chopin' section of Schumann's *Carnaval*) for a 'soirée.' Alexandra Danilova remembers a solo waltz done for her, possibly to Johann Strauss (she performed a Strauss waltz September 4 and 9, 1923, at the Svobodny Theater, Petrograd). She also recalls a solo to Scriabin (not the *Étude* pas de deux [30]). There is a possibility that Balanchine choreographed a pas de deux called *Dutch Dance* to the music of Grieg, but both he and Danilova think it equally possible that this dance, which appears on the programs for London performances of the Principal Dancers of the Russian State Ballet in 1924, might have been from Albert Lortzing's opera *Zar und Zimmermann*, with choreography by Pavel Petrov or Andrei Lopukhov. In published interviews, Balanchine has mentioned other early works: a ballet for eight boys in the Fokine style, done while he was still a student (*Dance Magazine*, June 1954, p. 148), a ballet to Stravinsky's *Ragtime* in 1922 (New York City Center: *Playbill* 1:10, December 2, 1957), and concert dances to music by Schumann (*Washington Post*, October 12, 1980).

See *110, 336, 356*

1921

4 POÈME

MUSIC: By Zdeněk Fibich.

PRODUCTION: Costumes by George Balanchine.

PREMIERE: Concert at the Petrograd Theater (Ballet) School some time prior to Balanchine's graduation on April 4, 1921.

CAST: Alexandra Danilova?, George Balanchine.

NOTE: The woman's costume, a light blue tunic, was unusual for the time: the standard costume was the tutu. It is not certain that Danilova danced the first performance of this work, but both the late Marietta Frangopoulo, Curator of the Museum of the Leningrad Academic Choreographic School, and the late Vera Kostrovitskaya, Senior Instructor of Classical Ballet and a slightly younger colleague of Balanchine's at the ballet school, have described Danilova in this ballet. She and Mikhail Dudko danced it at the Donon Restaurant, Petrograd, in 1923, and it was also included on the first Evening of the Young Ballet, June 1, 1923. The ballet continued to be performed for many years in the Soviet Union. The Soviet dance historian Vera Krasovskaya danced it at a school concert about 1932.

5 [FOXTROTS]

By 1921, the Bolsheviks had signed treaties with a number of European and Asian countries, renouncing claims to various border territories, guaranteeing mutual non-aggression in some cases, and resuming trade relations. Perhaps the most important of these was the Anglo-Soviet trade agreement of March 16, 1921, in which Lenin opened the ports of Petrograd to trade with the West. In celebration of this (or, perhaps, another similar treaty), a giant party was held; for entertainment there were actors, German music, and a foxtrot composed for the crowd by Balanchine.

A review in *Krasnaya gazeta*, May 20, 1924, mentions a foxtrot performed by the Young Ballet as part of a demonstration concert. This is almost certainly not the work composed for the public party; Pëtr Gusev suggests it may have been a solo created by Balanchine for Nicholas Efimov.

1922

6 WALTZ

MUSIC: By Riccardo Drigo.

PREMIERE: April 9, 1922, Petrograd Theater (Ballet) School graduation performance, State Theater of Opera and Ballet (formerly Maryinsky).

CAST: Anna Vorobieva.

NOTE: A Drigo *Waltz* was performed by Alexandra Danilova as a member of the Principal Dancers of the Russian State Ballet on the summer tour of Germany in 1924. It may have been this composition, but more probably was the waltz from Petipa's short ballet *The Lovely Pearl* (Drigo), which was in the repertory of the Young Ballet.

7 WALTZ AND ADAGIO

MUSIC: By George Balanchine.

PREMIERE: April 9, 1922, Petrograd Theater (Ballet) School graduation performance, State Theater of Opera and Ballet (formerly Maryinsky) [?].

CAST: Olga Mungalova, Pëtr Gusev.

NOTE: Information about the premiere was supplied by Gusev, a contemporary of Balanchine's at ballet school in St. Petersburg/Petrograd, in an unpublished interview with Poel Karp; however, the work does not appear on the printed program. A performance by Alexandra Danilova and Balanchine was reviewed on June 11, 1922, and the work is known to have been performed on the first Evening of the Young Ballet, June 1, 1923, probably by Gusev and Mungalova, who performed in the Young Ballet's first concert and often danced together.

8 ROMANZA

MUSIC: Music by George Balanchine. Lyrics by Evgeny Mravinsky.

PREMIERE: 1922, Pavlovsk?

CAST: Olga Mungalova, Pëtr Gusev.

NOTE: This work was created by Balanchine after his graduation in 1921; he thinks it was perhaps first performed at the summer resort of Pavlovsk, near Petrograd, with himself as the piano accompanist.

9 WALTZ

PREMIERE: August 15, 1922, resort at Sestroretsk, near Petrograd.

CAST: Alexandra Danilova, George Balanchine.

NOTE: Neither Balanchine nor Danilova remembers the music.

10 VALSE TRISTE

MUSIC: By Jean Sibelius (*Valse Triste* from incidental music for *Kuolema*, Op. 44, 1903).

PRODUCTION: Costume by Boris Erbshtein.

PREMIERE: August 15, 1922, resort at Sestroretsk, near Petrograd.

CAST: Lydia Ivanova.

NOTE: Also performed by Tamara Geva and Alexandra Danilova on the tour of Germany and during the London engagement of the Principal Dancers of the Russian State Ballet, in the summer and fall of 1924.

11 MATELOTTE (also called SAILOR'S HORNPIPE)

MUSIC: Traditional hornpipe music, arranged by Zuev.

PREMIERE: 1922?

CAST: Unavailable (a woman and two men).

NOTE: This little dance may have been given its first performance on August 15, 1922, at the resort at Sestroretsk, near Petrograd; Balanchine, Lydia Ivanova and Alexandra Danilova are known to have participated in a concert there on that date. The dance was included on the first Evening of the Young Ballet, June 1, 1923, at the Duma, Petrograd, when the musical arrangement of Zuev was first credited. It was apparently performed many times in the Soviet Union, but no casting for Soviet performances has been found. The work was in the repertory of the Principal Dancers of the Russian State Ballet in 1924, both for the summer German tour and the October performances at the Empire Theatre in London, where it was danced by Balanchine, Danilova and Nicholas Efimov.

12 ORIENTALIA

MUSIC: By César Cui (Op. 50, no. 9, 1912).

PREMIERE: Season of 1922-23.

CAST: *Young Oriental Dancer*, Nina Mlodzinskaya; *Blind Old Beggar*, George Balanchine.

NOTE: Yuri Slonimsky, in *Balanchine: The Early Years*, notes that this dance was choreographed when Balanchine had already received recognition in Petrograd. Mikhailov dates it 1922-23. There is record of a performance at the Hôtel d'Europe, Petrograd, on June 2, 1923, with Tamara Geva and Rostislav Slavianinov. The work was probably danced by the Principal Dancers of the Russian State Ballet on the 1924 tour of Germany, although newspaper announcements are unclear.

13 HUNGARIAN GYPSY DANCE

MUSIC: By Johannes Brahms.

PREMIERE: Season of 1922-23.

CAST: Tamara K. Leshevich, Rostislav Slavianinov.

NOTE: Balanchine thinks this work was first performed at Pavlovsk; he is quite sure the premiere was not on the formal stage of the State Theater of Opera and Ballet (formerly Maryinsky). Mikhailov gives 1922-23 as the premiere date. The Principal Dancers of the Russian State Ballet performed the work in 1924 during the summer German tour and the October performances at the Empire Theatre in London, where it was danced by Tamara Geva both with Balanchine and with Nicholas Efimov.

1923

14 VALSE CAPRICE

MUSIC: By Anton Rubinstein (Op. 118).

PREMIERE: April 2, 1923, Muzykalnaya Komediíà, Petrograd.

CAST: Xenia Maklezova, D. I. Beeness.

NOTE: First performed at the Thirty-fifth Year Jubilee benefit for
I. A. Smolyakov. In 1925, Balanchine rechoreographed Serafima
Astafieva's solo for Alicia Markova to this music.

See 37

15 COLUMBINE'S VEIL (DER SCHLEIER DER PIERRETTE)
Pantomime with Dances

MUSIC: By Ernst von Dohnanyi (produced 1910). Scenario by
Arthur Schnitzler.

PRODUCTION: Directed by N. A. Shcherbakov. Scenery by Vladimir
Dimitriev.

PREMIERE: May 9, 1923, Institute of Art History, Petrograd.

CAST: Unavailable.

16 LA MORT DU CYGNE

MUSIC: By Camille Saint-Saëns (*Le Cygne* [cello solo] from *Le Carnaval
des Animaux: Fantaisie Zoologique* for small orchestra, 1886).

CHOREOGRAPHY: By Michel Fokine (1905?); staged by George
Balanchine.

PREMIERE: June 1, 1923, Young Ballet, Alexandrinsky Hall, Duma,
Petrograd.

CAST: Nina Stukolkina.

NOTE: First performed on the opening program of the Young Ballet,
which also included the premiere of *Adagio* [17] and performances of
Romance [1, earlier titled *La Nuit*], *Waltz and Adagio* [7], *Matelotte* [11];
and may have included the premieres of *Spanish Dance* [18], *Marche
Funèbre* [19], *Waltz* [20], and *Extase* [21]. Works by Marius Petipa and
N. Lisovskaya were also performed. The concert seems not to have been
reviewed in the Soviet press or theater journals, but was announced
for this date by a poster which lists the following participants:
Alexandra Danilova, E. V. Eliseyeva, Lydia Ivanova, Vera Kostrovitskaya, N. Lisovskaya, Nina Mlodzinskaya, Olga Mungalova, N. A.

Nikitina, Nina Stukolkina, L. M. Tiuntina, Georgi Balanchivadze, L. Balashov, Pëtr Gusev, Nicholas Efimov, D. K. Kirsanov, Leonid Lavrovsky, and Mikhail Mikhailov.

See 263

17 ADAGIO

MUSIC: By Camille Saint-Saëns (adagio excerpt from the ballet *Javotte*, produced 1896).

PREMIERE: June 1, 1923, Young Ballet, Alexandrinsky Hall, Duma, Petrograd.

CAST: Alexandra Danilova, George Balanchine?

NOTE: Also performed by Danilova and Balanchine at the final concert of the Young Ballet, June 15, 1924, Pavlovsk.

18 SPANISH DANCE

MUSIC: Probably by Alexander Glazounov (from *Raymonda*, Op. 57, produced 1898).

PREMIERE: June 1, 1923, Young Ballet, Alexandrinsky Hall, Duma, Petrograd.

CAST: Nina Stukolkina, Mikhail Mikhailov.

NOTE: Although *Spanish Dance* does not appear on the poster announcing the first Evening of the Young Ballet, Slonimsky quotes Vera Kostrovitskaya's recollection that it was presented at the concert. *Adagio*, with Balanchine choreography to the music of Glazounov, does appear on the announcement poster; no other mention has been found: possibly it was retitled *Spanish Dance* for the performance.

See 233, 309, 339, 384

19 MARCHE FUNÈBRE

MUSIC: By Frédéric Chopin (second movement [1837] of Sonata No. 1 in B-flat minor, Op. 35, 1839).

PRODUCTION: Scenery by Boris Erbshtein. Costumes by Vladimir Dimitriev.

PREMIERE: June 1, 1923, Young Ballet, Alexandrinsky Hall, Duma, Petrograd.

CAST: FIRST MOVEMENT, TRAGIC: Olga Mungalova or Tamara Geva, 3 men, 6 women; SECOND MOVEMENT, LYRIC: Alexandra Danilova, ensemble; THIRD MOVEMENT, TRAGIC: Entire cast.

NOTE: Although *Marche Funèbre* is not listed on the announcements for the initial program of the Young Ballet, Balanchine planned it for the first performance and believes that it had its premiere June 1, 1923. It was mentioned (although not reviewed) on June 24, 1923, in *Krasnaya gazeta*. There is some indication that it was first performed as a school work. Soon after joining the Ballets Russes in 1924, Balanchine taught *Marche Funèbre* to members of the company for presentation to Serge Diaghilev, Boris Kochno and S. L. Grigoriev in the studio of Serafima Astafieva.

20 WALTZ

MUSIC: By Maurice Ravel (one of the waltzes from *Valses Nobles et Sentimentales*, 1911, orchestrated 1912).

PREMIERE: 1923?

CAST: Nina Stukolkina or Nina Mlodzinskaya, male partner.

NOTE: Balanchine recalls that this dance was originally performed on the first Evening of the Young Ballet, June 1, 1923, at the Duma, Petrograd, although the poster announcing the program does not list it.

See 277

21 EXTASE

MUSIC: By George Balanchine.

PREMIERE: 1923?

CAST: Unavailable (pas de deux for ballerina and partner).

NOTE: Balanchine does not remember for whom he created this pas de deux, which he thinks may possibly have been included in the first Evening of the Young Ballet, June 1, 1923, at the Duma, Petrograd, although it does not appear on the poster announcing the concert. Alexandra Danilova thinks it might have been made for Lydia Ivanova and Rostislav Slavianinov.

22 PAS DE DEUX

MUSIC: By Fritz Kreisler (*Liebesleid* from *Alt Wiener Tanzweisen*, 1911).

PREMIERE: July 31, 1923, evening with dancers from the academic theaters, Petrograd.

CAST: Lydia Ivanova, Nicholas Efimov.

NOTE: Newspapers do not specify the location of this concert or whether a special event was involved. All the dancers were participants in the Young Ballet, and were also members of the State Theater (formerly Maryinsky) company. Balanchine is known to have choreographed two works for the concert: this duet to music of Kreisler and a polka by Rachmaninoff for Ivanova [23]. He thinks he probably also choreographed a duet to Tschaikovsky's *Romance without Words* (Op. 40, no. 6) for Ivanova and Efimov, and may have created a dance for Efimov to Dulov's *Variation Classique*, presented the same evening.

See 2

23 POLKA

MUSIC: By Sergei Rachmaninoff.

PREMIERE: July 31, 1923, evening with dancers from the academic theaters, Petrograd.

CAST: Lydia Ivanova.

NOTE: See 22.

24 LE COQ D'OR

Opera in Three Acts by Nicolai Rimsky-Korsakov
ACT II VISION; ACT III MARCH

PRODUCTION: Directed by S. A. Samosud. Choreography and movement direction by George Balanchine (uncredited).

PREMIERE: September 15, 1923, Maly Opera Theater, Petrograd. Danced by the resident ballet troupe.

CAST: VISION: Uspenskaya. MARCH: Orlova, Uspenskaya, Kobeleva, Dikushina, Baranovich, Komarov, Rykhliakov, Chesnakov, Kobelev, Shuisky.

NOTE: Balanchine also devised movement sequences in Act II for the Queen of Shemakha, the choral group, and Dodon and the pupils.

See 172

25 ENIGMA

MUSIC: By Anton Arensky (*The Exit of Cleopatra* from *Egyptian Nights*, Op. 50, produced 1900).

PREMIERE: 1923?

CAST: Lydia Ivanova, George Balanchine.

NOTE: Danced in bare feet. Although no documentation has been found, Balanchine believes that he and Ivanova originally performed the work. He and Tamara Geva danced it at a benefit at the State Theater of Opera and Ballet (formerly Maryinsky); there are also records of their performing it in the floorshow at the Donon Restaurant in Petrograd on September 29, 1923. The work was danced by Geva and Balanchine during the Principal Dancers of the Russian State Ballet tour of Germany in the summer of 1924, at the Empire Theatre in London that October, and in audition for Diaghilev later that autumn in Paris. It was performed by Diaghilev's Ballets Russes at least three times in 1925 on programs of divertissements in the Nouvelle Salle de Musique (Salle Ganne) in the Casino at Monte Carlo. The work was still performed in the Soviet Union during the 1930s. *Enigma* is Balanchine's title for the work.

26 CAESAR AND CLEOPATRA

Play by George Bernard Shaw

MUSIC: By Yuri Shaporin.

CHOREOGRAPHY: Pantomime and dances choreographed by George Balanchine.

PRODUCTION: Produced and directed by V. R. Rappaport. Scenery and costumes by Vladimir A. Schouko.

PREMIERE: September 30, 1923, Petrograd Drama Theater [group], Maly Opera Theater, Petrograd.

CAST: *Cleopatra*, Eugenia Wolf-Israel; others.

NOTE: Balanchine choreographed the pantomime and dances in Act I, and movements for Cleopatra.

27 EUGENE THE UNFORTUNATE (THE BROKEN BROW)
Play by Ernst Toller, translated by Adrian Piotrovsky

PRODUCTION: Directed by Sergei Radlov. Pantomime directed by Levitsky. Scenery by Vladimir Dimitriev.

PREMIERE: December 15, 1923, Maly Opera Theater, Petrograd. Conductor: Max Kuper.

CAST: *Eugene Brokenbrow*, Vivien; *Margaret Brokenbrow, His Wife*, Yureneva; *Mrs. Brokenbrow, His Mother*, Gribunina; *Jock Rooster*, Andreivsky; and others. *Dancers*: Bezestorskaya, Orlova, Chazova, Dikushina, Rykhliakov, Shizyayev, Morosov, Petrushenko.

NOTE: Balanchine contributed Act II dances in silhouette.

28 CHORUS READING

PREMIERE: Late 1923?, Young Ballet, Duma, Petrograd.

CAST: 10-12 members of the Young Ballet.

NOTE: Choreography by Balanchine to the chanting of Alexander Blok's *The Twelve* and other poems by a chorus of fifty voices, without music, with the performers dressed in national costumes. This was a single number in an evening of works, the rest of which had music. No certain information regarding the premiere date or location has been obtained; the suggested date is provided by Bernard Taper in his biography of Balanchine. Possibly this work and others as yet undocumented were first performed on the second program of the Young Ballet. Pëtr Gusev recalls that this work, with *Marche Funèbre* [19], was given on a program at the Chensely Circus, Petrograd, by the Young Ballet.

64

29 [CABARET ENTERTAINMENT]

In December, 1923, The Carousel, an 'intellectual cabaret,' opened in Petrograd. For this occasion and subsequently, Balanchine devised movement for poems set to music. The Soviet periodical *Teatr* reported Balanchine's collaboration with the directors Evreinov, Petrov, Tversky, and Miklashevsky, the artists Akimov and Nicolas Benois, and also with Olga Mungalova, Armfeld and Volkov.

30 ÉTUDE

MUSIC: By Alexander Scriabin (probably *Caresse Dansée*, Op. 57, 1908, and one of the preludes, both for piano).

PREMIERE: 1923/24, Young Ballet.

CAST: Tamara Geva, George Balanchine.

NOTE: Pëtr Gusev recalls that Balanchine had intended a far more ambitious work, but was only able to complete the pas de deux. This was probably performed by Balanchine and Geva as an audition piece for Diaghilev in Paris in the autumn of 1924, and appears on matinee programs of divertissements performed by Diaghilev's Ballets Russes in the Nouvelle Salle de Musique (Salle Ganne) in the Casino at Monte Carlo. In 1925, Balanchine choreographed a new work to this music for Ruth Page and Chester Hale.

See 50

31 ORIENTAL DANCE

MUSIC: By Modest Moussorgsky (from the unfinished opera *Khovanshchina*, 1872-80, completed by Nicolai Rimsky-Korsakov, 1886).

PREMIERE: 1923/24, Young Ballet.

CAST: Tamara Geva, George Balanchine.

See 97

32 ELEGY

MUSIC: By Sergei Rachmaninoff (*Élégie* for piano, 1892).

PREMIERE: 1923/24, Young Ballet?

CAST: Unavailable (a woman and two men).

NOTE: No information about the premiere has been located. The ballet was danced at the final concert of the Young Ballet, Pavlovsk, June 15, 1924, by Tamara Geva, Nicholas Efimov and Balanchine. It was also performed on the German tour of the Principal Dancers of the Russian State Ballet in the summer of 1924, and may have been one of the audition pieces for Diaghilev in Paris in the autumn of 1924.

1924

33 PAS DE DEUX

MUSIC: By Alexander Glazounov (slow movement from one of the violin concertos).

PREMIERE: May 7, 1924, State Theater of Opera and Ballet (formerly Maryinsky), Petrograd.

CAST: Elizaveta Gerdt, Mikhail Dudko.

NOTE: This pas de deux followed a performance of *La Bayadère* at a benefit for Elizaveta Gerdt. Balanchine and Gerdt then danced a pas de deux (excluding the male variation) to the music of Nicolas Tcherepnine's *Le Pavillon d'Armide*, which may or may not have had choreography by Balanchine: Gerdt's variation was by Fokine, who had choreographed a complete ballet to this music in 1907; Balanchine's contribution, if he made one, would have been the opening adagio and the closing coda.

34 INVITATION TO THE DANCE

MUSIC: By Carl Maria von Weber (*Aufforderung zum Tanz* for piano, Op. 65, 1819).

PREMIERE: Spring, 1924.

CAST: Alexandra Danilova, George Balanchine, Mikhail Mikhailov.

NOTE: Premiere information and original casting are given by Mikhailov in *My Life in Ballet*. Balanchine thinks this was probably first performed at Pavlovsk, where there was an open-air platform for performances. The ballet was danced by the Principal Dancers of the Russian State Ballet during the tour of Germany in the summer of 1924. The music had been used by Fokine for *Le Spectre de la Rose* (1911), which Balanchine staged and performed in Copenhagen in 1930.

See 105

35 LE BŒUF SUR LE TOIT and PULCINELLA

During the period 1923-24, at least two works were rehearsed by Balanchine but not performed. The four-hand piano score to Stravinsky's *Pulcinella* had been smuggled into Russia; Balanchine began preparing the ballet in January 1924, but the project proved to be beyond the resources of the Young Ballet and had to be abandoned. He also rehearsed the Milhaud-Cocteau *Le Bœuf sur le Toit*.

See 379

1925

36 PIZZICATO POLKA

MUSIC: By Léo Delibes (from *Sylvia, ou la Nymphe de Diane*, produced 1876).

CHOREOGRAPHY: By George Balanchine after Serafima Astafieva.

PREMIERE: February 1925 (before February 21), the Royal Palace, Monte Carlo.

CAST: Alicia Markova.

NOTE: First performed at a party given by the Princesse Héréditaire. Earliest program found (February 21, 1925, matinee) lists the work, then entitled *Variation*, as part of the 'Suite de Danses' under the general title *Le Festin*, in the series of concert performances by Diaghilev's Ballets Russes given in the Nouvelle Salle de Musique (Salle Ganne) of the Monte Carlo Casino.

See 273, 350, 387

37 VALSE CAPRICE

MUSIC: By Anton Rubinstein (Op. 118).

CHOREOGRAPHY: By George Balanchine after Serafima Astafieva.

PREMIERE: February 1925 (before February 21), the Royal Palace, Monte Carlo.

CAST: Alicia Markova.

NOTE: First performed at a party given by the Princesse Héréditaire. Earliest program found (March 4, 1925, matinee) lists the work as part of the 'Suite de Danses' under the general title *L'Assemblée*, in the series of concert performances by Diaghilev's Ballets Russes given in the Nouvelle Salle de Musique (Salle Ganne) of the Monte Carlo Casino.

See 14

38 CARMEN

Opera in Four Acts by Georges Bizet
ACT II SEGUIDILLA

PREMIERE: January 25, 1925, Opéra de Monte-Carlo. Danced by Diaghilev's Ballets Russes.

CAST: 4 couples.

NOTE: Diaghilev's dancers were employed between ballet seasons as the resident company of the Opéra de Monte-Carlo, and his first assignments to Balanchine were opera divertissements. Balanchine has said that all choreography for operas in Monte Carlo during his tenure with Diaghilev was newly created by him; programs occasionally include no credits for choreography, and it may be that some dances by Nijinska, resident choreographer with Diaghilev at Monte Carlo in 1923 and 1924, remained during Balanchine's early years. When choreography credits appear in the opera programs between 1925 and 1929, they are variously given as 'Maître de ballet: Georges Balanchine,' 'Chorégraphie de Georges Balanchine,' or 'Ballet réglé par Georges Balanchine'; the significance of these differences is unknown.

See 127, 155, 248

39 THAÏS
Opera in Three Acts and Six Scenes by Jules Massenet
ACT I DIVERTISSEMENT

PREMIERE: January 27, 1925, Opéra de Monte-Carlo. Danced by Diaghilev's Ballets Russes. Conductor: Léon Jehin.

CAST: 13 women.

40 MANON
Opera in Four Acts by Jules Massenet
ACT III BALLET

PREMIERE: February 5, 1925, Opéra de Monte-Carlo. Danced by Diaghilev's Ballets Russes.

CAST: Alexandra Danilova, Thadée Slavinsky, corps de ballet.

See 122, 159

41 LE HULLA
Oriental Lyric Tale in Four Acts by Marcel Samuel-Rousseau
ACT III DIVERTISSEMENT

PREMIERE: February 12, 1925, Opéra de Monte-Carlo. Danced by Diaghilev's Ballets Russes. Conductor: Marcel Samuel-Rousseau.

CAST: Vera Nemtchinova, 4 women.

42 LE DÉMON

Fantastic Opera in Three Acts by Anton Rubinstein
ACT II BALLET

PREMIERE: February 14, 1925, Opéra de Monte-Carlo. Danced by Diaghilev's Ballets Russes. Conductor: Victor de Sabata.

CAST: Lubov Tchernicheva, Léon Woizikowsky, 8 men.

NOTE: The dance from *Le Démon*, a lezghinka, was performed as part of the 'Suite de Danses' under the general title *L'Assemblée* (March 7, 1925, matinee), in the series of concert performances by Diaghilev's Ballets Russes given in the Nouvelle Salle de Musique (Salle Ganne) of the Monte Carlo Casino.

43 HOPAC

MUSIC: By Modest Moussorgsky (from *The Fair at Sorochinsk*, 1874-80 [unfinished]).

PREMIERE: February 21, 1925 (matinee), Diaghilev's Ballets Russes, Nouvelle Salle de Musique (Salle Ganne), Monte Carlo Casino.

CAST: Lubov Tchernicheva, Nicolas Kremnev, 4 couples.

See 208

44 FAY-YEN-FAH

Opera in Three Acts by Joseph Redding
ACT II, SCENE I BALLET DIVERTISSEMENT; BALLET VOLANT

PREMIERE: February 26, 1925, Opéra de Monte-Carlo. Danced by Diaghilev's Ballets Russes. Conductor: Victor de Sabata.

CAST: BALLET DIVERTISSEMENT: *Lilies*, 6 women; *Veils*, 8 women; *Chinese Woman*, Vera Nemtchinova; *Chinese Man*, Nicolas Kremnev; *Poppies*, Nemtchinova, 6 women; *White Peacocks*, 2 women; *Gold Peacocks*, 4 women. BALLET VOLANT: 5 women.

NOTE: World premiere.

See 125

45 FAUST

Opera in Five Acts by Charles Gounod

ACT II KERMESSE

PREMIERE: March 5, 1925, Opéra de Monte-Carlo. Danced by Diaghilev's Ballets Russes. Conductor: Marc-César Scotto.

CAST: Corps de ballet.

See 117, 151, 227, 397, 413

46 HÉRODIADE

Opera in Four Acts and Six Scenes by Jules Massenet

ACT III BALLET

PREMIERE: March 7, 1925, Opéra de Monte-Carlo. Danced by Diaghilev's Ballets Russes. Conductor: Marc-César Scotto.

CAST: Lubov Tchernicheva, George Balanchine, Thadée Slavinsky, 14 women, 8 men.

See 119

47 UN DÉBUT

Opera in Two Acts by Philippe Bellenot

ACT II BALLET (DANCES IN RESTAURANT)

PREMIERE: March 21, 1925, Opéra de Monte-Carlo. Danced by Diaghilev's Ballets Russes. Conductor: Léon Jehin.

CAST: Corps de ballet.

NOTE: This brief opera was performed as curtain-raiser for the premiere of Maurice Ravel's *L'Enfant et les Sortilèges*.

48 L'ENFANT ET LES SORTILÈGES
Lyric Fantasy in Two Parts

MUSIC: By Maurice Ravel (1920-25). Libretto by Colette.

PRODUCTION: Directed by Raoul Gunsbourg. Scenery by Alphonse Visconti. Costumes by Georgette Vialet.

PREMIERE: March 21, 1925, Opéra de Monte-Carlo. Danced by Diaghilev's Ballets Russes. Conductor: Victor de Sabata.

CAST: Singers and dancers appeared together on stage. Individual dancers were listed for the first time in the program for February 15, 1926: ACT I: *Shepherds and Shepherdesses*, Alexandra Danilova, Constantin Tcherkas, 2 couples; *Ashes*, Alicia Markova; *3 Sheep*; *Goat*; *Dog*. ACT II: *Butterflies*, Danilova, Tcherkas, 2 women; *4 Squirrels*; *4 Dragonflies*; *5 Frogs*. Sung parts included *The Child, 2 Cats, Easy Chair, Princess, Mother, Nightingale, Fire, Chinese Cup, Dragonfly, Bat, Squirrel, Shepherd and Shepherdess, Teacher Arithmetic, Clock, Armchair, Teapot, Tree, Frog, 3 Beasts, Owl.*

NOTE: A naughty child, confined to his room, smashes the teapot, mistreats his pet squirrel, tears the wallpaper, assaults the fireplace, the clock, his school books. The objects come to life, assert themselves, rebuke him. Transported into a magic garden, the child is confronted by animals and trees that in the past have suffered from his cruelties; they attack him. During the fray a small squirrel is injured; moved to compassion, the child dresses its wound. The animals are astonished; when in despair the child cries out for his mother, they assist him, and lead him to her.

World premiere. Diaghilev's first major assignment to Balanchine, and the first of four Balanchine productions of this work, each a different staging with new décor; the 1981 version, conceived especially for television, used elements from the 1975 production.

OTHER VERSIONS: 1946, Ballet Society (*The Spellbound Child* [*L'Enfant et les Sortilèges*]). 1975, New York City Ballet (*L'Enfant et les Sortilèges*, Ravel Festival). 1981, for the PBS television series *Dance in America* (*The Spellbound Child / L'Enfant et les Sortilèges*).

See 235, 390, 416

49 LA DAMNATION DE FAUST

'La Taverne' and 'Les Sylphes' from the Opera by Hector Berlioz

BALLET VOLANT (LES SYLPHES)

PREMIERE: March 24, 1925, Opéra de Monte-Carlo. Danced by Diaghilev's Ballets Russes. Conductor: Léon Jehin.

CAST: Corps de ballet.

See 69

50 ÉTUDE

MUSIC: By Alexander Scriabin (probably *Caresse Dansée*, Op. 57, 1908, and one of the preludes, both for piano).

PREMIERE: March 1925, Monte Carlo.

CAST: Ruth Page, Chester Hale.

NOTE: *Étude* and *Polka Mélancolique* [51], the first works commissioned from Balanchine by an American, were choreographed at the request of the dancer Ruth Page during her brief time as a member of the Diaghilev company. They were given unofficial concert performances and were soon lost.

See 30

51 POLKA MÉLANCOLIQUE

MUSIC: By Anton Rubinstein.

PREMIERE: March 1925, Monte Carlo.

CAST: Ruth Page.

NOTE: See 50.

52 LE CHANT DU ROSSIGNOL
(also called THE SONG OF THE NIGHTINGALE)

Ballet in One Act, after Hans Christian Andersen's Fairy Tale

MUSIC: By Igor Stravinsky (symphonic poem for orchestra in three parts, 1917; adapted from his 1913 opera *Le Rossignol*).

CHOREOGRAPHY: Originally choreographed by Léonide Massine (1920); rechoreographed by George Balanchine.

PRODUCTION: Curtain, scenery and costumes by Henri Matisse (from the 1920 production).

PREMIERE: June 17, 1925, Diaghilev's Ballets Russes, Théâtre Gaieté Lyrique, Paris. Conductor: Marc-César Scotto.

CAST: *Nightingale*, Alicia Markova; *Death*, Lydia Sokolova; *Emperor*, Serge Grigoriev; *Mechanical Nightingale*, George Balanchine; *Japanese Maestro*, Nicolas Kremnev; *16 Ladies of the Court*; *6 Warriors*; *6 Mandarins*; *4 Chamberlains*.

NOTE: Stravinsky prefixed a ballet scenario to the score based on quotations from Andersen, with the following headings: 1. The Fête in the Emperor of China's Palace; 2. The Two Nightingales; 3. Illness and Recovery of the Emperor of China.

Balanchine's first choreography for performance in the regular seasons of Diaghilev's Ballets Russes, and his first choreography in the West to music by Stravinsky; in Leningrad he had choreographed *Ragtime* [3], and rehearsed *Pulcinella* [35]. On one occasion when Markova was ill, Balanchine danced the role of the Nightingale.

53 BARABAU
Ballet with Chorus

MUSIC: Music and book by Vittorio Rieti (expanded to an orchestral score with chorus from an existing *a cappella* cantata, *Barabau*, on commission from Serge Diaghilev, 1925).

PRODUCTION: Scenery and costumes by Maurice Utrillo. Scenery executed by Prince A. Schervashidze; costumes executed by Alias and Morris Angel.

PREMIERE: December 11, 1925, Diaghilev's Ballets Russes, Coliseum, London. Conductor: Roger Desormière.

CAST: *Barabau*, Léon Woizikowsky; *Sergeant*, Serge Lifar; *Servants of Barabau*, Alice Nikitina, Alexandra Danilova, Tamara Geva; *Peasants*, 3 men, 3 women; *6 Soldiers*. Chorus on stage.

NOTE: Balanchine's first original ballet for Diaghilev. Rieti based the plot on an Italian nursery rhyme: When a village party in Barabau's garden is disrupted by soldiers, Barabau feigns death; the villagers carry him mournfully to church, but as soon as the soldiers depart he revives, and they return him to his home in triumph.

REVISIONS: Soon after London opening, role of one female peasant enlarged, with additional solo to new music.

STAGINGS: 1931, Royal Danish.

1926

54 BORIS GODUNOV

Opera in Four Acts and Nine Scenes by Modest Moussorgsky

ACT III POLONAISE

PREMIERE: February 9, 1926, Opéra de Monte-Carlo. Danced by Diaghilev's Ballets Russes. Conductor: Victor de Sabata.

CAST: 9 women, 10 men.

See 298, 388

55 JUDITH

Opera in Three Acts and Four Scenes by Arthur Honegger

ACT III, SCENE 2 BALLET

PREMIERE: February 13, 1926, Opéra de Monte-Carlo. Danced by Diaghilev's Ballets Russes. Conductor: Arthur Honegger.

CAST: 12 women, 12 men.

NOTE: World premiere.

56 L'HIRONDELLE (LA RONDINE)

Opera in Three Acts by Giacomo Puccini

ACT II VALSE

PREMIERE: February 20, 1926, Opéra de Monte-Carlo. Danced by Diaghilev's Ballets Russes. Conductor: Victor de Sabata.

CAST: Lydia Sokolova, Léon Woizikowsky, corps de ballet.

See 161

57 LAKMÉ
Opera in Three Acts by Léo Delibes
ACT II BALLET

PREMIERE: March 2, 1926, Opéra de Monte-Carlo. Danced by Diaghilev's Ballets Russes. Conductor: Léon Jehin.

CAST: Lubov Tchernicheva, 12 women.

See 115, 153

58 LES CONTES D'HOFFMANN
Opera in Three Acts and Five Scenes by Jacques Offenbach
SCENE 2 BALLET

PREMIERE: March 7, 1926, Opéra de Monte-Carlo. Danced by Diaghilev's Ballets Russes. Conductor: Léon Jehin.

CAST: VALSE: 4 women; PAS DE DEUX: Alexandra Danilova, Stanislas Idzikowsky; VARIATION: Idzikowsky; VARIATION: Danilova; POLKA: Tamara Geva, Thadée Slavinsky; GRANDE VALSE: 6 couples.

See 112, 260

59 JEANNE D'ARC
Mystery in Seven Parts by Charles Gounod
ACT III BALLET

PREMIERE: March 28, 1926, Opéra de Monte-Carlo. Danced by Diaghilev's Ballets Russes. Conductor: Léon Jehin.

CAST: DANCE OF THE SOLDIERS AND BOHEMIAN WOMEN: 4 women, 4 men; DANCE OF THE KNIGHTS AND LADIES OF THE COURT: 8 couples.

NOTE: Presented with *La Fête du Printemps* from Ambroise Thomas' *Hamlet*.

60 HAMLET

'La Fête du Printemps' from the Opera by Ambroise Thomas
BALLET DIVERTISSEMENT

PREMIERE: March 28, 1926, Opéra de Monte-Carlo. Danced by Diaghilev's Ballets Russes. Conductor: Léon Jehin.

CAST: ANDANTINO: Lubov Tchernicheva, Léon Woizikowsky, 14 women; VARIATION: Woizikowsky; ALLEGRETTO: 9 women; VALSE-MAZURKA: 3 women; VARIATION: Nadejda Nicolaeva, 4 women; ADAGIO: Tchernicheva, Woizikowsky; VARIATION: Alexandra Danilova; VALSE: Tchernicheva; CODA: Tchernicheva, Woizikowsky, 5 women.

61 ROMEO AND JULIET

A Rehearsal, without Scenery, in Two Parts
ENTR'ACTE

MUSIC: By Constant Lambert (*Adam and Eve* ballet score, 1924-25, retitled by Diaghilev).

CHOREOGRAPHY: By Bronislava Nijinska; choreography of the entr'acte by George Balanchine.

PRODUCTION: 'Night' and 'Day' curtains by Max Ernst; front curtain and stage pieces by Joan Miró. Curtains and stage pieces executed by Prince A. Schervashidze; costumes executed by Georgette Vialet.

PREMIERE: May 4, 1926, Diaghilev's Ballets Russes, Opéra de Monte-Carlo. Conductor: Marc-César Scotto.

CAST: PART I: Tamara Karsavina, Serge Lifar; *Maestro*, Thadée Slavinsky; 14 women, 12 men. PART II: *Juliet*, Karsavina; *Romeo*, Lifar; *Nurse*, Lydia Sokolova; *Pierre, Servant to Capulet*, Léon Woizikowsky; *The Maestro, Rehearsing as Tybalt*, Slavinsky; *Paris*, Constantin Tcherkas; 14 women, 12 men.

NOTE: Balanchine's entr'acte was staged without music between the two parts. A drop-curtain was lowered to within a foot or two of the ground so that only the dancers' legs and feet were visible.

62 LA PASTORALE

MUSIC: By Georges Auric (1926, commissioned by Serge Diaghilev).
Book by Boris Kochno.

PRODUCTION: Curtain, scenery and costumes by Pedro Pruna. Curtain
and scenery executed by Prince A. Schervashidze; costumes executed by
La Maison Jules Muelle. Bicycle by Olympique.

PREMIERE: May 29, 1926, Diaghilev's Ballets Russes, Théâtre Sarah-
Bernhardt, Paris. Conductor: Roger Desormière.

CAST: *The Star*, Felia Doubrovska; *A Young Lady*, Tamara Geva;
4 Young Ladies; *Telegraph Boy*, Serge Lifar; *Régisseur*, Thadée Slavinsky;
2 Actors; *2 Operators*.

NOTE: While a telegraph delivery boy takes an impromptu swim, a
young girl as a prank steals his messages from his bicycle. The boy takes
a nap on the stream bank; a movie company appears and sets up a
scene; the boy awakens to find himself in a duet with the movie star.
Villagers seeking their telegrams disrupt the scene and the boy runs
away; returning at nightfall for his bicycle he finds the young girl,
and they ride off together.

63 JACK IN THE BOX

MUSIC: By Erik Satie (unpublished piano score for pantomime, 1899;
orchestrated after Satie's death in 1925 by Darius Milhaud).

PRODUCTION: Scenery and costumes by André Derain. Scenery
executed by Prince A. Schervashidze; costumes executed by La Maison
Jules Muelle.

PREMIERE: June 8, 1926, Diaghilev's Ballets Russes, Théâtre Sarah-
Bernhardt, Paris. Conductor: Roger Desormière.

CAST: *The Puppet*, Stanislas Idzikowsky; *The Black Dancer*, Alexandra
Danilova; *2 Dancers* (women); *2 Cloud Bearers* (men).

NOTE: The principal dancer is a comic puppet with whom the Black
Dancer and two others perform as if they are attending a ball. In the
background large cardboard clouds are moved by mimes.

64 THE TRIUMPH OF NEPTUNE
(also called LE TRIOMPHE DE NEPTUNE)
English Pantomime in Twelve Tableaux

MUSIC: By Lord Berners (1926, commissioned by Serge Diaghilev). Book by Sacheverell Sitwell.

PRODUCTION: Scenery and costumes after historical prints by George and Robert Cruikshank, Tofts, Honigold, and Webb, collected by B. Pollock and H. J. Webb. Costumes designed by Pedro Pruna; scenery and costumes adapted and executed by Prince A. Schervashidze.

PREMIERE: December 3, 1926, Diaghilev's Ballets Russes, Lyceum Theatre, London. Conductor: Henri Defosse.

CAST: *The Fairy Queen*, Alexandra Danilova; *Tom Tug, a Sailor*, Serge Lifar; *W. Brown, a Journalist*, Michael Fedorov; *Goddess [Britannia]*, Lydia Sokolova; *Emerald Fairy*; *Ruby Fairy*; *Fairies*, 16 women; *Sylphs*, Lubov Tchernicheva, Vera Petrova; *Street Dancer*, Tatiana Chamié; *The Sailor's Wife*; *The Sailor's Mother*; *Snowball, a Blackman*, George Balanchine; *Harlequins*, 6 men; *Pages*, 9 men; *Dandy*, Constantin Tcherkas; *2 Journalists*; *2 Policemen*; *Cab Driver*; *2 Telescope Keepers*; *Waiter*; *Beggar*; *2 Street Hawkers*; *3 Workmen*; *2 News Vendors*; *3 Newspaper Boys*; *Officer*; *Chimney Sweep*; *King of the Ogres*, Michel Pavloff; *10 Ogres*; *2 Clowns*; *3 Neptune Attendants*; *Voice*, Enrico Garcia.

Act I: CURTAIN [dance]. SCENE 1: London Bridge. SCENE 2: Cloudland. SCENE 3: Farewell. SCENE 4: Shipwreck. SCENE 5: Fleet Street. SCENE 6: The Frozen Wood.

Act II: CURTAIN [dance]. SCENE 7: The Giant Hand. SCENE 8: The Evil Grotto. SCENE 9: The Ogres' Castle. SCENE 10: Sunday Morning in London. SCENE 11: The Triumph of Neptune. SCENE 12: Apotheosis.

NOTE: Based on English pantomimes of the 1850s, the ballet follows the voyage to fairyland of a sailor and a journalist, and events back in London, where they are observed through a magic telescope. In the Apotheosis the sailor, deserted by his London wife, weds Neptune's daughter. Balanchine sometimes danced the roles of the tipsy Snowball, the Beggar and the leading Harlequin.

REVISIONS: 1927: *Cupid* (Stanislas Idzikowsky) added, with new variation. Within six months of the premiere (Paris, May 1927), Scenes 5, 8 and 9 had been deleted, as had several minor characters.

1927

65 AURORA'S WEDDING:
ARIADNE AND HER BROTHERS

In 1926 or 1927 Balanchine replaced the pas de trois for a man and two women in *Aurora's Wedding* (divertissements from Act III of Petipa's *The Sleeping Beauty* [Tschaikovsky]) known as 'Florestan and His Sisters,' with a pas de trois for a woman and two men called 'Ariadne and Her Brothers.' The earliest program found is for the January 10, 1927, performance of Diaghilev's Ballets Russes at La Scala, Milan.

Throughout his tenure as ballet master to Diaghilev, Balanchine made frequent adjustments to repertory pieces, from minor alterations to entire new variations; most of these changes are not noted on printed programs. During the frequent periods between the seasons of the Ballets Russes, Balanchine is also known to have created choreography for productions in provincial opera houses in France; these are no longer possible to document.

See 225, 259, 281, 404, 418

66 SAMSON ET DALILA

Opera in Three Acts and Four Scenes by Camille Saint-Saëns
ACT III DIVERTISSEMENT

PREMIERE: January 27, 1927, Opéra de Monte-Carlo. Danced by Diaghilev's Ballets Russes. Conductor: Léon Jehin.

CAST: Lubov Tchernicheva, 16 women.

See 116, 171, 228

67 LA TRAVIATA

Opera in Four Acts by Giuseppe Verdi
ACT III BALLET

PREMIERE: February 8, 1927, Opéra de Monte-Carlo. Danced by Diaghilev's Ballets Russes. Conductor: Victor de Sabata.

CAST: Vera Petrova, Nicholas Efimov, 6 couples.

See 123, 150, 252

68 TURANDOT

Opera in Three Acts and Four Scenes by Giacomo Puccini
ACT II DIVERTISSEMENT, LES PORCELAINES DE CHINE

PREMIERE: February 22, 1927, Opéra de Monte-Carlo. Danced by Diaghilev's Ballets Russes. Conductor: Victor de Sabata.

CAST: Lubov Tchernicheva, Alexandra Danilova, Stanislas Idzikowsky, Léon Woizikowsky, George Balanchine, corps de ballet.

See 120

69 LA DAMNATION DE FAUST

Opera in Five Acts and Ten Scenes by Hector Berlioz
SCENE 2 BALLET (PEASANT DANCE); SCENE 4 BALLET VOLANT

PREMIERE: February 26, 1927, Opéra de Monte-Carlo. Danced by Diaghilev's Ballets Russes. Conductor: Léon Jehin.

CAST: PEASANT DANCE: 6 couples. BALLET VOLANT: 5 women; *Sylphs*, 8 women; *Those with Lanterns*, 10 women.

See 49

70 IVAN LE TERRIBLE

Opera in Three Acts by Raoul Gunsbourg
ACT III BALLET DIVERTISSEMENT

PREMIERE: March 3, 1927, Opéra de Monte-Carlo. Danced by Diaghilev's Ballets Russes. Conductor: Léon Jehin.

CAST: Lydia Sokolova, Léon Woizikowsky, 12 women, 11 men.

71 OBÉRON

Comic and Fantastic Opera in Three Acts and Eleven Scenes
by Carl Maria von Weber
ACT II BALLET

PREMIERE: March 26, 1927, Opéra de Monte-Carlo. Danced by
Diaghilev's Ballets Russes. Conductor: Léon Jehin.

CAST: 21 women, 16 men.

72 LA CHATTE (also called THE CAT)

Ballet in One Act

MUSIC: By Henri Sauguet (1927, commissioned by Serge Diaghilev).
Book by Sobeka [Boris Kochno] (after one of Aesop's Fables).

PRODUCTION: Architecture and sculpture constructed by Naum Gabo
and Antoine Pevsner.

PREMIERE: April 30, 1927, Diaghilev's Ballets Russes, Opéra de Monte-
Carlo. Conductor: Marc-César Scotto.

CAST: *The Cat*, Olga Spessivtseva; *The Young Man*, Serge Lifar; *His
Companions*, 6 men.

NOTE: Deserting his male companions, a young man in love with a
cat persuades Aphrodite to change the cat into a beautiful girl. Tempted
by the goddess, the girl gives chase to a mouse, and is turned into a cat
again; the boy dies broken-hearted. The cast of seven men and one
woman danced around and through transparent Constructivist forms
against a black background. Lifar's 1933 version, which retained his solos
but little more, was produced without the collaboration of the
choreographer.

STAGINGS: 1933, Serge Lifar and His Russian Ballets (American tour).

73 GROTESQUE ESPAGNOL

MUSIC: By Isaac Albéniz (*Cordóba*).

PRODUCTION: Presented by F. Ray Comstock and Morris Guest.

PREMIERE: October 10, 1927, Balieff's Chauve-Souris (The Bat Theatre
of Moscow), Cosmopolitan Theater, New York.

CAST: Tamara Geva.

NOTE: *Grotesque Espagnol* and *Sarcasm* [74] were two of nineteen numbers in the 1927 version of Chauve-Souris, annual productions by Nikita Balieff of evenings of Russian cabaret which toured Europe and America. Balanchine choreographed the two pieces before the company departed from Paris for a New York season, where they became the first Balanchine works to be performed in America, and the first Balanchine choreography seen by Lincoln Kirstein.

74 SARCASM

MUSIC: By Sergei Prokofiev (Op. 17, 1912).

PRODUCTION: Presented by F. Ray Comstock and Morris Guest.

PREMIERE: October 10, 1927, Balieff's Chauve-Souris (The Bat Theatre of Moscow), Cosmopolitan Theater, New York.

CAST: Tamara Geva.

NOTE: See 73.

75 SWAN LAKE

At some time in the mid-1920s (1927?), Balanchine made minor alterations in Diaghilev's one-act *Swan Lake* (Tschaikovsky, choreographed by Ivanov and Petipa), deleting part of the Swan Queen's mime and rearranging ensemble movements for a decreased corps de ballet. Olga Spessivtseva was probably the first ballerina to dance the Swan Queen in this revised version.

See 191, 262, 285, 331, 367

1928

76 MIREILLE
Opera in Three Acts by Charles Gounod
ACT II FARANDOLE

PREMIERE: January 28, 1928, Opéra de Monte-Carlo. Danced by Diaghilev's Ballets Russes. Conductor: Marc-César Scotto.

CAST: Henriette Maikerska, Nicolas Kremnev, 8 couples.

77 LES MAÎTRES CHANTEURS
(DIE MEISTERSINGER VON NÜRNBERG)
Opera in Three Acts by Richard Wagner
ACT III DANSE

PREMIERE: February 5, 1928, Opéra de Monte-Carlo. Danced by Diaghilev's Ballets Russes. Conductor: Michel Steiman.

CAST: Dora Vadimova, Henriette Maikerska, Nicholas Efimov, Constantin Tcherkas.

See 163

78 VENISE
Opera in Three Acts and Four Scenes by Raoul Gunsbourg
ACT II, LE CARNAVAL

PREMIERE: February 23, 1928, Opéra de Monte-Carlo. Danced by Diaghilev's Ballets Russes. Conductor: Michel Steiman.

CAST: Alexandra Danilova, Léon Woizikowsky, 12 couples.

79 SIOR TODÉRO BRONTOLON

Comic Opera in One Act and Two Scenes by Gian Francesco Malipiero
BALLET

PREMIERE: March 8, 1928, Opéra de Monte-Carlo. Danced by
Diaghilev's Ballets Russes. Conductor: Michel Steiman.

CAST: 3 couples.

80 UN BAL MASQUÉ (UN BALLO IN MASCHERA)

Opera in Three Acts by Giuseppe Verdi
ACT III DIVERTISSEMENT

PREMIERE: March 10, 1928, Opéra de Monte-Carlo. Danced by
Diaghilev's Ballets Russes. Conductor: Marc-César Scotto.

CAST: 10 couples.

81 DON JUAN (DON GIOVANNI)

Opera in Three Acts and Seven Scenes by Wolfgang Amadeus Mozart
ACT II BALLET

PREMIERE: March 17, 1928, Opéra de Monte-Carlo. Danced by
Diaghilev's Ballets Russes. Conductor: Michel Steiman.

CAST: 4 couples.

See 181, 253

82 LA FILLE D'ABDOUBARAHAH

Comic Opera in One Act by Sanvel
BALLET

PREMIERE: March 20, 1928, Opéra de Monte-Carlo. Danced by
Diaghilev's Ballets Russes. Conductor: Florian Weiss.

CAST: Felia Doubrovska, Nicholas Efimov, Nicolas Kremnev, Michael
Fedorov, Jean Yazvinsky, corps de ballet.

83 ALEKO and POLKA GROTESQUE

Probably in the spring of 1928, when both the Pavlova and Diaghilev companies were in Paris, Balanchine choreographed *Aleko* (a gypsy dance to music by Sergei Rachmaninoff) and *Polka Grotesque* (music unknown) for Nina Kirsanova and Thadée Slavinsky, at the request of Anna Pavlova, for her company's tour to South America in the fall of that year. A Balanchine work for Pavlova herself, possibly to Scarlatti, was discussed but not choreographed.

84 APOLLON MUSAGÈTE
(also called APOLLO MUSAGETES; APOLLO, LEADER OF THE MUSES; APOLLO; APOLO MUSAGETA)
Ballet in Two Scenes

MUSIC: Music and book by Igor Stravinsky (*Apollo Musagetes*, 1927-28, commissioned by Mrs. Elizabeth Sprague Coolidge, 1927).

PRODUCTION: Scenery and costumes by André Bauchant. (New costumes by Chanel, 1929.) Scenery executed by Prince A. Schervashidze; costumes executed under the direction of Mme A. Youkine.

PREMIERE: June 12, 1928, Diaghilev's Ballets Russes, Théâtre Sarah-Bernhardt, Paris. Conductor: Igor Stravinsky. Violinist: Marcel Darrieux.

CAST: *Apollo*, Serge Lifar; *Terpsichore*, Alice Nikitina; *Calliope*, Lubov Tchernicheva; *Polyhymnia*, Felia Doubrovska; *2 Goddesses*; *Leto, Mother of Apollo*, Sophie Orlova.
  SCENE I: THE BIRTH OF APOLLO. SCENE 2: Apollo; PAS D'ACTION (Apollo and Muses): Calliope; Polyhymnia; Terpsichore; Apollo; PAS DE DEUX (Apollo and Terpsichore); CODA; APOTHEOSIS (Apollo and Muses).

NOTE: SCENE I: Leto's labor, and the birth and youth of Apollo; two goddesses present him with a lute and teach him music. SCENE 2: Apollo plays the lute and dances. The three Muses enter; he presents each with an emblem of her art: Calliope, receiving the stylus and tablet, personifies poetry and rhythm; Polyhymnia, finger to lips, represents mime; Terpsichore combines both poetry and gesture in dance and is honored by Apollo. He dances a solo variation and a pas de deux with Terpsichore. APOTHEOSIS: Apollo and the Muses join in a final dance and ascend toward Parnassus.

Stravinsky conceived and composed *Apollo Musagetes* as a ballet; the music was commissioned for a festival of contemporary music in Washington, D. C., with choreography by Adolph Bolm. Balanchine's production was his first collaboration with the composer; he later described the choreography as the turning point in his creative life.

REVISIONS: 1928, Ballets Russes: Variation for Alexandra Danilova (alternating as Terpsichore in the original production) differed from Nikitina's. 1978, Second International Dance Festival: SCENE 1 omitted. 1979, New York City Ballet: For a revival with Mikhail Baryshnikov as Apollo, SCENE 1 and Apollo's first variation omitted; ending of APOTHEOSIS rechoreographed to conclude with earlier tableau of Muses posing beside Apollo in arabesque, visually suggesting the sun and its rays, instead of ascending Mount Parnassus. 1980, New York City Ballet: Apollo's first variation restored.

NEW PRODUCTIONS BY BALANCHINE COMPANIES: 1937, American Ballet: Scenery and costumes by Stewart Chaney. 1941, American Ballet Caravan: Scenery and costumes by Tomás Santa Rosa. 1951, New York City Ballet: Costumes by Karinska. 1957, New York City Ballet: Danced in practice clothes with minimal scenery; scenery omitted entirely since 1979.

STAGINGS: 1931, Royal Danish; 1937, American Ballet; 1941, American Ballet Caravan; 1942, Colón; 1943, Ballet Theatre; 1946, Sociedad Pro-Arte Musical; 1947, Paris; 1948, Cuba; late 1940s?, La Plata; 1950, Ballet Nacional; 1951, New York City Ballet; 1955, San Francisco; 1958, Civic Ballet Society; 1960, Uruguay; 1962, Hamburg; 1965, Boston, São Paulo; 1966, Dutch National, Norway, Royal; 1967, Stuttgart, Vienna; 1969, Berlin, Geneva; 1970, Florence, Royal Ballet Touring; 1971, Düsseldorf, La Scala; 1973, Wisconsin, Rome; 1974, Nureyev and Friends, Munich, Royal Flemish; 1975, Palermo; 1976, Chicago Lyric Opera (excerpts), Turin; 1977, Gothenburg, Hungary; 1978, Second International Dance Festival, Catania; 1979, Bologna; 1981, San Juan.

TELEVISION: 1960 (CBC, Montreal); 1962 (BBC, London); 1963 (excerpts, Bell Telephone Hour, NBC); 1967 (rehearsal and performance, BBC, London); 1969 (L'Heure du Concert, CBC, Montreal); 1972 (rehearsal, PBS); ca. 1974 (German television; rebroadcast 1976, BBC, London); 1979 (pas de deux, The Magic of Dance, BBC, London).

See 176, 198, 284

85 THE GODS GO A-BEGGING
(also called LES DIEUX MENDIANTS)
Pastorale

MUSIC: By George Frederick Handel, arranged by Sir Thomas Beecham on commission from Serge Diaghilev (selections from the following compositions written between 1707 and 1739: *Rodrigo*; *Il Pastor Fido*; *Teseo*; *Admeto*; *Alcina* [four numbers]; two of the Opus 6 concerti grossi, including the Hornpipe movement from No. 7). Book by Sobeka [Boris Kochno].

PRODUCTION: Scenery by Léon Bakst (backcloth from first part of *Daphnis et Chloé* [Fokine], 1912). Costumes (with two exceptions) by Juan Gris (from *Les Tentations de la Bergère* [Nijinska], 1924).

PREMIERE: July 16, 1928, Diaghilev's Ballets Russes, His Majesty's Theatre, London. Conductor: Sir Thomas Beecham.

CAST: *The Serving Maid* and *The Shepherd* [divinities in disguise], Alexandra Danilova, Léon Woizikowsky; *Two Ladies*, Lubov Tchernicheva, Felia Doubrovska; *A Nobleman*, Constantin Tcherkas; *6 Ladies*; *6 Noblemen*; *4 Servants*.

NOTE: In the spirit of a *fête champêtre* by Watteau or Lancret. A shepherd wanders in among noble guests at an elaborate picnic; two aristocratic ladies invite him to dance with them, but he chooses to dance with a serving-girl. When indignant noblemen begin to chastise him, the shepherd and the maid cast off their humble dress and reveal themselves to be divinities in disguise.

STAGINGS: 1930, Ballet Club (Shepherd's hornpipe); 1931, Ballet Club (pas de deux, retitled *Shepherd's Wooing*).

TELEVISION: 1935 (excerpts, BBC, London).

1929

86 ROMÉO ET JULIETTE

Opera in Five Acts by Charles Gounod

ACT I DIVERTISSEMENT

PREMIERE: January 24, 1929, Opéra de Monte-Carlo. Danced by Diaghilev's Ballets Russes. Conductor: Gabriel Grovlez.

CAST: 8 couples.

See 124, 180

87 LA GIOCONDA

Opera in Four Acts by Amilcare Ponchielli

ACT I TARANTELLA; ACT III DANCE OF THE HOURS

PREMIERE: January 26, 1929, Opéra de Monte-Carlo. Danced by Diaghilev's Ballets Russes. Conductor: Michel Steiman.

CAST: TARANTELLA: Vera Petrova, Nicholas Efimov, 4 women. DANCE OF THE HOURS: *Morning (Dawn)*, Felia Doubrovska, Mezeslav Borovsky, 4 women; *Day*, Alexandra Danilova, Léon Woizikowsky, 4 women; *Evening*, Petrova, Efimov, 4 women; *Night*, Lubov Tchernicheva, Constantin Tcherkas, 4 women.

See 174

88 RIGOLETTO

Opera in Four Acts by Giuseppe Verdi

ACT I DIVERTISSEMENT

PREMIERE: February 28, 1929, Opéra de Monte-Carlo. Danced by Diaghilev's Ballets Russes. Conductor: Michel Steiman.

CAST: 6 couples.

See 121, 156

89 LA FEMME NUE

Opera in Four Acts by Henri Février
ACT II DIVERTISSEMENT

PREMIERE: March 23, 1929, Opéra de Monte-Carlo. Danced by Diaghilev's Ballets Russes. Conductor: Victor de Sabata.

CAST: Alexandra Danilova, Eugenia Lipkowska, Henriette Maikerska, corps de ballet.

NOTE: World premiere.

90 MARTHA

Opera in Four Acts by Friedrich von Flotow
SCENE 4 BALLET

PREMIERE: March 27, 1929, Opéra de Monte-Carlo. Danced by Diaghilev's Ballets Russes. Conductor: Marc-César Scotto.

CAST: Vera Petrova, Eugenia Lipkowska, Léon Woizikowsky, 8 couples.

91 WAKE UP AND DREAM!

Charles B. Cochran's 1929 Revue

MUSIC AND BOOK: Music and lyrics by Cole Porter. Book by John Hastings Turner.

CHOREOGRAPHY: Dances and ensembles by Tilly Losch, Max Rivers and George Balanchine (uncredited).

PRODUCTION: Produced under the personal direction of Charles B. Cochran. Staged by Frank Collins.

PREMIERE: March 29, 1929, London Pavilion. (Out-of-town preview: March 5, Palace Theatre, Manchester [titled *Charles B. Cochran's 1929 Revue*].)

CAST: Tilly Losch, Jessie Matthews, Sonnie Hale, Elsie Carlisle, Toni Birkmayer, and others.

NOTE: Balanchine's initial choreography for British and American musical revues.

WHAT IS THIS THING CALLED LOVE? (Part II, Scene 16): *Choreography*: By George Balanchine, credited to Tilly Losch. *Production*: Setting and The

Idol designed by Oliver Messel. *Cast*: *Singer*, Elsie Carlisle; *The Girl*,
Tilly Losch; *The Man*, Toni Birkmayer; *The Other Woman*, Alanova; *The Idol*, William Cavanagh.

OTHER PRODUCTIONS: New York premiere December 30, 1929, Selwyn
Theatre, produced by Arch Selwyn.

92 LA CROISADE DES DAMES (DIE VERSCHWORENEN)
Comic Opera in One Act by Franz Schubert
BALLET

PREMIERE: April 1, 1929, Opéra de Monte-Carlo. Danced by Diaghilev's
Ballets Russes. Conductor: Marc-César Scotto.

CAST: Felia Doubrovska, Vera Petrova, Eugenia Lipkowska,
corps de ballet.

93 LE BAL (also called THE BALL)
Ballet in Two Tableaux

MUSIC: By Vittorio Rieti (1928, commissioned by Serge Diaghilev).
Book by Boris Kochno (suggested by a story by Count Vladimir Sologub).

PRODUCTION: Scenery and costumes by Giorgio de Chirico. Costumes
executed under the direction of Mme A. Youkine.

PREMIERE: May 7, 1929, Diaghilev's Ballets Russes, Opéra de Monte-
Carlo. Conductor: Marc-César Scotto.

CAST: *The Lady*, Alexandra Danilova; *The Young Man*, Anton Dolin;
The Astrologer, André Bobrow; SPANISH ENTRANCE: Felia Doubrovska,
Léon Woizikowsky, George Balanchine; ITALIAN ENTRANCE: Eugenia
Lipkowska, Serge Lifar; *The Sylphides*, 4 women; *The Guests*, 12 women,
13 men; *The Statues*, 2 men.
    I. Prologue. II. The Ball.

NOTE: In the midst of a ball a Young Man seeks out a Lady accompanied by an Astrologer and begs her to remove her mask; she
complies, and to his horror reveals the face of an old woman; he flees,
she pursues him, and he hides. After the ball the Young Man is alone
in the ballroom. The Lady returns with the Astrologer, unmasks, but
then pulls off her face, which is only a second mask—and is revealed

as a young and beautiful woman. The Astrologer, too, unmasks and appears a handsome youth; he embraces the Lady and they depart, as the Young Man falls swooning.

REVISIONS: Two Archeologists added for London season, July 1929.

94 LE FILS PRODIGUE (also called PRODIGAL SON)
Ballet in Three Scenes

MUSIC: By Sergei Prokofiev (Op. 46, 1928-29, commissioned by Serge Diaghilev, 1927). Book by Boris Kochno (after the biblical parable).

PRODUCTION: Scenery and costumes by Georges Rouault. Scenery executed by Prince A. Schervashidze; costumes executed by Vera Soudeikina.

PREMIERE: May 21, 1929, Diaghilev's Ballets Russes, Théâtre Sarah-Bernhardt, Paris. Conductor: Sergei Prokofiev.

CAST: *The Prodigal Son*, Serge Lifar; *The Father*, Michael Fedorov; *The Siren*, Felia Doubrovska; *The Servants*, Eleanora Marra, Nathalie Branitzka; *Confidants of the Prodigal Son*, Léon Woizikowsky, Anton Dolin; *Friends of the Prodigal Son*, 12 men.

    I. 1. The Prodigal Son leaves the paternal home, accompanied by his two Confidants.

    II. 2. The Prodigal Son meets his friends and takes part in their festival. 3. Entry and dance of the Siren, which takes place beside the Prodigal Son. 4. The Confidants of the Prodigal Son entertain the guests. 5. The Prodigal Son dances with the Siren. 6. The Siren and the Friends of the Prodigal Son force him to drink. 7. The Confidants, the Friends and the Siren strip the sleeping Prodigal Son and take flight. 8. The awakening and lamentations of the Prodigal Son. 9. Promenade of the Siren, the Confidants, and the Friends of the Prodigal Son, laden with their spoils.

    III. 10. Return of the repentant Prodigal Son to the paternal home.

REVISIONS: After the death of Diaghilev and the disbanding of his Ballets Russes, the Balanchine choreography for *Le Fils Prodigue* was not seen until it was revived for the New York City Ballet in 1950 as *Prodigal Son*. At that time and subsequently the cast of characters was listed somewhat differently: Servants became Sisters; Confidants became

Servants; Friends became Drinking Companions. The number of Drinking Companions was smaller (12 in the original, 9 in the New York City Ballet revival). In 1977, the dances of the two Servants (men) were omitted from the New York City Ballet production; they were restored in the 1980 American Ballet Theatre staging. Long-time observers have noticed other changes, but Balanchine has said that the choreography remains essentially the same.

STAGINGS: 1950, New York City Ballet; 1966, Boston, Dutch National, Tokyo Ballet Geikijo; 1967, National; 1968, Royal Danish; 1973, Paris, Royal, Royal Ballet Touring; 1974, Houston, Geneva; 1975, Chicago; 1978, Pittsburgh; 1980, American Ballet Theatre.

TELEVISION: 1973 (Wide World of Entertainment, ABC); 1978 (Dance in America, PBS).

See 267

95 PAS DE DEUX (later called MOODS)

MUSIC: By Raie da Costa, orchestrated by De Caillaux.

PRODUCTION: Production supervised by Anton Dolin. Costumes by Phyllis Dolton, executed by Sims.

PREMIERE: September 2, 1929, Anton Dolin with Anna Ludmila and Company, Coliseum, London. Conductor: Alfred Dove.

CAST: Anton Dolin, Anna Ludmila.

NOTE: Anton Dolin formed a small company after the death of Diaghilev on August 19, 1929. For an engagement at the London Coliseum the troupe performed five numbers (of which the Balanchine pas de deux was the fifth) on a variety program with eleven other acts.

96 LES CRÉATURES DE PROMÉTHÉE
Ballet in Two Acts

MUSIC: By Ludwig van Beethoven (*Die Geschöpfe des Prometheus*, produced 1801, commissioned by Salvatore Viganò).

CHOREOGRAPHY: By George Balanchine and Serge Lifar.

PRODUCTION: Scenery and costumes by Quelvée. Scenery executed by Mouveau.

PREMIERE: December 30, 1929, Paris Opéra Ballet, Théâtre National de l'Opéra, Paris. Conductor: J.-E. Szyfer.

CAST: Olga Spessivtseva, Serge Lifar; Mlles Lorcia, Lamballe, Cérès, M. Peretti; 5 demi-soloists, 13 women, 9 men.

NOTE: Jacques Rouché, director of the Paris Opéra, engaged Balanchine to choreograph the ballet. Balanchine conceived the basic outline and created some of the dances, then became ill; Lifar completed the ballet and received credit on the printed program.

97 DARK RED ROSES

Film

PRODUCTION: Produced by Era Films; British International Film Distributors. Directed by Sinclair Hill. From a story by Stacy Aumonier.

RELEASED: 1929.

CAST: Stewart Rome, Frances Doble, Hugh Eden, Kate Cutler, Jack Clayton, Jill Clayton, Una O'Connor, Sydney Morgan, and others.

NOTE: The first feature-length talking motion picture made in England. During the filming, Balanchine, Dolin and Lopokova learned of Diaghilev's death in Venice.

TARTAR BALLET, 'JEALOUSY': *Music*: By Modest Moussorgsky (selections from *Khovanshchina*, 1872-80 [unfinished]). *Cast*: *Tartar*, George Balanchine; *His Wife*, Lydia Lopokova; *Minstrel*, Anton Dolin.

See 31

1930

98 AUBADE

MUSIC: By Francis Poulenc (*Aubade* for piano and 18 instruments, 1929, commissioned by Vicomte and Vicomtesse de Noailles).

PRODUCTION: Scenery and costumes by Angèles Ortiz, executed by Mme A. Youkine (uncredited).

PREMIERE: January 21, 1930, Ballets Russes de Vera Nemtchinova, Théâtre des Champs-Élysées, Paris. Conductor: Alexandre Labinsky. Pianist: Francis Poulenc.

CAST: *Diana*, Vera Nemtchinova; *Actaeon*, Alexis Dolinoff; *Diana's Companions*, 6 women.

NOTE: A Greek myth: At dawn, the hunter Actaeon surprises the goddess Diana bathing; she transforms him into a deer, wounds him, and turning her companions into dogs, sets them upon him. With a pang of regret, the goddess resumes her course through the forest; day has come.

STAGINGS: 1936, Les Ballets de Monte-Carlo (René Blum).

99 CHARLES B. COCHRAN'S 1930 REVUE

MUSIC AND BOOK: Music by Vivian Ellis and Beverley Nichols. Ballet music by Lord Berners and Henri Sauguet. Book by Beverley Nichols. Ballet libretti by Boris Kochno.

CHOREOGRAPHY: Dances and ensembles by George Balanchine, Serge Lifar and Ralph Reader.

PRODUCTION: Entire production under the personal direction of Charles B. Cochran. Staged by Frank Collins.

PREMIERE: March 27, 1930, London Pavilion. (Out-of-town preview: March 4, Palace Theatre, Manchester.)

CAST: Maisie Gay, Ada-May, Serge Lifar, Alice Nikitina, Fowler and Tamara, Roy Royston, Eric Marshall, and others.

IN A VENETIAN THEATRE (Part I, Scene 8): *Music*: By Vivian Ellis. *Production*: Costumes executed by Reville, Ltd. *Cast*: Mr. Cochran's Young Ladies.

LUNA PARK, OR THE FREAKS (Part I, Scene 10): *Music*: By Lord Berners. Book by Boris Kochno. *Production*: Scenery and costumes by Christopher Wood. Scenery executed by E. Delany; costumes executed by C. Alias, Ltd. *Cast*: *The Showman*, Nicholas Efimov; *The Three-headed Man*, Constantin Tcherkas; *The Three-legged Man*, Richard Domonsky; *The One-legged Woman*, Alice Nikitina; *The Six-armed Man*, Serge Lifar.

PICCADILLY, 1830 (Part I, Scene 13): *Music*: By Ivor Novello. *Production*: Scenery and costumes by Oliver Messel. Scenery executed by Alick Johnstone; costumes executed by C. Alias, Ltd. *Cast*: *The Dancers*, Fowler and Tamara; *The Singer*, Eric Marshall; *Some Promenaders*, Mr. Cochran's Young Ladies and Gentlemen; *A Highlander*, Lifar; *An Elderly Invalid*, Efimov; *His Wife*, Nikitina; *His Servants*, Tcherkas, Domonsky.

HEAVEN (Part I, Scene 14): *Music*: By Beverley Nichols and Ivor Novello. *Production*: Scenery and costumes by Oliver Messel. Scenery executed by Alick Johnstone; costumes executed by Eleanor Abbey. *Cast*: *Nell Gwynn*; *Lord Byron*; *Lady Hamilton*; *The Duke of Wellington*; *Mr. Gladstone*; *The Empress Josephine*; *Lola Montez*; *Lord Nelson*; *The Flower Woman*; *The Dancers*, Fowler and Tamara; *The Thieves*, Roy Royston, Ada-May; *A Policeman*; *The Lover and His Lady*, Lifar, Nikitina; *A Boy Scout*; *The Soldiers*, Mr. Cochran's Young Gentlemen; *Angels*, Mr. Cochran's Young Ladies; *2 Singers*.

THE WIND IN THE WILLOWS (Part II, Scene 20): *Music*: By Desmond Carter and Vivian Ellis. *Production*: Costumes by Ada Peacock; executed by H. & L. Nathan, Ltd. *Cast*: Royston, Mr. Cochran's Young Ladies.

REVISIONS: Programs of September 1930 include two additional pieces choreographed by Balanchine, which may have been added at an earlier date.

PAS DE DEUX (Part II, Scene 26): *Music*: By Peter Ilyitch Tschaikovsky. *Production*: Costumes by Oliver Messel. *Cast*: Nikitina, Efimov.

TENNIS (Part II, Scene 28): *Music*: By Vivian Ellis. *Production*: Scenery by Rex Whistler. Scenery executed by Alick Johnstone; costumes executed by Reville, Ltd. *Cast*: *Referee*, Efimov; *Tennis Players*, Mr. Cochran's Young Ladies.

100 [DUET and TRIO]

MUSIC: By Franz Liszt (*Liebestraum*, ca. 1850).

PREMIERE: September 16, 1930, members of the Royal Danish Ballet, Nimb's Restaurant, Tivoli Gardens, Copenhagen. Conductor: Victor Schiøler.

CAST: [DUET]: Elna Jørgen-Jensen, George Balanchine. [TRIO]: Elna Lassen, Ulla Poulsen, Balanchine.

NOTE: Untitled pieces performed once as part of Princess Margarethe's Høstfest (Harvest Festival).

See 107

101 DEN TREKANTEDE HAT (LE TRICORNE)

MUSIC: By Manuel de Falla (*El Sombrero de Tres Picos*, produced 1919).

CHOREOGRAPHY: Originally choreographed by Léonide Massine (1919); rechoreographed by George Balanchine.

PRODUCTION: Scenery and costumes by Kjeld Abell.

PREMIERE: October 12, 1930, Royal Danish Ballet, Royal Theater, Copenhagen. Conductor: Victor Schiøler.

CAST. *The Miller*, Leif Ørnberg; *The Miller's Wife*, Ulla Poulsen; *The Corregidor*, Karl Merrild; *The Corregidor's Wife*, Tony Madsen; *The Red Lady*, Ragnhild Rasmussen; *Policemen*; *Townspeople*.

NOTE: Performed, with *Schéhérazade* and *La Boutique Fantasque*, in the first of two Royal Danish Ballet series called *Ballet Evening by George Balanchine* presented during his six months as guest ballet master.

102 SCHÉHÉRAZADE

MUSIC: By Nicolai Rimsky-Korsakov (Op. 35, 1888).

CHOREOGRAPHY: Originally choreographed by Michel Fokine (1910); rechoreographed by George Balanchine.

PRODUCTION: Scenery and costumes by Kay Nielsen.

PREMIERE: October 12, 1930, Royal Danish Ballet, Royal Theater, Copenhagen. Conductor: Victor Schiøler.

CAST: *The Sultan*, Svend Methling (actor); *Sultan's Brother*, Richard Jensen; *Sultan's Wife*, Ulla Poulsen; *Sultan's Dancing Girls*, 3 women; *A Negro*, Leif Ørnberg; *A Eunuch*, Storm Petersen (actor); *Slave Girls*; *Wives*; *Negroes*; *Captives*.

NOTE: Balanchine changed the location from the original interior scene to a Persian garden, and included actors in the cast.

103 LEGETØJSBUTIKEN (LA BOUTIQUE FANTASQUE)

MUSIC: By Gioacchino Rossini (selections from *Les Péchés de Vieillesse*, orchestrated by Ottorino Respighi, 1918, on commission from Serge Diaghilev).

CHOREOGRAPHY: Originally choreographed by Léonide Massine (1919); rechoreographed by George Balanchine.

PRODUCTION: Scenery and costumes by Kjeld Abell.

PREMIERE: October 12, 1930, Royal Danish Ballet, Royal Theater, Copenhagen. Conductor: Victor Schiøler.

CAST: *Storekeeper*, Storm Petersen (actor); *Englishman*, Aage Winther-Jørgensen; *Wife*, Ragnhild Rasmussen; *Russian Merchant*, Richard Jensen; *His Wife*, Edel Pedersen; *Bananaman*; *Thief*; *Fop*; *Dolls*; *Dogs*; *Cossacks*; TARANTELLA: Elna Jørgen-Jensen, Leif Ørnberg; MAZURKA: Magda Allan Dahl, Gerda Karstens, Karl Merrild, Hans Brenaa; COSSACK DANCE: 5 men; DOGS DANCE: Maren Eschelsen, Niels Bjørn-Larsen; CAN-CAN: Kirsten Nellemose, Børge Ralov; INTERMEZZO: Else Højgaard, Gertrud Jensen, 12 women; GALOP: Entire cast.

104 FYRST IGOR (PRINCE IGOR)

Polovtsian Dances from the Opera 'Prince Igor'

MUSIC: By Alexander Borodin (1875).

CHOREOGRAPHY: By Michel Fokine (1909); staged by George Balanchine.

PRODUCTION: Scenery and costumes by K. Korovin.

PREMIERE: December 3, 1930, Royal Danish Ballet, Royal Theater, Copenhagen. Conductor: Victor Schiøler.

CAST: *Prince Igor*, Richard Jensen; *Khan Kontchak*, Albrecht Delfs; *Polovtsian Warrior Chief*, Karl Merrild; *16 Polovtsian Warriors*; *13 Polovtsian Women*; *17 Captured Persian Women*; *The Khan's Warriors*; *Polovtsian Women*; *Boys*.

NOTE: Balanchine appeared twice in the role of the Warrior Chief as guest artist in later performances.

See 383

105 ROSENDRØMMEN (LE SPECTRE DE LA ROSE)

MUSIC: By Carl Maria von Weber (*Aufforderung zum Tanz* for piano, Op. 65, 1819).

CHOREOGRAPHY: By Michel Fokine (1911); staged by George Balanchine.

PREMIERE: December 14, 1930, Koncert Palæet, Copenhagen.

CAST: Ulla Poulsen, George Balanchine.

NOTE: Given once, at the annual Christmas charity performance sponsored by the newspaper *Politiken*.

See 34

1931

106 JOSEF-LEGENDE (LA LÉGENDE DE JOSEPH)
Choreographic Narrative in Eight Scenes

MUSIC: By Richard Strauss (Op. 63, 1913-14, commissioned by Serge Diaghilev).

CHOREOGRAPHY: Originally choreographed by Michel Fokine (1914); rechoreographed by George Balanchine.

PRODUCTION: Scenery and costumes by Kjeld Abell. Scenery executed by Axel Bruun.

PREMIERE: January 18, 1931, Royal Danish Ballet, Royal Theater, Copenhagen. Conductor: Victor Schiøler.

CAST: *Josef*, Børge Ralov; *Father*, Karl Merrild; *Mother*, Edel Pedersen; *Josef's Brothers*, 10 men; *2 Young Women*; *3 Merchants*; *4 Slave Girls*; *Leader of Pharaoh's Bodyguard*, Richard Jensen; *His Wife*, Ulla Poulsen; *Bodyguards*; *Slaves*; *Guests*; *Onlookers*.
   SCENE 1: Joseph's Home. SCENE 2: The Well. SCENE 3: The Father. SCENE 4: The Masked Ball. SCENE 5: Interlude. SCENE 6: Temptation. SCENE 7: Interlude. SCENE 8: Pharaoh.

NOTE: Balanchine abandoned the original libretto by Hugo von Hofmannsthal (used by Fokine) and based his work on the story of

Joseph as recounted in the Old Testament. Presented with Balanchine's restaging of *Apollon Musagète* [84, with Leif Ørnberg] and *Barabau* [53, with Harald Lander] in the second of two Royal Danish Ballet series called *Ballet Evening by George Balanchine*.

107 DANCES FOR SIR OSWALD STOLL'S VARIETY SHOWS

A NOVEL INTERPRETATION OF LIEBESTRAUM: *Music*: By Franz Liszt (*Liebestraum*, ca. 1850). *Production*: Costumes by Hedley Briggs. Scenery by Frederick Stafford. *Premiere*: February 16, 1931, Sir Oswald Stoll's Variety Shows, Coliseum, London. *Cast*: 16 women. *Note*: LIEBESTRAUM appears on programs for the weeks beginning February 16, 23, and March 2, along with 'other dances produced by George Balanchine (Director of Serge Diaghileff's Russian Ballet).' The Coliseum was distinguished by having 'the finest revolving stage in the world.' In his setting of LIEBESTRAUM, Balanchine used the stage as a giant phonograph record, with a small dog in the center as 'His Master's Voice,' and the women as phonograph needles. *See 100*

WALTZ FANTASY IN BLUE: *Music*: By Mikhail Glinka (*Valse Fantaisie* in B minor, 1839; orchestrated 1856). *Premiere*: March 9, 1931, Sir Oswald Stoll's Variety Shows, Coliseum. *Cast*: Doris Sonne, corps de ballet. *Note*: Balanchine choreographed works to this music in 1953 (*Valse Fantaisie*) and 1967 (as a section of *Glinkiana*, soon after performed alone as *Valse Fantaisie*), both for the New York City Ballet. *See 293, 359, 366*

A SKIT ON MARLENE DIETRICH IN THE FILM 'THE BLUE ANGEL': *Music*: By Sammy Lerner and Frederick Hollander ('Falling in Love Again' from *The Blue Angel*, 1930). *Premiere*: March 9, 1931, Sir Oswald Stoll's Variety Shows, Coliseum. *Cast*: 6-8 women.

STATUES: *Music*: By Felix Mendelssohn (one of the *Songs without Words*). *Production*: Produced by Sir Oswald Stoll. *Premiere*: April?, 1931, *Varieties en Fête*, Alhambra, London. *Cast*: Hedley Briggs, Dorothy Jackson, Anna Roth.

PAPILLONS: *Music*: Perhaps by Frédéric Chopin (possibly the 'Butterfly' Étude in G-flat major, Op. 25, no. 9, 1832-34). *Production*: Produced by

Sir Oswald Stoll. *Premiere*: April?, 1931, *Varieties en Fête*, Alhambra.
Cast: Sonne, Natasha Gregorova, Maria Gaya, corps de ballet.
Note: Sonne remembers a pas de six to this étude, which may be
Papillons, or (as the program does not specify music) a separate work.

DIE FLEDERMAUS: *Music*: By Johann Strauss the Younger (overture to *Die
Fledermaus*, produced 1874). *Production*: Produced by Sir Oswald Stoll.
Premiere: May 18, 1931, *Varieties en Fête*, Alhambra. *Cast*: Bat, Sonne;
Pas de Deux: Jackson, Briggs; corps de ballet. *See 169, 199, 206, 294*

NOTE: In addition to these works documented from programs of Sir
Oswald Stoll's variety shows at the London Coliseum (February 16-
March 21) and Alhambra (April 6-May 30), reviews and conversations
with dancers identify the following: *Tango* (Sonne and Briggs); Rimsky-
Korsakov's *Flight of the Bumble Bee* (Gregorova, Sonne, Gaya); can-can
from Offenbach's *Orphée aux Enfers* for a corps of girls in front of the
curtain; a short jazz number for four women to the recorded music
of Jack Hilton and His Dance Orchestra, performed in front of the
curtain; an ensemble number to Tschaikovsky's *1812 Overture*, and a
pas de deux for Briggs and Betty Scorer to Lord Berners' *Scottish
Rhapsody*. Publicity material suggests that costumes were designed by
Hedley Brigg and scenery by Frederick Stafford, but Natasha Gregorova
remembers that Barbara Karinska was also involved with costuming.
Dennis Stoll (son of Sir Oswald) conducted some of the performances.
Balanchine's group of sixteen women (Hedley Briggs was the single
male performer) was variously billed as the Balanchine Ballet,
Balanchine's Girls, Balanchine's Sixteen Novelty Dancers, George
Balanchine's Sixteen Delightful Dancers, and 16 Delightful Balanchine
Girls 16. *See 109*

108 CHARLES B. COCHRAN'S 1931 REVUE

MUSIC: By Noel Coward and others.

CHOREOGRAPHY: Dances and ensembles by Buddy Bradley, Billy Pierce
and George Balanchine.

PRODUCTION: The whole produced under the direction of Charles B.
Cochran. Staged by Frank Collins.

PREMIERE: March 19, 1931, London Pavilion. (Out-of-town preview:
February 18, Palace Theatre, Manchester.)

CAST: Bobby Clark, Ada-May, Melville Cooper, Paul McCullough, Queenie Leonard, Edward Cooper, Effie Atherton, and others.

STEALING THROUGH (Part I, Scene 6): *Music and Sketch*: By Douglas Byng and Melville Gideon. *Production*: Scenery and costumes by Oliver Messel. Scenery executed by E. Delany; costumes executed by Reville, Ltd., Eleanor Abbey, L. & H. Nathan, Ltd. *Cast*: Ada-May, Mr. Cochran's Young Ladies; *A Satyr*, Bobby Clark.

SCARAMOUCHE: AN IMPRESSION OF THE COMMEDIA DELL'ARTE (Part I, Scene 11 [Finale]): *Music*: By Elsie April, from an air of Pergolesi. Lyrics by Douglas Byng. *Production*: Scenery and costumes by Oliver Messel. Scenery executed by Alick Johnstone; costumes executed by Eleanor Abbey and C. Alias, Ltd. *Cast*: *Scaramouche*, Bernardi; *Sylvia*, Kathryn Hamill; *Capitano*, Henry Mollison; *Pierrettes*, Mr. Cochran's Young Ladies, The John Tiller Girls; *Zanni*, 8 men; *Clown*, Charles Farey; *Sprite*, Eve; *2 Pages*; *Mezzetin*, Edward Cooper; *Coralline*, Jane Welsh; *Pantalone*, Melville Cooper; *Jacqueline*, Effie Atherton; *Arlochino*, John Mills; *Isabel*, Molly Molloy; *Pulcinella*, Al Marshall; *Trivellino*, Queenie Leonard; *Columbine*, Ada-May; *Two Sailors*, Clark, Paul McCullough.

109 ORPHÉE AUX ENFERS
Comic Opera in Three Acts and Nine Scenes

MUSIC: By Jacques Offenbach (produced 1874). Libretto by Hector Crémieux and Ludovic Halévy.

PRODUCTION: Produced by Les Frères Isola. Directed by Max Dearly.

PREMIERE: December 24, 1931, Théâtre Mogador, Paris. Danced by Les Ballets Russes de Georges Balanchine. Conductor: M. Diot.

CAST: *Jupiter*, Max Dearly; *Aristaeus-Pluto*, Lucien Muratore; *Eurydice*, Marise Beaujon; *Diana*, Jeanne Saint-Bonnet; *Public Opinion*, Rose Carday; *Orpheus*, Adrien Lamy; *Mercury*, Maurice Porterat; *Mars*, José Dupuis (fils); *Cupid*, Monette Diney; *Venus*, Raymonde Allain; *Juno*, Alice Soulie; *Morpheus*, Lucien Brouet; *John Styx*, Félix Oudart; *Premiere Danseuse* (and *Aurora*), Felia Doubrovska; *Premier Danseur*, Anatole Vilzak; *The Twelve Small Virtuosi* (child violinists); and others. Corps de ballet: 24 women, 4 men.

DIVERTISSEMENT PASTORALE (Act I): Corps de ballet.

DIVERTISSEMENT DES SONGES ET DES HEURES (Act II): Felia Doubrovska, corps de ballet.

GRAND BALLET DES NYMPHES (Act II): Doubrovska, Anatole Vilzak, Irina Baronova, Tatiana Semanova, Irène Lucezarska.

DIVERTISSEMENT DES MOUCHES (Act III): Corps de ballet.

CHŒUR INFERNAL (Act III, chorus and dance): Vilzak.

BACCHANALE (Act III): Doubrovska, Vilzak.

See 107

1932

110 LES AMOURS DU POÈTE
Comedy with Music in Five Acts by René Blum and G. Delaquys
ACT III SONG, LE PAUVRE PIERRE

MUSIC: By Robert Schumann ('Chopin' section of *Carnaval*, Op. 9, no. 3, 1834-35).

PRODUCTION: Scenery by Alphonse Visconti and Georges Geerts. Costumes by Georgette Vialet.

PREMIERE: January 5, 1932, Théâtre de Monte-Carlo [group], Opéra de Monte-Carlo. Danced by members of Ballets [Russes] de Monte-Carlo. Conductor: Marc-César Scotto.

CAST: 4 women, 2 men.

NOTE: Balanchine's first work as ballet master of the company that was to become Les Ballets Russes de Monte-Carlo. The play is about the poet Heinrich Heine; the chief characters in the song choreographed by Balanchine are lady admirers of the poet.

See 3

111 TANNHÄUSER

Opera in Three Acts and Four Scenes by Richard Wagner
ACT I VENUSBERG BALLET

PREMIERE: January 21, 1932, Opéra de Monte-Carlo. Danced by Ballets [Russes] de Monte-Carlo. Conductor: Gabriel Grovlez.

CAST: Valentina Lanina [Blinova], Léon Woizikowsky, 14 women, 7 men.

See 154

112 LES CONTES D'HOFFMANN

Opera in Three Acts with Prologue and Epilogue by Jacques Offenbach
SCENE 2 BALLET

PREMIERE: January 24, 1932, Opéra de Monte-Carlo. Danced by Ballets [Russes] de Monte-Carlo. Conductor: Gabriel Grovlez.

CAST: VALSE: 4 women; PAS DE DEUX: Valentina Blinova, Valentin Froman; POLKA: Eleanora Marra, Léon Woizikowsky; GRANDE VALSE: 6 couples.

See 58, 260

113 LE PROPHÈTE

Opera in Five Acts by Giacomo Meyerbeer
ACTS I, III, IV, V BALLETS

PREMIERE: January 26, 1932, Opéra de Monte-Carlo. Danced by Ballets [Russes] de Monte-Carlo. Conductor: Gabriel Grovlez.

CAST: ACT I VILLAGE BALLET: 4 couples. ACT III SKATING BALLET: 2 women, 4 men; *Two Skaters*, Eleanora Marra, Léon Woizikowsky; *Snow*, Valentina Blinova, Valentin Froman, 12 women. ACT IV, YOUNG GIRLS THROWING FLOWERS: 6 women. ACT V BACCHANALE: Marra, 10 women.

114 UNE NUIT À VENISE (EINE NACHT IN VENEDIG)

Comic Opera in Three Acts and Five Scenes by Johann Strauss the Younger

ACTS I, II, III BALLETS

PREMIERE: February 2, 1932, Opéra de Monte-Carlo. Danced by Ballets [Russes] de Monte-Carlo. Conductor: Gabriel Grovlez.

CAST: ACT I BALLET: 12 women. ACT II VALSE: 6 couples. ACT III MAZURKA: 3 couples. GRAND PAS CLASSIQUE: Valentina Blinova, Léon Woizikowsky, 3 women.

115 LAKMÉ

Opera in Three Acts by Léo Delibes

ACT II BALLET

PREMIERE: February 9, 1932, Opéra de Monte-Carlo. Danced by Ballets [Russes] de Monte-Carlo. Conductor: Marc-César Scotto.

CAST: Eleanora Marra, 12 women.

See 57, 153

116 SAMSON ET DALILA

Opera in Three Acts and Five Scenes by Camille Saint-Saëns

ACT I BALLET; ACT III BACCHANALE

PREMIERE: February 11, 1932, Opéra de Monte-Carlo. Danced by Ballets [Russes] de Monte-Carlo. Conductor: Gabriel Grovlez.

CAST: BALLET: 12 women. BACCHANALE: Eleanora Marra, 16 women.

See 66, 171, 228

117 FAUST

Opera in Five Acts by Charles Gounod

ACT II KERMESSE: VALSE

PREMIERE: February 13, 1932, Opéra de Monte-Carlo. Danced by Ballets [Russes] de Monte-Carlo. Conductor: Gabriel Grovlez.

CAST: 6 couples.

See 45, 151, 227, 397, 413

118 PATRIE

Opera-Ballet in One Act by Émile Paladilhe
BALLET

PREMIERE: February 20, 1932, Opéra de Monte-Carlo. Danced by
Ballets [Russes] de Monte-Carlo. Conductor: Marc-César Scotto.

CAST: NEAPOLITAN DANCE: Tatiana Lipkovska, Roland Guérard; INDIAN
DANCE: 1 woman, 3 men; AFRICAN DANCE: 5 women; FLEMISH DANCE:
2 couples; SPANISH DANCE: Eleanora Marra, Léon Woizikowsky;
CLASSICAL BALLET: Valentina Blinova, Tamara Toumanova, Valentin
Froman, 6 women; 'LA MONÉGASQUE' (music by Raoul Gunsbourg):
corps de ballet.

NOTE: Performed once, with Act III of *Hérodiade*, for the benefit of the
Caisse de Bienfaisance de la Colonie Française à Monaco.

119 HÉRODIADE

Act III of the Opera by Jules Massenet
DIVERTISSEMENT

PREMIERE: February 20, 1932, Opéra de Monte-Carlo. Danced by
Ballets [Russes] de Monte-Carlo. Conductor: Gabriel Grovlez.

CAST: 6 women.

See 46

120 TURANDOT

Opera in Three Acts and Four Scenes by Giacomo Puccini
ACT II DIVERTISSEMENT, LES PORCELAINES DE CHINE

PREMIERE: February 21, 1932, Opéra de Monte-Carlo. Danced by
Ballets [Russes] de Monte-Carlo. Conductor: Gabriel Grovlez.

CAST: Valentina Blinova, Tamara Toumanova, Léon Woizikowsky,
Marian Ladré, Roland Guérard, 16 women.

See 68

121 RIGOLETTO

Opera in Four Acts by Giuseppe Verdi
ACT I DIVERTISSEMENT

PREMIERE: February 23, 1932, Opéra de Monte-Carlo. Danced by Ballets [Russes] de Monte-Carlo. Conductor: Michel Steiman.

CAST: 4 couples.

See 88, 156

122 MANON

Opera in Four Acts by Jules Massenet
ACT III BALLET

PREMIERE: February 28, 1932, Opéra de Monte-Carlo. Danced by Ballets [Russes] de Monte-Carlo. Conductor: Gabriel Grovlez.

CAST: Valentina Blinova, Léon Woizikowsky, 6 couples.

See 40, 159

123 LA TRAVIATA

Opera in Four Acts by Giuseppe Verdi
ACT III BALLET

PREMIERE: March 3, 1932, Opéra de Monte-Carlo. Danced by Ballets [Russes] de Monte-Carlo. Conductor: Michel Steiman.

CAST: Tatiana Lipkovska, Metek [Mezeslav] Borovsky, 6 couples.

See 67, 150, 252

124 ROMÉO ET JULIETTE

Opera in Five Acts, Six Scenes and Prologue by Charles Gounod
ACT I DIVERTISSEMENT

PREMIERE: March 6, 1932, Opéra de Monte-Carlo. Danced by Ballets [Russes] de Monte-Carlo. Conductor: Gabriel Grovlez.

CAST: 8 couples.

See 86, 180

125 FAY-YEN-FAH

Opera in Three Acts and Four Scenes by Joseph Redding
SCENE 3 BALLET DIVERTISSEMENT; BALLET VOLANT

PREMIERE: March 8, 1932, Opéra de Monte-Carlo. Danced by Ballets [Russes] de Monte-Carlo. Conductor: Michel Steiman.

CAST: BALLET DIVERTISSEMENT: *Lilies*, 6 women; *Veils*, 6 women; *Chinese Woman*, Tamara Toumanova; *Chinese Man*, Marian Ladré; *Poppies*, Toumanova, 6 women; *White Peacocks*, 2 women; *Gold Peacocks*, 4 women. BALLET VOLANT: 5 women.

See 44

126 AÏDA

Opera in Four Acts by Giuseppe Verdi
ACTS I AND II BALLETS

PREMIERE: March 19, 1932, Opéra de Monte-Carlo. Danced by Ballets [Russes] de Monte-Carlo. Conductor: Alfredo Padovani.

CAST: ACT I BALLET: 8 women. ACT II BALLET: 12 women, 6 men.

See 152, 226, 255

127 CARMEN

Opera in Four Acts by Georges Bizet
ACT II SEGUIDILLA

PREMIERE: March 24, 1932, Opéra de Monte-Carlo. Danced by Ballets [Russes] de Monte-Carlo. Conductor: Michel Steiman.

CAST: 4 couples.

See 38, 155, 248

128 LA PÉRICHOLE

Comic Opera in Three Acts and Four Scenes by Jacques Offenbach
ACT III BALLET

PREMIERE: March 31, 1932, Opéra de Monte-Carlo. Danced by Ballets [Russes] de Monte-Carlo. Conductor: Michel Steiman.

CAST: 12 couples, Juan Martínez trio of Spanish Dancers.

129 COTILLON

Music: By Emmanuel Chabrier (*Dix Pièces Pittoresques*, 1880 [piano pieces, some orchestrated by Chabrier, others by Vittorio Rieti] and the third of the *Trois Valses Romantiques* for piano, 1883 [orchestrated by Felix Mottl]). Book by Boris Kochno.

Production: Scenery and costumes by Christian Bérard. Scenery executed by Prince A. Schervashidze; women's costumes executed by Karinska, men's costumes executed by Lidvall.

Premiere: April 12, 1932, Ballets Russes de Monte-Carlo, Opéra de Monte-Carlo. Conductor: Pierre Kolpikoff. (Preview: January 17, 1932, Ballets [Russes] de Monte-Carlo, Opéra de Monte-Carlo, with George Balanchine in the role later danced by David Lichine. Conductor: Marc-César Scotto.)

Cast: THE TOILETTE: THE BALLROOM, WHERE THE FINAL PREPARATIONS ARE INTERRUPTED BY THE ARRIVAL OF GUESTS: Tamara Toumanova, Natalie Strakhova, David Lichine; THE INTRODUCTIONS: Valentina Blinova, 12 women, 6 men; THE MASTER OF CEREMONIES RUNS IN LATE: Léon Woizikowsky; THE PLEASURE GARDEN: THE MASTER AND MISTRESS OF CEREMONIES DEMONSTRATE THE FIGURES OF THE FIRST DANCE, WHICH ARE REPEATED BY ALL THE GUESTS: Blinova, Woizikowsky, corps de ballet; NEW ENTRÉE AND DANCE OF HATS: *Harlequins, Jockeys and Spaniards*, Toumanova, Strakhova, 4 women; Lichine, 2 men; THE HANDS OF FATE: THE CAVALIER COMES UP TO THE CURTAIN TO CHOOSE ONE OF THE HANDS THAT ARE REVEALED ABOVE IT, BUT IS STOPPED BY THE SUDDEN APPARITION OF A HAND GLOVED IN BLACK: Lubov Rostova, Valentin Froman; THE MAGIC LANTERN: A YOUNG GIRL TELLS THE FORTUNES OF THE GUESTS; APPEARANCE OF THE BAT AND THE CUP OF CHAMPAGNE: Toumanova, Blinova, Rostova, Froman, Lichine, corps de ballet; GRAND ROND AND END OF COTILLION: Entire cast.

Note: Amid the program of festivities at a cotillion, Fate appears in the guise of a vampire wearing black gloves. A Young Girl telling fortunes is rebuffed by the Mistress of Ceremonies and runs off, but reappears to lead the Grand Rond, in which she pirouettes around the ballroom by herself, until the guests join her spinning and the curtain falls.

The preview performance marked the debut of the Ballets de Monte-Carlo, which within six weeks became the Ballets Russes de

Monte-Carlo. *Cotillon* and Balanchine's other major work for the company, *La Concurrence*, were performed by the several Ballets Russes companies in Europe, North America, Australia (and in the case of *Cotillon*, South America) until 1939 (*La Concurrence*) and 1943 (*Cotillon*), providing the base for Balanchine's early reputation in the United States.

In 1967, Balanchine choreographed Chabrier's *Trois Valses Romantiques* for the New York City Ballet.

STAGINGS (THE HANDS OF FATE pas de deux): 1954, Danilova Concert Company; 1968, Tulsa.

See 357

130 LA CONCURRENCE

MUSIC: By Georges Auric (1932, commissioned by René Blum). Book by André Derain.

PRODUCTION: Curtain, scenery and costumes by André Derain. Curtain executed by André Derain; scenery executed by Prince A. Schervashidze; costumes executed by Karinska, Paris.

PREMIERE: April 12, 1932, Ballets Russes de Monte-Carlo, Opéra de Monte-Carlo. Conductor: Marc-César Scotto.

CAST: *First Tailor*, Metek [Mezeslav] Borovsky; *Second Tailor*, Yurek Shabelevsky; *First Tailor's Wife*, Tatiana Lipkovska; *Second Tailor's Wife*, Gala Chabelska; *First Couple*, Louise Lyman, Roman Jasinsky; *Second Couple*, Lara Obidenna, Marian Ladré; *Their Daughter*, Irène Stepanova; *Two Friends*, Valentina Blinova, Eleanora Marra; *The Vagabond*, Léon Woizikowsky; *The Girl*, Tamara Toumanova; *The Girls*, 10 women; *Neighbors*, 6 women, 5 men.

NOTE: The theme is fashion and human vanity. Two rival tailors, both selling fashionable apparel in an imaginary town, vie for the attention of eager shoppers. The tailors begin to quarrel, and the customers are drawn into the commotion. Citizens of the town intervene and disperse the crowd; the two tailors, finding themselves alone with their profits, are pleased and become reconciled.

STAGINGS (VAGABOND DANCE, retitled *Hobo Dance*): 1945, Ballet Russe Highlights.

131 LE BOURGEOIS GENTILHOMME

MUSIC: By Richard Strauss (concert suite, ca. 1917). Book by Sobeka [Boris Kochno] after Molière.

PRODUCTION: Curtain, scenery and costumes by Alexandre Benois. Curtain executed by Georges Geerts; scenery executed by Prince A. Schervashidze; costumes executed by Karinska, Paris.

PREMIERE: May 3, 1932, Ballets Russes de Monte-Carlo, Opéra de Monte-Carlo. Conductor: Paul Paray.

CAST: *Cléonte*, David Lichine; *Covielle, His Valet*, Jasht Dolotine; *Two Gypsy Tailors*; *Monsieur Jourdain, le Bourgeois Gentilhomme*, Marian Ladré; *His Retinue*, 4 women, 2 men; *Cléonte's Friends Disguised as Slaves*, 4 men; *Lucille*, Tamara Toumanova; *Nicole, Her Servant*, Eleanora Marra; BALLET GIVEN BY M. JOURDAIN IN HONOR OF THE SON OF THE GRAND TURK: Valentina Blinova, 6 women; TURKISH DIVERTISSEMENT: I. Olga Morosova, Yurek Shabelevsky, Léonide Katchourovsky; II. Natalie Strakhova, Metek [Mezeslav] Borovsky; III. *Acrobats*, Roman Jasinsky, 3 women.

1. Cléonte disguises himself as the son of the Grand Turk. 2. Cléonte enters the house of Monsieur Jourdain. 3. Dance of Cléonte and his friends disguised as slaves. 4. Ballet given by Monsieur Jourdain in honor of the son of the Grand Turk. 5. Entrance of Lucille, accompanied by her servant Nicole. 6. Turkish ceremony to ennoble Monsieur Jourdain. 7. Turkish Divertissement. 8. Lucille, not recognizing Cléonte, attempts to flee. 9. Betrothal of Lucille to Cléonte, who removes his disguise.

OTHER VERSIONS (each subsequent version was a complete resetting of staging and décor): 1944, Ballet Russe de Monte Carlo. 1979, New York City Opera.

See 221, 410, 414

132 SUITES DE DANSE

MUSIC: By Mikhail Glinka.

PREMIERE: May 5, 1932, Ballets Russes de Monte-Carlo, Opéra de Monte-Carlo. Conductor: Marc-César Scotto.

CAST: JOTA ARAGONESA: Eleanora Marra, Léon Woizikowsky, 6 couples; TARANTELLA: Nina Verchinina, Lena Kirsova, David Lichine, Metek [Mezeslav] Borovsky, Yurek Shabelevsky; VALSE: Valentina Blinova, Tamara Toumanova, Tatiana Riabouchinska, 6 women; KOMARINSKAIA: Irène Kervily, Woizikowsky, 8 couples.

NOTE: In 1967, Balanchine choreographed the JOTA ARAGONESA as part of *Glinkiana* for the New York City Ballet.

See 359

133 NUMÉRO LES CANOTIERS

MUSIC: 'The Waves of the Danube' (a waltz tune popular in Russia).

PRODUCTION: Costumes by Christian Bérard (after Renoir).

PREMIERE: Spring?, 1932, costume ball at the Villa Blanche, home of Édouard and Denise Bourdet at Tamaris, near Toulon.

CAST: Mme Georges Auric, George Balanchine, Boris Kochno.

NOTE: Performed once, at the Bal de la Préfecture.

1933

134 MOZARTIANA

MUSIC: By Peter Ilyitch Tschaikovsky (Suite No. 4, *Mozartiana*, Op. 61, 1887; based on Mozart's Gigue in G major [K. 574], Minuet in D major [K. 355], the motet 'Ave, Verum Corpus' [K. 618], and variations on 'Les Hommes Pieusement' from Gluck's comic opera *La Rencontre Imprévue* [K. 455]).

PRODUCTION: Curtain, scenery and costumes by Christian Bérard.

PREMIERE: June 7, 1933, Les Ballets 1933, Théâtre des Champs-Élysées, Paris. Conductor: Maurice Abravanel.

CAST: GIGUE: Ludovic Matlinsky; MENUETTO: 6 women; PREGHIERA: Lucienne Kylberg; TEMA CON VARIAZIONI: Tamara Toumanova, Roman Jasinsky, corps de ballet; FINALE: Toumanova, Kylberg, Jasinsky, 7 women, 1 man.

NOTE: A suite of dances in stylized eighteenth-century costumes, set in an Italian town. A young man dances a solo and is joined by village girls. A sad girl enters carried by two veiled figures; she dances a gentle 'Prayer.' A series of dances follows featuring town characters, then a grand adagio, and a country-dance finale. The forecurtain showed a silhouette of the child Mozart seated at a harpsichord.

Mozartiana was one of six new ballets created by Balanchine during the six-months' existence of Les Ballets 1933, the company he formed with Boris Kochno. It was performed in Paris and London with *Les Sept Péchés Capitaux, Les Songes, Fastes, L'Errante, Les Valses de Beethoven,* and other musical works without choreography. In 1981, Balanchine choreographed a new ballet to *Mozartiana* for the New York City Ballet Tschaikovsky Festival, changing the order of the movements to place the PREGHIERA first.

REVISIONS: 1935, American Ballet: Sections originally danced by Toumanova and Jasinsky differently apportioned, with single pas de deux for leading couple; pas de six in THEME AND VARIATIONS danced by six women (three in men's costumes). 1945, Ballet Russe de Monte Carlo: Original form more closely followed, with two pas de deux for leading couple; corps de ballet entirely women; one male soloist instead of two. 1956, Danilova Concert Company: Presented without MENUETTO by cast of four dancers.

STAGINGS: 1935, American Ballet; 1945, Ballet Russe de Monte Carlo; 1956, Danilova Concert Company.

See 149, 417

135 LES SONGES

MUSIC: By Darius Milhaud (1933, commissioned by Boris Kochno).
Book by André Derain.

PRODUCTION: Scenery and costumes by André Derain.

PREMIERE: June 7, 1933, Les Ballets 1933, Théâtre des Champs-Élysées, Paris. Conductor: Maurice Abravanel.

CAST: *The Ballerina,* Tamara Toumanova; 1. POLKA: Kyra Blank, Karl Scheibe; 2. MONSTRE (ACROBAT): Roman Jasinsky; 3. THE KNAVES: Ludovic Matlinsky, Serge Ismaïloff; 4. THE CORYPHÉES: 5 women;

5. HIGH-LIFE AND THE DEMI-MONDE: Jasinsky, Lucienne Kylberg;
6. FINALE: Entire cast.

NOTE: Exhausted after a triumphant performance, the ballerina falls asleep and is assailed by nightmares and visions. The fragrance of flowers brings an intimation of loveliness; she awakens reassured to find herself in her own room.

STAGINGS (titled *Dreams*): 1935, American Ballet.

See 145

136 LES SEPT PÉCHÉS CAPITAUX (also called ANNA ANNA, OR THE SEVEN CAPITAL SINS)

MUSIC: By Kurt Weill (*Die sieben Todsünden*, produced 1933, commissioned by Boris Kochno and Edward James). Text by Bertolt Brecht from a suggestion by Boris Kochno and Edward James.

PRODUCTION: Produced and directed by George Balanchine. Scenery and costumes by Caspar Rudolph Neher.

PREMIERE: June 7, 1933, Les Ballets 1933, Théâtre des Champs-Élysées, Paris. Conductor: Maurice Abravanel.

CAST: *The Two Annas*, Lotte Lenya (singer), Tilly Losch; *The Family*, Heinrich Gretler, Otto Pasetti, Albert Peters, Erich Ruchs (singers); corps de ballet. Singers and dancers appeared together on stage.

I. Introduction. II. Sloth. III. Pride. IV. Anger. V. Gluttony. VI. Lust. VII. Avarice. VIII. Envy.

NOTE: An ironic morality play, the story of Anna, who leaves Louisiana to travel across the United States, intending to make her fortune and build a family home. Anna-Anna's double nature is portrayed by a dancer and a singer; in cabaret-style song and dance with pantomime, the two performers dramatize the opposing tendencies of Anna's nature: idealism and cynicism, generosity and meanness. As she goes from city to city (with her family onstage intoning Lutheran pieties) she betrays her art for success, love for money, justice for power.

OTHER VERSIONS: 1958, New York City Ballet (*The Seven Deadly Sins*).

See 322

137 FASTES

MUSIC: By Henri Sauguet (1933, commissioned by Boris Kochno).
Book by André Derain.

PRODUCTION: Scenery and costumes by André Derain.

PREMIERE: June 10, 1933, Les Ballets 1933, Théâtre des Champs-Élysées,
Paris. Conductor: Maurice Abravanel.

CAST: *The Genii*, Serge Ismaïloff, Ludovic Matlinsky; *The Matrons*,
6 women; *Two Persian Saltateurs*, Lucienne Kylberg, Tamara Sidorenko;
Two Buffoons, Ismaïloff, Matlinsky; *The Courtesan*, Tamara Tchinarova;
The Young Girl, Tamara Toumanova; *The Lupercalian Priest*, Roman
Jasinsky.

NOTE: The scene is a Latin feast in Etruscan Italy; two genii attend
pagan rites performed by matrons, buffoons, acrobats. The Young Girl
encounters a priest of Lupercal; wearing a three-faced mask, he dances
for her a parable of youth, maturity and old age. A final scene of orgy
ends in ridicule with the entrance of the donkey of Silenus.

138 L'ERRANTE (also called ERRANTE; ALMA ERRANTE;
THE WANDERER)

Choreographic Fantasy

MUSIC: By Franz Schubert (*The Wanderer*, fantasy for piano, Op. 15,
1822, transcribed by Franz Liszt, orchestrated by Charles Koechlin).
Book by Pavel Tchelitchew.

PRODUCTION: Costumes, lighting and dramatic effects by Pavel
Tchelitchew. Tilly Losch's dress by Molyneux.

PREMIERE: June 10, 1933, Les Ballets 1933, Théâtre des Champs-Élysées,
Paris. Conductor: Maurice Abravanel.

CAST: Tilly Losch; Roman Jasinsky; 8 women, 3 men; child.

NOTE: As in Schmidt von Lübeck's poem, set by Schubert, a wanderer
seeks lost love amid phantom dreams; she encounters figures of hope,
despair and memory in an atmosphere of dark shadow and diffused
light. Scenic effects achieved by lighting and silks dramatized the
actions of the dancers. In later productions, characters were identified
as Woman in Green, Youths, Shadows, Angels, Revolutionaries, and
others.

REVISIONS: 1935, American Ballet: A second male role made more prominent.

STAGINGS: 1935, American Ballet (*Errante*); 1941, American Ballet Caravan (*Alma Errante*); 1943, Ballet Theatre (*The Wanderer*).

See 143, 197

139 LES VALSES DE BEETHOVEN
(also called THE WALTZES OF BEETHOVEN)

MUSIC: By Ludwig van Beethoven (several waltzes, orchestrated by Nicolas Nabokov, and one of the *Scottish Songs* for cello and male voice).

PRODUCTION: Scenery and costumes by Emilio Terry.

PREMIERE: June 19, 1933, Les Ballets 1933, Théâtre des Champs-Élysées, Paris. Conductor: Maurice Abravanel.

CAST: *Daphne*, Tilly Losch; *The Elements, Companions of Daphne: Earth*, Diana Gould; *Water*, T. Ouchkova; *Air*, Prudence Hyman; *Fire*, Tamara Sidorenko; *Eros*, Lucienne Kylberg; *Apollo*, Roman Jasinsky; *The Train of Apollo*, 4 women; *The Shade of Apollo*, Fernando Gusso.

NOTE: A Greek myth: Eros, with an arrow shot from his bow, inflames the god Apollo with love for the maiden Daphne. Seeking to escape Apollo's embraces, Daphne prays to the gods and is transformed into a laurel tree. Apollo grieves his loss at the foot of the laurel and is mocked in song by his own shadow: The laurel is thereafter consecrated to poetry.

140 DANS L'ÉLYSÉE

MUSIC: By Jacques Offenbach.

PRODUCTION: Presented by Edward James.

PREMIERE: July 3, 1933, Ballets Serge Lifar, Savoy Theatre, London. Conductor: Alexander Labinsky.

CAST: Felia Doubrovska.

NOTE: Neither Balanchine nor Doubrovska remembers this piece, but a program for the Lifar engagement at the Savoy lists *Dans l'Élysée*, danced by Doubrovska, with choreography uncredited. A review of Lifar's London appearances (*Dancing Times*, August 1933, pp. 439-40) mentions a 'solo *sur les pointes* to music of Offenbach choreographed by Balanchine' for Doubrovska.

1935

141 SERENADE

MUSIC: By Peter Ilyitch Tschaikovsky (Serenade in C for string orchestra, Op. 48, 1880, first three movements; arranged and reorchestrated by George Antheil).

PRODUCTION: Scenery by Gaston Longchamp. Costumes by Jean Lurçat.

PREMIERE: March 1, 1935, American Ballet, Adelphi Theater, New York. Conductor: Sandor Harmati. (First performed by students of the School of American Ballet, June 10, 1934, at Woodland, the estate of Felix Warburg, near White Plains, New York, in rehearsal costumes; then by the Producing Company of the School of American Ballet, December 8, 1934, Avery Memorial Theater, Hartford, Connecticut, with costumes by William B. Okie, Jr.).

CAST: SONATINA: Leda Anchutina, Holly Howard, Elise Reiman, Elena de Rivas, 13 women; WALTZ: Anchutina, Howard, Sylvia Giselle [Gisella Caccialanza], Helen Leitch, Annabelle Lyon, 10 women; ELEGY: Howard, Kathryn Mullowny, Heidi Vosseler, Charles Laskey, 8 women, 4 men.

NOTE: Created for students during the first year of the School of American Ballet, *Serenade* is the first work Balanchine choreographed for American dancers; it has come to be considered the signature piece of the New York City Ballet and is one of Balanchine's most widely performed works. A ballet of patterns that newly explores academic ballet technique; the choreography, as the music, has overtones of love, loss, yearning. During the inaugural season of the American Ballet, the company formed by Balanchine, Lincoln Kirstein and Edward M. M. Warburg, *Serenade* was performed in repertory with *Alma Mater*,

Errante, Reminiscence, Dreams, and *Transcendence.* A ballet to the same music, Fokine's *Eros,* was in the repertory of the Maryinsky Theater during Balanchine's youth.

REVISIONS: 1936, American Ballet Ensemble at the Metropolitan Opera: male dancer added to WALTZ. 1940, Ballet Russe de Monte Carlo: solo parts (originally divided among several dancers) reworked for single ballerina, two male dancers and supporting female dancer (with full corps de ballet); fourth movement of the Serenade (*Tema Russo* [with some passages omitted]), called RUSSIAN DANCE, inserted before concluding ELEGY, danced by four demi-soloists and ballerina; Tschaikovsky's original scoring adopted, rather than Antheil's; these revisions incorporated in all subsequent stagings. 1970-71, New York City Ballet: Slight additions at beginning and extensive new material added at end of RUSSIAN DANCE, with all previous omissions in score of *Tema Russo* restored.

Although the steps have remained basically the same, solo measures have been allocated in various ways, most frequently to three ballerinas and two male dancers (New York City Ballet variations have included, among others, five ballerinas [1950, London]; four ballerinas [1953, 1955, 1958], three ballerinas [1959]).

NEW PRODUCTIONS BY BALANCHINE COMPANIES: From 1936, American Ballet: Performed without décor. 1941, American Ballet Caravan: Costumes by Candido Portinari. New York City Ballet: 1948, costumes uncredited, lighting by Jean Rosenthal; 1952, costumes by Karinska; 1964, lighting by Ronald Bates.

STAGINGS: 1940, Ballet Russe de Monte Carlo; 1941, American Ballet Caravan; 1947, Paris; 1948, New York City Ballet; 1952, San Francisco; 1957, Royal Danish; 1960, Hamburg, La Scala, Netherlands; 1961, Atlanta, Ballet Borealis; 1962, National Ballet of Canada; 1964, Ballet of Los Angeles, National, Utah, Royal; 1965, Munich; 1966, Boston, Düsseldorf, Tokyo Ballet Geikijo, Vienna; 1968, Ballet la Jeunesse; 1969, Pennsylvania; 1970, Australia, Berlin, Geneva, Norway, Royal Swedish; 1973, Cincinnati; 1974, Frankfurt; 1975, Israel, Les Grands Ballets Canadiens, New Zealand; 1976, Iran, Rome; 1977, Washington, Hungary; 1978, Pacific Northwest, Zagreb, Zürich; 1979, Dance Theatre of Harlem; 1981, Cleveland, Eglevsky; 1982, Kansas City, Milwaukee, Matsuyama.

TELEVISION: 1956 (excerpts, ABC); 1957 (L'Heure du Concert, CBC, Montreal).

See 193, 254

142 ALMA MATER

MUSIC: By Kay Swift, orchestrated by Morton Gould (1935, commissioned by Lincoln Kirstein and Edward M. M. Warburg). Book by Edward M. M. Warburg.

PRODUCTION: Scenery by Eugene Dunkel. Costumes by John Held, Jr. Scenery constructed and painted by New York Studios; costumes executed by Helene Pons Studio.

PREMIERE: March 1, 1935, American Ballet, Adelphi Theater, New York. Conductor: Sandor Harmati. (First performed by the Producing Company of the School of American Ballet, December 6, 1934, Avery Memorial Theater, Hartford, Connecticut.)

CAST: 1. INTRODUCTION: *The Heroine*, Sylvia Giselle [Gisella Caccialanza]; *The Villain*, William Dollar; *6 Girls*; 2. ENTRANCE OF THE HERO—SNAKE DANCE: *The Hero*, Charles Laskey; *The Photographer*, Eugene Loring; *6 Girls, 4 Boys*; 3. WALTZ: Giselle, Laskey, Dollar; 4. THE KNOCK-OUT-DREAM-WEDDING AND NIGHTMARE: *The Bride*, Heidi Vosseler; *The Groom*, Laskey; *14 Girls, 5 Boys*; 5. MORNING PAPERS, AND THE DUEL: *The Janitor*, Dollar; entire cast; 6. SALVATION RHUMBA: *Nell*, Kathryn Mullowny; 7. FINALE: Entire cast.

NOTE: Balanchine's first ballet with an American theme and American music: a fantasy satire on college life—the heroine a flapper, the hero a football halfback, the villain in a coonskin coat.

143 ERRANTE
Choreographic Fantasy

MUSIC: By Franz Schubert (*The Wanderer*, fantasy for piano, Op. 15, 1822, transcribed by Franz Liszt, orchestrated by Charles Koechlin). Book by Pavel Tchelitchew.

PRODUCTION: Costumes, lighting and dramatic effects by Pavel Tchelitchew (from the 1933 production).

PREMIERE: March 1, 1935, American Ballet, Adelphi Theater, New York.
Conductor: Sandor Harmati.

CAST: Tamara Geva (guest artist); William Dollar, Charles Laskey;
3 Youths; *Shadows, Angels, Revolutionaries, and Others*, 13 women, child.

NOTE: Originally presented by Les Ballets 1933, Paris.

See 138*, 197

144 REMINISCENCE

MUSIC: By Benjamin Godard, orchestrated by Henry Brant.

PRODUCTION: Scenery and costumes by Sergei Soudeikine. Scenery
constructed by New York Studios; costumes executed by Helene
Pons Studio.

PREMIERE: March 1, 1935, American Ballet, Adelphi Theater, New York.
Conductor: Sandor Harmati.

CAST: *Brighella*, Eugene Loring; ENTRÉE: 12 women; PAS D'ACTION: Kathryn
Mullowny, Charles Laskey, 4 men, 12 women; VALSE CHROMATIQUE:
Leda Anchutina; BARCAROLE: Elena de Rivas; CANZONETTA: Gisella
Caccialanza; FRAGMENT POÉTIQUE: Annabelle Lyon; TARANTELLA: Ruth-
anna Boris, Joseph Levinoff; SATURN: Paul Haakon (guest artist); PAS DE
TROIS: William Dollar, Holly Howard, Elise Reiman; FINALE: Entire cast.

NOTE: A classical divertissement set in a ballroom: A welcome to
the audience is followed by the entrée of the corps, principals in
variations, coda, grand finale.

REVISIONS: Role of Brighella deleted soon after premiere. 1936,
American Ballet Ensemble at the Metropolitan Opera: PAS D'ACTION
and SATURN dance omitted; MAZURKA added for Anatole Vilzak and
Rabana Hasburgh; VALSE and GRAND ADAGIO added.

145 DREAMS

MUSIC: By George Antheil (1935, commissioned by Lincoln Kirstein).
Book by André Derain.

PRODUCTION: Scenery and costumes by André Derain (from *Les
Songes* [135]).

PREMIERE: March 5, 1935, American Ballet, Adelphi Theater, New York. Conductor: Sandor Harmati. (First performed in America by students of the School of American Ballet, June 10, 1934, at Woodland, the estate of Felix Warburg, near White Plains, New York.)

CAST: *The Ballerina*, Leda Anchutina; THE POLKA: Gisella Caccialanza, Paul Haakon (guest artist); *The Acrobat*, William Dollar; THE MARCH: *The Knave*, Edward Caton; *2 Buffoons, 6 Pages* (women); THE CAN-CAN: Holly Howard, 8 women; *The Lady and the Prince*, Kathryn Mullowny, Charles Laskey; THE FINALE: Entire cast; EPILOGUE: *The Fairy Queen*, Mary Sale.

NOTE: Originally presented as *Les Songes* by Les Ballets 1933, Paris, with commissioned music by Darius Milhaud. Since this music could not be obtained for performance in America, a new score was commissioned; most of the choreography was from the 1933 production.

See 135

146 TRANSCENDENCE

MUSIC: By Franz Liszt ('Mephisto' Waltz; Ballade; 10th, 13th, 19th Hungarian Rhapsodies), arranged and orchestrated by George Antheil. Book by Lincoln Kirstein.

PRODUCTION: Scenery by Franklin Watkins (through union restrictions credited to Gaston Longchamp). Costumes by Franklin Watkins. Scenery constructed and painted by William H. Mensching Studios; costumes executed by Eaves Costume Company.

PREMIERE: March 5, 1935, American Ballet, Adelphi Theater, New York. Conductor: Sandor Harmati. (First performed by the Producing Company of the School of American Ballet, December 6, 1934, Avery Memorial Theater, Hartford, Connecticut.)

CAST: I. MEPHISTO WALTZ: *The Young Girl*, Elise Reiman; *The Young Man*, Charles Laskey; *The Man in Black*, William Dollar; 10 women, 4 men; II. BALLADE: THE MESMERISM: Reiman, Dollar; *Witches*, 15 women; THE END OF THE MAN IN BLACK: Dollar, 4 men; III. THE RESURRECTION: *The Possessed*: 16 women, 6 men.

NOTE: Inspired by the virtuosity of Liszt and Paganini, the ballet centers on the hypnotic powers of a virtuoso dancer; disguised as a monk, he mesmerizes a young girl. The girl's lover and friends manage to overcome him, but resurrected by his seemingly unlimited energy, the diabolical dancer leaps up and leads them all in a frenzied, Mephisthophelean finale.

147 [SOLO]

MUSIC: By Frédéric Chopin (unknown).

PREMIERE: May 3, 1935, Park Theater, New York.

CAST: William Dollar.

NOTE: Performed once; the single classical work in a modern dance concert, *Men in Dance*.

148 JEANNE D'ARC

MUSIC: By Claude Debussy?

PREMIERE: July 4, 1935, His Majesty's Theatre, London. Pianist: Stephen Kovacs.

CAST: Alanova.

NOTE: Balanchine recalls choreographing a work called *Joan of Arc* for Alanova, but does not think the music was by Debussy. The program for Alanova's solo recital of July 4, 1935, lists Debussy as the composer of a work called *Joan of Arc* but gives no choreographer.

149 MOZARTIANA

MUSIC: By Peter Ilyitch Tschaikovsky (Suite No. 4, *Mozartiana*, Op. 61, 1887; based on Mozart's Gigue in G major [K. 574], Minuet in D major [K. 355], the motet 'Ave, Verum Corpus' [K. 618], and variations on 'Les Hommes Pieusement' from Gluck's comic opera *La Rencontre Imprévue* [K. 455]).

PRODUCTION: Scenery and costumes by Christian Bérard (from the 1933 production). Costumes executed by Karinska.

PREMIERE: September 28, 1935, Westchester County Center, White Plains, New York. Conductor: Sandor Harmati. (First performed in America by students of the School of American Ballet, June 9, 1934, at

Woodland, the estate of Felix Warburg, near White Plains, New York; then by the Producing Company of the School of American Ballet, December 6, 1934, Avery Memorial Theater, Hartford, Connecticut.)

CAST: 1. GIGUE: Hortense Kahrklin, Joseph Levinoff, Jack Potteiger; 2. MENUET: 8 women; 3. PREGHIERA: Annabelle Lyon; 4. THEME AND VARIATIONS: PAS DE SIX: 6 women; PROMENADE: 5 women, 2 men; SCHERZANDO: Annia Breyman, Elise Reiman; PAS DE QUATRE: 4 women; CLOCHETTES: Gisella Caccialanza, Elena de Rivas, Potteiger; PAS DE DEUX: Holly Howard, Charles Laskey; 5. FINALE: Entire cast.

NOTE: Originally presented by Les Ballets 1933, Paris.

See 134*, 417

150 LA TRAVIATA

Opera in Four Acts by Giuseppe Verdi
ACT III BALLET DIVERTISSEMENT (GYPSY DANCE)

PREMIERE: December 16, 1935, Metropolitan Opera, New York. Danced by American Ballet Ensemble. Conductor: Ettore Panizza.

CAST: Anatole Vilzak, Gisella Caccialanza, Ruthanna Boris, Constantine Iolas, Joseph Levinoff, corps de ballet.

NOTE: Balanchine's first choreography for the Metropolitan Opera during the three-year residence of the American Ballet as American Ballet Ensemble.

See 67, 123, 252

151 FAUST

Opera in Four Acts and Five Scenes by Charles Gounod
ACT I, SCENE 2 INCIDENTAL DANCE (KERMESSE)

PREMIERE: December 19, 1935, Metropolitan Opera, New York. Danced by American Ballet Ensemble. Conductor: Louis Hasselmans.

CAST: Corps de ballet.

See 45, 117, 227, 397, 413

152 AÏDA

Opera in Four Acts by Giuseppe Verdi
ACTS I AND II BALLETS

PREMIERE: December 20, 1935, Metropolitan Opera, New York. Danced by American Ballet Ensemble. Conductor: Ettore Panizza.

CAST: ACT I, SCENE 2 TEMPLE DANCE: Corps de ballet. ACT II, SCENE I NEGRO DANCE: Corps de ballet. ACT II, SCENE 2 VICTORY DANCE: Daphne Vane, William Dollar, corps de ballet.

NOTE: At least three versions of *Aïda* were danced by the American Ballet Ensemble at the Metropolitan Opera. Choreography was variously credited to Balanchine, William Dollar, and Marius Petipa.

See 126, 226, 255

153 LAKMÉ

Opera in Three Acts by Léo Delibes
ACT II BALLET

PREMIERE: December 23, 1935, Metropolitan Opera, New York. Danced by American Ballet Ensemble. Conductor: Louis Hasselmans.

CAST: TERANA: Kathryn Mullowny, Betty Eisner, Nora Koreff [Kaye], Yvonne Patterson, Mary Sale; REKTAH: Elise Reiman, Lew Christensen, Douglas Coudy; PERSANE: Holly Howard, Charles Laskey; ENSEMBLE DANCE; FINALE: Entire cast.

See 57, 115

154 TANNHÄUSER

Opera in Three Acts and Four Scenes by Richard Wagner
ACT I BALLET

PREMIERE: December 26, 1935, Metropolitan Opera, New York. Danced by American Ballet Ensemble. Conductor: Artur Bodanzky.

CAST: BACCHANALE: Anatole Vilzak, Rabana Hasburgh, corps de ballet; VISION: Annia Breyman, Kathryn Mullowny, Helen Stuart, Heidi Vosseler, Charles Laskey.

REVISIONS: In the printed program for January 25, 1937, VISION is replaced by THREE GRACES, danced by Mullowny, Daphne Vane and Elise Reiman.

See 111

155 CARMEN

Opera in Four Acts by Georges Bizet
ACT IV BALLET

PREMIERE: December 27, 1935, Metropolitan Opera, New York. Danced by American Ballet Ensemble. Conductor: Louis Hasselmans.

CAST: GITANE: Ruthanna Boris, corps de ballet; FARUCCA: Anatole Vilzak, Betty Eisner, corps de ballet; FARANDOLE: Vilzak, Boris, Madeline Leweck, corps de ballet.

NOTE: Rosa Ponselle, who sang Carmen, was partnered by Lew Christensen; the choreography was not by Balanchine.

REVISIONS: A review dated December 31, 1936, states that Balanchine changed the FARUCCA. The program for January 2, 1937, lists a MENUETTO danced by Annabelle Lyon between the FARUCCA and the FARANDOLE.

See 38, 127, 248

156 RIGOLETTO

Opera in Four Acts by Giuseppe Verdi
ACT I INCIDENTAL DANCE

PREMIERE: December 28, 1935, Metropolitan Opera, New York. Danced by American Ballet Ensemble. Conductor: Ettore Panizza.

CAST: Corps de ballet.

See 88, 121

157 [PAS DE DEUX]

In the middle or late 1930s, for a party at the Persian Room of the Plaza Hotel, New York City, Balanchine choreographed a pas de deux for Marie-Jeanne and William Dollar to a Mozart adagio, with costumes by Pavel Tchelitchew.

1936

158 MIGNON

Opera in Three Acts and Four Scenes by Ambroise Thomas
GYPSY DANCE

PREMIERE: January 4, 1936, Metropolitan Opera, New York. Danced by American Ballet Ensemble. Conductor: Louis Hasselmans.

CAST: William Dollar, corps de ballet.

NOTE: Although programs give no act for the GYPSY DANCE, it probably occurred in Act I.

159 MANON

Opera in Five Acts by Jules Massenet

PREMIERE: January 10, 1936, Metropolitan Opera, New York. Conductor: Louis Hasselmans.

NOTE: Although choreographer and ballet cast are omitted from the printed program, reference in a review to 'a blithe ballet divertissement' indicates choreography by Balanchine for the American Ballet Ensemble. It may have occurred in Act III, Scene 1, COURS LA REINE.

See 40, 122

160 LA JUIVE

Opera in Four Acts and Five Scenes by Jacques Halévy
ACT I VALSE; ACT III BALLET PANTOMIME

PREMIERE: January 11?, 1936, Metropolitan Opera, New York. Danced by American Ballet Ensemble. Conductor: Wilfred Pelletier.

CAST: VALSE: Gisella Caccialanza, William Dollar, corps de ballet.
BALLET PANTOMIME: *Death*, Anatole Vilzak; *The Good Lady*, Annabelle Lyon; *The Imp*, Ruthanna Boris; *The Knights*, Dollar, Charles Laskey; *The Heralds*, Lew Christensen, Douglas Coudy; *The Acrobats*, Kathryn

Mullowny, Daphne Vane, Audrey Guerard; *Masked Ladies, Juggler, Musicians*, corps de ballet.

NOTE: The first performance of the 1936 revival of *La Juive* occurred on January 11; the printed program does not credit dancing. Balanchine's choreography may have been inadvertently omitted from the program, or may have been added to the production later, as listed in the program of January 20, 1936. The casting given here is from the program of a Grand Concert of the Metropolitan Opera on January 12, at which the ballets from *La Juive* were performed.

161 LA RONDINE

Opera in Three Acts by Giacomo Puccini
ACT II WALTZ

PREMIERE: January 17, 1936, Metropolitan Opera, New York. Danced by American Ballet Ensemble. Conductor: Ettore Panizza.

CAST: Kyra Blank, Daphne Vane, Douglas Coudy, corps de ballet.

See 56

162 ZIEGFELD FOLLIES: 1936 EDITION

A National Institution, Glorifying the American Girl
Revue in Two Acts and Twenty-four Scenes

MUSIC AND BOOK: Music by Vernon Duke. Lyrics by Ira Gershwin. Sketches by David Freedman. Orchestrations by Hans Spialek; additional orchestrations by Conrad Sallinger, Russell Bennett and Don Walker.

CHOREOGRAPHY: Ballets by George Balanchine. Modern dances by Robert Alton.

PRODUCTION: Produced by Lee Shubert. Sketches directed by Edward Clarke Lilley. Entire production staged by John Murray Anderson. Scenery and costumes by Vincente Minnelli. Scenery executed by James Surridge; costumes executed by Brooks Costume Company and others.

PREMIERE: January 30, 1936, Winter Garden, New York. Conductor: John McManus. (Out-of-town preview: December 30, 1935, Opera House, Boston.)

CAST: Fannie Brice, Bob Hope, Josephine Baker, Eve Arden, Harriet Hoctor, and others. Corps de ballet (7 women), Dancers (17 women), Boys (8 men). Dancers, in addition to those appearing in the Balanchine ballets, included the Nicholas Brothers.

WEST INDIES (Act I, Scene 5): Gertrude Niesen and The Varsity Eight (singers); Josephine Baker and ensemble (dancers).

WORDS WITHOUT MUSIC: A SURREALIST BALLET (Act I, Scene 7): *The Singer*, Niesen; *The Dancer*, Harriet Hoctor; *The Figures in Green*, Milton Barnett, George Church, Tom Draper; *The Figures in Black*, Gene Ashley, Eddie Browne, Prescott Brown, Howard Morgan; *The Figure with the Light*, Willem van Loon; corps de ballet.

NIGHT FLIGHT (Act I, Scene 10): Hoctor.

MOMENT OF MOMENTS (Act II, Scene 1, The Foyer of an Opera House in the 'Sixties'): Niesen and Rodney McLennan with The Varsity Eight (singers); *The Ballerina*, Hoctor; *Grand Duke*, Herman Belmonte; ensemble (dancers).

SENTIMENTAL WEATHER (Act II, Scene 2): *Production*: Costumes designed by Raoul Pène du Bois. *Cast*: Sung and danced by Cherry and June Preisser and Duke McHale.

5 A. M. (Act II, Scene 6): Sung and danced by Josephine Baker; *The Shadows*, 4 men.

163 DIE MEISTERSINGER VON NÜRNBERG
Opera in Three Acts and Four Scenes by Richard Wagner
ACT III, SCENE 2 INCIDENTAL DANCE (DANCE OF THE APPRENTICES)

PREMIERE: February 3, 1936, Metropolitan Opera, New York. Danced by American Ballet Ensemble. Conductor: Artur Bodanzky.

CAST: Corps de ballet.

See 77

164 SERENATA: 'MAGIC'

MUSIC: By Wolfgang Amadeus Mozart.

PRODUCTION: Scenery and costumes by Pavel Tchelitchew.

PREMIERE: February 14, 1936, Avery Memorial Theater, Hartford, Connecticut. Conductor: Alexander Smallens.

CAST: *The Lady*, Felia Doubrovska; *The Boy*, Lew Christensen; *5 Girls*.

NOTE: Performed once at the Hartford Festival. The music was an unidentified Mozart composition for eight instruments; the subtitle 'Magic' referred to illusionistic devices used in the décor.

165 CONCERTO (later called CLASSIC BALLET)

MUSIC: By Frédéric Chopin (Piano Concerto No. 2 in F minor, Op. 21, 1829).

CHOREOGRAPHY: By William Dollar and George Balanchine.

PREMIERE: March 8, 1936, American Ballet Ensemble, Metropolitan Opera, New York. Conductor: Wilfred Pelletier. Pianist: Nicholas Kopeikine.

CAST: MAESTOSO: Gisella Caccialanza, Rabana Hasburgh, Kathryn Mullowny, Yvonne Patterson, Daphne Vane, Annia Breyman; LARGHETTO: Holly Howard, Charles Laskey; William Dollar; ALLEGRO VIVACE: Leda Anchutina, Elise Reiman, Helen Leitch, Lew Christensen, corps de ballet.

NOTE: Balanchine choreographed the LARGHETTO.

166 ON YOUR TOES

Musical Comedy in Two Acts and Thirteen Scenes

MUSIC AND BOOK: Music by Richard Rodgers. Lyrics by Lorenz Hart. Book by Richard Rodgers, Lorenz Hart and George Abbott. Orchestrations by Hans Spialek.

CHOREOGRAPHY: By George Balanchine. Assistants to Mr. Balanchine: William Dollar and Herbert Harper.

PRODUCTION: Entire production under the supervision of Dwight Deere Wiman. Produced by Dwight Deere Wiman. Staged by

Worthington Miner. Scenery by Jo Mielziner. Costumes by Irene Sharaff. Scenery built by Turner Scenic Construction Company and painted by Triangle Scenic Studio; costumes executed by Helene Pons Studio, Brooks Costume Company, Eaves Costume Company, and others.

PREMIERE: April 11, 1936, Imperial Theatre, New York. Conductor: Gene Salzer. Pianists: Edgar Fairchild and Adam Carroll. (Out-of-town preview: March 21, Shubert Theatre, Boston.)

CAST: *Phil Dolan III*, Ray Bolger; *Frankie Frayne*, Doris Carson; *Vera Barnova*, Tamara Geva; *Peggy Porterfield*, Luella Gear; *Sergei Alexandrovitch*, Monty Woolley; and others. Dancers: Demetrios Vilan, George Church, 12 Ladies of the Ballet, 8 Gentlemen of the Ballet.

LA PRINCESSE ZENOBIA BALLET (Act I, Scene 8): *Princesse Zenobia*, Tamara Geva; *Beggar*, Demetrios Vilan; *Old Prince*, William Baker; *Young Prince*, George Church.

ON YOUR TOES (Act II, Scene 2): Doris Carson, Ray Bolger, David Morris, ensemble.

SLAUGHTER ON TENTH AVENUE BALLET (Act II, Scene 4): *Hoofer*, Bolger; *Strip Tease Girl*, Geva; *Big Boss*, Church.

NOTE: LA PRINCESSE ZENOBIA BALLET parodies the Oriental-style ballet. In SLAUGHTER ON TENTH AVENUE, a narrative ballet within the play, a nightclub stripteaser and a dancer fall in love; a rival arranges for the young man to be killed by a gangster, but the girl saves him.

At Balanchine's insistence, *On Your Toes* was the first Broadway musical to credit staged dances as choreography (a practice already customary in Europe), and is considered the first musical in which the dances were integrated into the plot, performed by dancers who were also dramatic characters. In choreographing for Broadway musicals, Balanchine often used ballet, tap and ballroom steps, in combination and separately.

OTHER PRODUCTIONS: February 5, 1937, Palace Theatre, London, and April 19, 1937, London Coliseum ('dances' by Andy Anderson; 'ballets' by William Baker, 'based on the choreography by George Balanchine'). Broadway revival October 11, 1954, Forty-sixth Street Theatre, New York (out-of-town preview September 25, Shubert Theatre, New Haven).

TELEVISION: 1956 (excerpts from SLAUGHTER ON TENTH AVENUE, Omnibus, ABC).

See 186, 361

167 THE BARTERED BRIDE
Opera in Three Acts by Bedřich Smetana
ACTS I, II AND III BALLETS

PREMIERE: May 15, 1936, Metropolitan Opera, New York. Danced by American Ballet Ensemble. Conductor: Wilfred Pelletier. (DANCE OF THE COMEDIANS first performed as a concert work on a Metropolitan Opera Gala Program, February 9, 1936.)

CAST: ACT I POLKA: Ruthanna Boris, William Dollar, corps de ballet. ACT II WALTZ: Helen Leitch, corps de ballet. ACT III DANCE OF THE COMEDIANS (Gala Program, February 9): Anatole Vilzak, Dollar, Rabana Hasburgh, Gisella Caccialanza, Leitch, Kyra Blank, Leda Anchutina, corps de ballet.

NOTE: DANCE OF THE COMEDIANS was given separately as part of a Metropolitan Opera Gala Program (principally of operatic arias) which also included a performance of *Serenade* [141].

REVISIONS: 1937, Metropolitan Opera: WALTZ replaced by FURIANTE.

168 LUCIA DI LAMMERMOOR
Opera in Three Acts and Four Scenes by Gaetano Donizetti
ACT III, SCENE I INCIDENTAL DANCE

PREMIERE: May 20, 1936, Metropolitan Opera, New York. Danced by American Ballet Ensemble. Conductor: Gennaro Papi.

CAST: Corps de ballet.

NOTE: Presented with the premiere performance of *The Bat*.

169 THE BAT (also called EL MURCIÉLAGO)
Character Ballet, from 'Die Fledermaus'

MUSIC: By Johann Strauss the Younger (from *Die Fledermaus*, produced 1874, with unidentified additions). Book by Lincoln Kirstein.

PRODUCTION: Costumes and lighting by Keith Martin.

PREMIERE: May 20, 1936, American Ballet Ensemble, Metropolitan Opera, New York. Conductor: Wilfred Pelletier.

CAST: *The Bat*, Holly Howard, Lew Christensen; *The Poet*, Charles Laskey; *The Masked (Identical) Ladies*, Leda Anchutina, Annabelle Lyon; *The Gypsies* (later called *Hungarian Dancers*), Helen Leitch, William Dollar; *The Can-Can Dancer*, Rabana Hasburgh; *The Ladies of Fashion*, 4 women; *2 Coachmen, Can-Can Dancers, Officers, Ladies and Gentlemen*, corps de ballet.

NOTE: Balanchine conceived The Bat as a couple, girl and boy, each wearing a huge spangled wing. The ballet is an evocation of Vienna, set in a park; a young poet seeking inspiration is confounded by two beautiful but identical ladies; a band of gypsies invades the scene. At the end the park is empty, except for the shadow of The Bat.

STAGINGS: 1941, American Ballet Caravan.

See 107, 199, 206, 294

170 ORPHEUS AND EURYDICE

Opera in Two Acts and Four Scenes

MUSIC: By Christoph Willibald Gluck (*Orfeo ed Euridice*, produced 1762, with ballet music from the Paris production of 1774). Libretto by Raniero da Calzabigi.

PRODUCTION: Stage production conceived by George Balanchine and Pavel Tchelitchew. Scenery and costumes by Pavel Tchelitchew. Scenery painted by Joseph Novak.

PREMIERE: May 22, 1936, Metropolitan Opera, New York. Danced by American Ballet Ensemble. Conductor: Richard Hageman.

CAST: SINGERS: *Orpheus*, Anna Kaskas; *Eurydice*, Jeanne Pengelly; *Amor*, Maxine Stellman; and others. DANCERS: *Orpheus*, Lew Christensen; *Eurydice*, Daphne Vane; *Amor*, William Dollar; *Shepherds and Nymphs, Furies and Ghosts from Hades, Heroes from Elysium, Followers of Orpheus*, corps de ballet.

Act I: SCENE 1. At the tomb of Eurydice. SCENE 2. Entrance to Hades.

Act II: SCENE 1. The Elysian Fields. SCENE 2. The Gardens of the Temple of Love.

NOTE: An original production staged by Balanchine at the Metropolitan; the singers were invisible in the orchestra pit while the dancers performed the action on stage; intense atmospheric scenic effects ended with a vast night-sky of stars. The innovative and controversial production was presented only twice.

Balanchine reconceived and directed *Orpheus and Eurydice* for the Hamburgische Staatsoper in 1963; this choreography, with some revision, was performed in a new production of the Théâtre National de l'Opéra, Paris, in 1973, and forms the basis for the ballet *Chaconne* [400], first presented by the New York City Ballet in 1976. Balanchine created different choreography for the Chicago Lyric Opera production of the opera in 1975.

OTHER VERSIONS: 1963, Hamburgische Staatsoper.

See 345, 399, 400

171 SAMSON ET DALILA

Opera in Three Acts and Four Scenes by Camille Saint-Saëns
ACT I INCIDENTAL DANCES; ACT III, SCENE 2 BACCHANALE

PREMIERE: December 26, 1936, Metropolitan Opera, New York. Danced by American Ballet Ensemble. Conductor: Maurice Abravanel.

CAST: INCIDENTAL DANCES: corps de ballet. BACCHANALE: Daphne Vane, corps de ballet.

See 66, 116, 228

1937

172 LE COQ D'OR

Opera in Three Acts

MUSIC: By Nicolai Rimsky-Korsakov (produced 1909). Libretto by Vladimir Bielski after a fairy tale by Alexander Pushkin.

PRODUCTION: Staged and choreographed by George Balanchine (uncredited). Stage direction by Herbert Graf. Scenery by Willy Pogany (uncredited). Miss Pons' costume by Mme Valentina (uncredited).

PREMIERE: February 4, 1937, Metropolitan Opera, New York. Danced by American Ballet Ensemble. Conductor: Gennaro Papi.

CAST: *The Queen of Shemakha*, Lily Pons; *King Dodon*, Ezio Pinza; *Prince Guidon*, Giordano Paltrinieri; *General Polk*, Norman Cordon; *Prince Aphron*, Wilfred Engelman; *Amelfa*, Doris Doe; *The Astrologer*, Nicholas Massue; *The Voice of the Golden Cockerel*, Thelma Votipka; and others.

NOTE: Although printed programs do not list dances or credit choreography, Balanchine choreographed and staged the production, which included a comic Russian dance for King Dodon, oriental movement for the Queen of Shemakha, and ensemble dances. Pons also consulted Michel Fokine about choreography for her role.

See 24

173 CAPONSACCHI

Opera in Three Acts with Prologue and Epilogue by Richard Hageman
ACT I BALLET

PREMIERE: February 4, 1937, Metropolitan Opera, New York. Danced by American Ballet Ensemble. Conductor: Richard Hageman.

CAST: TARANTELLA: Kyra Blank, Rabana Hasburgh, Joseph Levinoff, corps de ballet; ADAGIO: Elise Reiman, Charles Laskey, Heidi Vosseler, corps de ballet; VALSE: Leda Anchutina, William Dollar, Kathryn Mullowny, Daphne Vane, Lew Christensen, Douglas Coudy, corps de ballet.

174 LA GIOCONDA

Opera in Four Acts and Five Scenes by Amilcare Ponchielli
ACT I FURLANA; ACT III DANCE OF THE HOURS

PREMIERE: February 18, 1937, Metropolitan Opera, New York. Danced by American Ballet Ensemble. Conductor: Ettore Panizza. (DANCE OF THE HOURS first performed at a Metropolitan Opera Gala Concert, February 2, 1936.)

CAST: FURLANA: Corps de ballet. DANCE OF THE HOURS (Gala Concert, February 2): *Dawn*: Annia Breyman; *Morning*: Leda Anchutina; *Dusk*: Elise Reiman; *Night*: Rabana Hasburgh; *Day*: Anatole Vilzak, Gisella Caccialanza, Holly Howard, Kathryn Mullowny, corps de ballet.

NOTE: For the February 18th premiere, Mona Montes replaced Annia Breyman as *Dawn* in DANCE OF THE HOURS.

See 87

175 BABES IN ARMS

Musical Comedy in Two Acts and Fourteen Scenes

MUSIC AND BOOK: Music by Richard Rodgers. Lyrics by Lorenz Hart. Book by Richard Rodgers and Lorenz Hart. Orchestrations by Hans Spialek.

CHOREOGRAPHY: By George Balanchine. Assistant to Mr. Balanchine: Johnny Pierce.

PRODUCTION: Production under the supervision of Dwight Deere Wiman. Produced by Dwight Deere Wiman. Staged by Robert Sinclair. Scenery by Raymond Sovey. Costumes by Helene Pons. Scenery built by Turner Scenic Construction Company and painted by Robert Bergman Studio and Triangle Studio; costumes executed by Helene Pons Studio.

PREMIERE: April 14, 1937, Shubert Theatre, New York. Conductor: Gene Salzer. Pianists: Edgar Fairchild and Adam Carroll. (Out-of-town preview: March 25, Shubert Theatre, Boston.)

CAST: *Val LaMar*, Ray Heatherton; *Marshall Blackstone*, Alfred Drake; *Billie Smith*, Mitzi Green; *Lee Calhoun*, Dana Hardwick; *Peter*, Duke McHale; *Baby Rose*, Wynn Murray; *Ivor and Irving de Quincy*, Harold and Fayard Nicholas; and others.

LEE CALHOUN'S FOLLIES (Act I): *The Singer*, Wynn Murray; *The Child*, Douglas Perry; *The High Priest*, Alfred Drake; *The Priestess*, Elenore Tennis; *The Nubians*, The Nicholas Brothers; *The Acrobat*, Bobby Lane; *The Specialty Dancers*, Mitzi Green and Duke McHale; ensemble. This dance sequence included an Egyptian ballet.

ALL DARK PEOPLE (Act I): The Nicholas Brothers.

BALLET: PETER'S JOURNEY (Act II, Dream Ballet to the song 'Imagine'): *The Prince*, McHale; *His Attendants*, Kenneth Wilkins, Leroy James; *Rockefeller*, Rolly Pickert; *The Mermaid*, Tennis; *Greta Garbo*, Gedda Petry; *Marlene Dietrich*, Ursula Seiler; *Clark Gable*, Ted Gary; ensemble.

DUET (untitled): Grace and Ray McDonald.

NOTE: PETER'S JOURNEY is considered to be the first dream ballet on Broadway, introducing a form that was to become popular in American musicals. Peter dreams an imaginary journey around the world, to Hollywood, to Europe, to the African wilds, and back to reality.

176 APOLLON MUSAGÈTE

MUSIC: Music and book by Igor Stravinsky (*Apollo Musagetes*, 1927-28, commissioned by Mrs. Elizabeth Sprague Coolidge).

PRODUCTION: Scenery and costumes by Stewart Chaney. Scenery executed by Studio Alliance; costumes executed by Helene Pons Studio. Wigs executed by Barris.

PREMIERE: April 27, 1937, American Ballet, Metropolitan Opera, New York. Conductor: Igor Stravinsky.

CAST: *Apollo, Leader of the Muses*, Lew Christensen; *Terpsichore*, Elise Reiman; *Calliope*, Daphne Vane; *Polyhymnia*, Holly Howard; *2 Nymphs*; *Leto, Mother of Apollo*, Jane Burkhalter.

NOTE: Originally presented by Diaghilev's Ballets Russes, Paris, 1928. Performed with the new works *The Card Party* and *Le Baiser de la Fée* as a Stravinsky Festival (April 27 and 28, 1937) by the American Ballet while in residence at the Metropolitan Opera House as the American Ballet Ensemble.

See 84*, 198, 284

177 THE CARD PARTY
(also called THE CARD GAME, POKER GAME)
A Ballet in Three Deals

MUSIC: By Igor Stravinsky (*Jeu de Cartes – A Card Game – Das Kartenspiel*, 1936, commissioned by Lincoln Kirstein and Edward M. M. Warburg). Book by Igor Stravinsky and M. Malaieff.

PRODUCTION: Scenery and costumes by Irene Sharaff. Scenery executed by Triangle Scenic Studio and painted by Joseph Novak; costumes executed by Eaves Costume Company and the American Ballet Studio: Eudoxia Mironova, Marie Striga. Wigs by Lucien.

PREMIERE: April 27, 1937, American Ballet, Metropolitan Opera, New York. Conductor: Igor Stravinsky.

CAST: *Joker*, William Dollar; *Queens: Hearts*, Annabelle Lyon; *Spades*, Leda Anchutina; *Diamonds*, Ariel Lang [Helen Leitch]; *Clubs*, Hortense Kahrklin; *4 Aces* (women); *4 Kings*; *4 Jacks*; *10, 9, 8, 7, 6, 5 of Hearts*; *10, 9, 8, 7 of Spades*.

NOTE: Conceived by Stravinsky: The principal characters are the chief cards in a game of poker; each of the three deals is complicated by the endless tricks of the perfidious Joker, who believes himself invincible because of his ability to become any desired card.

REVISIONS: In later productions by the Ballet Russe de Monte Carlo and the New York City Ballet, the Aces were danced by men.

STAGINGS: 1940, Ballet Russe de Monte Carlo (*Poker Game*); 1951, New York City Ballet (*The Card Game*).

See 275

178 LE BAISER DE LA FÉE (also called THE FAIRY'S KISS)
Ballet-Allegory in Four Scenes

MUSIC: Music and book by Igor Stravinsky (1928, commissioned by Ida Rubinstein, dedicated to Peter Ilyitch Tschaikovsky). Based on a tale by Hans Christian Andersen (*The Ice Maiden*).

PRODUCTION: Scenery and costumes by Alice Halicka. Scenery painted by Joseph Novak; costumes executed by Theatrical Costume Company and American Ballet Studio: Eudoxia Mironova, Marie Striga.

PREMIERE: April 27, 1937, American Ballet, Metropolitan Opera, New York. Conductor: Igor Stravinsky.

CAST: *The Fairy*, Kathryn Mullowny; *The Bride*, Gisella Caccialanza; *Her Friend*, Leda Anchutina; *The Bridegroom*, William Dollar; *His Mother*, Annabelle Lyon. FIRST TABLEAU, PROLOGUE: *Mother*; *2 Winds*; *Snowflakes*, Anchutina, 21 women; *Fairy*; *Her Shadow*, Rabana Hasburgh; *8 Mountaineers*. SECOND TABLEAU, THE VILLAGE FESTIVAL:

Peasant Boys and Girls; *Bridegroom*; *Bride*; *Bridesmaids*, Anchutina,
7 women; *A Gypsy (Disguised Fairy)*. THIRD TABLEAU, INSIDE THE MILL:
DANCE OF THE PEASANT GIRLS: Anchutina, 16 women; PAS DE DEUX;
BRIDE'S VARIATION; CODA (*Bride, Bridegroom, Friend*, corps de ballet);
SCENE: *Fairy, Bridegroom*. FOURTH TABLEAU, EPILOGUE (BERCEUSE DE
DEMEURES ETERNELLES): *Fairy, Bridegroom*.

NOTE: Stravinsky used the story of *The Ice Maiden*, with its theme of
the muse's fatal kiss, to compose an homage to Tschaikovsky. The Fairy
implants her magic kiss on a child at birth. When the child has
grown to young manhood and good fortune, the Fairy reappears at his
wedding fête; repeating the kiss, she leads the young man (the artist in
allegory) to abandon his bride and dwell with her forever.

The score was first choreographed by Bronislava Nijinska in 1928 for
Ballets Ida Rubinstein. Balanchine created a new ballet in 1937. In 1972,
he choreographed *Divertimento from 'Le Baiser de la Fée'* for the New
York City Ballet Stravinsky Festival, using *Divertimento*, a concert suite
Stravinsky based on the ballet, with additions from the full ballet score.

REVISIONS: 1940, Ballet Russe de Monte Carlo: Final scene changed
several times. 1947, Paris Opéra: Final scene changed. 1950, New York
City Ballet: Dance sequences in entr'actes between the tableaux
lengthened; new pas de deux for Bride and Bridegroom; new EPILOGUE
(changed several times to better create illusion of Fairy and Bridegroom
swimming through space).

STAGINGS: 1940, Ballet Russe de Monte Carlo; 1947, Paris; 1950, New
York City Ballet; 1953, La Scala.

See 271, 376

179 MÂROUF

Opera in Four Acts by Henri Rabaud
ACT II ORIENTAL DANCES

PREMIERE: May 21, 1937, Metropolitan Opera, New York. Danced by
American Ballet Ensemble. Conductor: Wilfred Pelletier.

CAST: Ruthanna Boris, Rabana Hasburgh, Eugene Loring, corps
de ballet.

See 204

180 ROMÉO ET JULIETTE

Opera in Five Acts and Seven Scenes by Charles Gounod

ACT I INCIDENTAL DANCE

PREMIERE: December 16, 1937, Metropolitan Opera, New York. Danced by American Ballet Ensemble. Conductor: Maurice Abravanel.

CAST: Corps de ballet.

See 86, 124

1938

181 DON GIOVANNI

Opera in Two Acts and Ten Scenes by Wolfgang Amadeus Mozart

ACT II INCIDENTAL DANCE

PREMIERE: January 1, 1938, Metropolitan Opera, New York. Danced by American Ballet Ensemble. Conductor: Ettore Panizza.

CAST: Corps de ballet.

See 81, 253

182 I MARRIED AN ANGEL

Musical Comedy in Two Acts and Eleven Scenes

MUSIC AND BOOK: Music by Richard Rodgers. Lyrics by Lorenz Hart. Book by Richard Rodgers and Lorenz Hart, adapted from the play by John Vaszary. Orchestrations by Hans Spialek.

PRODUCTION: Produced by Dwight Deere Wiman. Staged by Joshua Logan. Scenery by Jo Mielziner. Costumes by John Hambleton. Scenery executed by Turner Scenic Construction Company; costumes executed by Mildred Manning, George Pons and Eaves Costume Company.

PREMIERE: May 11, 1938, Shubert Theatre, New York. Conductor: Gene Salzer. (Out-of-town preview: April 14, Shubert Theatre, New Haven.)

CAST: *Peter Mueller*, Charles Walters; *Count Willy Palaffi*, Dennis King; *Countess Peggy Palaffi*, Vivienne Segal; *Anna Murphy*, Audrey Christie; *Angel*, Vera Zorina; *Harry Mischka Szigetti*, Walter Slezak; and others. *Premier Danseur*, Charles Laskey; 19 Ladies of the Ballet, 10 Gentlemen of the Ballet.

HONEYMOON BALLET (Act I, Scene 4): Vera Zorina, Dennis King, Charles Laskey, corps de ballet.

HOW TO WIN FRIENDS AND INFLUENCE PEOPLE (Act I, Scene 6): Audrey Christie, Charles Walters, corps de ballet.

ROXY'S MUSIC HALL (Act II, Scene 4): Christie, Vivienne Segal, Zorina, Laskey, other cast members, corps de ballet.

SOLO ('Charlie McCarthy'): Walters.

183 THE BOYS FROM SYRACUSE
Musical Comedy in Two Acts and Nine Scenes

MUSIC AND BOOK: Music by Richard Rodgers. Lyrics by Lorenz Hart. Book by George Abbott, based on Shakespeare's *The Comedy of Errors*. Orchestrations by Hans Spialek.

CHOREOGRAPHY: By George Balanchine. Assistants to Mr. Balanchine: David Jones and Duke McHale.

PRODUCTION: Produced and directed by George Abbott. Scenery and lighting by Jo Mielziner. Costumes by Irene Sharaff. Scenery built by T. B. McDonald Construction Company and painted by Studio Alliance; costumes executed by Helene Pons.

PREMIERE: November 23, 1938, Alvin Theatre, New York. Conductor: Harry Levant. (Out-of-town preview: November 3, Shubert Theatre, New Haven.)

CAST: *Antipholus of Ephesus*, Ronald Graham; *Dromio of Ephesus*, Teddy Hart; *Antipholus of Syracuse*, Eddie Albert; *Dromio of Syracuse*, Jimmy Savo; *Luce*, Wynn Murray; *Adriana*, Muriel Angelus; *Luciana*, Marcy Wescott; *Dancing Policeman*, George Church; *Courtezan*, Betty Bruce; *Secretary to Courtezan*, Heidi Vosseler; and others. Dancers: 17 women, 11 men.

DEAR OLD SYRACUSE (Act I, Scene 1): Eddie Albert, Alice Craig, Vivien Moore, Lita Lede, dancers.

SHORTEST DAY OF THE YEAR (Act I, Scene 3): Betty Bruce, Heidi Vosseler, George Church.

LADIES OF THE EVENING (Act II, Scene 1): Vosseler, Church.

THE BALLET (Act II, Scene 2): Jimmy Savo, Albert, Buddy Douglas, Vosseler, Robert Howard, Wynn Murray, dancers.

SING FOR YOUR SUPPER (Act II, Scene 3): Bruce, ensemble.

OH, DIOGENES (Act II, Scene 4): Church, Bruce, ensemble.

184 GREAT LADY

Musical Comedy in Two Acts and Fourteen Scenes

MUSIC AND BOOK: Music by Frederick Loewe. Lyrics by Earle Crooker. Book by Earle Crooker and Lowell Brentano. Orchestrations by Hans Spialek.

CHOREOGRAPHY: By George Balanchine (for contractual reasons credited in the printed program to William Dollar).

PRODUCTION: Produced by Dwight Deere Wiman and J. H. Del Bondio by arrangement with Frank Crumit. Staged by Bretaigne Windust. Scenery by Albert R. Johnson. Costumes by Lucinda Ballard and Scott Wilson. Scenery built by Turner Scenic Construction Company and painted by Studio Alliance, Inc.; costumes executed by Brooks Costume Company.

PREMIERE: December 1, 1938, Majestic Theatre, New York. Conductor: John Fredhoven. (Out-of-town preview: October 21, Forrest Theatre, Philadelphia.)

CAST: *Eliza Bowen (later Elsa de la Croix)*, Norma Terriss; *Stephen Jumel*, Tullio Carminati; *Madame Colette*, Irene Bordoni; and others. *Premier Danseur*, André Eglevsky; *Premieres Danseuses*, Leda Anchutina, Annabelle Lyon; 19 Ladies of the Ballet, 11 Gentlemen of the Ballet.

MADAME COLETTE'S DRESSMAKING SHOP (Act I, Scene 5): *Floorwalker*, André Eglevsky; *Shop Forewoman*, Annabelle Lyon; *Shop Assistant*, Leda Anchutina; *Betty Bowen*, Norma Terriss; corps de ballet.

SISTERS UNDER THE SKIN (Act II, Scene 3): Helen Ford, Gentlemen of the Ballet.

ELSA'S REVERIE: THERE HAD TO BE THE WALTZ (Act II, Scene 3): *1. The Waltz: Napoleon*, Ray Schultz; corps de ballet. *2. Pas de Sept*: Holly

Howard; Albia Kavan, Yvonne Patterson, Nora Kaye, Olga Suárez, Hortense Kahrklin, Doris Jane Solly. *3. Pas de Trois and Variations*: Anchutina, Lyon, Eglevsky.

185 GOLDWYN FOLLIES

Film

PRODUCTION: United Artists. Produced by Samuel Goldwyn. Associate Producer: George Haight. Directed by George Marshall. Screenplay by Ben Hecht.

MUSIC: By George Gershwin. Lyrics by Ira Gershwin. Ballet music and additional songs by Vernon Duke (WATER NYMPH BALLET orchestrated by Ray Golden and Sid Kuller).

CHOREOGRAPHY: By George Balanchine. Tap Consultant: Sammy Lee.

RELEASED: 1938.

CAST: Adolphe Menjou, Ritz Brothers, Vera Zorina, Kenny Baker, Andrea Leeds, Helen Jepson, Phil Baker, Ella Logan, Bobby Clark, Jerome Cowan, Edgar Bergen and 'Charlie McCarthy,' and others.

ROMEO AND JULIET BALLET: Vera Zorina, William Dollar, corps de ballet.

WATER NYMPH BALLET: Zorina, Dollar, corps de ballet.

NOTE: Balanchine directed the filming of the choreography for his first Hollywood work. The corps de ballet was composed of members of the American Ballet. In the ROMEO AND JULIET BALLET, the Montagues (ballet dancers) and the Capulets (tap dancers) engage in a mock duel. In the WATER NYMPH BALLET, Zorina rises out of a pool; this dance was later the model for the dance of the hippos and ostriches (to the DANCE OF THE HOURS from *La Gioconda*) in Walt Disney's film *Fantasia* (RKO Radio, 1940). Balanchine also created a ballet to Gershwin's *An American in Paris*, which Goldwyn rejected.

1939

186 ON YOUR TOES

Film

PRODUCTION: Warner Brothers. Produced by Hal B. Wallis and Robert Lord. Directed by Ray Enright. Screenplay by Jerry Wald and Richard Macaulay from the Broadway show by George Abbott, Richard Rodgers and Lorenz Hart. Art direction by Robert Haas. Costumes by Orry-Kelly.

MUSIC: By Richard Rodgers. Lyrics by Lorenz Hart. Musical direction by Leo F. Forbstein.

RELEASED: 1939.

CAST: *Vera*, Vera Zorina; *Phil Dolan, Jr.*, Eddie Albert; *Sergei Alexandrovitch*, Alan Hale; *Konstantine Morrosine*, Erik Rhodes; *Phil Dolan, Sr.*, James Gleason; *Mrs. Dolan*, Queenie Smith; *Peggy Porterfield*, Gloria Dickson; *Ivan Boultonoff*, Leonid Kinsky; and others.

LA PRINCESSE ZENOBIA BALLET: Vera Zorina and others.

SLAUGHTER ON TENTH AVENUE BALLET: Zorina, Eddie Albert; Lew Christensen, André Eglevsky and others.

NOTE: Balanchine directed the filming of his dance sequences. He describes the choreography as essentially the same as that for the stage play of 1936.

See 166*, 361

1940

187 KEEP OFF THE GRASS

Revue in Two Acts

MUSIC AND BOOK: Music by James McHugh. *Raffles* ballet music by

Vernon Duke. Lyrics by Al Dubin. Sketches by Mort Lewis, Parke Levy and Alan Lipscott, S. Jay Kaufman, and Panama and Frank. Orchestrations by Hans Spialek and Don Walker. Vocal arrangements by Anthony R. Morelli.

PRODUCTION: Produced by the Shuberts. Book directed by Edward Duryea Dowling. Staged by Fred de Cordova. Scenery and costumes by Nat Karson. Scenery built by Nolan Brothers and painted by Van Ackerman Scenic Studios; costumes executed by Veronica. Lighting by Edward Duryea Dowling.

PREMIERE: May 23, 1940, Broadhurst Theatre, New York. Conductor: John McManus. (Out-of-town preview: April 30, Shubert Theatre, Boston.)

CAST: Jimmy Durante, Ray Bolger, Jane Froman, Ilka Chase, and others. Dancers: Betty Bruce, Sunnie O'Dea, José Limón, Daphne Vane, Marjorie Moore, 15 Dancing Young Ladies, 8 Dancing Young Men.

THIS IS SPRING (Act I): José Limón, Daphne Vane, Marjorie Moore, The Dancing Young Ladies [as ponies].

CRAZY AS A LOON (Act I): Ray Bolger, Sunnie O'Dea.

I'LL APPLAUD YOU WITH MY FEET (Act I): Betty Bruce, dancers.

THE FOUNTAIN (Act I): Bolger and others.

A LATIN TUNE, A MANHATTAN MOON, AND YOU (Act I): Bolger, Bruce, Limón, Vane, Moore, ensemble.

CLEAR OUT OF THIS WORLD (Act I): Limón, Vane, Moore, ensemble.

LOOK OUT FOR MY HEART (Act II): Bruce, Limón, The Dancing Young Ladies [as a chorus of fencers].

OLD JITTERBUG (Act II): Bolger, O'Dea, Moore, ensemble.

I'M IN THE MOOD (Act II): Bruce, Vane, Limón, Henry Dick.

RAFFLES (Act II): *Music:* By Vernon Duke. *Cast:* Bolger, Bruce, Vane, Moore, ensemble.

THIS IS WINTER (Act II): Bolger, Limón, Vane, Moore, entire company.

188 LOUISIANA PURCHASE

Musical Comedy in Two Acts and Fifteen Scenes

MUSIC AND BOOK: Music and lyrics by Irving Berlin. Book by Morrie Ryskind, based on a story by B. G. De Sylva. Orchestral arrangements by Russell Bennett. Vocal arrangements by Hugh Martin.

CHOREOGRAPHY: Ballets by George Balanchine. Modern dances by Carl Randall.

PRODUCTION: Produced by B. G. De Sylva. Book staged by Edgar MacGregor. Scenery and costumes by Tom Lee. Scenery built by Vail Scenic Construction Company and painted by Triangle Scenic Studios; costumes executed by Helene Pons and Eaves Costume Company.

PREMIERE: May 28, 1940, Imperial Theatre, New York. Conductor: Robert Emmett Dolan. (Out-of-town preview: May 2, Shubert Theatre, New Haven.)

CAST: *Marina Van Linden*, Vera Zorina; *Jim Taylor*, William Gaxton; *Madame Bordelaise*, Irene Bordoni; *Senator Oliver P. Loganberry*, Victor Moore; and others. *Premier Danseur*, Charles Laskey; 19 Dancing Girls, 15 Dancing Boys.

TONIGHT AT THE MARDI GRAS (Act I): *Queen of the Mardi Gras / Queen of the Creoles*, Vera Zorina; *Premier Danseur*, Charles Laskey.

OLD MAN'S DARLING—YOUNG MAN'S SLAVE? (Act II): *Marina*, Zorina; *Spirit of Jim Taylor*, Laskey; *Spirit of Senator Loganberry*, Harold Haskins.

NOTE: The film version of *Louisiana Purchase* (1941), with which Balanchine was not personally involved, included his Mardi Gras ballet but did not credit the choreographer.

189 PAS DE DEUX—BLUES

MUSIC: By Vladimir Dukelsky [Vernon Duke].

PREMIERE: August 6, 1940, Winter Garden, New York. Pianists: Vladimir Dukelsky and George Balanchine.

CAST: Vera Zorina, Anton Dolin.

NOTE: Performed once at an *All Star Dance Gala* for British War Relief.

190 CABIN IN THE SKY
Musical Comedy in Two Acts and Nine Scenes

MUSIC AND BOOK: Music by Vernon Duke. Lyrics by John Latouche. Book by Lynn Root. Orchestrations by Domenico Savino, Charles Cooke, Fudd Livingston, Nathan van Cleve. Vocal arrangements by Hugh Martin.

CHOREOGRAPHY: By George Balanchine in collaboration with Katherine Dunham.

PRODUCTION: Produced by Albert Lewis in association with Vinton Freedley. Entire production staged by George Balanchine. Dialogue directed by Albert Lewis. Scenery and costumes by Boris Aronson. Scenery executed by Studio Alliance; costumes executed by Karinska.

PREMIERE: October 25, 1940, Martin Beck Theatre, New York. Conductor: Max Meth.

CAST: *Petunia Jackson*, Ethel Waters; *'Little Joe' Jackson*, Dooley Wilson; *Georgia Brown*, Katherine Dunham; *Lucifer, Jr.*, Rex Ingram; *The Lawd's General*, Todd Duncan; and others. Katherine Dunham Dancers: 17 men and women.

DO WHAT YOU WANNA DO (Act I): *Lucifer, Jr.*, Rex Ingram; *Imps*, Archie Savage, Jieno Moxzer, Rajah Chardieno, Alexander McDonald.

EGYPTIAN BALLET (VISION) (Act II): Katherine Dunham and the Dunham Dancers.

LAZY STEPS (Act II): The Dunham Dancers.

BOOGY WOOGY (Act II): The Dunham Dancers.

SAVANNAH (Act II): *Petunia*, Ethel Waters; Savage.

NOTE: For this musical with a black cast, featuring the Katherine Dunham dancers, Balanchine combined classical ballet technique with their own highly developed dance forms and choreographed special dances for the leading players.

191 I WAS AN ADVENTURESS
Film

PRODUCTION: Twentieth-Century Fox. Produced by Darryl F. Zanuck. Associate Producer: Nunnally Johnson. Directed by Gregory Ratoff. Screenplay by Karl Tunberg, Don Ettlinger and John O'Hara.

Music: Ballet music by Peter Ilyitch Tschaikovsky (primarily from *Swan Lake*, Act II, Op. 20, 1875-76).

Released: 1940.

Cast: *Countess Tanya Vronsky*, Vera Zorina; *Paul Vernay*, Richard Greene; *André Desormeaux*, Erich von Stroheim; *Polo*, Peter Lorre; and others.

BALLET: *Swan Queen*, Vera Zorina; *Prince*, Lew Christensen; *Evil One*, Charles Laskey; 18 swans.

Note: An extremely abbreviated, rechoreographed version of *Swan Lake*, Act II, using elaborate camera techniques developed with the choreographer's collaboration. Some of the ideas for the corps de ballet were later used in the finale of Balanchine's New York City Ballet version of *Swan Lake* [285]. There are also rehearsal sequences with Zorina. Under the stage name Fortunio Bonanova, Balanchine plays the Orchestra Leader and is seen conducting.

See 75, 262, 285, 331, 367

1941

192 BALUSTRADE

Music: By Igor Stravinsky (Concerto in D for violin and orchestra, 1931, commissioned by Blair Fairchild).

Production: Scenery and costumes by Pavel Tchelitchew. Scenery executed by Eugene Dunkel; costumes executed by Karinska.

Premiere: January 22, 1941, Original Ballet Russe, Fifty-first Street Theatre, New York. Conductor: Igor Stravinsky. Violinist: Samuel Dushkin.

Cast: FIRST MOVEMENT, TOCCATA: Tatiana Leskova, Roman Jasinsky, 8 women; SECOND MOVEMENT, ARIA: Marina Svetlova, Paul Petroff, Sonia Orlova, Irina Zarova, 8 women; THIRD MOVEMENT, ARIA: Tamara Toumanova, Jasinsky, Petroff; FOURTH MOVEMENT, CAPRICCIO: Toumanova, Leskova, Svetlova, Jasinsky, Petroff, 12 women.

NOTE: A fantasy of contrasting moods expressed in a series of dialogues of movement, without story. The costumes and setting were surreal: two skeletal trees glowed as blood-red nerve ganglia. The title derives from a low balustrade onstage framing the action. In 1972, for the New York City Ballet Stravinsky Festival, Balanchine choreographed *Violin Concerto* (since 1973 called *Stravinsky Violin Concerto*), an entirely new work to this music performed in practice clothes without scenery.

See 374

193 SERENATA (SERENADE)

MUSIC: By Peter Ilyitch Tschaikovsky (Serenade in C for string orchestra, Op. 48, 1880, with third and fourth movements reversed).

PRODUCTION: Costumes by Candido Portinari.

PREMIERE: June 25, 1941, American Ballet Caravan, Teatro Municipal, Rio de Janeiro. Conductor: Emanuel Balaban.

CAST: Marie-Jeanne, William Dollar, Lorna London, corps de ballet.
SONATINA; WALTZ; TEMA RUSSO; ELEGY.

NOTE: Originally presented by the American Ballet, New York, 1935. At the invitation of Nelson A. Rockefeller, Co-ordinator of Inter-American Affairs, Balanchine and Lincoln Kirstein formed American Ballet Caravan, bringing together members of the former American Ballet and of Ballet Caravan for a five-months' tour of South America. *Serenade* was presented in repertory with other ballets, including Balanchine's *Ballet Imperial, Concerto Barocco, Divertimento, Errante, Apollo, The Bat,* and *Fantasia Brasileira.*

See 141*, 254

194 BALLET IMPERIAL (from 1973 called TSCHAIKOVSKY PIANO CONCERTO NO. 2)

MUSIC: By Peter Ilyitch Tschaikovsky (Piano Concerto No. 2 in G major, Op. 44, 1879, abridged, rewritten and rearranged by Alexander Siloti).

PRODUCTION: Scenery and costumes by Mstislav Doboujinsky.

PREMIERE: June 25, 1941, American Ballet Caravan, Teatro Municipal, Rio de Janeiro. Conductor: Emanuel Balaban. Pianist: Simon Sadoff. (Open dress rehearsal: May 29, Little Theatre of Hunter College, New York. Conductor: Fritz Mahler.)

CAST: Marie-Jeanne, William Dollar; Gisella Caccialanza; Fred Danieli, Nicholas Magallanes; 2 female demi-soloists; 16 women, 6 men.
ALLEGRO BRILLANTE–ANDANTE; ANDANTE NON TROPPO; ALLEGRO CON FUOCO.

NOTE: A tribute to St. Petersburg, Petipa and Tschaikovsky, set in the grandeur of a palace, the scenic view suggesting the splendors of the Imperial capital of Russia.

REVISIONS: 1950, Sadler's Wells [later Royal Ballet]: Pantomime deleted and new pas de deux added in second movement; somewhat different groupings in third movement; new scenery and costumes by Eugene Berman.

NEW PRODUCTIONS BY BALANCHINE COMPANIES: New York City Ballet: 1964, 1941 version with augmented corps de ballet and minor revisions, with new scenery by Rouben Ter-Arutunian (based on the 1941 production) and new costumes by Karinska; 1973, 1950 version (titled *Piano Concerto No. 2*, then *Tschaikovsky Piano Concerto No. 2*), staged without scenery, with new costumes by Karinska (classical tutus replaced by chiffon skirts), and lighting by Ronald Bates.

STAGINGS: 1942, New Opera Company; 1944, Ballet Russe de Monte Carlo; 1950, Sadler's Wells; 1952, La Scala; 1964, New York City Ballet; 1967, Australia; 1968, Berlin; 1973, Geneva; 1975, Naples; 1976, Norway; 1980, Mexico.

See 349, 382

195 CONCERTO BAROCCO

MUSIC: By Johann Sebastian Bach (Double Violin Concerto in D minor, B.W.V. 1043).

PRODUCTION: Scenery and costumes by Eugene Berman.

PREMIERE: June 27, 1941, American Ballet Caravan, Teatro Municipal, Rio de Janeiro. Conductor: Emanuel Balaban. Violinists: Edmundo

Blois, Salvador Piersant. (Open dress rehearsal: May 29, Little Theatre of Hunter College, New York. Conductor: Fritz Mahler.)

CAST: Marie-Jeanne, William Dollar; Mary Jane Shea; 8 women.

VIVACE; LARGO MA NON TANTO; ALLEGRO.

NOTE: The work was begun as a School of American Ballet exercise in stagecraft. When it entered the repertory of the Ballet Russe de Monte Carlo in 1945 the dancers were dressed in practice clothes, probably the first appearance of what has come to be regarded as the ballet uniform pioneered by Balanchine. Presented with *Orpheus* [246] and *Symphony in C* [244] at the first performance of the New York City Ballet, October 11, 1948.

NEW PRODUCTIONS BY BALANCHINE COMPANIES: New York City Ballet: 1948, using Berman's original costumes, molded of synthetic rubber; 1951, performed without scenery, in practice clothes (black for the women until ca. 1963; white thereafter).

STAGINGS: 1943, American Concert Ballet; 1945, Ballet Russe de Monte Carlo; 1948, New York City Ballet, de Cuevas; 1953, San Francisco; 1955, Royal Danish; 1956, Netherlands; 1960, Hamburg; 1961, Washington, La Scala, National Ballet of Canada; 1963, Paris; 1964, Boston, Pennsylvania; 1965, San Diego, Utah; 1967, National; 1968, Ballet la Jeunesse; 1969, Dayton, Cologne, Munich; 1970, Dallas, Geneva; 1971, Dance Theatre of Harlem, Houston; 1972, Cincinnati; 1973, Garden State, Los Angeles; 1974, Ballet Victoria, New Zealand; 1975, Chicago, Eglevsky; 1976, Chicago Lyric Opera, Les Grands Ballets Canadiens; 1977, Pacific Northwest, Frankfurt, Royal Ballet Touring; 1978, Minnesota, North Carolina, Zürich; 1979, Cleveland; 1980, Atlanta, Ohio, Belgrade, Bologna, Israel; 1981, Norway, Taller Coreográfico; 1982, Ballet Oklahoma, San Juan, Tulsa.

TELEVISION: 1964 (excerpts, Bell Telephone Hour, NBC); 1969 (L'Heure du Concert, CBC, Montreal); 1976 (second movement, Dance in America, PBS).

See 250

196 DIVERTIMENTO

MUSIC: By Gioacchino Rossini (*Matinées Musicales*; *Soirées Musicales*, 1830-35; overture to *La Cenerentola*, produced 1817; selected and orchestrated by Benjamin Britten at the request of Lincoln Kirstein).

PRODUCTION: Scenery and costumes by André Derain (from *Les Songes* [135]).

PREMIERE: June 27, 1941, American Ballet Caravan, Teatro Municipal, Rio de Janeiro. Conductor: Emanuel Balaban.

CAST: MARCH: *King*, Todd Bolender; *6 Attendants*; CANZONETTA: *Flower Lady*, Marjorie Moore; TYROLEAN DANCE: Marie-Jeanne; POLKA: *Couple in Black and White*, Gisella Caccialanza, John Kriza; BOLERO: *Lady in White*, Olga Suárez; TARANTELLA: *Ladies in Red*, 9 women; NOCTURNE: Marie-Jeanne, Fred Danieli; FINALE: Entire cast.

NOTE: A series of costume dances at a party. Near the end a guest costumed as a rat is chased by other guests; unmasked, he is discovered to be an acrobat. On at least one occasion, Balanchine appeared as the rat. Made for the South American tour and not performed elsewhere.

197 ALMA ERRANTE (ERRANTE)
Ballet Fantástico

MUSIC: By Franz Schubert (*The Wanderer*, fantasy for piano, Op. 15, 1882, transcribed by Franz Liszt, orchestrated by Charles Koechlin). Book by Pavel Tchelitchew.

PRODUCTION: Costumes, lighting and dramatic effects by Pavel Tchelitchew (from the 1933 production).

PREMIERE: June 27, 1941, American Ballet Caravan, Teatro Municipal, Rio de Janeiro. Conductor: Emanuel Balaban.

CAST: Marjorie Moore, William Dollar; *Shadows, Angels, Revolutionaries*, and others.

NOTE: Originally presented by Les Ballets 1933, Paris.

See 138*, 143

198 APOLO MUSAGETA (APOLLON MUSAGÈTE)

Ballet in Two Scenes

MUSIC: Music and book by Igor Stravinsky (*Apollo Musagetes*, 1927-28, commissioned by Mrs. Elizabeth Sprague Coolidge).

PRODUCTION: Scenery and costumes by Tomás Santa Rosa.

PREMIERE: June 30, 1941, American Ballet Caravan, Teatro Municipal, Rio de Janeiro. Conductor: Emanuel Balaban.

CAST: *Apollo*, Lew Christensen; *Terpsichore*, Marie-Jeanne; *Calliope*, Olga Suárez; *Polyhymnia*, Marjorie Moore; *2 Goddesses*.

NOTE: Originally presented by Diaghilev's Ballets Russes, Paris, 1928.

See 84*, 176, 284

199 EL MURCIÉLAGO (THE BAT)

MUSIC: By Johann Strauss the Younger (from *Die Fledermaus*, produced 1874, with unidentified additions). Book by Lincoln Kirstein.

PRODUCTION: Costumes and lighting by Keith Martin.

PREMIERE: June 30, 1941, American Ballet Caravan, Teatro Municipal, Rio de Janeiro. Conductor: Emanuel Balaban.

CAST: *The Bat*, Helen Kramer, Todd Bolender; *The Poet*, Lew Christensen; *The Masked (Identical) Ladies*, Gisella Caccialanza, Olga Suárez; *Hungarian Dancers* (formerly called *Gypsies*), Marie-Jeanne, William Dollar; *The Can-Can Dancer*, Beatrice Tompkins; *The Ladies of Fashion*, 4 women; *2 Coachmen*; *Can-Can Dancers, Officers, Ladies and Gentlemen*, corps de ballet.

NOTE: Originally presented by the American Ballet, New York, 1936.

See 107, 169*, 206, 294

200 FANTASIA BRASILEIRA

MUSIC: By Francisco Mignone (*Brazilian Fantasy No. 4*, 1941, commissioned by Lincoln Kirstein).

PRODUCTION: Scenery and costumes by Erico Bianco.

PREMIERE: August 27, 1941, American Ballet Caravan, Teatro Municipal, Santiago de Chile. Conductor: Emanuel Balaban. Pianist: Simon Sadoff.

CAST: Olga Suárez, Fred Danieli, Nicholas Magallanes, corps de ballet.

NOTE: The choreography employed Brazilian folk-dance motifs. Performed only in South America.

1942

201 THE LADY COMES ACROSS
Musical Comedy in Two Acts and Twelve Scenes

MUSIC AND BOOK: Music and lyrics by Vernon Duke and John Latouche. Book by Fred Thompson and Dawn Powell. Orchestrations supervised by Domenico Savino. Musical arrangements by Domenico Savino, Charles L. Cooke and staff.

CHOREOGRAPHY: By George Balanchine. Choreographic Assistant: William Holbrook.

PRODUCTION: Production under the supervision of Morrie Ryskind. Produced by George Hale in association with Charles R. Rogers and Nelson Seabra. Book directed by Romney Brent. Scenery and costumes by Stewart Chaney. Scenery built by Vail Construction Company and painted by Robert W. Bergman Studios, Inc.; costumes executed by Mme Karinska, Mme Berthe and Brooks Costume Company.

PREMIERE: January 9, 1942, Forty-fourth Street Theatre, New York. Conductor: Jacques Rabiroff. Pianist/Organist: Adam Carroll. (Out-of-town preview: December 17, 1941, Shubert Theatre, Boston.)

CAST: *Jill Charters*, Evelyn Wyckoff (Jessie Matthews, Boston); *Otis Kibber*, Joe E. Lewis; *Ernie Bustard*, Mischa Auer; *Mrs. Riverdale*, Ruth Weston; *Babs Appleway*, Wynn Murray; *Campbell*, Gower Champion; *Kay*, Jeanne Tyler; and others. *Ballerina Comique*, Eugenia Delarova; *Ballerina*, Lubov Rostova; *The Phantom Lover*, Marc Platt; Dancing Ensemble of 17 women and 8 men.

HIT THE RAMP (Act I, Scene 3): Wynn Murray, Mischa Auer, ensemble.

TANGO (Act I, Scene 4): Auer, Eugenia Delarova, ensemble.

CONEY ISLAND BALLET (Act II, Scene 1): Delarova, Lubov Rostova, Marc Platt, ensemble.

LADY (Act II, Scene 1): Gower Champion, Jeanne Tyler.

THIS IS WHERE I CAME IN (Act II, Scene 2): Champion, Tyler.

DAYBREAK (Act II, Scene 5): Evelyn Wyckoff (Jessie Matthews, Boston); *The Phantom Lover*, Platt.

202 THE BALLET OF THE ELEPHANTS

MUSIC: By Igor Stravinsky (*Circus Polka*, 1942, written at the request of George Balanchine, with the dedication 'For a young elephant').

PRODUCTION: Staged by John Murray Anderson. Costumes by Norman Bel Geddes. Elephants trained by Walter McClain.

PREMIERE: April 9, 1942, Ringling Brothers and Barnum & Bailey Circus, Madison Square Garden, New York. Conductor: Merle Evans.

CAST: The elephant Modoc as 'premiere ballerina,' and 'fifty elephants and fifty beautiful girls in an original choreographic *tour de force.*'
In early performances, including an Armed Forces benefit, Vera Zorina rode at the head of the troupe in a specially choreographed addition to the circus routine.

NOTE: In 1945, for a program entitled *Adventure in Ballet*, Balanchine choreographed another work to this music with an all-human cast.

See 230

203 PAS DE TROIS FOR PIANO AND TWO DANCERS

MUSIC: By Theodore Chanler (1942, commissioned by Lincoln Kirstein).

PRODUCTION: Produced by Lincoln Kirstein. Costumes by Pavel Tchelitchew.

PREMIERE: May 10, 1942, Alvin Theatre, New York. Pianist: Theodore Chanler.

CAST: Mary Ellen Moylan, Nicholas Magallanes.

NOTE: Performed once on a program entitled *Music at Work*, in aid of Russian War Relief.

204 MARUF (MÂROUF)

Opera in Four Acts by Henri Rabaud

ACT II HAREM BALLET

PREMIERE: August 7, 1942, Opera of the Teatro Colón, Buenos Aires, Argentina. Conductor: A. Wolff.

CAST: Leticia de la Vega, Yurek Shabelevsky, corps de ballet.

NOTE: Presented with the premiere performance of *Concierto de Mozart* during Balanchine's two months as guest director of the ballet of the Teatro Colón. The season included a production of *Apollon Musagète* designed by Pavel Tchelitchew.

See 179

205 CONCIERTO DE MOZART (also called CONCIERTO)

MUSIC: By Wolfgang Amadeus Mozart (Violin Concerto in A major, K. 219, 1775).

PRODUCTION: Scenery and costumes by Pavel Tchelitchew.

PREMIERE: August 7, 1942, Ballet of the Teatro Colón, Buenos Aires, Argentina. Conductor: Juan José Castro. Violinist: Carlos Pessina.

CAST: ALLEGRO APERTO: Maria Ruanova, Michel [Mezeslav] Borovsky; Nelida Cendra, Estela Deporte, Jorge Tomin; 11 women, 11 men; ADAGIO: Ruanova, Yurek Shabelevsky; Tomin; 15 women, 7 men; MINUETO: Ruanova, Borovsky, Shabelevsky; Cendra, Deporte, Tomin; 19 women, 7 men.

NOTE: At least one section of this work has been seen in the United States, the pas de deux from the ADAGIO, performed in 1964 in Washington, D. C., and Montevideo, Minnesota.

STAGINGS: 1955, La Plata; 1960, Berliner Ballett; 1964, Uruguay; 1965, São Paulo; 1980, Belo Horizonte.

206 ROSALINDA (DIE FLEDERMAUS)

Operetta in Three Acts and a Prologue

MUSIC AND BOOK: Music by Johann Strauss the Younger (produced 1874), in a version by Max Reinhardt (1920s). Music from other Strauss scores interpolated by Erich Wolfgang Korngold, including *Tales from the Vienna Woods*, *Knight Pazman* and *Wine, Women and Song*. Lyrics by Paul Kerby.

CHOREOGRAPHY: By George Balanchine. Ballet Master: William Dollar.

PRODUCTION: Produced by Lodewick Vroom. Staged by Felix Brentano and George Balanchine (uncredited). Scenery by Oliver Smith. Costumes by Ladislas Czettel. Scenery built by Vail Construction Company and painted by E. B. Dunkel Studios; costumes executed by Brooks Costume Company. Lighting by Jean Rosenthal.

PREMIERE: October 28, 1942, New Opera Company, Forty-fourth Street Theatre, New York. Conductor: Erich Wolfgang Korngold.

CAST: *Rosalinda von Eisenstein*, Dorothy Sarnoff; *Gabriel von Eisenstein*, Ralph Herbert; *Adele*, Virginia MacWatters; *Prince Orlofsky*, Oscar Karlweis; and others. *Premier Danseur*, José Limón; *Premiere Danseuse*, Mary Ellen Moylan; 10 women dancers, 7 men dancers.

WAITERS DANCE (Act I): Todd Bolender, Douglas Coudy.

BALLETS IN BALLROOM SCENE, INCLUDING GRAND WALTZ FINALE (Act II): Mary Ellen Moylan, José Limón, ensemble.

DANCE OF DRUNKEN GENTLEMEN IN PRISON (Act III): Male ensemble with flying ballerinas.

NOTE: Created during Balanchine's year-long association with the New Opera Company, for which he choreographed opera divertissements and mounted a production of *Ballet Imperial*.

See 107, 169, 199, 294

207 THE OPERA CLOAK
Operatic Fantasy in One Act by Walter Damrosch
RAGTIME BALLET [?]

PREMIERE: November 3, 1942, New Opera Company, Broadway Theatre, New York. Conductor: Walter Damrosch.

NOTE: World premiere and only performance. The RAGTIME BALLET was announced in press releases, but programs credit neither choreographer nor dancers. Balanchine recalls some association with this production. Presented with *The Fair at Sorochinsk*.

208 THE FAIR AT SOROCHINSK
Opera in Three Acts by Modest Moussorgsky
ACT III HOPAK BALLET

PREMIERE: November 3, 1942, New Opera Company, Broadway
Theatre, New York. Conductor: Emil Cooper.

CAST: Gisella Caccialanza, William Dollar, 10 women, 4 men.

See 43

209 LA VIE PARISIENNE
Comic Opera in Three Acts and Four Scenes by Jacques Offenbach
ACT II, SCENE 2 BALLET

CHOREOGRAPHY: Dances staged by William Dollar under the
supervision of George Balanchine.

PREMIERE: November 10, 1942, New Opera Company, Broadway
Theatre, New York. Conductor: Paul Breisach.

CAST: Gisella Caccialanza, 10 women, 4 men.

210 THE QUEEN OF SPADES (PIQUE DAME)
Opera in Three Acts and Seven Scenes by Peter Ilyitch Tschaikovsky
ACT II, SCENE I BALLET

CHOREOGRAPHY: Dances staged by William Dollar under the
supervision of George Balanchine.

PREMIERE: November 24, 1942, New Opera Company, Broadway
Theatre, New York. Conductor: Emil Cooper.

CAST: Gisella Caccialanza, William Dollar, 10 women, 4 men.

211 MACBETH
Opera in Four Acts and Nine Scenes by Giuseppe Verdi
ACT I, SCENE I, AND ACT III, SCENE I DANCES OF THE WITCHES

CHOREOGRAPHY: Dances staged by William Dollar under the
supervision of George Balanchine.

PREMIERE: December 2, 1942, New Opera Company, Broadway Theatre, New York. Conductor: Fritz Stiedry.

CAST: 10 women, 4 men.

212 [SOLO]

Gisella Caccialanza remembers performing a dance with Balanchine choreography to music by Prokofiev at the U. S. O. headquarters in New York City in 1942.

213 STAR SPANGLED RHYTHM
Film

PRODUCTION: Paramount Pictures. Produced by Joseph Sistrom. Directed by George Marshall. Screenplay by Melvin Frank, Norman Panama and Harry Tugend. Art direction by Hans Dreier and Ernst Fegte. Scenery by Stephen Seymour. Costumes by Edith Head.

MUSIC: Music and lyrics by Harold Arlen and Johnny Mercer. Musical Director: Robert Emmett Dolan, assisted by Arthur Franklin.

CHOREOGRAPHY: By George Balanchine, Danny Dare and Katherine Dunham.

RELEASED: 1942.

CAST: *Pop Webster*, Victor Moore; *Polly Judson*, Betty Hutton; *Jimmy Webster*, Eddie Bracken; and others. Stars playing themselves in the benefit performance scene include Bing Crosby, Bob Hope, Fred MacMurray, Franchot Tone, Ray Milland, Dorothy Lamour, Paulette Goddard, Vera Zorina, Mary Martin, Veronica Lake, Alan Ladd, Katherine Dunham, Cecil B. De Mille, and others.

THAT OLD BLACK MAGIC (sung by Johnny Johnston): Vera Zorina.

1943

214 HELEN OF TROY

Michel Fokine's last ballet, *Helen of Troy* (choreographed to excerpts from Offenbach's *La Belle Hélène*), was substantially revised by David Lichine, whose version was first performed by Ballet Theatre at the Masonic Auditorium, Detroit, November 29, 1942. Before the New York performances in April 1943, Balanchine assisted Lichine in devising a new ending for the ballet.

215 THE CRUCIFIXION OF CHRIST

MUSIC: By Johann Sebastian Bach (*St. Matthew Passion*, 1729).

PRODUCTION: Performance conceived by Leopold Stokowski, Robert Edmond Jones and George Balanchine. Groupings devised by George Balanchine.

PREMIERE: April 9, 1943, Metropolitan Opera, New York. Conductor: Leopold Stokowski.

CAST: Students of the School of American Ballet on stage, singers in the orchestra pit. *Maria Magdalena*, Lillian Gish; students from the School of American Ballet miming the roles of Peter, Pilate, the High Priest, Judas, Soldiers, the Crowd.

NOTE: Described in announcements as a modern form of miracle play, the work was performed once as a benefit for the American Friends Service Committee.

216 THE MERRY WIDOW
Operetta in Three Acts

MUSIC AND BOOK: Music by Franz Lehár (produced 1905). New musical version by Robert Stolz. Lyrics by Adrian Ross. Special lyrics by Robert Gilbert. New book by Sidney Sheldon and Ben Roberts.

PRODUCTION: Produced by Yolanda Mero-Irion. Directed by Felix
Brentano. Scenery by Howard Bay. Costumes by Walter Florell.
Scenery built by William Kellam Company and painted by Centre
Studios; costumes executed by Eaves and Brooks Costume Companies.

PREMIERE: August 4, 1943, New Opera Company, Majestic Theatre,
New York. Conductor: Robert Stolz.

CAST: *Sonia Sadoya*, Marta Eggerth; *Prince Danilo*, Jan Kiepura; *Popoff*,
Melville Cooper; *Jolidon*, Robert Field; *Natalie*, Ruth Matteson; *Clo-Clo*,
Lisette Verea; and others. *Premieres Danseuses*, Lubov Roudenko,
Milada Mladova; *Premiers Danseurs*, Chris Volkoff, James Starbuck;
6 women dancers, 5 men dancers.

POLKA (Act I): Lubov Roudenko, James Starbuck.

MARSOVIAN DANCE (Act II): Milada Mladova, Chris Volkoff, corps
de ballet.

THE WOMEN (Act II): Melville Cooper, 6 men, 2 women dancers, 6
women singers.

I LOVE YOU SO (Act II): Mladova, Volkoff, corps de ballet.

THE GIRLS AT MAXIM'S [CAN-CAN] (Act III): Roudenko, ballet girls.

NOTE: The production featured the choreography, and added music
for dance numbers not in the original score.

OTHER PRODUCTIONS: October 7, 1944 (New Opera Company) and
April 9, 1957 (New York City Center Light Opera Company).
Although Balanchine was not personally involved in these stagings,
his name appears on the printed programs and his choreography
was used, with modifications.

217 WHAT'S UP
Musical Comedy in Two Acts and Nine Scenes

MUSIC AND BOOK: Music by Frederick Loewe. Lyrics by Alan Jay Lerner.
Book by Alan Jay Lerner and Arthur Pierson. Orchestrations by Van
Cleave. Vocal arrangements by Bobby Tucker.

PRODUCTION: Produced by Mark Warnow. Book directed by Robert
H. Gordon. Staged and choreographed by George Balanchine. Scenery
by Boris Aronson. Costumes by Grace Houston. Scenery executed by

Studio Alliance, Inc.; costumes executed by Eaves Costume Company. Lighting by Al Alloy.

PREMIERE: November 11, 1943, National Theatre, New York. Conductor: Will Irwin. (Out-of-town preview: October 22, Playhouse, Wilmington, Delaware.)

CAST: *Rawa of Tanglinia*, Jimmy Savo; *Sgt. Moroney*, Johnny Morgan; *Virginia Miller*, Gloria Warren; and others. Featured dancers included Phyllis Hill, Don Weissmuller, Sondra Barrett, Kenneth Buffett, Honey Murray, Robert Bay, Jack Baker.

JOSHUA (Act I, Scene 3): Ensemble of men and women.

BALLET (Act I, Scene 4): Jimmy Savo, Phyllis Hill.

HOW FLY TIMES (Act I, Scene 4): Don Weissmuller.

YOU WASH AND I'LL DRY (Act II, Scene 1): Sondra Barrett, Kenneth Buffett, Honey Murray.

THE ILL-TEMPERED CLAVICHORD (Act II, Scene 3): Ensemble of men and women. Dance specialty: Robert Bay.

REPRISE: YOU'VE GOT A HOLD ON ME (Act II, Scene 3): Hill, Jack Baker.

NOTE: Among the dance numbers were two dream ballets: In JOSHUA, U. S. Army soldiers in pajamas dance with schoolgirls in nighties, combining ballet and tap styles; in BALLET, a pas de deux, the mime-comedian Jimmy Savo, small, pursues a large ballerina, his dream-girl.

1944

218 DREAM WITH MUSIC
Musical Comedy in Two Acts and Fourteen Scenes

MUSIC AND BOOK: Music by Clay Warnick (based on themes from Saint-Saëns' Violin Concerto in B minor, Rimsky-Korsakov's *Schéhérazade*, Schubert's Symphony No. 9, Beethoven's Symphony No. 7, Weber's *Oberon*, Grieg's Piano Concerto in A minor, Beethoven's Symphony No. 1, Borodin's *Prince Igor*, Moussorgsky's *A Night on Bald Mountain*, Wagner's 'Ride of the Valkyries' from *Die Walküre*, Chopin's

Twenty-four Preludes, Gluck's ballet music, Schumann's Piano Concerto, Dvořák's 'New World' Symphony, Haydn's Symphony No. 1, and Tschaikovsky's *The Nutcracker*.) Lyrics by Edward Eager. Book by Sidney Sheldon, Dorothy Kilgallen and Ben Roberts. Orchestrations by Russell Bennett, Hans Spialek, Ted Royal, and Clay Warnick. Vocal arrangements by Clay Warnick.

CHOREOGRAPHY: Ballet choreography by George Balanchine. Tap routines by Henry Le Tang.

PRODUCTION: Produced and directed by Richard Kollmar. Scenery by Stewart Chaney. Costumes by Miles White. Scenery built by Martin Turner and painted by Kaj Velden; costumes executed by Brooks Costume Company, Karinska and others.

PREMIERE: May 18, 1944, Majestic Theatre, New York. Conductor: Max Meth. (Out-of-town preview: April 17, Shubert Theatre, Boston.)

CAST: *Dinah*, Vera Zorina; *Michael*, Ronald Graham; *Marian*, Joy Hodges (June Knight, Boston). IN THE DREAM: *Scheherazade*, Zorina; *Jasmin*, Hodges; *Sultan*, Robert Brink; *Aladdin*, Graham; *Sinbad*, Leonard Elliott; and others. Dancers: Peter Birch and corps de ballet of 9 women and 4 men, 6 tap dancers.

SCHEHERAZADE'S DANCE (Act I): Vera Zorina, singing ensemble.

BE GLAD YOU'RE ALIVE (Act I): Alex Rotov, Peter Birch, ensemble.

I'LL TAKE THE SOLO (Act I): Corps de ballet, tap dancers.

BALLET IN THE CLOUDS (Act I): Zorina, Birch, Sunny Rice, corps de ballet.

THE LION AND THE LAMB (Act II): Ensemble.

219 SONG OF NORWAY
Operetta in Two Acts and Seven Scenes

MUSIC AND BOOK: Music by Edvard Grieg, adapted by Robert Wright and George Forrest. Lyrics by Robert Wright and George Forrest. Book by Milton Lazarus from a play by Homer Curran (based on the life of Grieg). Orchestral and vocal arrangements by Arthur Kay.

CHOREOGRAPHY: Choreography and vocal ensembles staged by George Balanchine.

PRODUCTION: Produced by Edwin Lester. Book directed by Charles K. Freeman. Scenery by Lemuel Ayers. Costumes by Robert Davison. Scenery supervised by Carl Kent. Scenery built by Curran Productions and painted by Harry Dworkin and Fritz Kraencke; costumes executed by Walter J. Israel.

PREMIERE: June 12, 1944, Los Angeles and San Francisco Civic Light Operas, Philharmonic Auditorium, Los Angeles, California. Conductor: Arthur Kay. Pianist: Rachel Chapman. (First New York performance, August 21, Imperial Theatre. Pianist: Louis Teicher.)

CAST: *Edvard Grieg*, Walter Cassel (Lawrence Brooks, New York); *Rikard Nordraak*, Robert Shafer; *Nina Hagerup*, Helena Bliss; *Count Peppi Le Loup*, Sig Arno; *Louisa Giovanni*, Irra Petina; *Maestro Pisoni*, Charles Judels (Robert Bernard, New York); *Freddy/Tito*, Frederic Franklin; *Adelina*, Alexandra Danilova; and others. Dancing ensemble from Ballet Russe de Monte Carlo: 11 women, 11 men.

IN THE HOLIDAY SPIRIT (Act I, Scene 2): Ruthanna Boris, Anna Istomina, Leon Danielian, Alexander Goudovitch, and others.

FREDDY AND HIS FIDDLE (Act I, Scene 2): *Music*: Adapted from *Norwegian Dances*, Op. 38, 1881. *Cast*: *Einar*, Kent Edwards; *Sigrid*, Janet Hamer; *Freddy*, Frederic Franklin; singers.

MARCH OF THE TROLLGERS (THE CAKE LOTTERY) (Act I, Scene 2): *Music*: Adapted from *Mountaineers Song*, *Halling* in G minor, and *March of the Dwarfs*. *Cast*: Singing and dancing ensemble.

CHOCOLATE PAS DE TROIS (Act II, Scene 2): *Music*: Adapted from *Fra Monte Pincio*, Op. 39, 1870, and *Rigaudon* from *Holberg Suite*, Op. 4, 1884. *Cast*: *Tito*, Franklin; *His Employees*, corps de ballet.

WALTZ ETERNAL (Act II, Scene 3): *Music*: Adapted from *Waltz Caprice*, Op. 37, 1883. *Cast*: Corps de ballet.

PEER GYNT BALLET (Act II, Scene 3): *Music*: Adapted from *Peer Gynt Suites* I and II, Opp. 46 and 55, 1876. *Cast*: Alexandra Danilova, Nathalie Krassovska, Danielian, corps de ballet. SOLVEIG'S SONG: Krassovska, Danielian; HALL OF THE DOVRE KING: Male ensemble; ANITRA'S DANCE: Danilova.

THE SONG OF NORWAY (Act II, Scene 5): *Music*: Adapted from A minor

Concerto, 1868. *Cast*: Danilova, Franklin, Nicholas Magallanes, corps de ballet.

NOTE: The production featured the Ballet Russe de Monte Carlo ensemble and its principal dancers, Danilova and Franklin.

OTHER PRODUCTIONS: May 26, 1952, Philharmonic Auditorium, Los Angeles. Although the choreography is credited to Balanchine and Aida Broadbent, Balanchine was not involved.

220 DANSES CONCERTANTES
(also called DANCE CONCERTO)

MUSIC: By Igor Stravinsky (*Danses Concertantes* for chamber orchestra, 1941-42, commissioned by Werner Janssen).

PRODUCTION: Scenery and costumes by Eugene Berman. Scenery executed by E. B. Dunkel Studios; costumes executed by Karinska, Inc.

PREMIERE: September 10, 1944, Ballet Russe de Monte Carlo, City Center of Music and Drama, New York. Conductor: Emanuel Balaban.

CAST: Alexandra Danilova, Frederic Franklin; I. VARIATION: Gertrude Svobodina, Nikita Talin, Nora White; II. VARIATION: Ruthanna Boris, Alexander Goudovitch, Dorothy Etheridge; III. VARIATION: Lillian Lanese, Herbert Bliss, Pauline Goddard; IV. VARIATION: Maria Tallchief, Nicholas Magallanes, Mary Ellen Moylan; PAS DE DEUX: Danilova, Franklin; FINALE: Entire cast.

NOTE: Stravinsky wrote the music for concert performance; Balanchine choreographed the score as his first new work for the Ballet Russe de Monte Carlo at the beginning of his two-year association with that company as choreographer.

REVISIONS: 1972, New York City Ballet (Stravinsky Festival): Choreography entirely reworked, but resembling the first production in style and effect, using Berman's original costumes and scenery.

See 375

221 LE BOURGEOIS GENTILHOMME

Music: By Richard Strauss (concert suite, ca. 1917). Libretto after Molière.

Production: Scenery and costumes by Eugene Berman. Scenery executed by E. B. Dunkel Studios; costumes executed by Karinska, Inc.

Premiere: September 23, 1944, Ballet Russe de Monte Carlo, City Center of Music and Drama, New York. Conductor: Emanuel Balaban.

Cast: *Cléonte*, Nicholas Magallanes; *Coviel, His Valet*, Peter Deign; *M. Jourdain*, Michel Katcharoff; *Lucile, His Daughter*, Nathalie Krassovska; *Nicola, Her Maid*, Vida Brown; *4 Ladies in Waiting*; *4 Blackamoors*; divertissements: *Fencers*, 2 men; pas de sept: Mary Ellen Moylan, 6 women; harlequinade: Ruthanna Boris, Leon Danielian, Nikita Talin; danse indienne: Maria Tallchief, Yurek Lazowski; pas de deux d'amour: Krassovska, Magallanes.

Revisions: 1945, Ballet Russe de Monte Carlo: Reviews imply some reworking.

Other versions: 1932, Ballets Russes de Monte-Carlo. 1979, New York City Opera.

See 131*, 410, 414

222 WALTZ ACADEMY

Music: By Vittorio Rieti (orchestrated by the composer from his two-piano suite *Second Avenue Waltzes*, 1944, on commission from Ballet Theatre).

Production: Scenery by Oliver Smith. Costumes by Alvin Colt. Scenery executed by Eugene B. Dunkel Studios; costumes executed by Karinska.

Premiere: October 5, 1944, Ballet Theatre, Opera House, Boston. Conductor: Antal Dorati.

Cast: pas de six: Margaret Banks, Mildred Ferguson, Barbara Fallis, Rozsika Sabo, June Morris, Fern Whitney; pas de quatre: Janet Reed, Albia Kavan, Harold Lang, Fernando Alonso; pas de trois: Miriam Golden, Diana Adams, John Kriza; pas de trois: Nora Kaye, John

Taras, Rex Cooper; PAS DE DEUX: Nana Gollner, Paul Petroff; FINALE: Entire cast.

NOTE: A suite of waltz variations, opening with morning ballet practice in a rehearsal room; the set suggested a loft under a cupola. Balanchine's first original work for Ballet Theatre.

REVISIONS: 1948, Ballet Theatre: Revised, retitled *Six Waltzes*.

223 SENTIMENTAL COLLOQUY

MUSIC: By Paul Bowles.

CHOREOGRAPHY: By George Balanchine, credited to André Eglevsky.

PRODUCTION: Scenery and costumes by Salvador Dali. Costumes executed by Karinska.

PREMIERE: October 30, 1944, Ballet International, International Theatre, New York. Conductor: Alexander Smallens.

CAST: Marie-Jeanne, André Eglevsky; 2 men.

NOTE: Titled after a poem by Verlaine and choreographed for two figures veiled in white who dance in surreal surroundings with a bicyclist and a figure costumed as a turtle. Dali's backdrop, filled with images of bearded bicyclists and a grand piano spouting water, was designed to suggest extreme loneliness experienced in the midst of a crowd.

1945

224 THE TEMPEST

Play by William Shakespeare

MUSIC: By David Diamond.

PRODUCTION: Produced by Cheryl Crawford, based on a production idea by Eva Le Gallienne. Directed by Margaret Webster. Scenery and costumes by Motley. Scenery built by Nolan Brothers and painted by Centre Studios; men's costumes executed by Eaves Costume

Company; other costumes executed by Edith Lutyens. Lighting by
Moe Hack.

PREMIERE: January 25, 1945, Alvin Theatre, New York. Conductor:
David Diamond. (Out-of-town preview: December 26, 1944, Shubert
Theatre, Philadelphia.)

CAST: *Alonso*, Philip Huston; *Gonzalo*, Paul Leyssac; *Antonio*, Berry
Kroeger; *Sebastian*, Eugene Stuckmann; *Prospero*, Arnold Moss; *Miranda*,
Frances Heflin; *Ariel*, Vera Zorina; *Caliban*, Canada Lee; *Ferdinand*, Vito
Christi; *Trinculo*, George Voskovec; *Stephano*, Jan Werich; and others.

NOTE: Although his name does not appear on the printed program,
Balanchine arranged movement sequences for Vera Zorina.

See 308

225   PAS DE DEUX (also called GRAND ADAGIO)

MUSIC: By Peter Ilyitch Tschaikovsky (entr'acte from *The Sleeping
Beauty*, 1890, orchestrated by Ivan Boutnikoff).

PREMIERE: March 14, 1945, Ballet Russe de Monte Carlo, City Center of
Music and Drama, New York. Conductor: Emanuel Balaban.

CAST: Alexandra Danilova, Frederic Franklin.

NOTE: In 1955, Balanchine interpolated this music in its original form
as a violin cadenza into Act I of his production of *The Nutcracker* for the
New York City Ballet.

See 65, 259, 281, 302, 404, 418

226   AÏDA

Opera in Four Acts and Seven Scenes by Giuseppe Verdi
BALLET

CHOREOGRAPHY: By George Balanchine and William Dollar.

PREMIERE: ca. June 8, 1945, Ópera Nacional, Palacio de Bellas Artes,
Mexico City. Danced by advanced students from the School of American
Ballet and guest soloists. Conductor: Carl Alwin.

NOTE: Accompanying Balanchine and Dollar to Mexico were
Marie-Jeanne, Nicholas Magallanes, and twelve girls from the School

of American Ballet. Printed programs do not list dances or dancers. Balanchine choreographed *Aïda*, *Faust* and *Samson et Dalila*. He may also have choreographed *Carmen* and *Rigoletto*, but no documentation has been located. *Concerto Barocco* [195], *Apollo* [84], and Dollar's *Constantia* and staging of *Les Sylphides* were also performed.

See 126, 152, 255

227 FAUSTO (FAUST)

Opera in Four Acts by Charles Gounod
WALPURGISNACHT BALLET

PREMIERE: June 26, 1945, Ópera Nacional, Palacio de Bellas Artes, Mexico City. Danced by advanced students from the School of American Ballet and guest soloists. Conductor: Jean Morel.

NOTE: Patricia Wilde remembers performing a solo.

See 45, 117, 151, 397, 413

228 SANSÓN Y DALILA (SAMSON ET DALILA)

Opera in Three Acts by Camille Saint-Saëns
BALLETS

PREMIERE: July 3, 1945, Ópera Nacional, Palacio de Bellas Artes, Mexico City. Danced by advanced students from the School of American Ballet and guest soloists. Conductor: Jean Morel.

NOTE: Traditional choreography for *Samson et Dalila* includes the DANCE OF THE PRIESTESSES in Act I and BACCHANALE in Act III.

See 66, 116, 171

229 MR. STRAUSS GOES TO BOSTON

Musical Comedy in Two Acts and Nine Scenes

MUSIC AND BOOK: Music by Robert Stolz. Lyrics by Robert Sour. Book by Leonard L. Levinson, based on an original story by Alfred Gruenwald and Geza Herczeg. Orchestrations by George Lessner. Musical arrangements of Johann Strauss the Younger's melodies by Robert Stolz and George Lessner.

PRODUCTION: Produced, staged and directed by Felix Brentano. Scenery by Stewart Chaney. Costumes by Walter Florell. Scenery built by Vail Scenic Construction Company and painted by Robert Bergman Studios; costumes executed by Eaves Costume Company.

PREMIERE: September 6, 1945, Century Theatre, New York. Conductor: Robert Stolz. (Out-of-town preview August 13, Shubert Theatre, Boston.)

CAST: *Johann Strauss*, George Rigaud; *Brook Whitney*, Virginia MacWatters; *Dapper Dan Pepper*, Ralph Dumke; *Hetty Strauss*, Ruth Matteson; and others. *Solo Dancers*, Harold Lang, Babs Heath, Margit Dekova; corps de ballet of 9 women, 5 men.

RADETZKY MARCH-FANTASIE (Act I, music by Strauss): The Dancing Girls.

MIDNIGHT WALTZ (Act I, music by Strauss): Babs Heath, Harold Lang, corps de ballet.

THE GOSSIP POLKA (Act I, music by Strauss): Heath, Lang, corps de ballet; singers.

REPRISE: YOU NEVER KNOW WHAT COMES NEXT (Act II): Lang.

REPRISE: INTO THE NIGHT (Act II): Lang, Margit Dekova, corps de ballet.

THE GRAND AND GLORIOUS FOURTH (Act II): Lang, Helen Gallagher, corps de ballet.

WALTZ FINALE (Act II, music by Strauss): Entire company.

230 CIRCUS POLKA

MUSIC: By Igor Stravinsky (1942, written at the request of George Balanchine, with the dedication 'For a young elephant').

PREMIERE: November 5, 1945, Carnegie Hall, New York. National Orchestral Society, Leon Barzin, musical director. Danced by students of the School of American Ballet.

CAST: *A Little Elephant*, Judy Kursch; corps de ballet.

NOTE: Performed once, on a program arranged by Lincoln Kirstein entitled *Adventure in Ballet*, which also included *Élégie* [245] and *Symphonie Concertante* [241], danced by students of the School of American Ballet, with Todd Bolender as guest artist.

See 202

1946

231 RESURGENCE

MUSIC: By Wolfgang Amadeus Mozart (from the Quintet in G minor, K. 516 [movements 1, 3, 4?]).

PREMIERE: January 22, 1946, Waldorf-Astoria Hotel, New York. Danced by students of the School of American Ballet.

CAST: *The Dancer*, Tanaquil Le Clercq; *4 Friends* (girls); *Children*; *The Teacher*, Elise Reiman; *The Angel*, Dorothy Bird; *Threat of Polio*, George Balanchine.

NOTE: Performed once at a March of Dimes benefit fashion show and luncheon, in which Vera Zorina and Gertrude Lawrence also participated.

232 THE NIGHT SHADOW
(also called NIGHT SHADOW, NIGHT SHADOWS, LA SOMNAMBULE, LA SONNAMBULA)

MUSIC: Music and book by Vittorio Rieti, based on themes from operas by Vincenzo Bellini (1830-35, including *La Sonnambula, I Puritani, Norma,* and *I Capuletti ed i Montecchi*).

PRODUCTION: Scenery and costumes by Dorothea Tanning. Scenery executed by E. B. Dunkel Studios; costumes executed by Karinska.

PREMIERE: February 27, 1946, Ballet Russe de Monte Carlo, City Center of Music and Drama, New York. Conductor: Emanuel Balaban.

CAST: *The Sleepwalker*, Alexandra Danilova; *The Poet*, Nicholas Magallanes; *The Coquette*, Maria Tallchief; *The Host* (Husband of the Sleepwalker), Michel Katcharoff; *Guests at the Ball*, 8 couples; ENTERTAINERS AT THE BALL: SHEPHERDS' DANCE: 2 couples; BLACKAMOORS' DANCE: Ruthanna Boris, Leon Danielian; HARLEQUIN DANCE: Marie-Jeanne; HOOP DANCE: 4 women.

NOTE: At a masked ball with entertainments, the Poet pays suit to the Coquette, who is escorted by the Host. After the guests go in to supper an apparition in white enters, a beautiful Sleepwalker. Entranced, the Poet tries to wake her, but she eludes him. The jealous Coquette informs the Host who, enraged, stabs the Poet. The Sleepwalker reappears and bears the Poet's body away.

REVISIONS: The Entertainers' dances (also called DIVERTISSEMENTS) have been changed often by the many companies that have staged the ballet. Examples in three principal companies include: Grand Ballet du Marquis de Cuevas: MOORISH DANCE sometimes substituted for BLACKAMOORS' DANCE; until about 1950, HARLEQUIN DANCE omitted; 1950, SHEPHERDS' DANCE (PASTORALE) changed from two couples to one, HOOP DANCE replaced by ACROBATS' DANCE for three (various combinations of men and women). New York City Ballet: 1960, name changed from *Night Shadow* to *La Sonnambula*, HARLEQUIN DANCE restored (for a man instead of a woman; frequently altered for various performers), ACROBATS' DANCE retained from de Cuevas production (HOOP DANCE omitted); 1967, SHEPHERDS' DANCE (PASTORALE) changed from two couples to a pas de trois for a virtuoso man and two women; 1979, BLACKAMOORS' DANCE eliminated. American Ballet Theatre, 1981: HOOP DANCE rechoreographed by John Taras as GYPSY DANCE, BLACKAMOORS' DANCE retitled DANSE EXOTIQUE.

STAGINGS: 1948, de Cuevas; 1955, Netherlands, Royal Danish; 1957, Ballets de Pâques; 1960, New York City Ballet; 1961, Ballet Rambert; 1964, Geneva; 1965, National; 1967, London Festival; 1972, Bordeaux (excerpt); 1973, San Juan; 1974, San Francisco; 1976, Paris (Sleepwalker pas de deux); 1977, Louisville, Turin; 1978, Ballet Théâtre Français; 1979, Dallas; 1980, Boston; 1981, American Ballet Theatre.

TELEVISION: 1948 (British television); 1958 (BBC, London); 1960s (Sleepwalker pas de deux, BBC); 1963 (Sleepwalker pas de deux, NBC); 1966 (excerpt, Camera Three, CBS).

See 328

233 RAYMONDA
Ballet in Three Acts

MUSIC: By Alexander Glazounov (Op. 57, produced 1898).

CHOREOGRAPHY: By George Balanchine and Alexandra Danilova after Marius Petipa.

PRODUCTION: Scenery and costumes by Alexandre Benois. Scenery executed by E. B. Dunkel Studios; costumes executed by Karinska.

PREMIÈRE: March 12, 1946, Ballet Russe de Monte Carlo, City Center of Music and Drama, New York. Conductor: Ivan Boutnikoff. Violinist: Earle Hummel. Harpist: Marjorie Call.

CAST: *Raymonda*, Alexandra Danilova; *Jean de Brienne*, Nicholas Magallanes; *Emir Abd-er-Raham, the Saracen Knight*, Nikita Talin. ACT I: *Raymonda*; *Brienne*; *Friends of Raymonda*, 3 women; *Raymonda's Page*; *Two Noblemen, Friends of Brienne*; *The White Lady, Protectress of the Castle*, Joy Williams; *The Seneschal of the Castle*, G. Alexandroff; *Peasant Girls*, Marie-Jeanne, Gertrude Tyven [Gertrude Svobodina], 8 women; *4 Knights*. ACT II: *Raymonda*; *Brienne*; *Emir*; *Emir's Favorite Slave*, Leon Danielian; *Slaves*, Pauline Goddard, 4 women, 2 men; *4 Jongleurs*; *Jongleuses*, Marie-Jeanne, 4 women. ACT III: DIVERTISSEMENTS: CZARDAS: Goddard, Stanley Zompakos, 6 couples; PAS DE TROIS: Tyven, Patricia Wilde, Danielian; PAS CLASSIQUE HONGROIS: Danilova, Magallanes; Marie-Jeanne, Ruthanna Boris, Maria Tallchief, Yvonne Chouteau, Herbert Bliss, Talin, Robert Lindgren, Ivan Ivanov (VARIATIONS: I. Tallchief; II. Chouteau; III. 4 men; IV. Marie-Jeanne; V. Boris; VI. Magallanes; VII. Danilova); FINALE: Entire cast.

NOTE: This version derives from the Petipa original at the Maryinsky as remembered by Balanchine and Danilova, abbreviated and rechoreographed by Balanchine, retaining the Petipa style. The male pas de quatre and the ballerina's variation in Act III (VARIATIONS III and VI of the PAS CLASSIQUE HONGROIS) are particularly close to the Petipa choreography. The original was a full evening's ballet, choreographed for more than two hundred performers; the Balanchine-Danilova version lasts three-quarters of an evening, omitting much of the Petipa mime, and used the entire Ballet Russe de Monte Carlo company of about forty dancers. The central pas de deux from the Act III PAS CLASSIQUE HONGROIS, usually called *Pas de Deux from*

Raymonda (and as often credited to Petipa as to Balanchine, who staged the Petipa choreography for Diaghilev in 1925), is frequently performed by a ballerina and cavalier as a concert piece.

In 1955, Balanchine choreographed *Pas de Dix* [309] for the New York City Ballet, using much of the PAS CLASSIQUE HONGROIS music, but adding a fast finale (coda). The choreography, for the most part new, retained VARIATION III exactly; VARIATION VII was retained in essence, although made more brilliant. In 1973, Balanchine incorporated this heightened VARIATION VII into *Cortège Hongrois* [384], a new work for the New York City Ballet using much of the *Pas de Dix* music.

In 1961, Balanchine choreographed a completely different work to other selections from the *Raymonda* score for the New York City Ballet: *Valses et Variations* [339, retitled *Raymonda Variations* in 1963].

REVISIONS: Ballet Russe de Monte Carlo: Numerous small revisions including omission of some Act III VARIATIONS on tour; by September, 1946, intermission between Acts I and II eliminated; 1947, White Lady and possibly other mime roles deleted; 1948, Act III given as *Divertissements from Raymonda*, although complete ballet remained in repertory.

STAGINGS (material from Act III divertissements performed under varying *Raymonda* titles [distinct from *Valses et Variations* (339, later retitled *Raymonda Variations*)]; most stagings include material from *Pas de Dix* [309]; choreography often not credited to Balanchine): 1959, Washington; 1961, American Ballet Theatre (titled *Grand Pas—Glazounov*); 1962, San Juan; 1964, National; 1967, Oklahoma City; 1969, Minnesota; 1970, North Carolina; 1972, Delta Festival; 1974, Chicago; 1975, Fairfax; 1976, Cincinnati; 1977, Louisville; 1978, Maryland; 1979, Princeton; 1980, Atlanta; 1982, Tulsa.

See 18, 309, 339, 384

234 GISELLE: ACT II GRAVE SCENE

MUSIC: By Adolphe Adam (produced 1841).

CHOREOGRAPHY: By Dimitri Romanoff, with contributions by George Balanchine and Antony Tudor.

PRODUCTION: Scenery and costumes by Eugene Berman.

PREMIERE: October 15, 1946, Ballet Theatre, Broadway Theatre, New York. Conductor: Max Goberman.

CAST: *Giselle*, Alicia Alonso; *Albrecht*, Igor Youskevitch; *Hilarion*, Stanley Herbertt; *Myrtha*, Nora Kaye; and others.

NOTE: Balanchine arranged the traditional Maryinsky staging of Giselle's grave scene in Act II: Albrecht prevents Giselle from disappearing into her grave and lays her on a bed of flowers; but Giselle sinks away, and only the flowers remain.

235 THE SPELLBOUND CHILD
(L'ENFANT ET LES SORTILÈGES)
Lyric Fantasy in Two Parts

MUSIC: By Maurice Ravel (1920-25). Libretto by Colette (translated by Lincoln Kirstein and Jane Barzin).

PRODUCTION: Scenery and costumes by Aline Bernstein. Costumes executed by Karinska. Lighting by Jean Rosenthal.

PREMIERE: November 20, 1946, Ballet Society, Central High School of Needle Trades, New York. Conductor: Leon Barzin.

CAST: Each role was performed by a singer off stage and a dancer on stage. *Child* (sung and danced), Joseph Connolly; *His Mother*; *Armchair*; *Bergère*; *Clock*; *Tea Pot*; *Chinese Cup*; *Fire*, Elise Reiman; *2 Shepherdesses*; *2 Shepherds*; *Princess*, Tanaquil Le Clercq; *Teacher Arithmetic*; *10 Numbers*; *Black Cat*, William Dollar; *White Cat*, Georgia Hiden; *Big Frog*; *4 Little Frogs*; *Tree* (sung only); *7 Dragonflies*; *Nightingale*; *Bat*; *Squirrel*; *Little Squirrel*; *Owl*.

NOTE: Presented with *The Four Temperaments* on the initial program of Ballet Society, the membership-supported non-profit organization formed by Balanchine and Lincoln Kirstein.

OTHER VERSIONS: 1925, Opéra de Monte-Carlo (*L'Enfant et les Sortilèges*, danced by Diaghilev's Ballets Russes). 1975, New York City Ballet (*L'Enfant et les Sortilèges*, Ravel Festival). 1981, for the PBS television series Dance in America (*The Spellbound Child/L'Enfant et les Sortilèges*).

See 48*, 390, 416

236 THE FOUR TEMPERAMENTS

MUSIC: By Paul Hindemith (*Theme with Four Variations [According to the Four Temperaments]* for string orchestra and piano, 1940, commissioned by George Balanchine).

PRODUCTION: Scenery and costumes by Kurt Seligmann. Lighting by Jean Rosenthal.

PREMIERE: November 20, 1946, Ballet Society, Central High School of Needle Trades, New York. Conductor: Leon Barzin. Pianist: Nicholas Kopeikine.

CAST: A. THEME: 1. Beatrice Tompkins, José Martinez; 2. Elise Reiman, Lew Christensen; 3. Gisella Caccialanza, Francisco Moncion; B. FIRST VARIATION: MELANCHOLIC: William Dollar; Georgia Hiden, Rita Karlin, 4 women; C. SECOND VARIATION: SANGUINIC: Mary Ellen Moylan, Fred Danieli, 4 women; D. THIRD VARIATION: PHLEGMATIC: Todd Bolender, 4 women; E. FOURTH VARIATION: CHOLERIC: Tanaquil Le Clercq, 3 THEME couples, Moylan, Danieli; Dollar, Bolender, entire cast.

NOTE: The three main themes are stated in the opening section by three successive couples. The variations are named after the four temperaments of medieval cosmology. The score, commissioned by Balanchine and completed in 1940, was partially choreographed during the 1941 American Ballet Caravan tour of South America for an entirely different ballet titled *The Cave of Sleep*; Pavel Tchelitchew created complete costumes and décor, but the work was never produced.

REVISIONS: The original MELANCHOLIC VARIATION was more acrobatic than it later became. Balanchine has made numerous changes in the finale, the most radical in 1977 for the Dance in America telecast; most television changes were retained in the stage version.

NEW PRODUCTIONS BY BALANCHINE COMPANIES: New York City Ballet: 1951, danced in practice clothes without scenery; 1964, lighting by David Hays.

STAGINGS: 1960, Netherlands, Royal Swedish; 1962, Hamburg, La Scala; 1963, Paris, Royal Danish; 1964, National, Vienna; 1966, Düsseldorf; 1967, Rome; 1968, Boston, Norway; 1969, Pennsylvania, National Ballet of Canada; 1970, Berlin, Geneva; 1973, Royal; 1974, San Francisco, Frankfurt, Les Grands Ballets Canadiens; 1975, Ballet West; 1976, Chicago Lyric Opera, Ballet Théâtre Contemporain, Royal Ballet

Touring, Strasbourg; 1977, Gothenburg, Zagreb Zürich; 1978,
Pacific Northwest, East Berlin; 1979, Dance Theatre of Harlem; 1980,
New York Dance Theatre (FIRST THEME), Munich; 1982, Los Angeles.

TELEVISION: 1962 (Dutch television); 1963 (excerpt, NBC); 1964
(L'Heure du Concert, CBC, Montreal); 1977 (Dance in America, PBS).

1947

237 RENARD

Ballet-Burlesque for Singers and Dancers

MUSIC: Music and libretto by Igor Stravinsky (*Le Renard*, 1915-16,
commissioned by Princesse Edmond de Polignac). Derived from a tale
by Alexander Afanasiev. English version by Harvey Officer.

PRODUCTION: Scenery and costumes by Esteban Francés. Scenery
painted by Centre Studios under the supervision of Gilbert Hancox,
and built by Martin Turner; costumes executed by Karinska. Lighting
by Jean Rosenthal.

PREMIERE: January 13, 1947, Ballet Society, Hunter College Playhouse,
New York. Conductor: Leon Barzin. Singers: William Hess, William
Upshaw (tenors); William Gephart, Leon Lishner (baritones).

CAST: *The Fox*, Todd Bolender; *The Rooster*, Lew Christensen; *The Cat*,
Fred Danieli; *The Ram*, John Taras.

NOTE: *Le Renard* was first choreographed by Bronislava Nijinska for
Diaghilev's Ballets Russes in 1922, and rechoreographed for that
company by Serge Lifar in 1929. Balanchine's version was first presented
on the second Ballet Society program, which also included the premiere
of *Divertimento*.

REVISIONS: 1955, San Francisco Ballet: Rechoreographed by Lew
Christensen, based on Balanchine's version.

238 DIVERTIMENTO

MUSIC: By Alexei Haieff (*Divertimento* for small orchestra, 1944).

PRODUCTION: Lighting by Jean Rosenthal.

PREMIERE: January 13, 1947, Ballet Society, Hunter College Playhouse, New York. Conductor: Leon Barzin.

CAST: Mary Ellen Moylan, Francisco Moncion; Gisella Caccialanza, Tanaquil Le Clercq, Elise Reiman, Beatrice Tompkins, Todd Bolender, Lew Christensen, Fred Danieli, John Taras.

PRELUDE; ARIA; SCHERZO; LULLABY; FINALE.

NOTE: Choreographed for a leading couple and four supporting couples, each dancer a principal with solos, and featuring a blues pas de deux. The ballet combines popular American dance idioms and modern concert dance with classic ballet.

239 THE CHOCOLATE SOLDIER
Operetta in Three Acts

MUSIC AND BOOK: Music by Oscar Straus. Book by Rudolph Bernauer and Leopold Jacobson. American version by Stanislaus Stange. Revised book by Guy Bolton. Revised and additional lyrics by Bernard Hanighen. Orchestrations by Jay Blackton.

CHOREOGRAPHY: By George Balanchine. Assistant to Mr. Balanchine: Edward Brinkman.

PRODUCTION: Produced by J. H. Del Bondio and Hans Bartsch for the Delvan Company. Directed by Felix Brentano. Scenery and lighting by Jo Mielziner. Costumes by Lucinda Ballard. Scenery built by Martin Turner Studios and painted by Studio Alliance; costumes executed by Eaves Costume Company.

PREMIERE: March 12, 1947, New Century Theatre, New York. Conductor: Jay Blackton. (Out-of-town preview: February 6, Forrest Theatre, Philadelphia.)

CAST: *Nadina*, Frances McCann; *Mascha*, Gloria Hamilton; *Bumerli*, Keith Andes; *Popoff*, Billy Gilbert; and others. *Premiere Danseuse*, Mary Ellen Moylan; *Premier Danseur*, Francisco Moncion; 7 Ladies of the Ballet, 7 Gentlemen of the Ballet.

SLAVIC DANCE (Act II): Mary Ellen Moylan, Francisco Moncion, corps de ballet.

WALTZ BALLET (Act III): Moylan, Moncion, corps de ballet.

AFTER TODAY GALA POLKA (Act III): Moylan, Moncion, corps de ballet.

240 LE PALAIS DE CRISTAL (later called SYMPHONY IN C)

MUSIC: By Georges Bizet (Symphony No. 1 in C major, 1855).

PRODUCTION: Scenery and costumes by Leonor Fini.

PREMIERE: July 28, 1947, Paris Opéra Ballet, Théâtre National de l'Opéra, Paris. Conductor: Roger Desormière.

CAST: FIRST MOVEMENT (ALLEGRO VIVO): Lycette Darsonval, Alexandre Kalioujny; SECOND MOVEMENT (ADAGIO): Tamara Toumanova, Roger Ritz; THIRD MOVEMENT (ALLEGRO VIVACE): Micheline Bardin, Michel Renault; FOURTH MOVEMENT (ALLEGRO VIVACE): Madeleine Lafon, Max Bozzoni (in each movement: 2 demi-solo couples, 6 women); FINALE: Entire cast.

NOTE: During six months as guest ballet master for the Paris Opéra, Balanchine choreographed Bizet's Symphony in C, and staged *Apollo*, *Serenade* and *Le Baiser de la Fée*. *Le Palais de Cristal* was staged for Ballet Society as *Symphony in C* [244] the following year, and was presented with *Concerto Barocco* [195] and *Orpheus* [246] at the first performance of the New York City Ballet, October 11, 1948. When the Paris Opéra Ballet performed this work at the Bolshoi Theater, Moscow, in June 1958, it became the first ballet made by Balanchine in the West to be seen in the Soviet Union since his departure in 1924.

REVISIONS: 1948, Ballet Society (titled *Symphony in C*): Original corps of 48 reduced, with doubling of corps members from movement to movement due to limited size of company. New York City Ballet: By 1968, larger company eliminated duplication of cast, allowing full finale; 8 corps members in FIRST MOVEMENT instead of 6; by 1971, 8 corps members in FOURTH MOVEMENT for total cast of 52; 1971?, musical repeat in FOURTH MOVEMENT, danced by FIRST MOVEMENT cast in exact repetition of FOURTH MOVEMENT cast steps (cut entirely at various times), completely rechoreographed for FIRST MOVEMENT cast. Male solos in FIRST and THIRD MOVEMENTS rechoreographed several times for various performers.

STAGINGS (in America, and usually in other countries, titled *Symphony in C*): 1948, Ballet Society, New York City Ballet; 1952, Royal Danish; 1955, La Scala; 1960, Royal Swedish; 1961, San Francisco; 1962, Dutch National; 1965, Garden State (FIRST, SECOND and THIRD MOVEMENTS), Hamburg; 1967, Ballet of Los Angeles, Boston, Pennsylvania, Norway; 1968, Atlanta, Ballet West, Memphis (SECOND MOVEMENT); 1969, Berlin; 1970, Geneva, Kirov (THIRD MOVEMENT); 1972, Rome, Vienna; 1973, Tokyo; 1975, Munich; 1976, East Berlin, Stuttgart; 1977, Hungary; 1978, Zürich.

TELEVISION: 1963 (SECOND and FOURTH MOVEMENTS, CBS); ca. 1963 (Dutch television).

See 244

241 SYMPHONIE CONCERTANTE
Classic Ballet in One Act

MUSIC: By Wolfgang Amadeus Mozart (Symphonie Concertante in E-flat for violin, viola and orchestra, K. 364, 1779).

PRODUCTION: Scenery and costumes by James Stewart Morcom. Costumes executed by Edith Lutyens. Lighting by Jean Rosenthal.

PREMIERE: November 12, 1947, Ballet Society, City Center of Music and Drama, New York. Conductor: Leon Barzin. Violinist: Hugo Fiorato. Violist: Karl Braunstein.

CAST: ALLEGRO MAESTOSO: Tanaquil Le Clercq, Maria Tallchief, 22 women; ANDANTE: Le Clercq, Tallchief, Todd Bolender, 6 women; PRESTO: Le Clercq, Tallchief, Bolender, 22 women.

NOTE: Created for students a year before its professional premiere to show the relationship between a classical symphony and classical dance. Originally presented (with *Élégie* [245] and *Circus Polka* [230]) on the program of the National Orchestral Society entitled *Adventure in Ballet*, November 5, 1945, danced by students of the School of American Ballet, with Todd Bolender as guest artist. The scenery for the Ballet Society production was a literal transcription of a design by the Baroque artist Giuseppe Galli Bibiena.

242 THEME AND VARIATIONS

MUSIC: By Peter Ilyitch Tschaikovsky (final movement of Suite No. 3 for orchestra in G major, 1884).

PRODUCTION: Scenery and costumes by Woodman Thompson. Scenery executed by Eugene B. Dunkel Studios; costumes executed by Karinska.

PREMIERE: November 26, 1947, Ballet Theatre, City Center of Music and Drama, New York. Conductor: Max Goberman.

CAST: Alicia Alonso, Igor Youskevitch; Anna Cheselka, Melissa Hayden, Paula Lloyd, Cynthia Riseley, Fernando Alonso, Eric Braun, Fernand Nault, Zachary Solov; 8 women, 8 men.

NOTE: An intensive development of the classic ballet lexicon. In 1970, incorporated (with minor revisions) as the fourth movement of the full *Suite No. 3* [369, later called *Tschaikovsky Suite No. 3*].

REVISIONS: Choreography for male principal changed several times for various performers.

STAGINGS: 1960, New York City Ballet; 1967, Mexico; 1969, Les Grands Ballets Canadiens; 1970, Cuba (pas de deux); 1971, Geneva; 1981, Dutch National.

TELEVISION: 1978 (American Ballet Theatre: Live from Lincoln Center, PBS).

See 330, 369

1948

243 THE TRIUMPH OF BACCHUS AND ARIADNE
Ballet-Cantata

MUSIC: By Vittorio Rieti (1947, commissioned by Ballet Society). Words from a Florentine carnival song by Lorenzo de' Medici.

PRODUCTION: Scenery and costumes by Corrado Cagli.

PREMIERE: February 9, 1948, Ballet Society, City Center of Music and

Drama, New York. Conductor: Leon Barzin. Singers: Ellen Faull, soprano; Leon Lishner, bass; chorus of 40.

CAST: INTRODUCTION (PRELUDE AND CHORUS): *Major Domo*, Lew Christensen; *Spectators*, 6 couples; BACCHUS AND ARIADNE (CHORUS): *Bacchus*, Nicholas Magallanes; *Ariadne*, Tanaquil Le Clercq; SATYRS AND NYMPHS (TARANTELLA WITH CHORUS): *Satyr*, Herbert Bliss; *Nymph*, Marie-Jeanne; *6 Satyrs, 6 Nymphs*; SILENUS (ARIA FOR SOLO BASS): *Silenus*, Charles Laskey; MIDAS (CHORUS): *Midas*, Francisco Moncion; *2 Discoboles*; *Little Girl*, Claudia Hall; *Young Girl*, Pat McBride; INVITATION TO THE DANCE (ARIA FOR SOLO SOPRANO); BACCHANALE (CHORUS): Ensemble.

NOTE: The work consists of songs and pageantry, and dance episodes celebrating Youth and Age and sacred and profane love, in an Italianate setting. At the premiere, the singers were visible in the windows of the scenic façade; in later performances they sang from the orchestra pit.

244 SYMPHONY IN C
Classic Ballet

MUSIC: By Georges Bizet (Symphony No. 1 in C major, 1855).

PRODUCTION: Lighting by Jean Rosenthal.

PREMIERE: March 22, 1948, Ballet Society, City Center of Music and Drama, New York. Conductor: Leon Barzin.

CAST: FIRST MOVEMENT (ALLEGRO VIVO): Maria Tallchief, Nicholas Magallanes; SECOND MOVEMENT (ADAGIO): Tanaquil Le Clercq, Francisco Moncion; THIRD MOVEMENT (ALLEGRO VIVACE): Beatrice Tompkins, Herbert Bliss; FOURTH MOVEMENT (ALLEGRO VIVACE): Elise Reiman, John Taras (in each movement, 2 demi-solo couples, 6 women; FINALE: Entire cast.

NOTE: Originally presented by the Paris Opéra Ballet, 1947, titled *Le Palais de Cristal*. Presented with *Concerto Barocco* [195] and *Orpheus* [246] at the first performance of the New York City Ballet, October 11, 1948.

NEW PRODUCTIONS BY BALANCHINE COMPANIES: 1950, New York City Ballet: Costumes by Karinska.

See 240*

245 ÉLÉGIE

MUSIC: By Igor Stravinsky (*Élégie-Elegy* for solo viola, 1944).

PREMIERE: April 28, 1948, Ballet Society, City Center of Music and Drama, New York. Violist: Emanuel Vardi.

CAST: Tanaquil Le Clercq, Pat McBride.

NOTE: As described by the choreographer, the music is reflected through the interlaced bodies of two dancers rooted to a central spot on the stage; referred to by the composer as a kind of preview of the *Orpheus* pas de deux. Originally presented (with *Symphonie Concertante* [241] and *Circus Polka* [230]) on the program of the National Orchestral Society entitled *Adventure in Ballet*, November 5, 1945, danced by students of the School of American Ballet, with Todd Bolender as guest artist. The Ballet Society premiere was part of an evening which included the premiere of *Orpheus*.

In 1966, and in 1982 for the New York City Ballet Stravinsky Centennial Celebration, Balanchine choreographed new works to this music, also called *Élégie*.

See 355, 423

246 ORPHEUS

Ballet in Three Scenes

MUSIC: By Igor Stravinsky (1947, commissioned by Ballet Society).

PRODUCTION: Scenery and costumes by Isamu Noguchi. Lighting by Jean Rosenthal.

PREMIERE: April 28, 1948, Ballet Society, City Center of Music and Drama, New York. Conductor: Igor Stravinsky.

CAST: *Orpheus*, Nicholas Magallanes; *Dark Angel*, Francisco Moncion; *Eurydice*, Maria Tallchief; *Leader of the Furies*, Beatrice Tompkins; *Leader of the Bacchantes*, Tanaquil Le Clercq; *Apollo*, Herbert Bliss; *Pluto*; *Satyr*; *Nature Spirits*; *Friends to Orpheus*; *Furies*, 9 women; *Lost Souls*, 7 men; *Bacchantes*, 8 women.

Synopsis of the action (from Stravinsky's score): SCENE 1: 1. Orpheus weeps for Eurydice. He stands motionless, with his back to the audience. Some friends pass, bringing presents and offering him sympathy.

2. AIR DE DANSE. 3. DANCE OF THE ANGEL OF DEATH. The Angel leads Orpheus to Hades. 4. *Interlude*. The Angel and Orpheus reappear in the gloom of Tartarus.

SCENE 2: 5. PAS DE FURIES (their agitation and their threats). 6a. AIR DE DANSE (Orpheus). 7. *Interlude*. The tormented souls in Tartarus stretch out their fettered arms toward Orpheus and implore him to continue his song of consolation. 6b. AIR DE DANSE (concluded). Orpheus continues his air. 8. PAS D'ACTION. Hades, moved by the song of Orpheus, grows calm. The Furies surround him, bind his eyes, and return Eurydice to him. (Veiled curtain.) 9. PAS DE DEUX (Orpheus and Eurydice before the curtain). Orpheus tears the bandage from his eyes. Eurydice falls dead. 10. *Interlude* (veiled curtain, behind which the décor of the first scene is placed). 11. PAS D'ACTION. The Bacchantes attack Orpheus, seize him, and tear him to pieces.

SCENE 3: 12. ORPHEUS' APOTHEOSIS. Apollo appears. He wrests the lyre from Orpheus and raises his song heavenwards.

NOTE: In composing *Orpheus*, Stravinsky worked in close collaboration with Balanchine. The ballet led Morton Baum, chairman of the Executive Committee of the City Center of Music and Drama, to invite Ballet Society to become its permanent ballet company: the New York City Ballet. *Orpheus* was presented with *Concerto Barocco* [195] and *Symphony in C* [244] at the first performance of the New York City Ballet, October 11, 1948.

REVISIONS: 1980, New York City Ballet: DANCE OF THE FURIES slightly revised by Peter Martins.

NEW PRODUCTIONS BY BALANCHINE COMPANIES: 1972, New York City Ballet (Stravinsky Festival): Designs rescaled by Noguchi for the New York State Theater.

STAGINGS: 1962, Hamburg; 1964, La Scala; 1974, Paris.

TELEVISION: 1956 (pas de deux, CBS); 1960 (CBC, Montreal).

247 PAS DE TROIS CLASSIQUE

MUSIC: By Léon Minkus (from *Paquita*, 1881).

PRODUCTION: Costumes by Jean Robier.

PREMIERE: August 9, 1948, Grand Ballet du Marquis de Cuevas, Royal Opera House, Covent Garden, London.

CAST: Rosella Hightower, Marjorie Tallchief, André Eglevsky.

NOTE: Balanchine considers his *Pas de Trois Classique* essentially a restaging of Petipa's pas de trois from *Paquita*. He changed some steps for the 1951 New York City Ballet version; the ballet possibly contains additional original Balanchine choreography, as is usual in his remounting of the classics.

REVISIONS: 1951, New York City Ballet: Variation created for Marjorie Tallchief revised.

STAGINGS (variant names include *Minkus Pas de Trois* and *Paquita Pas de Trois*; most stagings incorporate 1951 revisions; choreography credited to André Eglevsky in some later stagings): 1951, New York City Ballet; 1954, Rio de Janeiro; 1955, Ballet Russe de Monte Carlo; 1958, Vienna; 1961, Eglevsky; 1963, San Juan; 1965, Grand Ballet Classique de France, Hamburg, Uruguay; 1967, Joffrey; by 1967, Ballets Janine Charrat; 1968, Harkness, London Festival; 1970, Minnesota, Bordeaux; 1971, American Ballet Theatre, Newburgh, Paris; 1972, New Jersey; 1974, Augusta, Israel; 1975, Dover; 1976, Chicago Lyric Opera; 1979, Bernhard; 1982, Delta Festival.

TELEVISION: 1963 (Bell Telephone Hour, NBC).

See 276

248 CARMEN

Opera in Four Acts by Georges Bizet
ACT II TAVERN SCENE BALLET

PREMIERE: October 10, 1948, New York City Opera, City Center of Music and Drama, New York. Danced by New York City Ballet. Conductor: Jean Morel.

CAST: Maria Tallchief, Francisco Moncion, 2 women.

NOTE: Balanchine's first work for the New York City Ballet, which for two seasons served as resident ballet company for the New York City Opera.

See 38, 127, 155

249 WHERE'S CHARLEY?

Musical Comedy in Two Acts and Nine Scenes

MUSIC AND BOOK: Music and lyrics by Frank Loesser. Book by George Abbott, based on the play *Charley's Aunt*, by Brandon Thomas. Orchestrations by Ted Royal, Hans Spialek and Phil Lang. Vocal arrangements and direction by Gerry Dolin.

CHOREOGRAPHY: By George Balanchine, assisted by Fred Danieli.

PRODUCTION: Produced by Cy Feuer and Ernest H. Martin in association with Gwen Rickard. Directed by George Abbott. Scenery and costumes by David Ffolkes. Scenery executed by Studio Alliance; costumes executed by Brooks Costume Company.

PREMIERE: October 11, 1948, St. James Theatre, New York. Conductor: Max Goberman. (Out-of-town preview: September 13, Forrest Theatre, Philadelphia.)

CAST: *Charley Wykeham*, Ray Bolger; *Amy Spettigue*, Allyn McLerie; *Jack Chesney*, Byron Palmer; *Kitty Verdun*, Doretta Morrow; and others. Dancers: 9 women, 9 men.

THE NEW ASHMOLEAN MARCHING SOCIETY AND STUDENTS' CONSERVATORY BAND (Act I, Scene 2): Byron Palmer, Allyn McLerie, Doretta Morrow, Bobby Harrell, ensemble.

MAKE A MIRACLE (Act I, Scene 3): Ray Bolger, McLerie.

PERNAMBUCO (Act I, Scene 4): Bolger, McLerie, ensemble.

ONCE IN LOVE WITH AMY (Act II, Scene 2): Bolger.

AT THE RED ROSE COTILLION (Act II, Scene 4): Bolger, McLerie, ensemble.

OTHER PRODUCTIONS: January 21, 1951, Broadway Theatre, New York. Basically unchanged; ONCE IN LOVE WITH AMY performed with audience participation and expanded dance sequence.

250 CONCERTO BAROCCO

MUSIC: By Johann Sebastian Bach (Double Violin Concerto in D minor, B.W.V. 1043).

PRODUCTION: Scenery and costumes by Eugene Berman, executed by Centre Studios and Karinska under the supervision of George Balanchine. Lighting by Jean Rosenthal.

PREMIERE: October 11, 1948, New York City Ballet, City Center of Music and Drama, New York. Conductor: Leon Barzin.

CAST: Marie-Jeanne, Francisco Moncion; Ruth Gilbert; 8 women.

NOTE: Originally presented by American Ballet Caravan, Rio de Janeiro, 1941. *Concerto Barocco* was the first ballet danced by the New York City Ballet in its inaugural performance, October 11, 1948, which also included *Orpheus* [246] and *Symphony in C* [244].

See 195*

251 THE MARRIAGE OF FIGARO (LE NOZZE DI FIGARO)

Opera in Four Acts by Wolfgang Amadeus Mozart
ACT III FANDANGO

PREMIERE: October 14, 1948, New York City Opera, City Center of Music and Drama, New York. Danced by New York City Ballet. Conductor: Joseph Rosenstock.

CAST: Corps de ballet.

252 LA TRAVIATA

Opera in Four Acts by Giuseppe Verdi
ACT III BALLET

PREMIERE: October 17, 1948, New York City Opera, City Center of Music and Drama, New York. Danced by New York City Ballet. Conductor: Jean Morel.

CAST: Marie-Jeanne, Herbert Bliss, 4 women.

See 67, 123, 150

253 DON GIOVANNI

Opera in Two Acts and Six Scenes by Wolfgang Amadeus Mozart
ACT II DANCE

PREMIERE: October 21, 1948, New York City Opera, City Center of

Music and Drama, New York. Danced by New York City Ballet. Conductor: Laszlo Halasz.

CAST: Corps de ballet.

See 81, 181

254 SERENADE

MUSIC: By Peter Ilyitch Tschaikovsky (Serenade in C for string orchestra, Op. 48, 1880, with third and fourth movements reversed).

PRODUCTION: Lighting by Jean Rosenthal.

PREMIERE: October 26, 1948, New York City Ballet, City Center of Music and Drama, New York. Conductor: Leon Barzin.

CAST: Marie-Jeanne, Pat McBride, Herbert Bliss, Nicholas Magallanes; 4 female demi-soloists; 12 women, 4 men.

   SONATINA; WALTZ; TEMA RUSSO; ELEGY.

NOTE: Originally presented by the American Ballet, New York, 1935.

See 141*, 193

255 AÏDA

Opera in Three Acts by Giuseppe Verdi
ACT II, SCENE 2 TRIUMPHAL BALLET

PREMIERE: October 28, 1948, New York City Opera, City Center of Music and Drama, New York. Danced by New York City Ballet. Conductor: Laszlo Halasz.

CAST: Maria Tallchief, Nicholas Magallanes, 6 women, 4 men.

NOTE: In addition to the Scene 2 ballet, reviews mention the Ritual of the Priestesses and dance entertainment for Amneris.

See 126, 152, 226

256 EUGEN ONEGIN
Opera in Three Acts and Six Scenes by Peter Ilyitch Tschaikovsky
INCIDENTAL SOCIAL DANCES

PREMIERE: November 7, 1948, New York City Opera, City Center of
Music and Drama, New York. Danced by New York City Ballet.
Conductor: Laszlo Halasz.

CAST: 4 couples.

See 341

257 THE MADWOMAN OF CHAILLOT
(LA FOLLE DE CHAILLOT)
Play by Jean Giraudoux, adapted by Maurice Valency

MUSIC: By Albert Hague (mazurka, Act I) and Alexander Haas ('La
Belle Polonaise,' Act II), arranged by Alexander Haas.

PRODUCTION: Produced and directed by Alfred de Liagre, Jr. Movement
direction by George Balanchine (uncredited). Scenery and costumes
by Christian Bérard (from the Paris production, 1945). American
reproductions of original French costumes executed by Karinska.
Lighting by Samuel Leve.

PREMIERE: December 27, 1948, Belasco Theatre, New York. Conductor:
Alexander Haas.

CAST: *Countess Aurelia, the Madwoman of Chaillot,* Martita Hunt; *The
Ragpicker,* John Carradine; *Mme Constance, the Madwoman of Passy,*
Estelle Winwood; *The Prospector,* Vladimir Sokoloff; *The President,*
Clarence Derwent; *Mlle Gabrielle, the Madwoman of St. Sulpice,* Nydia
Westman; *Mme Josephine, the Madwoman of La Concorde,* Doris Rich;
The Deaf Mute, Martin Kosleck; and others.

1949

258 TROUBLED ISLAND

Opera in Three Acts by William Grant Still

ACT II, SCENE 2 COURT BALLET

PREMIERE: March 31, 1949, New York City Opera, City Center of Music and Drama, New York. Danced by the company of Jean-Léon Destiné. Conductor: Laszlo Halasz.

NOTE: World premiere. The printed program does not list dancers.

259 PRINCESS AURORA

MUSIC: By Peter Ilyitch Tschaikovsky (excerpts from *The Sleeping Beauty*, produced 1890, most from Act III).

CHOREOGRAPHY: Originally choreographed by Marius Petipa; staged and adapted by George Balanchine. Choreography of the THREE IVANS by Bronislava Nijinska.

PRODUCTION: Scenery by Michel Baronoff and costumes by Barbara Karinska after designs by Léon Bakst (1921).

PREMIERE: April 2, 1949, Ballet Theatre, Opera House, Chicago. Conductor: Max Goberman.

CAST: *Princess Aurora*, Nana Gollner; *Prince Charming*, John Kriza; *The Queen*, Charlyne Baker; *The King*, Peter Rudley; *Master of Ceremonies*, Edward Caton; *Six Fairies*, Lillian Lanese, Janet Reed, Dorothy Scott, Ruth Ann Koesun, Diana Adams, Mary Burr (the first five danced VARIATIONS I-V); 6 *Attendants*; PAS DE TROIS: Norma Vance, Jocelyn Vollmar, Wallace Seibert; BLUEBIRD AND THE PRINCESS: Maria Tallchief, Igor Youskevitch; THREE IVANS: Eric Braun, Fernand Nault, Nicolas Orloff; 4 *Pages*; *Ensemble*, 4 women, 4 men.

NOTE: The printed program indicates that this selection of excerpts from *The Sleeping Beauty* included the FAIRY VARIATIONS from the PROLOGUE and divertissements from Act III. Balanchine staged Petipa's choreography of the BLUEBIRD pas de deux, but altered much of the rest. A duet (presumably for two fairies, which would have given each of the six Fairies a variation) is mentioned in a review by Lillian Moore (*Dancing Times*, June 1949, p. 497); printed programs list only five solo variations.

REVISIONS: 1950, Ballet Theatre: One, later two, FAIRY VARIATIONS omitted.

See 65, 225, 281, 404, 418

260 THE TALES OF HOFFMANN
(LES CONTES D'HOFFMANN)
Opera in Three Acts with Prologue and Epilogue by Jacques Offenbach
BALLET

PREMIERE: April 6, 1949, New York City Opera, City Center of Music and Drama, New York. Danced by New York City Ballet. Conductor: Jean Morel.

NOTE: The printed program does not list dances or dancers.

See 58, 112

261 CINDERELLA
Made for Television

MUSIC: By Peter Ilyitch Tschaikovsky (excerpts from Symphonies No. 1 [1866, revised 1874] and 2 [1872, revised 1879]; adagio from Symphony No. 3 [1875]).

PRODUCTION: Produced by Paul Belanger.

FIRST TELECAST: April 25, 1949, Through the Crystal Ball, CBS.

CAST: *Cinderella,* Tanaquil Le Clercq; *Fairy,* Jimmy Savo; *Ugly Sisters,* Ruth Sobotka, Pat McBride; *Prince,* Herbert Bliss; corps de ballet.

262 DON QUIXOTE and SWAN LAKE (BLACK SWAN) PAS DE DEUX

During the 1949 Ballet Theatre spring tour and New York season, Balanchine staged and to some degree altered the pas de deux from

Don Quixote (Minkus, choreographed by Petipa), danced by Maria Tallchief and John Kriza, and the Black Swan pas de deux from *Swan Lake* Act III (Tschaikovsky, choreographed by Petipa), danced by Tallchief and Igor Youskevitch.

See 75, 191, 285, 331, 367

263 LA MORT DU CYGNE

MUSIC: By Camille Saint-Saëns (*Le Cygne* [cello solo] from *Le Carnaval des Animaux: Fantaisie Zoologique* for small orchestra, 1886).

CHOREOGRAPHY: Choreographed by Michel Fokine (1905?); staged by George Balanchine.

PREMIERE: June 20, 1949, Grand Ballet du Marquis de Cuevas, Stadsschouwburg, Amsterdam.

CAST: Tamara Toumanova.

NOTE: Performed at the Holland Festival, 1949.

See 16

264 FIREBIRD

MUSIC: By Igor Stravinsky (1909-10, dedicated to Andrei Rimsky-Korsakov [third ballet suite, for reduced orchestra, 1945]). Derived from ancient Russian legends and fairy tales.

PRODUCTION: Scenery and costumes by Marc Chagall (from the Ballet Theatre production, 1945). Scenery executed by Eugene B. Dunkel Studios; costumes executed by Edith Lutyens. Lighting by Jean Rosenthal.

PREMIERE: November 27, 1949, New York City Ballet, City Center of Music and Drama, New York. Conductor: Leon Barzin.

CAST: *Firebird*, Maria Tallchief; *Prince Ivan*, Francisco Moncion; *Prince's Bride*, Pat McBride; *Kastchei*, Edward Bigelow; *Chief Monster*, Beatrice Tompkins; *8 Maidens, 19 Monsters*.

NOTE: Balanchine's 1949 production of *Firebird* was made with the assistance of Stravinsky. Balanchine had seen Lopukhov's production in Petrograd in 1921, and during his years with Diaghilev's Ballets

Russes performed Kastchei in Fokine's ballet, which was the original from 1910; Lincoln Kirstein saw him dance this role in 1926.

REVISIONS: New York City Ballet: 1970, largely rechoreographed; choreography for Monsters by Jerome Robbins; 1972 (Stravinsky Festival), choreography for Firebird made more stately, with few dance steps; new costume with long train and large wings (modified in 1974); 1980, revised choreography for Firebird incorporating some passages from 1949 version; gold costume and lighter train.

NEW PRODUCTIONS BY BALANCHINE COMPANIES: New York City Ballet: 1970, new scenery from Chagall designs executed under the supervision of Volodia Odinokov, costumes by Karinska, lighting by Ronald Bates; 1972, 1980, new costumes for Firebird by Karinska (uncredited on programs).

STAGINGS (based on 1949 version): 1965, Ballet of Los Angeles; 1981, Chicago City; 1982, Kansas City.

TELEVISION: 1952? (pas de deux, BBC, London); 1954 (pas de deux, NBC); 1956 (BERCEUSE, CBS).

265 BOURRÉE FANTASQUE

MUSIC: By Emmanuel Chabrier (*Marche Joyeuse*, 1888; *Bourrée Fantasque*, 1891; 'Prélude' from the opera *Gwendoline*, 1885; 'Fête Polonaise' from the opera *Le Roi Malgré Lui*, 1887).

PRODUCTION: Costumes by Karinska.

PREMIERE: December 1, 1949, New York City Ballet, City Center of Music and Drama, New York. Conductor: Leon Barzin.

CAST: BOURRÉE FANTASQUE: Tanaquil Le Clercq, Jerome Robbins; 8 women, 4 men; PRÉLUDE: Maria Tallchief, Nicholas Magallanes; 2 female demi-soloists; 8 women; FÊTE POLONAISE: Janet Reed, Herbert Bliss; 2 demi-solo couples; 6 women, 4 men; followed by full cast.

STAGINGS: 1960, London Festival; 1961, La Scala; 1963, Paris, Royal Danish; 1981, American Ballet Theatre.

See 403

266 [PAS DE DEUX]
Made for Television

In the late 1940s or early 1950s, Balanchine choreographed a pas de deux for Tanaquil Le Clercq and Nicholas Magallanes, telecast by CBC Television, Montreal. The ballet had elements of the *Coppélia* story.

See 291, 387

1950

267 PRODIGAL SON
Ballet in Three Scenes

MUSIC: By Sergei Prokofiev (Op. 46, 1928-29, commissioned by Serge Diaghilev, 1927). Book by Boris Kochno (after the biblical parable).

PRODUCTION: Lighting by Jean Rosenthal.

PREMIERE: February 23, 1950, New York City Ballet, City Center of Music and Drama, New York. Conductor: Leon Barzin.

CAST: *Prodigal Son*, Jerome Robbins; *Siren*, Maria Tallchief; *Father*, Michael Arshansky; *Servants to the Prodigal Son*, Frank Hobi, Herbert Bliss; *Two Sisters*, Jillana, Francesca Mosarra; *Drinking Companions*, 9 men.

NOTE: Originally presented by Diaghilev's Ballets Russes, Paris, 1929, titled *Le Fils Prodigue*. The New York City Ballet production was danced in improvised costumes from February 1950 until July, when scenery and costumes were added for the Company's first London season, recreated by Esteban Francés from Rouault sketches in the Wadsworth Atheneum, Hartford, Connecticut. For the 1978 Dance in America television production, the costume for the Prodigal Son was redesigned following that of the original Diaghilev production and was used for a limited period in staged performances. From time to time Balanchine appeared in the role of the Father.

See 94*

268 PAS DE DEUX ROMANTIQUE

MUSIC: By Carl Maria von Weber (Concertino for clarinet and orchestra, 1811).

PRODUCTION: Costumes by Robert Stevenson, executed by Angie Costumes, Inc.

PREMIERE: March 3, 1950, New York City Ballet, City Center of Music and Drama, New York. Conductor: Leon Barzin.

CAST: Janet Reed, Herbert Bliss.

269 JONES BEACH

MUSIC: By Jurriaan Andriessen (*Berkshire Symphonies* [Symphony No. 1], 1949, commissioned by the Royal Government of the Netherlands, dedicated to Serge Koussevitsky).

CHOREOGRAPHY: By George Balanchine and Jerome Robbins.

PRODUCTION: Bathing suits by Jantzen.

PREMIERE: March 9, 1950, New York City Ballet, City Center of Music and Drama, New York. Conductor: Leon Barzin.

CAST: SUNDAY [ALLEGRO]: Melissa Hayden, Yvonne Mounsey, Beatrice Tompkins, Herbert Bliss, Frank Hobi, 22 women, 9 men; RESCUE FROM DROWNING [ANDANTE]: Tanaquil Le Clercq, Nicholas Magallanes, 2 couples; WAR WITH MOSQUITOES [SCHERZO]: William Dollar, Hobi, Roy Tobias, 7 women; HOT DOGS [ALLEGRO]: Maria Tallchief, Jerome Robbins, entire cast.

NOTE: In SUNDAY, a small aggressive female gives chase to a big handsome male; RESCUE includes artificial respiration and a love duet; seven mosquitoes dance on pointe in WAR WITH MOSQUITOES; in the HOT DOGS finale, ballabile technique is employed in scenes of male rivalry over a hot dog and a girl. Balanchine's first collaboration with Robbins; both worked on all sections.

270 TRUMPET CONCERTO

MUSIC: By Franz Joseph Haydn (Trumpet Concerto in E-flat major, 1796).

PRODUCTION: Scenery and costumes by Vivienne Kernot. Scenery painted by Alick Johnstone; costumes executed under the direction of Eileen Anderson.

PREMIERE: September 14, 1950, Sadler's Wells Theatre Ballet, Opera House, Manchester. (First London performance, Sadler's Wells, September 19. Trumpet: Harry Wild.)

CAST: Svetlana Beriosova, David Blair; Elaine Fifield, Maryon Lane; David Poole, Pirmin Trecu; 8 women.

NOTE: *Trumpet Concerto* was choreographed at the request of Ninette de Valois, founder and director of the Sadler's Wells Ballet.

271 THE FAIRY'S KISS (LE BAISER DE LA FÉE)
Ballet-Allegory in Four Scenes

MUSIC: Music and book by Igor Stravinsky (1928, commissioned by Ida Rubinstein, dedicated to Peter Ilyitch Tschaikovsky). Based on a tale by Hans Christian Andersen (*The Ice Maiden*).

PRODUCTION: Scenery and costumes by Alice Halicka (from the 1937 production). Lighting by Jean Rosenthal.

PREMIERE: November 28, 1950, New York City Ballet, City Center of Music and Drama, New York. Conductor: Leon Barzin.

CAST: *The Fairy*, Maria Tallchief; *The Bride*, Tanaquil Le Clercq; *Her Friend*, Patricia Wilde; *The Bridegroom*, Nicholas Magallanes; *His Mother*, Beatrice Tompkins; *Shadow*, Helen Kramer; *Winds, Snowflakes, Mountaineers, Bridesmaids, Peasants*.

NOTE: Originally presented by the American Ballet (Stravinsky Festival), New York, 1937.

See 178*, 376

272 MAZURKA FROM 'A LIFE FOR THE TSAR'

MUSIC: By Mikhail Glinka (*A Life for the Tsar*, produced 1836).

PRODUCTION: Costumes by Karinska. Lighting by Jean Rosenthal.

PREMIERE: November 30, 1950, New York City Ballet, City Center of Music and Drama, New York. Conductor: Leon Barzin.

CAST: Janet Reed, Yurek Lazowski (guest artist); Vida Brown, George Balanchine; Barbara Walczak, Harold Lang; Dorothy Dushock, Frank Hobi.

NOTE: A brief character dance in which Balanchine performed on opening night.

273 SYLVIA: PAS DE DEUX

MUSIC: By Léo Delibes (from *Sylvia, ou la Nymphe de Diane*, produced 1876 [Act I VALSE LENTE and Act III pas de deux]).

PRODUCTION: Costumes by Karinska.

PREMIERE: December 1, 1950, New York City Ballet, City Center of Music and Drama, New York. Conductor: Leon Barzin.

CAST: Maria Tallchief, Nicholas Magallanes.

NOTE: In the tradition of a grand pas de deux, with entrée, adagio, two solos, and coda. In 1965, incorporated (with minor changes) into *Pas de Deux and Divertissement* [350], choreographed for the New York City Ballet. The male variation is reproduced in the Balanchine-Danilova *Coppélia* [387], Act III (PEACE pas de deux).

STAGINGS (choreography credited to André Eglevsky in some later stagings): 1963, National; 1964, American Ballet Theatre; 1965, Eglevsky; 1968, Harkness; 1979, Royal Winnipeg; 1980, Pennsylvania; 1981, Matsuyama.

TELEVISION: 1950 (CBS); 1955 (Ed Sullivan Show, CBS); 1959-60 (excerpts, PBS); 1960 (ABC); 1963 (CBC, Montreal); 1965 (Bell Telephone Hour, NBC).

See 36, 350, 387

1951

274 MUSIC AND DANCE:
NUMBERS IV, VI, VII, VIII, IX, XI, XII

MUSIC: As given below.

CHOREOGRAPHY: By George Balanchine (eight of thirteen dances), Todd Bolender, Frank Hobi, and Francisco Moncion.

PRODUCTION: Presented by the National Orchestral Society, Leon Barzin, Musical Director. Artistic Director: George Balanchine. Lighting Director: Jean Rosenthal.

PREMIERE: February 10, 1951, Carnegie Hall, New York. Danced by members of the New York City Ballet and students of the School of American Ballet. Conductor: Leon Barzin.

CAST: IV. SARABANDE from *Louis XIV Suite* (François Couperin, orchestrated by Wood-Hill): 4 women; VI. MINUET from Symphony No. 39, K. 543 (Wolfgang Amadeus Mozart): Doris Breckenridge, Robert Barnett; VII. GAVOTTE from *Ladies of the Ballet* (Alfred Edward Moffat): 2 couples; VIII. BOURRÉE from *Concerto for String Orchestra* (Jean-Baptiste Lully): 2 couples; IX. RIGAUDON from the Lully *Concerto*: 4 couples; XI. WALTZ from *Naïla* (*La Source*, Léo Delibes): Maria Tallchief, 11 women; XII. TANGO from *Le Carnaval d'Aix* (Darius Milhaud): Tanaquil Le Clercq.

NOTE: Each musical selection was played by the orchestra alone and then repeated with dances. *Mazurka from 'A Life for the Tsar'* [272] was performed as Number XIII, closing the program.

See 350, 364, 387

275   THE CARD GAME (THE CARD PARTY)
A Ballet in Three Deals

MUSIC: By Igor Stravinsky (*Jeu de Cartes–A Card Game–Das Kartenspiel*, 1936, commissioned by Lincoln Kirstein and Edward M. M. Warburg). Book by Igor Stravinsky and M. Malaieff.

PRODUCTION: Scenery and costumes by Irene Sharaff.

PREMIERE: February 15, 1951, New York City Ballet, City Center of Music and Drama, New York. Conductor: Leon Barzin.

CAST: *Joker*, Todd Bolender; *Queens*: *Hearts*, Janet Reed; *Spades*, Jillana; *Diamonds*, Patricia Wilde; *Clubs*, Doris Breckenridge; *4 Aces* (men); *4 Kings*; *4 Jacks*; *10, 9, 8, 7, 6, 5 of Hearts*; *10, 9, 8, 7 of Spades*.

NOTE: Originally presented by the American Ballet (Stravinsky Festival), New York, 1937.

REVISIONS: On at least one occasion, Joker danced by a woman (Janet Reed).

*See 177**

276 PAS DE TROIS

MUSIC: By Léon Minkus (from *Paquita*, 1881).

PRODUCTION: Costumes by Karinska. Lighting by Jean Rosenthal.

PREMIERE: February 18, 1951, New York City Ballet, City Center of Music and Drama, New York. Conductor: Leon Barzin.

CAST: Nora Kaye, Maria Tallchief, André Eglevsky.

NOTE: Originally presented (in somewhat different form) by the Grand Ballet du Marquis de Cuevas, London, 1948, as *Pas de Trois Classique*.

*See 247**

277 LA VALSE

MUSIC: By Maurice Ravel (*Valses Nobles et Sentimentales*, 1911, orchestrated 1912; *La Valse*, 1920, commissioned by Serge Diaghilev).

PRODUCTION: Costumes by Karinska. Lighting by Jean Rosenthal.

PREMIERE: February 20, 1951, New York City Ballet, City Center of Music and Drama, New York. Conductor: Leon Barzin.

CAST: VALSES NOBLES ET SENTIMENTALES: FIRST WALTZ, Overture (not danced); SECOND WALTZ: Vida Brown, Edwina Fontaine, Jillana; THIRD WALTZ: Patricia Wilde, Frank Hobi; FOURTH WALTZ: Yvonne Mounsey, Michael Maule; FIFTH WALTZ: Diana Adams, Herbert Bliss; SIXTH WALTZ: Adams; SEVENTH WALTZ: Bliss, Brown, Fontaine, Jillana; EIGHTH WALTZ: Tanaquil Le Clercq, Nicholas Magallanes; LA VALSE: Le Clercq, Magallanes, Francisco Moncion, 16 women, 9 men.

NOTE: The eight *Valses Nobles et Sentimentales* establish a mood of disturbed gaiety and impending catastrophe. In *La Valse* the stage becomes a ballroom of waltzing couples. The figure of Death, in black, enters; a girl in white dances with him. Waltzing ever faster, unable to resist, she dies.

REVISIONS: 1974, New York City Ballet: Figure of Death makes momentary appearance in EIGHTH WALTZ, foreshadowing events of LA VALSE.

STAGINGS: 1965, Stuttgart; 1966, Royal Swedish; 1967, Dutch National, Hamburg; 1969, Geneva; 1975, Paris; 1977, Berlin, Frankfurt; 1978, East Berlin, Vienna, Zürich; 1981, Pacific Northwest.

TELEVISION: 1951 (excerpts, CBS, on first commercial color telecast).

See 20

278 ROMEO AND JULIET

Play by William Shakespeare

MUSIC: By David Diamond.

PRODUCTION: Produced by Dwight Deere Wiman. Directed by Peter Glenville. Scenery and costumes by Oliver Messel. Scenery executed by Studio Alliance; costumes executed by Karinska.

PREMIERE: March 10, 1951, Broadhurst Theatre, New York. Conductor: Robert Stanley. (Out-of-town preview: January 22, Cass Theatre, Detroit.)

CAST: *Romeo*, Douglas Watson; *Juliet*, Olivia de Havilland; *Mercutio*, Jack Hawkins; *Tybalt*, William Smithers; *Capulet*, Malcolm Keen; *Lady Capulet*, Isobel Elsom; *Nurse to Juliet*, Evelyn Varden; *Friar Laurence*, James Hayter; and others.

NOTE: Balanchine choreographed a pavane for the Capulet ball, Act I, Scene 5.

See 325

279 CAPRICCIO BRILLANT

MUSIC: By Felix Mendelssohn (*Capriccio Brillant* for piano and orchestra, Op. 22, 1825-26).

PRODUCTION: Costumes by Karinska. Lighting by Jean Rosenthal.

PREMIERE: June 7, 1951, New York City Ballet, City Center of Music and Drama, New York. Conductor: Leon Barzin. On-stage pianist: Nicholas Kopeikine.

CAST: Maria Tallchief, André Eglevsky; Barbara Bocher, Constance Garfield, Jillana, Irene Larsson.

280 COURTIN' TIME
Musical Comedy in Two Acts and Nine Scenes

MUSIC AND BOOK: Music and lyrics by Jack Lawrence and Don Walker. Book by William Roos, based on the play *The Farmer's Wife*, by Eden Phillpotts. Musical and vocal arrangements by Don Walker.

PRODUCTION: Produced by James Russo and Michael Ellis in association with Alexander H. Cohen. Directed by Alfred Drake. Scenery and lighting by Ralph Alswang. Costumes by Saul Bolasni. Scenery built by Nolan Brothers and painted by Triangle Studios; costumes executed by Eaves Costume Company.

PREMIERE: June 13, 1951, National Theatre, New York. Conductor: Bill Jonson. (Out-of-town preview: April 9, Shubert Theatre, Boston.)

CAST: *Samuel Rilling*, Joe E. Brown (Lloyd Nolan, Boston); *Araminta*, Billie Worth; *Theresa Tapper*, Carmen Mathews; and others. Dancers: Gloria Patrice, Peter Conlow, 6 women, 6 men.

TODAY AT YOUR HOUSE, TOMORROW AT MINE (Act I): Gloria Patrice, Peter Conlow, ensemble.

REPRISE: THE WISHBONE SONG (Act I): Patrice, Conlow.

CHOOSE YOUR PARTNER (Act I): Patrice, Conlow, ensemble.

BALLET: JOHNNY AND THE PUCKWUDGIES (Act II): *Johnny-Ride-the-Sky*, Conlow; Patrice, ensemble.

NOTE: CHOOSE YOUR PARTNER, a square dance around a gazebo, used the American dance form on which Balanchine later based a ballet [315].

281 THE SLEEPING BEAUTY:
VARIATION from AURORA'S WEDDING

In the summer of 1951, at Jacob's Pillow, Diana Adams performed a variation from *Aurora's Wedding* (divertissements from Act III of *The Sleeping Beauty* [Tschaikovsky]), with choreography credited to Balanchine.

See 65, 225, 259, 404, 418

282 À LA FRANÇAIX

MUSIC: By Jean Françaix (*Serenade for Small Orchestra*, 1934).

PRODUCTION: Scenery by Raoul Dufy. Lighting by Jean Rosenthal.

PREMIERE: September 11, 1951, New York City Ballet, City Center of Music and Drama, New York. Conductor: Leon Barzin.

CAST: Janet Reed, Maria Tallchief, André Eglevsky; Frank Hobi, Roy Tobias.

NOTE: As the pun of the title implies, a humorous and anecdotal ballet: A tennis-playing athlete flirts with a pretty girl until a ballerina dressed as a winged sylph appears and fascinates him; in the end the sylph, stripping down to a bathing suit, reveals herself to be an athlete, too.

STAGINGS: 1953, San Francisco; 1964, Eglevsky; 1965, San Diego; 1981, American Festival; 1982, Kansas City.

TELEVISION: 1953 (Kate Smith Hour, NBC).

283 TYL ULENSPIEGEL

MUSIC: By Richard Strauss (*Till Eulenspiegels lustige Streiche*, Op. 28, 1895).

PRODUCTION: Scenery and costumes by Esteban Francés. Scenery executed by Triangle Studios and Nolan Brothers. Lighting by Jean Rosenthal.

PREMIERE: November 14, 1951, New York City Ballet, City Center of Music and Drama, New York. Conductor: Leon Barzin.

CAST: *Tyl Ulenspiegel*, Jerome Robbins; *Nell, His Wife*, Ruth Sobotka; *Philip II, King of Spain*, Brooks Jackson; *Duke and Duchess*, Frank Hobi,

Beatrice Tompkins; *Woman*, Tomi Wortham; *Tyl as a Child*, Alberta Grant; *Philip II as a Child*, Susan Kovnat; *Spanish Nobility*, 2 women, 2 men; *Soldiers*, 6 men; *Peasants*, 8 women; *Inquisitors*, 4 men; *Crowd*, 8 women.

NOTE: Fantastic pantomime-ballet depicting the medieval prankster as liberator of Flanders from Spanish invaders; set in elaborate décor, with many changes of costume.

284 APOLLO, LEADER OF THE MUSES
Ballet in Two Scenes

MUSIC: Music and book by Igor Stravinsky (*Apollo Musagetes*, 1927-28, commissioned by Mrs. Elizabeth Sprague Coolidge).

PRODUCTION: Costumes by Karinska. Lighting by Jean Rosenthal.

PREMIERE: November 15, 1951, New York City Ballet, City Center of Music and Drama, New York. Conductor: Leon Barzin.

CAST: *Apollo*, André Eglevsky; *Terpsichore*, Maria Tallchief; *Calliope*, Diana Adams; *Polyhymnia*, Tanaquil Le Clercq; *Leto*, Barbara Milberg; *Handmaidens*, Irene Larsson, Jillana.

NOTE: Originally presented by Diaghilev's Ballets Russes, Paris, 1928, titled *Apollon Musagète*. From 1957, titled *Apollo*.

See 84*, 176, 198

285 SWAN LAKE

MUSIC: By Peter Ilyitch Tschaikovsky (excerpts from *Swan Lake*, Op. 20, 1875-76).

CHOREOGRAPHY: By George Balanchine after Lev Ivanov.

PRODUCTION: Scenery and costumes by Cecil Beaton. Scenery executed by Triangle Studios and Nolan Brothers; costumes executed by Karinska. Lighting by Jean Rosenthal.

PREMIERE: November 20, 1951, New York City Ballet, City Center of Music and Drama, New York. Conductor: Leon Barzin.

CAST: *Odette, Queen of the Swans*, Maria Tallchief; *Prince Siegfried*, André Eglevsky; *Benno, the Prince's Friend*, Frank Hobi; PAS DE TROIS: Patricia

Wilde, 2 women; PAS DE NEUF: Yvonne Mounsey, 8 women; *Von Rothbart, a Sorcerer*, Edward Bigelow; *Swans*, 24 women; *Hunters*, 8 men.

NOTE: Balanchine's version of *Swan Lake* is essentially Act II of the original four-act production, reproducing Ivanov's WHITE SWAN ADAGIO (the pas de deux), the Swan Queen's solo and coda entrance, and the DANCE OF THE FOUR CYGNETS (the pas de quatre); the entrance of the Swans derives from traditional versions. Balanchine removed all mime, greatly enlarged the role of the corps de ballet, and choreographed a new finale to music from Act IV.

REVISIONS: New York City Ballet, changes from first years in repertory: 1956, traditional ending of pas de deux replaced by coda for corps de ballet (to Tschaikovsky's original score rather than the traditional Drigo interpolation); 1959, PAS DE TROIS omitted and new Prince's solo added to that music (Grand Waltz from Act II) replacing original Prince's solo to fourth variation of pas de six (Act III), and traditional entrance of Swan Queen in coda rechoreographed; 1964, traditional Swan Queen solo replaced by new choreography (to *Un Poco di Chopin*, Op. 72, no. 15, 1893, orchestrated by Drigo) and subsequently changed several times, Prince's solo rechoreographed (to music from Act I pas de trois) and subsequently changed several times and often omitted, pas de quatre (DANCE OF THE FOUR CYGNETS) replaced by WALTZ BLUETTE for 12 Swans (to orchestrated version of a composition for piano in E-flat), role of Benno omitted; 1980, traditional Swan Queen solo and entrance in coda restored.

NEW PRODUCTIONS BY BALANCHINE COMPANIES: 1964, New York City Ballet: New scenery, costumes and lighting by Rouben Ter-Arutunian for the New York State Theater.

STAGINGS: 1954, San Francisco; 1961, La Scala; 1965, Ballet of Los Angeles; 1979, Los Angeles; 1981, Eglevsky; 1982, Kansas City.

TELEVISION: 1954 (excerpt, Kate Smith Show, NBC); 1956 (pas de deux, CBS); 1959-60 (pas de deux, PBS).

See 75, 191, 262, 331, 367

1952

286 CARACOLE

MUSIC: By Wolfgang Amadeus Mozart (Divertimento No. 15 in B-flat major, K. 287, second minuet [fifth movement] and andante from sixth movement omitted).

PRODUCTION: Costumes by Christian Bérard (from *Mozartiana* [134]). Lighting by Jean Rosenthal.

PREMIERE: February 19, 1952, New York City Ballet, City Center of Music and Drama, New York. Conductor: Leon Barzin.

CAST: Diana Adams, Melissa Hayden, Tanaquil Le Clercq, Maria Tallchief, Patricia Wilde, André Eglevsky, Nicholas Magallanes, Jerome Robbins, 8 women.

ALLEGRO; THEME AND VARIATIONS; MINUET; ANDANTE; FINALE.

NOTE: The French title denotes a form of turning or circling, and is used as a term in horsemanship, to which the costumes made reference. The ballet, an intricate work set to music for which Balanchine has expressed special admiration, could not be remembered in 1956 when a revival was planned. Balanchine then choreographed a new ballet to the same score, titled *Divertimento No. 15*, without programmatic context.

See 314

287 BAYOU

MUSIC: By Virgil Thomson (*Acadian Songs and Dances*, 1947).

PRODUCTION: Scenery and costumes by Dorothea Tanning. Costumes executed by Karinska. Lighting by Jean Rosenthal.

PREMIERE: February 21, 1952, New York City Ballet, City Center of Music and Drama, New York. Conductor: Leon Barzin.

CAST: *Boy of the Bayou*, Francisco Moncion; *Girl of the Bayou*, Doris Breckenridge; *Leaves and Flowers*, Melissa Hayden, Hugh Laing, 2 couples; *Starched White People*, Diana Adams, Herbert Bliss, 2 couples.

NOTE: At the opening and close, the Boy poles a small boat through the mysterious bayou; the dancers are Acadians from country and town whom the Boy encounters. The music was composed for Robert Flaherty's documentary film *Louisiana Story*.

288 SCOTCH SYMPHONY

MUSIC: By Felix Mendelssohn (Symphony No. 3 in A minor, Op. 56, 'Scotch,' 1842 [first movement omitted]).

PRODUCTION: Scenery by Horace Armistead; painted by Scenic Studios. Women's costumes by Karinska. Men's costumes by David Ffolkes. Lighting by Jean Rosenthal.

PREMIERE: November 11, 1952, New York City Ballet, City Center of Music and Drama, New York. Conductor: Leon Barzin.

CAST: Maria Tallchief, André Eglevsky; Patricia Wilde; 8 couples.

NOTE: An homage to Scotland in the form of a classic ballet, with allusions to the elusive sylph of Romantic ballet.

STAGINGS: 1962, New England Civic; 1963, Paris; 1964, Munich; 1965, Pennsylvania, La Scala; 1966, San Francisco; 1967, Joffrey, Hamburg; 1970, Eglevsky (pas de deux); 1971, Geneva; 1973, San Juan; 1976, Pacific Northwest; 1978, Washington; 1979, Milwaukee; 1980, Los Angeles; 1982, Atlanta.

TELEVISION: 1959 (excerpts, Bell Telephone Hour, NBC).

289 METAMORPHOSES

MUSIC: By Paul Hindemith (*Symphonic Metamorphoses on Themes of Carl Maria von Weber*, 1943).

PRODUCTION: Costumes by Karinska. Décor by Jean Rosenthal.

PREMIERE: November 25, 1952, New York City Ballet, City Center of Music and Drama, New York. Conductor: Leon Barzin.

CAST: Tanaquil Le Clercq, Todd Bolender, Nicholas Magallanes, 16 women, 8 men.

ALLEGRO; TURANDOT SCHERZO; ANDANTINO; MARCH.

NOTE: A fantasy on insectile life: The dancers are costumed as bug-inspired, winged beings with antennae, in a décor formed of series of light-reflective coat hangers and Chinese panels. The adagio features a beetle and a sort of butterfly; the sky-swept finale, wings in motion. A principal theme of Hindemith's music is based on a Chinese melody used by Weber.

290 HARLEQUINADE PAS DE DEUX

MUSIC: By Riccardo Drigo (from *Les Millions d'Arlequin*, Act I, produced 1900).

PRODUCTION: Costumes by Karinska. Lighting by Jean Rosenthal.

PREMIERE: December 16, 1952, New York City Ballet, City Center of Music and Drama, New York. Conductor: Leon Barzin.

CAST: Maria Tallchief, André Eglevsky.

NOTE: In 1965, Balanchine choreographed the complete *Harlequinade* for the New York City Ballet, creating new choreography for this pas de deux.

STAGINGS: 1961, Eglevsky (female variation, retitled *Columbine*).

See 351

291 ONE, YULETIDE SQUARE
Made for Television

MUSIC: By Léo Delibes (from *Coppélia, ou la Fille aux Yeux d'Émail*, produced 1870).

PRODUCTION: Produced by L. Leonidoff. Costumes by Karinska.

FIRST TELECAST: December 25, 1952, NBC.

CAST: *Swanilda/Coppélia*, Tanaquil Le Clercq; *Frantz*, Jacques d'Amboise; *Dr. Coppélius*, Robert Helpmann; corps de ballet.

NOTE: An abridged treatment of the *Coppélia* story.

See 266, 387

292 CONCERTINO

MUSIC: By Jean Françaix (Concertino for piano and orchestra, 1932).

PRODUCTION: Costumes by Karinska. Lighting by Jean Rosenthal.

PREMIERE: December 30, 1952, New York City Ballet, City Center of Music and Drama, New York. Conductor: Leon Barzin. Pianist: Nicholas Kopeikine.

CAST: Diana Adams, Tanaquil Le Clercq, André Eglevsky.

NOTE: The two ballerinas, costumed as can-can dancers in black tutus, keep the male dancer, in formal dress, close company throughout; they permit him one brief solo variation.

1953

293 VALSE FANTAISIE

MUSIC: By Mikhail Glinka (*Valse Fantaisie* in B minor, 1839; orchestrated 1856).

PRODUCTION: Costumes by Karinska. Lighting by Jean Rosenthal.

PREMIERE: January 6, 1953, New York City Ballet, City Center of Music and Drama, New York. Conductor: Leon Barzin.

CAST: Diana Adams, Melissa Hayden, Tanaquil Le Clercq, Nicholas Magallanes.

NOTE: The three ballerinas, wearing headdresses reminiscent of Glinka's Russia, move together in a *perpetuum mobile*, attended by the male dancer.

STAGINGS (sometimes as *Waltz Fantasy*): 1964, Eglevsky; 1970, San Juan; 1974, Philippines; 1982, New York Dance Theatre.

See 107*, 359, 366

294 THE COUNTESS BECOMES THE MAID
Made for Television

MUSIC: By Johann Strauss the Younger (excerpts from *Die Fledermaus*, produced 1874).

FIRST TELECAST: February 3, 1953, Kate Smith Hour, NBC.

CAST: *Countess*, Melissa Hayden; *Maid*, Janet Reed; André Eglevsky.

See 107, 169, 199, 206

295 THE RAKE'S PROGRESS
Opera in Three Acts and Nine Scenes

MUSIC: By Igor Stravinsky (produced 1951). Libretto by W. H. Auden and Chester Kallman, a fable and epilogue after William Hogarth's paintings.

PRODUCTION: Stage direction by George Balanchine. Scenery and costumes by Horace Armistead. Scenery constructed by Metropolitan Opera Studio and painted by Studio Alliance; costumes executed by Helene Pons Studio.

PREMIERE: February 14, 1953, Metropolitan Opera, New York. Conductor: Fritz Reiner.

CAST: *Trulove*, Norman Scott; *Anne*, Hilde Gueden; *Tom Rakewell*, Eugene Conley; *Nick Shadow*, Mack Harrell; *Mother Goose*, Martha Lipton; *Baba the Turk*, Blanche Thebom; *Sellem, Auctioneer*, Paul Franke; *Keeper of the Madhouse*, Lawrence Davidson; and others.

NOTE: American premiere. Although the staging was noted for its choreographic qualities, particularly in the brothel scene at Mother Goose's house and the last act in the Madhouse, there were no actual dance sequences.

296 [COTILLION PROMENADE]

On February 20, 1953, Tanaquil Le Clercq and Jacques d'Amboise led some five hundred couples in a promenade arranged by Balanchine for the Negro Debutante Ball, at the 369th Armory, Harlem, New York City, an event sponsored by the *New Amsterdam News*.

297 LA FAVORITA

Opera in Four Acts and Five Scenes by Gaetano Donizetti

BALLET

PREMIERE: April 16, 1953, Teatro alla Scala, Milan. Conductor: Antonino Votto.

CAST: Olga Amati, Giulio Perugini, Vera Colombo, Gilda Maiocchi, Mario Pistoni.

NOTE: The ballet probably occurred in the Act II scene in the gardens of the Palace of the Alcazar.

298 BORIS GODUNOV

Opera in Prologue, Four Acts and Seven Scenes by Modest Moussorgsky

POLONAISE

PREMIERE: April 20, 1953, Teatro alla Scala, Milan. Conductor: Antonino Votto.

NOTE: Although the printed program credits no dance or dancers, the ballet was probably a POLONAISE performed in the scene set in the Polish castle.

See 54, 388

299 ADRIANA LECOUVREUR

Opera in Four Acts by Francesco Cilea

BALLET

PREMIERE: May 7, 1953, Teatro alla Scala, Milan. Conductor: Carlo Maria Giulini.

CAST: *Paris,* Walter Marconi; *Mercury,* Mario Pistoni; *Juno,* Tilde Baroni; *Pallas,* Gilda Maiocchi; *Venus,* Carla Calzati; *Wisdom,* Nuccy Muti; *Purity,* Maria Bazzolo; corps de ballet.

NOTE: The ballet occurred in Act III, in the scene set in the palace of the Prince of Bouillon.

300 AMAHL AND THE NIGHT VISITORS

Opera in One Act by Gian Carlo Menotti

SHEPHERDS' DANCE

PREMIERE: May 9, 1953, Teatro della Pergola, Florence. Conductor: Leopold Stokowski.

CAST: Raimonda Orselli, Alberto Moro.

NOTE: Performed at the XVI° Maggio Musicale.

1954

301 OPUS 34

MUSIC: By Arnold Schoenberg (*Accompaniment-Music for a Motion Picture*, Op. 34, 1930).

PRODUCTION: Costumes by Esteban Francés. Scenery and lighting by Jean Rosenthal.

PREMIERE: January 19, 1954, New York City Ballet, City Center of Music and Drama, New York. Conductor: Leon Barzin.

CAST: THE FIRST TIME: Diana Adams, Patricia Wilde, Nicholas Magallanes, Francisco Moncion, 9 women; THE SECOND TIME: Tanaquil Le Clercq, Herbert Bliss, 6 women, 10 men.

NOTE: The sections of the twelve-tone score are titled 'Threat,' 'Danger,' 'Fear,' 'Catastrophe.' The music is performed twice without pause. THE FIRST TIME is performed in an extreme vocabulary of dance motion. THE SECOND TIME is an endurance of horror, a grisly symbolic surgery in pantomime, with dancers costumed in bandages and as cadavers.

302 THE NUTCRACKER

Classic Ballet in Two Acts, Four Scenes, and Prologue

MUSIC: By Peter Ilyitch Tschaikovsky (*The Nutcracker*, produced 1892; violin cadenza from *The Sleeping Beauty* added 1955). Based on the Alexandre Dumas *père* version of E. T. A. Hoffmann's tale, *The Nutcracker and the Mouse King* (1816).

CHOREOGRAPHY: By George Balanchine. CANDY CANE variation (TREPAK) and Little Prince's mime choreographed by Lev Ivanov. BATTLE BETWEEN THE NUTCRACKER AND THE MOUSE KING choreographed by Jerome Robbins.

PRODUCTION: Scenery by Horace Armistead, executed by Century Scenic Studios. Costumes by Karinska. Masks by Vlady. Lighting and production by Jean Rosenthal.

PREMIERE: February 2, 1954, New York City Ballet with students from the School of American Ballet, City Center of Music and Drama, New York. Conductor: Leon Barzin.

CAST: ACT I, SCENE 1, CHRISTMAS PARTY AT THE HOME OF DR. STAHLBAUM, NUREMBERG, CA. 1816: *Dr. and Frau Stahlbaum*, Frank Hobi, Irene Larsson; *Their Children, Clara and Fritz*, Alberta Grant, Susan Kaufman; *Maid*; *Guests*: *4 Parents, 11 Children, 2 Grandparents*; *Herr Drosselmeyer*, Michael Arshansky; *His Nephew (The Nutcracker)*, Paul Nickel; *Toys*: *Harlequin and Columbine*, Gloria Vauges, Kaye Sargent; *Toy Soldier*, Roy Tobias; SCENE 2, THE BATTLE BETWEEN THE NUTCRACKER AND THE MOUSE KING: *Mouse King*, Edward Bigelow; *Nutcracker*; *Clara*; *8 Mice*; *19 Child Soldiers*; SCENE 3, THE WHITE FOREST AND THE SNOWFLAKE WALTZ: *Nutcracker*; *Clara*; *Snowflakes*, 16 women. Boys choir (40 voices) from St. Thomas Episcopal Church. ACT II, CONFITUERENBURG (THE KINGDOM OF THE SUGAR PLUM FAIRY): *Sugar Plum Fairy*, Maria Tallchief; *Her Cavalier*, Nicholas Magallanes; *Little Princess*, Grant; *Little Prince*, Nickel; *Angels*, 8 girls; DIVERTISSEMENTS: HOT CHOCOLATE (SPANISH DANCE): Yvonne Mounsey, Herbert Bliss, 4 couples; COFFEE (ARABIAN DANCE): Francisco Moncion, 4 children; TEA (CHINESE DANCE): George Li, 2 women; CANDY CANES (BUFFOONS): Robert Barnett, 6 girls; MARZIPAN SHEPHERDESSES (MIRLITONS): Janet Reed, 4 women; BONBONNIÈRE (MOTHER GINGER AND HER POLICHINELLES): Bigelow, 8 children; WALTZ OF THE CANDY FLOWERS: *Dewdrop*, Tanaquil Le Clercq; *Flowers*, 2 demi-soloists; 12 women.

NOTE: Balanchine danced the roles of The Nutcracker/Little Prince, Mouse King, and others in productions by the Maryinsky Theater in Petrograd (later State Theater of Opera and Ballet), and was especially noted for his solo in the BUFFOONS' DANCE (TREPAK [CANDY CANE] variation). He chose the ballet to be the first full-length work presented by the New York City Ballet; the overwhelming success of his production, with elaborate scenic effects, helped assure the permanence of the Company. The use of children from the School of American Ballet, recalling Balanchine's early experience at the Maryinsky, set a precedent for future New York City Ballet works. *The Sleeping Beauty* cadenza, interpolated into Act I by Balanchine in 1955, has the same theme as the 'tree growing' music from *The Nutcracker* which occurs later in Act I.

REVISIONS: New York City Ballet: 1955, violin cadenza from *The Sleeping Beauty* added to extended pantomime in Act I; 1958, GRAND PAS DE DEUX (Sugar Plum Fairy and Cavalier, end of Act II), replaced by PAS DE CINQ with Cavalier omitted and Sugar Plum Fairy supported in adagio by men from CHOCOLATE, COFFEE, TEA, CANDY CANES; variation for Sugar Plum Fairy moved to beginning of Act II from traditional placement at climax of GRAND PAS DE DEUX; 1959, adagio and coda of GRAND PAS DE DEUX restored with Cavalier, replacing PAS DE CINQ, but without variation for Cavalier; Sugar Plum Fairy variation retained at beginning of Act II; 1964, COFFEE (ARABIAN DANCE), formerly featuring hookah-smoking nobleman fanned by four parrots, rechoreographed as solo for a woman; 1968, introduction of mechanical device allowing Sugar Plum Fairy to glide across stage on one pointe; 1972, eight child mice added; 1979, opening section of SNOWFLAKE WALTZ revised; COFFEE (ARABIAN DANCE) substantially rechoreographed.

NEW PRODUCTIONS BY BALANCHINE COMPANIES: 1964, New York City Ballet: New scenery and lighting by Rouben Ter-Arutunian for the New York State Theater, executed by Feller Scenery Studios, tree by Decorative Plant Corporation; some new costumes by Karinska.

STAGINGS: 1959, Atlanta (ACT I, SCENE 3 and ACT II), Joffrey (pas de deux); 1965, Cologne; 1966, Atlanta (full length); 1968, Pennsylvania (ACT II); 1973, Geneva (ACT II); 1976, Pacific Northwest (pas de deux); 1977, Prince George's (pas de deux); 1978, Chicago Lyric Opera (excerpts).

TELEVISION: 1954 (pas de deux, NBC); 1955 (Sugar Plum Fairy variation, NBC); 1956 (excerpts, rehearsal, CBS); 1956 (pas de deux, Ed Sullivan Show, CBS); 1957 (full length, Seven Lively Arts, CBS); 1957? (pas de deux, L'Heure du Concert, CBC, Montreal); 1958 (full length, with Balanchine as Drosselmeyer, Playhouse 90, CBS); 1959 (pas de deux, ABC); 1959-60 (pas de deux, PBS); 1961 (pas de deux, Bell Telephone Hour, NBC); 1963 (pas de deux, NBC); 1971 (excerpts, NBC).

See 225

303 WESTERN SYMPHONY

MUSIC: By Hershy Kay (1954, commissioned by the New York City Ballet; themes: 'Red River Valley,' 'Old Taylor,' 'Rye Whiskey,' 'Lolly-Too-Dum,' 'Good Night, Ladies,' 'Oh, Dem Golden Slippers,' 'The Girl I Left Behind Me').

PRODUCTION: Lighting by Jean Rosenthal.

PREMIERE: September 7, 1954, New York City Ballet, City Center of Music and Drama, New York. Conductor: Leon Barzin.

CAST: FIRST MOVEMENT, ALLEGRO: Diana Adams, Herbert Bliss, 8 women, 4 men; SECOND MOVEMENT, ADAGIO: Janet Reed, Nicholas Magallanes, 4 women; THIRD MOVEMENT, SCHERZO: Patricia Wilde, André Eglevsky, 4 women; FOURTH MOVEMENT, RONDO: Tanaquil Le Clercq, Jacques d'Amboise, 4 couples.

NOTE: A ballet deriving its flavor and character from the American West while moving rigorously within the framework of classic dance technique and the symphony form. Initially presented without scenery, in practice clothes.

REVISIONS: ca. 1960, New York City Ballet: SCHERZO permanently eliminated.

NEW PRODUCTIONS BY BALANCHINE COMPANIES: New York City Ballet: 1955, scenery by John Boyt (executed by Eugene B. Dunkel Studios), costumes by Karinska; 1968, scenery and costumes renewed in the same style, executed by Nolan Scenery Studios and Karinska.

STAGINGS: 1976, Geneva; 1978, Zürich; 1982, Pacific Northwest, San Francisco.

TELEVISION: 1958 (RONDO, Australian television).

304 IVESIANA

MUSIC: By Charles Ives, as given below (for chamber orchestra except as noted).

PRODUCTION: Lighting by Jean Rosenthal.

PREMIERE: September 14, 1954, New York City Ballet, City Center of Music and Drama, New York. Conductor: Leon Barzin.

CAST: CENTRAL PARK IN THE DARK (1906): Janet Reed, Francisco Moncion,

20 women; HALLOWE'EN (1907?, string quartet and piano): Patricia
Wilde, Jacques d'Amboise, 4 women; THE UNANSWERED QUESTION (1906):
Allegra Kent, Todd Bolender, 4 men; OVER THE PAVEMENTS (1906-13):
Diana Adams, Herbert Bliss, 4 men; IN THE INN (1904-6?): Tanaquil
Le Clercq, Bolender; IN THE NIGHT (1906): Entire cast.

NOTE: A series of dances to brief compositions, each presenting a
dramatic situation in the manner of a tone poem. This homage to the
composer was choreographed soon after his death; the music had
rarely been performed prior to its use for the ballet.

REVISIONS: New York City Ballet: 1955, HALLOWE'EN replaced by
ARGUMENTS (second movement of String Quartet No. 2, 1907); later that
year ARGUMENTS replaced by BARN DANCE (from *Washington's Birthday*,
1909); 1961, OVER THE PAVEMENTS and BARN DANCE eliminated, IN THE INN
rechoreographed, presented in the order CENTRAL PARK IN THE DARK,
THE UNANSWERED QUESTION, IN THE INN, IN THE NIGHT; 1978, Peter
Martins' *Calcium Light Night* (also to Ives) included in several performances presented in the order CENTRAL PARK IN THE DARK, IN THE INN,
THE UNANSWERED QUESTION, CALCIUM LIGHT NIGHT, IN THE NIGHT.

STAGINGS: 1968, Dutch National; 1971, Berlin; 1975, Los Angeles.

TELEVISION: 1964 (L'Heure du Concert, CBC, Montreal).

305 HOUSE OF FLOWERS
Musical Comedy in Two Acts and Thirteen Scenes

MUSIC AND BOOK: Music by Harold Arlen. Lyrics by Truman Capote
and Harold Arlen. Book by Truman Capote. Orchestrations by
Ted Royal.

CHOREOGRAPHY: By George Balanchine. Banda dance choreographed by
Geoffrey Holder.

PRODUCTION: Produced by Saint Subber. Directed by Peter Brook.
Scenery and costumes by Oliver Messel. Scenery built by Messmore &
Damon and painted by E. B. Dunkel Studios; costumes executed by
Brooks Costume Company. Lighting by Jean Rosenthal.

PREMIERE: November 25, 1954, Erlanger Theatre, Philadelphia.
Conductor: Jerry Arlen.

CAST: *Madame Fleur*, Pearl Bailey; *Ottilie alias Violet*, Diahann Carroll;

Madame Tango, Juanita Hall; *Tulip*, Josephine Premice; *Royal*, Rawn Spearman; and others.

WAITING (Act I): *Pansy*, Enid Mosier; *Tulip*, Josephine Premice; *Gladiola*, Ada Moore; *Do*, Winston George Henriques; *Don't*, Solomon Earl Green.

BAMBOO CAGE (Act I): *The Champion*, Geoffrey Holder; Henriques, Green; *Watermelon*, Phillip Hepburn; Mosier, Premice, Moore; *Madame Tango*, Juanita Hall; *Chief of Police*, Don Redman; ensemble.

TWO LADIES IN DE SHADE OF DE BANANA TREE (Act I): Premice, Moore, male ensemble.

CARNIVAL (Act I): Mosier, Premice, Moore, ensemble.

VOUDOU (Act II): *The Drummers*, Joseph Comadore, Michael Alexander, Alphonso Marshall; *Duchess of the Sea*, Miriam Burton; *Octopus*, Albert Popwell; *Shark*, Walter Nicks, Arthur Mitchell, Marshall; *Turtle*, Comadore, ensemble; *Baron of the Cemetery* (Banda dance), choreographed and danced by Geoffrey Holder.

MADAME TANGO'S TANGO (Act II): Hall, Tango Belles.

THE TURTLE SONG (Act II): *Royal*, Rawn Spearman; Henriques, Green, Hepburn, Holder, ensemble.

NOTE: Balanchine withdrew from the show before the New York opening. Herbert Ross rearranged some of the choreography, some was deleted, and the sequence of the numbers was changed.

1955

306 ROMA

MUSIC: By Georges Bizet (three of the four movements from *Roma Suite*, 1861-68: Andante omitted).

PRODUCTION: Scenery and costumes by Eugene Berman. Lighting by Jean Rosenthal.

PREMIERE: February 23, 1955, New York City Ballet, City Center of Music and Drama, New York. Conductor: Leon Barzin.

CAST: Tanaquil Le Clercq, André Eglevsky; Barbara Milberg, Barbara Walczak, Roy Tobias, John Mandia; 12 women, 8 men.

SCHERZO; ADAGIO (pas de deux); CARNAVAL (TARANTELLA).

NOTE: A celebration of Italy, the set combining vistas of a lofty ruin and a slum square.

307 PAS DE TROIS

MUSIC: By Mikhail Glinka (ballet music from *Ruslan and Ludmilla* [Act II vision scene], produced 1842).

PRODUCTION: Costumes by Karinska. Lighting by Jean Rosenthal.

PREMIERE: March 1, 1955, New York City Ballet, City Center of Music and Drama, New York. Conductor: Leon Barzin.

CAST: Melissa Hayden, Patricia Wilde, André Eglevsky.

STAGINGS (choreography credited to André Eglevsky in some later stagings): 1965, Pennsylvania; 1969, Eglevsky; 1971, Downtown; 1972, Dance Repertory Company, North Carolina; 1974, Georgia Dance Theatre; 1975, Syracuse; 1977, Royal Winnipeg; 1979, American Ballet Theatre; 1980, Ballet West.

See 365

308 THE TEMPEST

Play by William Shakespeare

MUSIC: By Ernst Bacon.

PRODUCTION: Produced by Chandler Cowles. Directed by Denis Carey. Scenery by Horace Armistead. Costumes by Robert Fletcher. Scenery executed by Chester Rakeman Studios; costumes executed by Brooks Costume Company. Lighting by Jean Rosenthal.

PREMIERE: August 1, 1955, American Shakespeare Festival, Stratford, Connecticut. Danced by members of the Festival company. Conductor and pianist: Andrew Heath. (Preview: July 26.)

CAST: *Prospero*, Raymond Massey; *Antonio*, Fritz Weaver; *Ferdinand*, Christopher Plummer; *Caliban*, Jack Palance; *Miranda*, Joan Chandler; *Ariel*, Roddy McDowall; and others. BALLET MASQUE (speaking roles):

Iris, Dorothy Whitney; *Ceres*, Leora Dana; *Juno*, Virginia Baker.

NOTE: Balanchine choreographed the ballet masque for nymphs and reapers in Act IV, Scene 1.

See 224

309 PAS DE DIX

MUSIC: By Alexander Glazounov (*Raymonda*, excerpts from Act III, Op. 57, produced 1898).

CHOREOGRAPHY: By George Balanchine, after Marius Petipa.

PRODUCTION: Costumes by Esteban Francés. Lighting by Jean Rosenthal.

PREMIERE: November 9, 1955, New York City Ballet, City Center of Music and Drama, New York. Conductor: Leon Barzin.

CAST: Maria Tallchief, André Eglevsky; Barbara Fallis, Constance Garfield, Jane Mason, Barbara Walczak, Shaun O'Brien, Roy Tobias, Roland Vazquez, Jonathan Watts.

NOTE: Using much of the same music as the PAS CLASSIQUE HONGROIS from Act III of *Raymonda* [233], the work is composed of solos, two pas de deux, a duet for two women, and a quartet for four men, concluding with bravura measures for the ballerina. In 1960, for the San Francisco Ballet *Variations de Ballet*, parts of *Pas de Dix* were combined with choreography by Lew Christensen to Glazounov's suite *Scènes de Ballet*, Op. 52 (revised 1981).

REVISIONS: Often performed without male pas de quatre and sometimes without first two of three variations for female soloists.

STAGINGS (occasionally titled *Raymonda*, *Raymonda Pas de Dix* or *Raymonda Variations* [distinct from *Valses et Variations* (339, later retitled *Raymonda Variations*)]; see also note and stagings list for *Raymonda* [233]; choreography credited to Petipa in later stagings): 1960, Joffrey, San Francisco (as part of Christensen's *Variations de Ballet*); 1961, New England Civic; 1962, Eglevsky, Hamburg, Royal Winnipeg; 1963, Pennsylvania; 1964, Dutch National; 1965, Ballet of Los Angeles, Cologne; 1968, Huntington Dance Ensemble; 1969, Houston; 1970, Dance Repertory Company; 1972, Pittsburgh; 1973, Ballet West; 1974, Los Angeles, New Zealand; 1975, Milwaukee, Stars of American Ballet; 1976, Arizona, Dallas, National Academy, Pacific

Northwest; 1977, Chicago Lyric Opera, Louisville; 1978, Garden State, Philippines; 1980, Makarova and Company; 1981, Kansas City; 1982, Mesa Civic, North Carolina.

TELEVISION: 1957 (L'Heure du Concert, CBC, Montreal).

See 18, 233*, 339, 384

310 JEUX D'ENFANTS

MUSIC: By Georges Bizet (*Jeux d'Enfants*, 12 pieces for piano duet, Opp. 22-26, nos. 2, 3, 6, 11, and 12, 1871, orchestrated by the composer as *Petite Suite d'Orchestre*, 1873; remaining sections orchestrated by an unidentified English composer).

CHOREOGRAPHY: By George Balanchine, Francisco Moncion and Barbara Milberg.

PRODUCTION: Scenery and costumes by Esteban Francés. Scenery executed by Messmore & Damon; costumes executed by Helene Pons Studio. Lighting by Jean Rosenthal.

PREMIERE: November 22, 1955, New York City Ballet, City Center of Music and Drama, New York. Conductor: Leon Barzin.

CAST: 1. OVERTURE; 2. BADMINTON: Barbara Fallis, Richard Thomas, Jonathan Watts; 3. HOBBY HORSES: 2 couples; 4. PAPER DOLLS: 4 women; *Scissors*, 1 man; 5. THE LION AND THE MOUSE: Ann Crowell, Eugene Tanner; 6. THE MUSIC BOX: Una Kai, Walter Georgov, Roland Vazquez; 7. THE AMERICAN BOX: 5 women; 8. THE TOPS: Barbara Walczak, Robert Barnett; 9. THE SOLDIER: Roy Tobias; 10. THE DOLL: Melissa Hayden; 11. PAS DE DEUX: Hayden, Tobias; 12. GALOP: Entire cast.

NOTE: A set of dances for toys and playthings which come to life, with costumes and décor based on eighteenth- and nineteenth-century wooden toys, and American playthings from the early part of the twentieth century. In 1975, Balanchine choreographed the Marche, Berceuse, Duo, and Galop (nos. 6, 3, 11, 12) from *Jeux d'Enfants* as a pas de deux, *The Steadfast Tin Soldier*, for the New York City Ballet, retaining the woman's variation from the 1955 work.

REVISIONS: 1959, New York City Ballet: Restaged with choreography credited to Francisco Moncion (2-8) and George Balanchine (9-12).

See 398

1956

311 THE MAGIC FLUTE (DIE ZAUBERFLÖTE)
Made for Television

MUSIC: By Wolfgang Amadeus Mozart (*Die Zauberflöte*, K. 620, produced 1791). Libretto by Emanuel Schikaneder and Karl Ludwig Giesecke. English translation and adaptation by W. H. Auden and Chester Kallman. Conductor and Artistic Director: Peter Herman Adler.

PRODUCTION: Produced by Samuel Chotzinoff. Associate Producer: Charles Polacheck. Special Production Assistant: Lincoln Kirstein. Directed by Kirk Browning. Stage Direction by George Balanchine.

FIRST TELECAST: January 15, 1956, NBC Opera Theatre.

CAST: *Queen of the Night*, Laurel Hurley; *Pamina*, Leontyne Price; *Sarastro*, Yi-kwei Sze; *Papageno*, John Reardon; *Tamino*, William Lewis; *Papagena*, Adelaide Bishop; *Monostatos*, Andrew McKinley; *Three Ladies* (singers), Frances Paige, Joan Maynagh, Helen Vanni; *Three Ladies* (dancers), Françoise Martinet, Barbara Milberg, Eda Lioy.

NOTE: Balanchine created dance sequences for the Queen of the Night's Three Ladies, and in the staging emphasized fluidity of action and clarity of vocal placement.

312 ALLEGRO BRILLANTE

MUSIC: By Peter Ilyitch Tschaikovsky (Piano Concerto No. 3 in E-flat major, Op. 75, 1892 [unfinished]).

PRODUCTION: Costumes by Karinska (uncredited). Lighting by Jean Rosenthal; David Hays (1964-70); Ronald Bates (from 1971).

PREMIERE: March 1, 1956, New York City Ballet, City Center of Music and Drama, New York. Conductor: Leon Barzin. Pianist: Nicholas Kopeikine.

CAST: Maria Tallchief, Nicholas Magallanes, 4 couples.

NOTE: A concentrated essay in the extended classical vocabulary.

STAGINGS: 1961, Joffrey; 1962, La Scala; 1964, Les Grands Ballets Canadiens; 1965, Pennsylvania, Stuttgart; 1966, Boston, Cologne, Royal Swedish; 1967, Ballet of Los Angeles, Garden State; 1970, Eglevsky; 1971, Hamburg, Noverre; 1973, Royal Ballet Touring; 1974, Los Angeles, Geneva; 1975, Dance Theatre of Harlem, Norway; 1976, Chicago Lyric Opera, Pacific Northwest; 1977, Hartford, North Carolina, Caracas, Frankfurt; 1978, Atlanta; 1979, Ballet West, San Francisco; 1980, Louisville, Milwaukee, Minnesota; 1981, Ballet Metropolitan, Matsuyama, Reggio Emilia, West Australian, Zürich; 1982, Tulsa, Royal Flemish.

TELEVISION: 1964 (excerpts, Bell Telephone Hour, NBC); 1979 (Dance in America, PBS).

313 A MUSICAL JOKE

MUSIC: By Wolfgang Amadeus Mozart (*Ein musikalischer Spaß*, sextet for strings and horns in F major, K. 522, 1787).

PRODUCTION: Costumes by Karinska. Lighting by Jean Rosenthal.

PREMIERE: May 31, 1956, Mozart Festival, American Shakespeare Festival Theatre, Stratford, Connecticut. Danced by members of the New York City Ballet. Musical Director: Erich Leinsdorf. Conductor: Hugo Fiorato.

CAST: Diana Adams, Tanaquil Le Clercq, Patricia Wilde, Herbert Bliss, Nicholas Magallanes, Francisco Moncion.

NOTE: Performed twice, with the ballet *Divertimento No. 15* [314] and the Mozart Serenade for 13 Wind Instruments (K. 361). The program, titled *A Serenade of Music and Dance*, was presented during the five-day bicentennial Mozart Festival of the American Shakespeare Festival.

314 DIVERTIMENTO NO. 15

MUSIC: By Wolfgang Amadeus Mozart (Divertimento No. 15 in B-flat major, K. 287; second minuet [fifth movement] and andante from sixth movement omitted; new cadenza for violin and viola by John Colman added late 1960s).

PRODUCTION: Scenery by James Stewart Morcom (from *Symphonie Concertante* [241]). Costumes by Karinska. Lighting by Jean Rosenthal.

PREMIERE: May 31, 1956, Mozart Festival, American Shakespeare Theatre, Stratford, Connecticut. Danced by members of the New York City Ballet. Musical Director: Erich Leinsdorf. Conductor: Hugo Fiorato. (First New York City Ballet performance December 19, City Center of Music and Drama, New York. Conductor: Leon Barzin.)

CAST: ALLEGRO: Diana Adams, Melissa Hayden, Allegra Kent, Tanaquil Le Clercq, Patricia Wilde, Herbert Bliss, Nicholas Magallanes, Roy Tobias, 8 women; THEME AND VARIATIONS: Bliss, Tobias; FIRST VARIATION: Kent; SECOND VARIATION: Hayden; THIRD VARIATION: Adams; FOURTH VARIATION: Le Clercq; FIFTH VARIATION: Magallanes; SIXTH VARIATION: Wilde; MINUET: 8 women; ANDANTE: 8 principals; FINALE: Entire cast.

NOTE: Balanchine planned to present *Caracole* [286] for the American Shakespeare Theatre bicentennial Mozart Festival. When he found that neither he nor the dancers could recall the choreography, he created a new work using some of the former steps. It was initially performed under the title *Caracole*, and titled *Divertimento No. 15* from the first New York performance.

REVISIONS: Late 1960s, New York City Ballet: Choreography to new cadenza by John Colman added at end of ANDANTE section; VARIATIONS and ANDANTE reworked with minor changes for different casts.

NEW PRODUCTIONS BY BALANCHINE COMPANIES: New York City Ballet: 1966, new scenery and lighting by David Hays (scenery executed by Nolan Brothers), new costumes by Karinska; from mid-1970s, performed without scenery.

STAGINGS: 1969, Vienna; 1970, Munich; 1971, Cologne, Dutch National, Geneva, Hamburg; 1975, Frankfurt; 1977, Pacific Northwest; 1978, Chicago Lyric Opera, Pennsylvania, Paris, Royal Danish; 1979, San Francisco, Les Grands Ballets Canadiens.

TELEVISION: 1961 (L'Heure du Concert, CBC, Montreal); 1977 (excerpt, Dance in America, PBS).

See 286

1957

315 SQUARE DANCE

Music: By Antonio Vivaldi (Concerto Grosso in B minor, Op. 3, no. 10; Concerto Grosso in E major, Op. 3, no. 12 [first movement]) and Arcangelo Corelli (*Sarabanda, Badinerie e Giga* [second and third movements]).

Production: Lighting by Nananne Porcher.

Premiere: November 21, 1957, New York City Ballet, City Center of Music and Drama, New York. Leader of on-stage string ensemble: Louis Graeler.

Cast: Patricia Wilde, Nicholas Magallanes, 6 couples. Square dance caller: Elisha C. Keeler.

Note: Balanchine adapted patterns from the American folk dance to classic ballet, setting them to seventeenth- and eighteenth-century music, with fiddlers on stage and rhymed directions invented by the square dance caller.

Revisions: 1976, New York City Ballet: Staged with musicians (augmented chamber ensemble) in orchestra pit, no longer with caller; new male solo choreographed to first movement of Corelli's *Sarabanda, Badinerie e Giga*, not used in 1957; lighting by Ronald Bates.

Stagings (incorporating new male solo after 1976): 1962, Joffrey; 1972, Geneva; 1973, Ballet West; 1980, Eglevsky; 1981, Atlanta, North Carolina, Pacific Northwest, Pennsylvania.

Television: 1963 (Bell Telephone Hour, NBC).

316 AGON

Music: By Igor Stravinsky (1953-56, commissioned by the New York City Ballet with funds from the Rockefeller Foundation and dedicated to Lincoln Kirstein and George Balanchine).

Production: Lighting by Nananne Porcher.

PREMIERE: December 1, 1957, New York City Ballet, City Center of Music and Drama, New York. Conductor: Leon Barzin. (Preview: March of Dimes Benefit, November 27.)

CAST: PART I: PAS DE QUATRE: 4 men; DOUBLE PAS DE QUATRE: 8 women; TRIPLE PAS DE QUATRE: 8 women, 4 men; PART II: FIRST PAS DE TROIS: SARABANDE: Todd Bolender; GAILLIARD: Barbara Milberg, Barbara Walczak; CODA: Milberg, Walczak, Bolender; SECOND PAS DE TROIS: BRANSLE SIMPLE: Roy Tobias, Jonathan Watts; BRANSLE GAY: Melissa Hayden; BRANSLE DOUBLE (DE POITOU): Hayden, Tobias, Watts; PAS DE DEUX: Diana Adams, Arthur Mitchell; PART III: DANSE DES QUATRE DUOS: 4 duos; DANSE DES QUATRE TRIOS: 4 trios; CODA: 4 men.

NOTE: *Agon* is the Greek word for contest; the movements of the ballet are named after French court dances. Although when commissioned the work was intended to complete a triad of ballets (with *Apollo* and *Orpheus*) on Greek themes, Stravinsky and Balanchine have noted that the historical references are pretexts. The composer and the choreographer together designed the structure of the ballet during the creation of the music. The outline for the score specifies in detail, with exact timings, the basic movements for twelve dancers.

REVISIONS: 1970s, New York City Ballet: Final arm sequence in GAILLIARD changed; final pose of ballet (in CODA) changed—four men face toward back of stage (repeating opening pose) rather than each other, following Stravinsky's original schematic manuscript indications in the outline for the score.

STAGINGS: 1967, San Francisco; 1970, Geneva, Hamburg, Stuttgart; 1971, Dance Theatre of Harlem; 1973, Royal; 1974, Dutch National, Paris; 1975, Israel (pas de deux); 1977, Berlin; 1978, Zürich; 1979, Hungary; 1980, New York Dance Theatre (pas de deux); 1982, Reggio Emilia.

TELEVISION: 1960 (CBC, Montreal); 1966 (excerpts, PBS); 1969 (excerpt, NBC).

1958

317 GOUNOD SYMPHONY

MUSIC: By Charles Gounod (Symphony No. 1 in D major, 1855).

PRODUCTION: Scenery by Horace Armistead (from *Lilac Garden* [Tudor], 1951). Costumes by Karinska. Scenery executed by Nolan Brothers. Lighting by Nananne Porcher.

PREMIERE: January 8, 1958, New York City Ballet, City Center of Music and Drama, New York. Conductor: Leon Barzin.

CAST: FIRST MOVEMENT, ALLEGRO MOLTO: Maria Tallchief, Jacques d'Amboise, 20 women, 10 men; SECOND MOVEMENT, ALLEGRETTO: Tallchief, d'Amboise, 8 women; THIRD MOVEMENT, MINUETTO: 6 couples; FOURTH MOVEMENT, ADAGIO AND ALLEGRO VIVACE: Entire cast.

NOTE: French in spirit, the ballet was choreographed soon after Gounod's First Symphony came to public attention following a century of neglect.

STAGINGS: 1959, Paris (retitled *Symphonie*).

318 STARS AND STRIPES

Ballet in Five Campaigns

MUSIC: By John Philip Sousa (as given below), adapted and orchestrated by Hershy Kay.

PRODUCTION: Scenery by David Hays. Costumes by Karinska. Lighting by Nananne Porcher (1958); David Hays (1964).

PREMIERE: January 17, 1958, New York City Ballet, City Center of Music and Drama, New York. Conductor: Leon Barzin.

CAST: FIRST CAMPAIGN, *1st Regiment* ('Corcoran Cadets'): Allegra Kent, 12 women; SECOND CAMPAIGN, *2nd Regiment* ('Thunder and Gladiator'): Robert Barnett, 12 men; THIRD CAMPAIGN, *3rd Regiment* ('Rifle Regiment'): Diana Adams, 12 women; FOURTH CAMPAIGN ('Liberty Bell' and 'El Capitan'): Melissa Hayden, Jacques d'Amboise; FIFTH CAMPAIGN, *All Regiments* ('Stars and Stripes').

NOTE: A kind of balletic parade based on the themes of Sousa's patriotic marching band music. The campaigns or movements feature each regiment in turn; following a grand pas de deux all combine in the finale as a giant American flag appears. Dedicated to the memory of Fiorello H. La Guardia, Mayor of New York City and founder of the City Center of Music and Drama.

REVISIONS: New York City Ballet: Order of Second and Third Campaigns reversed shortly after premiere.

STAGINGS (pas de deux unless otherwise noted): 1967, Garden State; 1969, Boston (complete); 1974, New York Dance Theatre; 1975, Dover; 1976, U. S. Terpsichore, Geneva; 1977, Princeton, Australia; ca. 1978, Eglevsky; 1979, Chicago Lyric Opera, Prince George's; 1981, New Jersey, San Francisco (complete).

TELEVISION: 1959 (excerpts, Bell Telephone Hour, NBC); 1963 (pas de deux, NBC); 1964 (excerpts, CBS); n.d. (pas de deux, German television).

319 A MIDSUMMER NIGHT'S DREAM
Play by William Shakespeare

MUSIC: By Marc Blitzstein.

PRODUCTION: Directed by Jack Landau. Scenery by David Hays. Costumes by Thea Neu. Lighting by Tharon Musser.

PREMIERE: June 20, 1958, American Shakespeare Festival, Stratford, Connecticut. Danced by members of the Festival company. Singer: Russell Oberlin.

CAST: *Titania*, June Havoc; *Oberon*, Richard Waring; *Puck*, Richard Easton; *Bottom*, Hiram Sherman; *Theseus*, Jack Bittner; and others.

NOTE: Balanchine choreographed dance passages for the fairies.

STAGINGS: American Shakespeare Festival, 1959, 1960 (Boston).

320 THE WINTER'S TALE
Play by William Shakespeare

MUSIC: By Marc Blitzstein.

PRODUCTION: Directed by John Houseman and Jack Landau. Scenery by David Hays. Costumes by Dorothy Jeakins. Lighting by Jean Rosenthal.

PREMIERE: July 20, 1958, American Shakespeare Festival, Stratford, Connecticut. Danced by members of the Festival company. Singer: Russell Oberlin.

CAST: *Polixenes*, Richard Waring; *Leontes*, John Colicos; *Hermione*, Nancy Wickwire; *Autolycus*, Earle Hyman; *Florizel*, Richard Easton; *Perdita*, Inga Swenson; and others.

NOTE: Balanchine choreographed dances in the pastoral scene, Act IV, Scene 3.

321 WALTZ-SCHERZO

MUSIC: By Peter Ilyitch Tschaikovsky (Waltz-Scherzo for violin and orchestra, Op. 34, 1877).

PRODUCTION: Costumes by Karinska. Lighting by Nananne Porcher.

PREMIERE: September 9, 1958, New York City Ballet, City Center of Music and Drama, New York. Conductor: Robert Irving. Violinist: Louis Graeler.

CAST: Patricia Wilde, André Eglevsky.

REVISIONS: 1964, New York City Ballet: Minor changes, including addition of some lifts.

322 THE SEVEN DEADLY SINS
Sloth, Pride, Anger, Gluttony, Lust, Avarice, Envy

MUSIC: By Kurt Weill (*Die sieben Todsünden*, produced 1933, commissioned by Boris Kochno and Edward James). Text by Bertolt Brecht, from a suggestion by Boris Kochno and Edward James, translated by W. H. Auden and Chester Kallman (translation commissioned by Lincoln Kirstein).

PRODUCTION: Scenery, costumes and lighting by Rouben Ter-Arutunian. Scenery executed by T. B. McDonald Construction Company.

PREMIERE: December 4, 1958, New York City Ballet, City Center of Music and Drama, New York. Conductor: Robert Irving.

CAST: *Anna I* (singer), Lotte Lenya; *Anna II* (dancer), Allegra Kent; *Characters* (dancers), 16 women, 15 men. *Family* (singers): *Mother*,

Stanley Carlson; *Father*, Gene Hollman; *Brother I*, Frank Poretta; *Brother II*, Grant Williams. Singers and dancers appeared together on stage.

NOTE: First presented by Les Ballets 1933, Paris. This revival for the New York City Ballet was sponsored by Ballet Society to celebrate the twenty-fifth year of association between Lincoln Kirstein and George Balanchine; Lotte Lenya played the role created for her in 1933. The staging, noted for its masque-like characteristics, consisted primarily of stylized movement rather than balletic dancing.

STAGINGS: 1964, San Francisco (based on Balanchine's 1958 version with new choreography by Lew Christensen).

OTHER VERSIONS: 1933, Les Ballets 1933 (*Les Sept Péchés Capitaux*).

See 136*

1959

323 NATIVE DANCERS

MUSIC: By Vittorio Rieti (Symphony No. 5, 1945).

PRODUCTION: Scenery and lighting by David Hays. Women's costumes by Peter Larkin. Jockey silks by H. Kauffman & Sons Saddlery Company.

PREMIERE: January 14, 1959, New York City Ballet, City Center of Music and Drama, New York. Conductor: Robert Irving.

CAST: Patricia Wilde, Jacques d'Amboise; 6 women, 6 men.
ALLEGRO GIOCOSO; ANDANTE TRANQUILLO; PRESTO.

NOTE: Named after the famous race horse. The ladies are horses, with ponytails and jingling harnesses, put through their paces by men as jockeys.

324 EPISODES

MUSIC: By Anton Webern (complete orchestral works, as given below).

CHOREOGRAPHY: By Martha Graham (Part I) and George Balanchine (Part II).

PRODUCTION: Scenery and lighting by David Hays. Costumes for Part I by Karinska. Scenery executed by Chester Rakeman Studios, S. C. Hansen and Decorator Plant Company; later by Nolan Brothers.

PREMIERE: May 14, 1959, New York City Ballet, City Center of Music and Drama, New York. Conductor: Robert Irving.

CAST: Part I. (*Passacaglia*, Op. 1, 1906, and *Six Pieces*, Op. 6, 1910): *Mary, Queen of Scots*, Martha Graham; *Bothwell*, Bertram Ross; *Elizabeth, Queen of England*, Sallie Wilson (of the New York City Ballet); *The Four Marys*, 4 women; *Darnley, Riccio, Chastelard*, 3 men; *Executioner*; *2 Heralds*.

Part II. SYMPHONY (Op. 21, 1928): Violette Verdy, Jonathan Watts, 3 couples; FIVE PIECES (Op. 10, 1911-13): Diana Adams, Jacques d'Amboise; CONCERTO (Op. 24, 1934): Allegra Kent, Nicholas Magallanes, 4 women; VARIATIONS (Op. 30, 1940): Paul Taylor (of the Martha Graham Dance Company); RICERCATA (in 6 voices from Bach's *Musical Offering*, 1935): Melissa Hayden, Francisco Moncion, 14 women.

NOTE: A Ballet Society production. Conceived by Balanchine as an homage to the atonal composer Webern, *Episodes* is set to his complete orchestral works. Martha Graham by invitation choreographed Part I (a narrative, in period costume) for her company; Balanchine choreographed Part II (plotless, danced in practice clothes) for the New York City Ballet. The VARIATIONS FOR ORCHESTRA consists of a theme and six variations for a single male dancer, choreographed for Paul Taylor, then a member of the Graham Company. The final part, the RICERCATA, is a tribute by Webern to the music of Johann Sebastian Bach. The full ballet was performed by both companies for two seasons. In 1960, the New York City Ballet presented its part alone as *Episodes II*; from 1961 this was performed as *Episodes*, without the solo created for Paul Taylor.

STAGINGS (Part II): 1969, Berlin; 1971, Geneva; 1973, Dutch National; 1978, Chicago Lyric Opera (FIVE PIECES).

Television: 1963 (concerto, NBC); 1970 (five pieces, CBC, Montreal); 1978 (BBC, London).

325 ROMEO AND JULIET
Play by William Shakespeare

Music: By David Amram.

Production: Directed by Jack Landau. Scenery by David Hays. Costumes by Dorothy Jeakins. Lighting by Tharon Musser.

Premiere: June 12, 1959, American Shakespeare Festival, Stratford, Connecticut. Danced by members of the Festival company.

Cast: *Romeo*, Richard Easton; *Juliet*, Inga Swenson; *Mercutio*, William Smithers; *Tybalt*, Jack Bittner; *Capulet*, Morris Carnovsky; *Lady Capulet*, Nancy Wickwire; *Nurse*, Aline MacMahon; *Friar Laurence*, Hiram Sherman; and others.

Note: Balanchine choreographed dances for the Capulet ball, Act I, Scene 5.

See 278

326 THE MERRY WIVES OF WINDSOR
Play by William Shakespeare

Music: By Irwin Bazelon.

Production: Directed by John Houseman and Jack Landau. Scenery by Will Steven Armstrong. Costumes by Motley. Lighting by Tharon Musser.

Premiere: July 2, 1959, American Shakespeare Festival, Stratford, Connecticut. Danced by members of the Festival company.

Cast: *Falstaff*, Larry Gates; *Mistress Page*, Nancy Marchand; *Mistress Ford*, Nancy Wickwire; *Mistress Quickly*, Sada Thompson; *Fenton*, Lowell Harris; *Anne Page*, Barbara Barrie; and others.

Note: Balanchine choreographed the fairies' dances in Windsor Park, Act V, Scene 5.

327 THE WARRIOR

MUSIC: By Sergei Rachmaninoff (Prelude in G minor, Op. 33, no. 5, 1911).

CHOREOGRAPHY: Originally choreographed by Léonide Massine (1945); rechoreographed by George Balanchine.

CAST: André Eglevsky.

NOTE: André Eglevsky recalled dancing this solo once in Miami during the 1950s.

1960

328 NIGHT SHADOW (from 1960 called LA SONNAMBULA)

MUSIC: Music and book by Vittorio Rieti, based on themes from operas by Vincenzo Bellini (1830-35, including *La Sonnambula*, *I Puritani*, *Norma*, and *I Capuletti ed i Montecchi*).

CHOREOGRAPHY: By George Balanchine. Staged by John Taras.

PRODUCTION: Scenery and lighting by Esteban Francés. Costumes by André Levasseur (from the Grand Ballet du Marquis de Cuevas production, 1948). Scenery and costumes executed by Nolan Brothers. Jewelry by Emmons.

PREMIERE: January 6, 1960, New York City Ballet, City Center of Music and Drama, New York. Conductor: Robert Irving.

CAST: *The Coquette*, Jillana; *The Baron*, John Taras; *The Poet*, Erik Bruhn; *The Sleepwalker*, Allegra Kent; *The Guests*, 8 couples; DIVERTISSEMENTS: PASTORALE: 2 couples; THE BLACKAMOORS: Suki Schorer, William Weslow; HARLEQUIN: Edward Villella; ACROBATS: 3 women.

NOTE: Originally presented as *The Night Shadow* by the Ballet Russe de Monte Carlo, New York, 1946.

*See 232**

329 PANAMERICA: NUMBERS II, IV, VIII

MUSIC: By Latin American composers (as given below), edited by Carlos Chávez.

CHOREOGRAPHY: By George Balanchine (three of eight dances), Gloria Contreras, Francisco Moncion, John Taras, and Jacques d'Amboise.

PRODUCTION: Scenery and lighting by David Hays. Costumes for Numbers II and VIII by Esteban Francés, executed by Brooks Costume Company; costumes for Number IV by Karinska.

PREMIERE: January 20, 1960, New York City Ballet, City Center of Music and Drama, New York. Conductor: Robert Irving. Guest Conductor for SINFONÍA NO. 5: Carlos Chávez.

CAST: II. PRELUDIOS PARA PERCUSIÓN (COLOMBIA), composed by Luis Escobar: Patricia Wilde, Erik Bruhn; IV. SINFONÍA NO. 5, FOR STRING ORCHESTRA (MEXICO), composed by Carlos Chávez: Diana Adams, Nicholas Magallanes, 6 couples; VIII. DANZAS SINFÓNICAS (CUBA), composed by Julián Orbón: Maria Tallchief, Conrad Ludlow, Arthur Mitchell, Edward Villella, 20 women, 10 men.

NOTE: A Ballet Society production. This salute to Pan America took the form of an evening-long collection of eight short ballets. During the following season (spring 1960), Number II, retitled *Colombia*, and Number VIII, retitled *Cuba*, were performed as independent works.

330 THEME AND VARIATIONS

MUSIC: By Peter Ilyitch Tschaikovsky (final movement of Suite No. 3 for orchestra in G major, 1884).

PRODUCTION: Costumes by Karinska (from *Symphony in C* [244]). Lighting by David Hays.

PREMIERE: February 5, 1960, New York City Ballet, City Center of Music and Drama, New York. Conductor: Robert Irving.

CAST: Violette Verdy, Edward Villella; Susan Borree, Judith Green, Francia Russell, Carol Sumner, Conrad Ludlow, Richard Rapp, Roy Tobias, William Weslow; 8 women, 8 men.

NOTE: Originally presented by Ballet Theatre, New York, 1947.

See 242*, 369

331 PAS DE DEUX
(also called TSCHAIKOVSKY PAS DE DEUX)

MUSIC: By Peter Ilyitch Tschaikovsky (*Swan Lake*, Op. 20, 1875-76; pas de deux originally intended for Act III, subsequently lost from 1877 until 1953).

PRODUCTION: Costumes by Karinska. Lighting by Jack Owen Brown; subsequently by David Hays.

PREMIERE: March 29, 1960, New York City Ballet, City Center of Music and Drama, New York. Conductor: Robert Irving.

CAST: Violette Verdy, Conrad Ludlow.

NOTE: A display piece for two leading dancers, choreographed to lost music intended for the third act of *Swan Lake*, rediscovered in 1953 in the Bolshoi archives. A fifty-second excerpt from this pas de deux appears in the film *The Turning Point* (Twentieth-Century Fox, 1977).

REVISIONS: Male variation and coda differ from performer to performer.

STAGINGS: 1962, Les Grands Ballets Canadiens; 1963, Royal Danish; 1964, Royal; 1969, Boston; 1970, American Ballet Theatre, Houston; 1971, Ballet West; 1972, San Francisco, London Festival; 1973, Los Angeles, Geneva; 1976, Joffrey, Caracas; ca. 1976, Eglevsky; 1977, Dance Theatre of Harlem, U. S. Terpsichore, Washington; 1978, Arizona, North Carolina; 1980, Connecticut, New Jersey, New York Dance Theatre, Alberta, Belgrade, La Scala, Matsuyama, Paris; 1981, Baltimore; 1982, Ballet Metropolitan, Kansas City.

TELEVISION: 1962 (Voice of Firestone, ABC); 1962 (BBC, London); 1964 (Bell Telephone Hour, NBC); 1965 (CBS); 1965 (CBC, Montreal); 1966 (PBS); 1968 (excerpts, Bell Telephone Hour, NBC); 1969 (WTTW, Chicago); 1970 (CBC, Montreal); 1979 (Dance in America, PBS).

See 75, 191, 262, 285, 367

332 THE FIGURE IN THE CARPET
Ballet in Five Scenes

MUSIC: By George Frederick Handel (from the *Royal Fireworks Music*, 1749, and *Water Music*, ca. 1717). Book by George Lewis; underlying

ideas in the organization of the sequence of scenes suggested by
Dr. Arthur Upham Pope.

PRODUCTION: Scenery, costumes and lighting by Esteban Francés.
Scenery executed by Nolan Brothers; costumes executed by Karinska.

PREMIERE: April 13, 1960, New York City Ballet, City Center of Music
and Drama, New York. Conductor: Robert Irving.

CAST: SCENE I, THE SANDS OF THE DESERT: Violette Verdy, 18 women;
SCENE II, THE WEAVING OF THE CARPET (PAS D'ACTION): Verdy, 12 women;
Nomad Tribesmen, Conrad Ludlow, 6 men; SCENE III, THE BUILDING OF THE
PALACE: ENTRANCE OF THE IRANIAN COURT: *Prince and Princess of Persia*,
Jacques d'Amboise, Melissa Hayden; *Their Courtiers*, 8 couples; THE
RECEPTION OF THE FOREIGN AMBASSADORS: *France: The Prince and Princesses
of Lorraine*, Edward Villella, Susan Borree, Suki Schorer; *Spain: The
Duke and Duchess of Granada*, Francisco Moncion, Judith Green;
America: The Princess of the West Indies, Francia Russell, 6 women; *China:
The Duke and Duchess of L'an L'ing*, Nicholas Magallanes, Patricia
McBride, 4 women; *Africa: The Oni of Ife and His Consort*, Arthur
Mitchell, Mary Hinkson (guest artist); *Scotland: The Four Lairds of the
Isles and Their Lady*, Diana Adams, 4 men; GRAND PAS DE DEUX: Hayden,
d'Amboise; SCENE IV, FINALE: THE GARDENS OF PARADISE; SCENE V,
APOTHEOSIS: THE FOUNTAINS OF HEAVEN.

NOTE: Devised in the style of an eighteenth-century court ballet, based
on Dr. Pope's relation of Handel's musical counterpoint to Persian
carpet weaving of the period. The title is from a tale by Henry James.
SCENE I evokes a desert atmosphere; in the APOTHEOSIS a large
fountain plays on stage; the décor and costumes for SCENES III, IV and V
were derived from Persian designs. Presented in honor of the
Fourth International Congress of Iranian Art and Archeology. In 1976,
Balanchine used the Scottish theme from the *Water Music* for the
Royal Canadian Air Force variation in *Union Jack* [401].

333 VARIATIONS FROM DON SEBASTIAN
(from 1961 called DONIZETTI VARIATIONS)

MUSIC: By Gaetano Donizetti (from *Dom Sébastien*, produced 1843).

PRODUCTION: Scenery and lighting by David Hays. Women's costumes
by Karinska; men's by Esteban Francés (from *Panamerica* [329]).

PREMIERE: November 16, 1960, New York City Ballet, City Center of Music and Drama, New York. Conductor: Robert Irving.

CAST: Melissa Hayden, Jonathan Watts, 6 women, 3 men.

NOTE: The premiere was part of a special *Salute to Italy*, which also included the premiere of *Monumentum pro Gesualdo*, and performances of *La Sonnambula* [232] and Lew Christensen's *Con Amore*.

REVISIONS: 1971, New York City Ballet: Some new choreography for principals.

NEW PRODUCTIONS BY BALANCHINE COMPANIES: 1971, New York City Ballet: Costumes by Karinska; lighting by Ronald Bates.

STAGINGS (usually titled *Donizetti Variations*): 1964, Boston, Pennsylvania; 1966, Joffrey; 1967, Hamburg; 1968, Royal Danish; 1972, Geneva; 1976, Dutch National; 1977, Maryland; 1978, Eglevsky; 1979, Chicago Lyric Opera; 1981, Connecticut, Louisville, New Jersey, Reggio Emilia.

TELEVISION: 1961 (excerpts, Omnibus, NBC).

334 MONUMENTUM PRO GESUALDO

MUSIC: By Igor Stravinsky (three madrigals by Gesualdo, recomposed for instruments, 1960).

PRODUCTION: Scenery and lighting by David Hays (1960); lighting by Ronald Bates (1974).

PREMIERE: November 16, 1960, New York City Ballet, City Center of Music and Drama, New York. Conductor: Robert Irving.

CAST: Diana Adams, Conrad Ludlow, 6 couples.

NOTE: Stravinsky made orchestral versions of Gesualdo's madrigals to honor the four-hundredth anniversary of the composer's birth. The ballet is in three parts, each lasting just over two minutes. Occasionally since 1965, and consistently since 1966, performed with *Movements for Piano and Orchestra* [344].

335 LIEBESLIEDER WALZER

Ballet in Two Parts

MUSIC: By Johannes Brahms (*Liebeslieder*, Op. 52, 1869, and *Neue Liebeslieder*, Op. 65, 1874, waltzes for piano duet and vocal quartet, all set to poems by Friedrich Daumer, except the last, by Goethe).

PRODUCTION: Scenery and lighting by David Hays. Costumes by Karinska.

PREMIERE: November 22, 1960, New York City Ballet, City Center of Music and Drama, New York. Pianists: Louise Sherman, Robert Irving. Singers: Angeline Rasmussen, Mitzi Wilson, Frank Poretta, Herbert Beattie.

CAST: Diana Adams, Bill Carter; Melissa Hayden, Jonathan Watts; Jillana, Conrad Ludlow; Violette Verdy, Nicholas Magallanes.

NOTE: Dancers and musicians in period costumes are on stage together. During the first set of eighteen waltzes the four couples, wearing formal evening dress and dancing slippers, dance in interweaving combinations in an intimate ballroom. After a brief lowering of the curtain they dance fourteen waltzes under a starry sky, the women wearing ballet dresses and toe shoes. They leave the stage; returning in the original costumes, they pause to listen to the final waltz. Within the strict three-quarter beat of music and dance, personal and romantic associations between the couples are implied.

STAGINGS: 1977, Vienna; 1979, Royal; 1981, Zürich.

TELEVISION: 1961 (L'Heure du Concert, CBC, Montreal).

336 RAGTIME (I)

MUSIC: By Igor Stravinsky (*Ragtime for Eleven Instruments*, 1918).

PRODUCTION: Scenery by Robert Drew (from *Blackface* [L. Christensen], 1947). Costumes by Karinska. Lighting by David Hays.

PREMIERE: December 7, 1960, New York City Ballet, City Center of Music and Drama, New York. Conductor: Robert Irving.

CAST: Diana Adams, Bill Carter.

NOTE: The choreography is jazz-inspired, in a cabaret style. One of a quartet of works by Balanchine, Todd Bolender, Francisco Moncion, and John Taras, collectively titled *Jazz Concert*. Balanchine first used this music for a dance in 1922; in 1966, he choreographed another work to this score, titled *Ragtime (II)*.

See 3, 356

1961

337 MODERN JAZZ: VARIANTS

MUSIC: By Gunther Schuller (*Variants* for orchestra and the Modern Jazz Quartet, 1960, commissioned by the New York City Ballet).

PRODUCTION: Lighting by David Hays.

PREMIERE: January 4, 1961, New York City Ballet, City Center of Music and Drama, New York. Conductor: Gunther Schuller. Modern Jazz Quartet: John Lewis (piano), Percy Heath (bass), Milt Jackson (vibraharp), Connie Kay (drums).

CAST: INTRODUCTION (orchestra): Diana Adams, Melissa Hayden, John Jones (guest artist), Arthur Mitchell, 6 women, 6 men; VARIANT 1 (piano): Adams, Jones; VARIANT 2 (bass): Adams, 6 men; VARIANT 3 (vibraharp): Hayden, Mitchell; VARIANT 4 (drums): Hayden; VARIANT 5 (quartet): Adams, Hayden, Jones, Mitchell; FINALE: Entire cast.

NOTE: The Modern Jazz Quartet played on stage, accompanied by a twelve-tone score performed by the orchestra. The choreography combines ballet with jazz action.

338 ELECTRONICS

MUSIC: Electronic tape by Remi Gassmann in collaboration with Oskar Sala (commissioned by Philip Johnson).

PRODUCTION: Scenery and lighting by David Hays. Scenery executed by Nolan Brothers. Fabrics by Dazian's.

PREMIERE: March 22, 1961, New York City Ballet, City Center of Music and Drama, New York.

CAST: Diana Adams, Violette Verdy, Jacques d'Amboise, Edward Villella, 8 women.

NOTE: The score is composed of sound material itself electronically created, not derived or adapted from conventional sound sources. The stage action takes place in an atmosphere of science fiction, the setting cellophane, the costumes white, silver, gold, black.

339 VALSES ET VARIATIONS
(from 1963 called RAYMONDA VARIATIONS)

MUSIC: By Alexander Glazounov (from *Raymonda*, Op. 57, produced 1898).

PRODUCTION: Scenery by Horace Armistead (from *Lilac Garden* [Tudor], 1951). Costumes by Karinska. Lighting by David Hays.

PREMIERE: December 7, 1961, New York City Ballet, City Center of Music and Drama, New York. Conductor: Robert Irving.

CAST: VALSE: Patricia Wilde, 12 women; PAS DE DEUX: Wilde, Jacques d'Amboise; VARIATION I: Victoria Simon; VARIATION II: Suki Schorer; VARIATION III: d'Amboise; VARIATION IV: Wilde; VARIATION V: Gloria Govrin; VARIATION VI: Carol Sumner; VARIATION VII: Patricia Neary; VARIATION VIII: d'Amboise; VARIATION IX: Wilde; CODA AND FINALE: Wilde, d'Amboise, ensemble.

NOTE: To selections from the score of *Raymonda*, Balanchine developed in his twentieth-century terms the heritage of the three-act Petipa original of 1898.

STAGINGS (distinct from the numerous stagings of excerpts from Act III of *Raymonda* [233] and *Pas de Dix* [309], also often performed under the title *Raymonda Variations*): 1966, Eglevsky; 1967, Atlanta; 1969, Geneva; 1971, Houston (titled *Waltz and Variations*), Pennsylvania; 1973, Los Angeles; 1976, Chicago Lyric Opera; 1982, Alabama.

See 18, 233*, 309, 384

1962

340 A MIDSUMMER NIGHT'S DREAM
Ballet in Two Acts and Six Scenes

MUSIC: By Felix Mendelssohn (Overture and incidental music to *Ein Sommernachtstraum*, Opp. 21 and 61, 1826, 1842; Overture to *Athalie*, Op. 74, 1845; Concert overture *Die schöne Melusine*, Op. 32, 1833; *Die erste Walpurgisnacht*, Op. 60; Symphony No. 9 for strings [first three of four movements], 1823; Overture to *Die Heimkehr aus der Fremde*, Op. 89, 1829).

PRODUCTION: Scenery and lighting by David Hays, assisted by Peter Harvey. Costumes by Karinska.

PREMIERE: January 17, 1962, New York City Ballet with children from the School of American Ballet, City Center of Music and Drama, New York. Conductor: Robert Irving. Singers: Veronica Tyler (soprano), Marija Kova (mezzo-soprano), 4 women.

CAST: ACT I: *Butterflies*, Suki Schorer, 4 women, 8 children; *Puck*, Arthur Mitchell; *Helena, in love with Demetrius*, Jillana; *Oberon, King of the Fairies*, Edward Villella; *Oberon's Pages*; *Titania, Queen of the Fairies*, Melissa Hayden; *Titania's Cavalier*, Conrad Ludlow; *Titania's Page*; *Bottom, a Weaver*, Roland Vazquez; *Bottom's Companions*, 4 men; *Theseus, Duke of Athens*, Francisco Moncion; *Courtiers to Theseus*; *Hermia, in love with Lysander*, Patricia McBride; *Lysander, beloved of Hermia*, Nicholas Magallanes; *Demetrius, Suitor to Hermia*, Bill Carter; *Titania's Retinue*, 12 women; *Oberon's Kingdom: Butterflies and Fairies*, 13 children; *Hippolyta, Queen of the Amazons*, Gloria Govrin; *Hippolyta's Hounds*, 6 women; ACT II: *Courtiers*, 18 women, 8 men; DIVERTISSEMENT: Violette Verdy, Ludlow, 6 couples.

NOTE: Balanchine's first wholly original full-length ballet. Act I relates the story of Shakespeare's play. Act II is a wedding divertissement, concluding with a brief return to the enchanted forest, and Shakespeare's ending. A film of the entire work, produced by Oberon Productions, Ltd., was released in 1967.

REVISIONS: New York City Ballet: Act II, third movement of Symphony

No. 9 deleted almost immediately; 1964, Act II, new choreography for courtiers, divertissement shortened (to first two movements of Symphony No. 9, omitting second movement fugue); 1978, Act I, new choreography for Hippolyta's Hounds.

NEW PRODUCTIONS BY BALANCHINE COMPANIES: New York City Ballet: 1964, scenery and costumes redesigned by David Hays and Karinska for the New York State Theater, with color scheme in Act II changed from white and gold to red; 1980, scenery adapted by David Hays to facilitate use in repertory, lighting by Ronald Bates.

STAGINGS: 1979, Zürich.

TELEVISION: n.d. (pas de deux from DIVERTISSEMENT, German television).

341 EUGEN ONEGIN
Opera in Three Acts and Six Scenes

MUSIC: By Peter Ilyitch Tschaikovsky (*Eugen Onegin*, produced 1879). Libretto based on a poem by Alexander Pushkin. German text by A. Bernhard and M. Kalbeck.

PRODUCTION: Directed and choreographed by George Balanchine. Scenery and costumes designed by H. M. Crayon.

PREMIERE: February 27, 1962, Hamburgische Staatsoper, Hamburg. Danced by Ballett der Hamburgischen Staatsoper. Conductor: Horst Stein.

CAST: *Larina*, Maria v. Ilosvay; *Tatiana*, Melitta Muszely; *Olga*, Cvetka Ahlin; *Filipevna*, Ursula Boese; *Eugen Onegin*, Vladimir Ruzdak; *Lensky*, Heinz Hoppe; *Count Gremin*, Arnold van Mill; and others.

NOTE: Printed programs list no dances or dancers; the choreography included the ball scenes in Acts II and III.

STAGINGS: 1971, Opéra du Grand Théâtre de Genève.

See 256

342 NOAH AND THE FLOOD

Made for Television

MUSIC: Dance-drama by Igor Stravinsky (*The Flood*, 1962). Text chosen and arranged by Robert Craft from *Genesis*, the *Te Deum* and *Sanctus* hymns, the fifteenth-century York and Chester miracle plays, and for Satan's final *Arietta* from several sources including Shakespeare and Dylan Thomas. Prologue written by Jack Richardson.

PRODUCTION: Produced by Sextant, Inc. Directed by Kirk Browning. Production Designer: Rouben Ter-Arutunian.

FIRST TELECAST: June 14, 1962, CBS. Danced by New York City Ballet. Columbia Symphony Orchestra and Chorus. Conductors: Igor Stravinsky and Robert Craft. Chorus Director: Gregg Smith.

CAST: VOICES: *Narrator*, Laurence Harvey; *Noah*, Sebastian Cabot; *Mrs. Noah*, Elsa Lancaster; *Caller*, Paul Tripp; *The Voice of God*, John Reardon and Robert Oliver; *Satan*, Robert Robinson. DANCERS: *Adam* and *Lucifer*, Jacques d'Amboise; *Eve*, Jillana; *Satan*, Edward Villella; *Noah*, Ramon Segarra; *Mrs. Noah*, Joysanne Sidimus; 8 women, 8 men.

NOTE: Conceived and written for television. Balanchine worked closely with the composer during the composition and production. The work is divided into six parts. Four sections are sung: *Prelude* (including the Creation, the Expulsion from the Garden, and God's Command to Noah), *The Catalogue of the Animals*, *The Comedy* (Noah and his wife and sons), and *The Covenant of the Rainbow*; two sections are choreographed: *The Building of the Ark* and *The Flood*. Balanchine did not choreograph a subsequent stage performance until the 1982 New York City Ballet production for the Stravinsky Centennial Celebration.

See 422

1963

343 BUGAKU

MUSIC: By Toshiro Mayuzumi (1962, commissioned by the New York City Ballet).

PRODUCTION: Scenery and lighting by David Hays. Costumes by Karinska. Scenery executed by Nolan Brothers.

PREMIERE: March 20, 1963, New York City Ballet, City Center of Music and Drama, New York. Conductor: Robert Irving.

CAST: Allegra Kent, Edward Villella, 4 couples.

NOTE: Following the appearance of the Imperial Gagaku company of musicians and dancers from Japan on programs of the New York City Ballet in 1959, Mayuzumi was invited to compose a piece in the spirit of Japanese court music (Bugaku), but with Western instrumentation. The ballet, in three movements, suggests ceremonial rites of courtship and marriage.

STAGINGS: 1975, Dance Theatre of Harlem; 1980, Zürich.

TELEVISION: 1977 (pas de deux, Dance in America, PBS); 1978 (CBC, Montreal).

344 MOVEMENTS FOR PIANO AND ORCHESTRA

MUSIC: By Igor Stravinsky (1958-59, dedicated to Margrit Weber).

PRODUCTION: Lighting by Peter Harvey.

PREMIERE: April 9, 1963, New York City Ballet, City Center of Music and Drama, New York. Conductor: Robert Irving. Pianist: Gordon Boelzner.

CAST: Suzanne Farrell, Jacques d'Amboise, 6 women.

NOTE: The music uses serial combinations and is divided into five concise parts. Stravinsky described the ballet as a double concerto for male and female solo dancers, both identified with the piano solo, accompanied by a corps de ballet. Occasionally since 1965, and consistently since 1966, performed with *Monumentum pro Gesualdo* [334].

TELEVISION: 1963 (CBS); 1971 (CBC, Montreal).

345 ORPHEUS UND EURYDIKE (ORFEO ED EURIDICE)
Opera in Three Acts and Five Scenes

MUSIC: By Christoph Willibald Gluck (*Orfeo ed Euridice*, produced 1762, with ballet music from the Paris production of 1774). Libretto by Raniero da Calzabigi, translated by Hans Swarowsky.

PRODUCTION: Directed and choreographed by George Balanchine. Scenery and costumes designed by Rouben Ter-Arutunian.

PREMIERE: November 16, 1963, Hamburgische Staatsoper, Hamburg. Danced by Ballett der Hamburgischen Staatsoper. Conductor: Janos Kulka.

CAST: SINGERS: *Orpheus*, Ursula Boese; *Eurydike*, Doris Jung; *Amor*, Ria Urban; and others. DANCERS: SCENE 1: *Shepherds and Shepherdesses*, 7 women, 4 men. SCENE 2: *Furies*, 12 women, 12 men. SCENE 3: *Night*, Angèle Albrecht; 8 *Spirits* (women), 4 *Shadows* (women). SCENE 5: CHACONNE: Christa Kempf, Heinz Clauss; Albrecht; Erika Czarnecki, Falco Kapuste; Wilfried Schumann; 9 women, 6 men; PAS DE TROIS: Uta Graf, Heidi Korf, Helmut Baumann; CUPID AND CHERUBS (PAS DE CINQ): Henni Vanhaiden, 4 women; PAS DE DEUX: Dulce Anaya, Rainer Kochermann; Marilyn Burr, Peter van Dyk.

NOTE: The CHACONNE of this production, directed and choreographed by Balanchine at the invitation of Rolf Liebermann, formed the basis for the ballet *Chaconne* [400], first performed by the New York City Ballet in 1976.

REVISIONS: 1973, Théâtre National de l'Opéra, Paris: Choreography from Hamburg, 1963, performed in a new production of the opera (not directed by Balanchine); changes included some new choreography in principal (second) pas de deux, pas de cinq, and ensemble passages.

STAGINGS (ballet sequences only): 1965, Hamburg; 1974, Geneva.

OTHER VERSIONS: 1936, Metropolitan Opera (danced by American Ballet, as American Ballet Ensemble).

See 170*, 399, 400

346 MEDITATION

MUSIC: By Peter Ilyitch Tschaikovsky (*Meditation*, Op. 42, no. 1, from *Souvenir d'un Lieu Cher*, three pieces for piano and violin, 1878, orchestrated by Alexander Glazounov).

PRODUCTION: Costumes by Karinska.

PREMIERE: December 10, 1963, New York City Ballet, City Center of Music and Drama, New York. Conductor: Robert Irving. Violinist: Marilyn Wright.

CAST: Suzanne Farrell, Jacques d'Amboise.

NOTE: On the darkened stage a solitary, troubled young man enters and kneels. He is approached by a young woman who seeks to comfort him. They dance together and embrace; in the end she departs, and he is again alone.

STAGINGS: 1973, Ballet du XXe Siècle.

TELEVISION: 1966 (PBS).

1964

347 TARANTELLA

MUSIC: By Louis Moreau Gottschalk (*Grande Tarantelle*, ca. 1866, reconstructed and orchestrated by Hershy Kay).

PRODUCTION: Costumes by Karinska.

PREMIERE: January 7, 1964, New York City Ballet, City Center of Music and Drama, New York. Conductor: Robert Irving. Pianist: Jean-Pierre Marty.

CAST: Patricia McBride, Edward Villella.

STAGINGS: 1973, Los Angeles, Geneva; 1974, Boston; 1975, Dayton; 1977, Arizona, Garden State, Joffrey; 1978, North Carolina, Zürich; 1979, Eglevsky; 1980, Royal.

TELEVISION: 1966 (PBS); 1968 (excerpts, Bell Telephone Hour, NBC); 1971 (CBC, Montreal); 1979 (WETA, Washington, D.C.).

348 CLARINADE

MUSIC: By Morton Gould (*Derivations for Clarinet and Jazz Band*, 1954-55, composed for Benny Goodman).

PRODUCTION: Costumes (practice clothes) assembled by Karinska in consultation with George Balanchine (uncredited).

PREMIERE: April 29, 1964, New York City Ballet, New York State Theater. Conductor: Robert Irving. Clarinetist: Benny Goodman.

CAST: WARM-UP: Gloria Govrin, Arthur Mitchell, 5 couples; CONTRA-PUNTAL BLUES: Suzanne Farrell, Anthony Blum, 2 couples; RAG: Govrin, 4 women; RIDE-OUT: Entire cast.

NOTE: The first work choreographed by Balanchine for the New York City Ballet after the move from City Center of Music and Drama to establish residency at the New York State Theater, Lincoln Center.

349 BALLET IMPERIAL (from 1973 called TSCHAIKOVSKY PIANO CONCERTO NO. 2)

MUSIC: By Peter Ilyitch Tschaikovsky (Piano Concerto No. 2 in G major, Op. 44, 1879, abridged, rewritten and rearranged by Alexander Siloti).

CHOREOGRAPHY: By George Balanchine. Staged by Frederic Franklin.

PRODUCTION: Scenery by Rouben Ter-Arutunian (based on the 1941 production). Costumes by Karinska.

PREMIERE: October 15, 1964, New York City Ballet, New York State Theater. Conductor: Robert Irving. Pianist: Gordon Boelzner.

CAST: Suzanne Farrell, Jacques d'Amboise; Patricia Neary; Frank Ohman, Earle Sieveling; 2 female demi-soloists; 16 women, 6 men.
ALLEGRO BRILLANTE–ANDANTE; ANDANTE NON TROPPO; ALLEGRO CON FUOCO.

NOTE: Originally presented by American Ballet Caravan, Rio de Janeiro, 1941. This production used the original choreography with minor revisions and an augmented corps de ballet.

See 194*, 382

1965

350 PAS DE DEUX AND DIVERTISSEMENT

MUSIC: By Léo Delibes (excerpts from *La Source* [*Naïla*], 1866, and *Sylvia, ou la Nymphe de Diane*, 1876).

PRODUCTION: Costumes by Karinska. Lighting by David Hays.

PREMIERE: January 14, 1965, New York City Ballet, New York State Theater. Conductor: Robert Irving.

CAST: VALSE LENTE AND PAS DE DEUX: Melissa Hayden, André Prokovsky; ALLEGRO VIVACE: Suki Schorer, 8 women; VARIATION: Prokovsky; PIZZICATI: Hayden; VALSE DES FLEURS: Entire cast.

NOTE: VALSE LENTE AND PAS DE DEUX was originally choreographed for the New York City Ballet in 1950, titled *Sylvia: Pas de Deux* [273]. In 1969, the ALLEGRO VIVACE and VALSE DES FLEURS were incorporated in *La Source* [364], choreographed for the New York City Ballet.

See 36, 273*, 274, 364, 387

351 HARLEQUINADE

Ballet in Two Acts

MUSIC: By Riccardo Drigo (from *Les Millions d'Arlequin*, produced 1900).

PRODUCTION: Scenery (partially from the New York City Opera production of *La Cenerentola*, 1953), costumes and lighting by Rouben Ter-Arutunian. Scenery executed by Feller Scenery Studios.

PREMIERE: February 4, 1965, New York City Ballet with children from the School of American Ballet, New York State Theater. Conductor: Robert Irving.

CAST: *Harlequin*, Edward Villella; *Colombine*, Patricia McBride; *Pierrot, Servant to Cassandre*, Deni Lamont; *Pierrette, Wife of Pierrot*, Suki Schorer; *Cassandre, Father of Colombine*, Michael Arshansky; *Léandre, Wealthy Suitor to Colombine*, Shaun O'Brien; *La Bonne Fée*, Gloria Govrin; *Les Scaramouches, Friends to Harlequin*, 4 couples; *Les Sbires, Hired by Cassandre to Capture Harlequin*, 3 men; *La Patrouille*, 5 men; *Le Laquais*; *Alouettes*, Carol Sumner, 8 women; *Les Petits Harlequins*, 8 children.

    Act I: House of Cassandre
    Act II: An Enchanted Park

NOTE: As a student in Petrograd, Balanchine danced in Petipa's *Les Millions d'Harlequin*. Balanchine's production follows the tradition of the commedia dell'arte, in the spirit of Petipa. In Act I, Harlequin outwits his adversaries, and with the help of the Good Fairy wins Colombine's hand. Act II is a divertissement of celebration. The décor was taken from Pollock's toy theaters of London.

REVISIONS: New York City Ballet: 1966, CARNIVAL NUMBER added to Act I, BALLABILE DES INVITÉS (8 couples) added to Act II; 1973, lengthened version using complete score, with addition of 12 couples, 24 children.

TELEVISION: 1966 (pas de deux, Bell Telephone Hour, NBC); 1968 (pas de deux, Bell Telephone Hour, NBC); 1979 (pas de deux, PBS).

See 290

352 DON QUIXOTE
Ballet in Three Acts

MUSIC: By Nicolas Nabokov (commissioned by the New York City Ballet).

PRODUCTION: Scenery, costumes and lighting by Esteban Francés, assisted by Peter Harvey. Scenery executed by Feller Scenery Studios; costumes executed by Karinska. Giant by Kermit Love and Peter Saklin. Masks and armor by Lawrence Vlady.

PREMIERE: May 28, 1965, New York City Ballet with children from the School of American Ballet, New York State Theater. Conductor: Robert Irving. (Preview: Annual New York City Ballet Gala Benefit, May 27, with George Balanchine as Don Quixote.)

CAST: *Don Quixote*, Richard Rapp; *Dulcinea*, Suzanne Farrell; *Sancho Panza*, Deni Lamont. PROLOGUE (DON QUIXOTE'S STUDY): *Don Quixote*; *Dulcinea*; *Sancho Panza*; *Fantasies*, 6 children. ACT I, SCENE 1 (LA MANCHA): *Don Quixote*; *Sancho Panza*; *A Peasant*; *A Boy*; *6 Slaves*; *2 Guards*; SCENE 2 (A VILLAGE SQUARE): *3 Market Vendors*; *2 Waitresses*; *Cafe Proprietor*; *Townspeople*, 16 women, 8 men; *Dead Poet*; *His Friend*; *2 Pallbearers*; *Marcela*, Farrell; *2 Policemen*; *Organ Grinder*; *Puppeteer*; *Puppets* (children): *5 Saracens, Christian Girl, Christian Boy*; *4 Palace Guards*; *2 Ladies in Waiting*; *2 Gentlemen in Waiting*; *Duke*, Nicholas Magallanes; *Duchess*, Jillana. ACT II (THE PALACE): *Don Quixote*; *Sancho Panza*; *Vision of Dulcinea*; *Duke*; *Duchess*; *2 Ladies in Waiting*; *Major Domo*; *Ladies and Gentlemen of the Court*, 8 couples; *Merlin*, Francisco Moncion; DIVERTISSEMENTS: DANZA DE LA CACCIA: Patricia Neary, Conrad Ludlow, Kent Stowell; PAS DE DEUX MAURESQUE: Suki Schorer, John Prinz; COURANTE SICILIENNE: Sara Leland, Kay Mazzo, Carol Sumner, Frank Ohman, Robert Rodham, Earle Sieveling; RIGAUDON FLAMENCO: Gloria Govrin,

Arthur Mitchell; RITORNEL: Patricia McBride, child. ACT III, SCENE I
(A GARDEN OF THE PALACE): *Don Quixote*; *Sancho Panza*; PAS D'ACTION:
Knight of the Silver Moon, Ludlow; *Maidens*, Marnee Morris, Mimi Paul,
16 women; *Cavaliers*, Anthony Blum, Ohman; VARIATION I: Paul;
VARIATION II: Morris; VARIATION III: Blum; VARIATION IV: Farrell; *Merlin*;
Night Spirit, Govrin; SCENE 2 (LA MANCHA): *Don Quixote*; *Sancho Panza*;
Pigs; *4 Bearers*; SCENE 3 (DON QUIXOTE'S STUDY): *Don Quixote*; *Sancho
Panza*; *Housekeeper*; *Priest*; entire cast.

Prologue and Act I: In which Don Quixote reads—Dreams and
fantasies—Vision of Dulcinea—The attainment of knighthood and
beginning of the quest—Incident of the boy and the peasant—Adventure of the slaves—Sancho's adventure in the market place—Marcela
and the murdered poet—Performance at the puppet theater—Arrival
of the Duke and Duchess.

Act II: In which Don Quixote and Sancho Panza come to Court—
Entertainment at Court—A Masque and other diversions—Merlin
makes magic—Vision of Dulcinea.

Act III: Of knights, ladies and sorcery—Further adventures and a
stampede—How Don Quixote comes home—Apotheosis and death.

NOTE: The Balanchine-Nabokov full-length production is an original
work without reference to nineteenth-century Russian versions. The
ballet depicts episodes in the hero's search for perfection, and for his
ideal woman, Dulcinea, who appears as housemaid, shepherdess, the
Virgin Mary, and in other guises. Balanchine performed the role of Don
Quixote on several occasions.

REVISIONS: There were many revisions, including the composition of
additional music and scenery alterations. Major changes:

ACT I, SCENE 2 (A VILLAGE SQUARE): 1967, Role of Zoraida (Dulcinea)
added, with gypsy solo, JUGGLER'S DANCE added, Dead Poet omitted;
1968, Zoraida omitted; 1969, RIGAUDON FLAMENCO from Act II inserted
(restored to Act II in 1972), Juggler omitted; 1972, PAS CLASSIQUE
ESPAGNOL added (pas de deux with ensemble of 12 women), Belly
Dancer added; 1973, four variations added to PAS CLASSIQUE ESPAGNOL,
including one for leading man and one for leading woman; 1978, JOTA
added as prelude to PAS CLASSIQUE ESPAGNOL.

ACT II (THE PALACE): 1965, order of divertissements changed, DANZA DE
LA CACCIA changed from pas de trois to pas de deux; 1969, RIGAUDON

FLAMENCO inserted in Act I, Scene 2 (restored to Act II in 1972).

ACT III, SCENE I (A GARDEN OF THE PALACE): VARIATION III (male) changed several times; eliminated in 1975.

1966

353 VARIATIONS

MUSIC: By Igor Stravinsky (*Variations in Memory of Aldous Huxley*, 1965).

PRODUCTION: Lighting by Ronald Bates.

PREMIERE: March 31, 1966, New York City Ballet, New York State Theater. Conductor: Robert Irving.

CAST: I. 12 women; II. 6 men; III. Suzanne Farrell.

NOTE: The music is played three times, each time with different choreography and cast. In 1982, for the New York City Ballet Stravinsky Centennial Celebration, Balanchine rechoreographed the solo; it was presented alone, titled *Variations for Orchestra*.

See 425

354 BRAHMS–SCHOENBERG QUARTET

MUSIC: By Johannes Brahms (Piano Quartet No. 1 in G minor, Op. 25, 1861, orchestrated by Arnold Schoenberg, 1937).

PRODUCTION: Scenery by Peter Harvey, executed by Feller Scenery Studios. Costumes by Karinska. Lighting by Ronald Bates.

PREMIERE: April 21, 1966, New York City Ballet, New York State Theater. Conductor: Robert Irving. (Preview: Annual New York City Ballet Gala Benefit, April 19.)

CAST: ALLEGRO: Melissa Hayden, André Prokovsky; Gloria Govrin; 8 women, 4 men; INTERMEZZO: Patricia McBride, Conrad Ludlow, 3 women; ANDANTE: Allegra Kent, Edward Villella, 3 female demi-soloists, 12 women; RONDO ALLA ZINGARESE: Suzanne Farrell, Jacques d'Amboise, 8 couples.

NOTE: Brahms' First Piano Quartet was given the power of the full orchestra by Schoenberg; it was choreographed by Balanchine for dancers in ballroom gowns, court uniforms and gypsy regalia.

355 ÉLÉGIE

MUSIC: By Igor Stravinsky (*Élégie-Elegy* for solo viola, 1944).

PREMIERE: July 15, 1966, Philharmonic Hall, New York. Violist: Jesse Levine. (First New York City Ballet performance July 28, Saratoga Performing Arts Center. Violist: Jesse Levine.)

CAST: Suzanne Farrell.

NOTE: The premiere formed part of *A Festival of Stravinsky: His Heritage and His Legacy*, directed by Lucas Foss, which also included the premiere of Balanchine's *Ragtime* (II).

See 245*, 423

356 RAGTIME (II)

MUSIC: By Igor Stravinsky (*Ragtime for Eleven Instruments*, 1918).

PREMIERE: July 15, 1966, Philharmonic Hall, New York. Conductor: Richard Dufallo. (First New York City Ballet performance January 17, 1967, New York State Theater.)

CAST: Suzanne Farrell, Arthur Mitchell.

See 3, 336*

1967

357 TROIS VALSES ROMANTIQUES

MUSIC: By Emmanuel Chabrier (*Trois Valses Romantiques* for piano, 1883, orchestrated by Felix Mottl).

PRODUCTION: Costumes by Karinska (from *Bourrée Fantasque* [265], with additions). Lighting by Ronald Bates.

PREMIERE: April 6, 1967, New York City Ballet, New York State Theater. Conductor: Hugo Fiorato.

CAST: Melissa Hayden, Arthur Mitchell; Gloria Govrin, Frank Ohman; Marnee Morris, Kent Stowell; 6 couples.

REVISIONS: 1968, New York City Ballet: Music performed by two pianists on stage, without orchestra.

See 129

358 JEWELS

MUSIC: EMERALDS: By Gabriel Fauré (from *Pelléas et Melisande*, 1898, and *Shylock*, 1889). RUBIES: By Igor Stravinsky (*Capriccio* for piano and orchestra, 1929). DIAMONDS: By Peter Ilyitch Tschaikovsky (from Symphony No. 3 in D major, Op. 29, 1875 [first movement omitted]).

PRODUCTION: Scenery by Peter Harvey, executed by Feller Scenery Studios. Costumes by Karinska. Lighting by Ronald Bates.

PREMIERE: April 13, 1967, New York City Ballet, New York State Theater. Conductor: Robert Irving. Pianist: Gordon Boelzner.

CAST: EMERALDS: Violette Verdy, Conrad Ludlow; Mimi Paul, Francisco Moncion; Sara Leland, Suki Schorer, John Prinz; 10 women.
RUBIES: Patricia McBride, Edward Villella; Patricia Neary; 8 women, 4 men.
DIAMONDS: Suzanne Farrell, Jacques d'Amboise; 4 demi-solo couples; 12 women, 12 men.

NOTE: Each section is a separate work, the costumes green for EMERALDS, red for RUBIES, white for DIAMONDS. The ballet lasts a full evening.

REVISIONS: 1976, New York City Ballet: EMERALDS extended by new pas de deux (to additional music from *Shylock*) and new pas de sept (to additional music from *Pelléas et Melisande*); second ballerina variation altered.

STAGINGS: RUBIES (usually retitled *Capriccio*): 1974, Paris; 1977, Dutch National; 1980, Les Grands Ballets Canadiens, Zürich; 1981, Chicago City; 1982, Los Angeles.

TELEVISION: 1968 (RUBIES pas de deux, Bell Telephone Hour, NBC); 1977 (excerpts, Dance in America, PBS); 1979 (RUBIES pas de deux, PBS).

359 GLINKIANA (later called GLINKAIANA)

MUSIC: By Mikhail Glinka.

PRODUCTION: Scenery, costumes and lighting by Esteban Francés.

PREMIERE: November 23, 1967, New York City Ballet, New York State Theater. Conductor: Robert Irving.

CAST: POLKA: Violette Verdy, Paul Mejia, 3 couples; VALSE FANTAISIE: Mimi Paul, John Clifford, 4 women; JOTA ARAGONESE: Melissa Hayden, 6 women, 8 men; DIVERTIMENTO BRILLANTE: Patricia McBride, Edward Villella.

NOTE: The curtain was lowered after each section and the décor changed. *Glinkiana* was seldom performed with the full four movements. From June 1, 1969, *Valse Fantaisie* was presented as a separate work; the other movements were eliminated.

STAGINGS: See 366.

TELEVISION: 1968 (DIVERTIMENTO BRILLANTE, Bell Telephone Hour, NBC); 1969 (DIVERTIMENTO BRILLANTE, L'Heure du Concert, CBC, Montreal).

See 107*, 132, 293, 366

1968

360 METASTASEIS & PITHOPRAKTA

MUSIC: By Iannis Xenakis (*Metastaseis*, 1953-54; *Pithoprakta*, 1955-56).

PRODUCTION: Lighting by Ronald Bates.

PREMIERE: January 18, 1968, New York City Ballet, New York State Theater. Conductor: Robert Irving.

CAST: METASTASEIS: 22 women, 6 men; PITHOPRAKTA: Suzanne Farrell, Arthur Mitchell, 7 women, 5 men.

NOTE: The music of both brief pieces by the modern Greek composer-architect is based on a calculus of sound, the orchestra of sixty-one instruments playing sixty-one different parts. In the ballet METASTASEIS (Greek, meaning 'a state of standstill') the dancers, in white, form a mass in the shape of a giant wheel that moves and changes, ending as it began. In PITHOPRAKTA (meaning 'action by probabilities'), the two leading dancers, dressed in white and gold, perform a pas de deux during which they simulate partnering but seldom touch; the corps is in black.

361 SLAUGHTER ON TENTH AVENUE

MUSIC: By Richard Rodgers (from *On Your Toes*, 1936, with new orchestration by Hershy Kay).

PRODUCTION: Scenery and lighting by Jo Mielziner, executed by Feller Scenery Studios. Costumes by Irene Sharaff.

PREMIERE: May 2, 1968, New York City Ballet, New York State Theater. Conductor: Robert Irving. (Preview: Annual New York City Ballet Gala Benefit, April 30.)

CAST: *Hoofer*, Arthur Mitchell; *Strip Tease Girl*, Suzanne Farrell; *Big Boss*, Michael Steele; *2 Bartenders*; *Thug*; *3 Policemen*; *Morosine, Premier Danseur Noble*, Earle Sieveling; *Gangster*; *7* Ladies of the Ballet; *4* Gentlemen of the Ballet.

NOTE: Originally choreographed in 1936 for the Broadway musical *On Your Toes*, the ballet was mounted for the New York City Ballet as a separate work, following the original ideas but with different steps.

STAGINGS: 1974, New York Dance Theatre (pas de trois).

TELEVISION: 1969 (excerpt, NBC).

See 166*, 186

362 REQUIEM CANTICLES

In Memoriam: Martin Luther King, Jr. (1929-68)

MUSIC: By Igor Stravinsky (*Requiem Canticles* for contralto, bass, chorus, and orchestra, 1966).

PRODUCTION: Costumes and candelabra by Rouben Ter-Arutunian. Lighting by Ronald Bates.

PREMIERE: May 2, 1968, New York City Ballet, New York State Theater. Conductor: Robert Irving. Singers: Margaret Wilson (contralto); John Ostendorf (bass).

CAST: Suzanne Farrell, Arthur Mitchell, corps de ballet.

NOTE: Choreographed as a religious ceremony and performed once. The corps de ballet, in long white robes and bearing three-branched candelabra, moved on the darkened stage; a lone woman seemed to search among them, and at the end a figure in purple representing Martin Luther King, Jr. was raised aloft.

363 DIANA AND ACTAEON PAS DE DEUX
Made for Television

MUSIC: By Cesare Pugni?

FIRST TELECAST: June 2, 1968, Ed Sullivan Show, CBS.

CAST: Patricia McBride, Edward Villella.

364 LA SOURCE
(briefly called PAS DE DEUX: LA SOURCE)

MUSIC: By Léo Delibes (excerpts from *La Source* [Naïla], 1866).

PRODUCTION: Costumes by Karinska. Lighting by Ronald Bates.

PREMIERE: November 23, 1968, New York City Ballet, New York State Theater. Conductor: Robert Irving.

CAST: Violette Verdy, John Prinz.

NOTE: Varying the conventional structure of a pas de deux, *La Source* begins with solos for the man and woman rather than a supported adagio.

REVISIONS: 1969, New York City Ballet: Expanded to include ALLEGRO VIVACE for female soloist and ensemble of 8 women and VALSE DES FLEURS from *Pas de Deux and Divertissement* [350].

STAGINGS: 1971, San Francisco, Geneva; 1982, Los Angeles.

See 274, 350, 387

1969

365 RUSLAN UND LUDMILLA

Opera in Three Acts

MUSIC: By Mikhail Glinka (produced 1842). Libretto based on the work by Alexander Pushkin. German version by Kurt Honolka.

PRODUCTION: Directed and choreographed by George Balanchine. Scenery and costumes by Nicolas Benois.

PREMIERE: March 30, 1969, Hamburgische Staatsoper, Hamburg. Danced by the Ballett der Hamburgischen Staatsoper. Conductor: Charles Mackerras.

CAST: SINGERS: *Svetosar*, Carl Schultz; *Ludmilla*, Jeanette Scovotti; *Ruslan*, Hubert Hofmann; *Ratmir*, Ursula Boese; *Farlaf*, Noël Mangin; *Gorislava*, Judith Beckmann; *Finn*, Helmut Melchert; *Naïna*, Maria v. Ilosvay; and others. DANCERS: ACT II VISION: 3 women; ACT III ORIENTAL DANCES: 5 women, 5 men.

See 307

366 VALSE FANTAISIE

MUSIC: By Mikhail Glinka (*Valse Fantaisie* in B minor, 1839; orchestrated 1856).

PRODUCTION: Scenery, costumes and lighting by Esteban Francés.

PREMIERE: June 1, 1969, New York City Ballet, New York State Theater. Conductor: Robert Irving.

CAST: Suki Schorer, John Prinz, 4 women.

NOTE: *Valse Fantaisie* was originally presented by the New York City Ballet in 1967 as the second section of *Glinkiana* [359].

STAGINGS (sometimes as *Waltz Fantasy*): 1968, Boston; 1973, Garden State, Los Angeles; 1975, Pacific Northwest; 1976, U. S. Terpsichore; 1977, Stars of American Ballet; 1978, Berkshire, Chicago Lyric Opera,

Dallas, North Carolina, Princeton; 1979, Connecticut; 1980, New Jersey; 1981, American Festival, Baltimore, Richmond; 1982, Kansas City, Festival, Toledo.

See 107*, 293, 359

367 LE LAC DES CYGNES
Ballet in Four Acts

MUSIC: By Peter Ilyitch Tschaikovsky (*Swan Lake*, 1875-76).

CHOREOGRAPHY: Staged by George Balanchine after Lev Ivanov, Marius Petipa, and Nicholas Beriozoff. Choreography for the WALTZ (Act I) and for the MAZURKA, CZARDAS and DANCE OF THE PRINCESSES (Act III) by George Balanchine.

PRODUCTION: Scenery and costumes by Alexandre Benois, executed in the workshops of La Scala, Milan, and by Marie Gromtseff.

PREMIERE: September 11, 1969, Ballet du Grand Théâtre, Geneva. Conductor: Jean Meylan.

CAST: *Odette, Queen of the Swans*, Patricia Neary; *The Evil Genius*, Carlos Kloster; *Prince Siegfried*, Karl Musil; *Jester*, Jean-Marie Sosso; corps de ballet.

See 75, 191, 262, 285, 331

1970

368 WHO CARES?

MUSIC: By George Gershwin (songs as given below), orchestrated by Hershy Kay.

PRODUCTION: Costumes by Karinska. Lighting by Ronald Bates.

PREMIERE: February 5, 1970, New York City Ballet, New York State Theater. Conductor: Robert Irving. Pianist on opening night (orchestration had been completed only for *Strike Up the Band* and *I Got Rhythm*): Gordon Boelzner. *Clap Yo' Hands* played by George Gershwin, recorded.

CAST: Karin von Aroldingen, Patricia McBride, Marnee Morris, Jacques d'Amboise, 15 women, 5 men.

STRIKE UP THE BAND (1927): Ensemble. SWEET AND LOW DOWN (1925): Ensemble. SOMEBODY LOVES ME (1924): Deborah Flomine, Susan Hendl, Linda Merrill, Susan Pilarre, Bettijane Sills. BIDIN' MY TIME (1930): Deni Lamont, Robert Maiorano, Frank Ohman, Richard Rapp, Earle Sieveling. 'S WONDERFUL (1927): Pilarre, Rapp. THAT CERTAIN FEELING (1925): Flomine, Lamont; Sills, Sieveling. DO DO DO (1926): Hendl, Ohman. LADY BE GOOD (1924): Merrill, Maiorano. REPEAT: Ensemble. THE MAN I LOVE (1924): McBride, d'Amboise. I'LL BUILD A STAIRWAY TO PARADISE (1922): von Aroldingen. EMBRACEABLE YOU (1930): Morris, d'Amboise. FASCINATIN' RHYTHM (1924): McBride. WHO CARES? (1931): von Aroldingen, d'Amboise. MY ONE AND ONLY (1927): Morris. LIZA (1929): d'Amboise. CLAP YO' HANDS (1926): von Aroldingen, McBride, Morris, d'Amboise. I GOT RHYTHM (1930): Entire cast.

NOTE: Balanchine and Gershwin had discussed a collaboration before the composer's death in 1937. Thirty-three years later, Balanchine selected and formed into this ballet seventeen of Gershwin's classic songs from Broadway musicals. First presented with costumes but without décor; from November, 1970, with scenery by Jo Mielziner.

REVISIONS: 1976, New York City Ballet: CLAP YO' HANDS eliminated.

STAGINGS: 1980, Zürich; 1982, Chicago City (excerpts).

TELEVISION: 1971 (CBC, Montreal); 1975 (THE MAN I LOVE, NBC).

369 SUITE NO. 3

(from 1971 called TSCHAIKOVSKY SUITE NO. 3)

MUSIC: By Peter Ilyitch Tschaikovsky (Suite No. 3 in G major, Op. 55, 1884).

PRODUCTION: Scenery and costumes by Nicolas Benois; costumes for TEMA CON VARIAZIONI later redesigned by Ben Benson. Lighting by Ronald Bates.

PREMIERE: December 3, 1970, New York City Ballet, New York State Theater. Conductor: Robert Irving.

CAST: ÉLÉGIE: Karin von Aroldingen, Anthony Blum, 6 women; VALSE MÉLANCOLIQUE: Kay Mazzo, Conrad Ludlow, 6 women; SCHERZO:

Marnee Morris, John Clifford, 8 women; TEMA CON VARIAZIONI: Gelsey Kirkland, Edward Villella, 4 demi-solo couples, 8 women, 8 men.

NOTE: Danced until the final movement in a darkened ballroom, the women's dresses long and flowing, their hair unbound; in the first movement they are barefoot. In the finale the stage brightens, the women appear in tutus and tiaras, and the men are dressed as cavaliers.

TELEVISION: 1979 (ÉLÉGIE, Dance in America, PBS).

See 242*, 330

1971

370 CONCERTO FOR JAZZ BAND AND ORCHESTRA

MUSIC: By Rolf Liebermann (Concerto for jazz band and orchestra, 1954).

CHOREOGRAPHY: By George Balanchine and Arthur Mitchell.

PRODUCTION: Lighting by Ronald Bates.

PREMIERE: May 6, 1971 (Annual New York City Ballet Gala Benefit), New York City Ballet and Dance Theatre of Harlem, New York State Theater. Conductor: Robert Irving. On stage: Tonight Show orchestra, conducted by 'Doc' Severinsen.

CAST: 21 New York City Ballet dancers, 23 Dance Theatre of Harlem dancers. I. INTRODUCTION AND JUMP: New York City Ballet women, men from both companies; II. SCHERZO I: New York City Ballet; III. BLUES: Dance Theatre of Harlem; IV. SCHERZO II: New York City Ballet women; V. BOOGIE WOOGIE: Dance Theatre of Harlem; VI. INTERLUDIUM: women from both companies, Dance Theatre of Harlem men; VII. MAMBO: Entire cast.

NOTE: Performed once, in practice clothes.

371 PAMTGG

MUSIC: By Roger Kellaway (based on themes by Stan Applebaum and Sid Woloshin, commissioned by the New York City Ballet).

PRODUCTION: Scenery and lighting by Jo Mielziner. Costumes by Irene Sharaff.

PREMIERE: June 17, 1971, New York City Ballet, New York State Theater. Conductor: Robert Irving.

CAST: Kay Mazzo, Victor Castelli, 24 women, 16 men; Karin von Aroldingen, Frank Ohman, 6 women, 6 men; Sara Leland, John Clifford, 16 women, 12 men.

NOTE: The title is an acronym of a radio and television jingle for an airline commercial; the ballet, a futuristic fantasy on airport procedures.

1972

372 SONATA

MUSIC: By Igor Stravinsky (Scherzo from Sonata in F-sharp minor, 1903-4).

PREMIERE: June 18, 1972, New York City Ballet, New York State Theater. Pianist: Madeleine Malraux. (Annual New York City Ballet Gala Benefit.)

CAST: Sara Leland, John Clifford.

NOTE: Unlisted in the program, *Sonata* was presented as a surprise, the first danced work of the Stravinsky Festival of the New York City Ballet (detailed in *Festivals Directed by Balanchine*, page 311), which included the premieres of ten Balanchine works [372-381].

373 SYMPHONY IN THREE MOVEMENTS

MUSIC: By Igor Stravinsky (1942-45, dedicated to the New York Philharmonic).

PRODUCTION: Lighting by Ronald Bates.

PREMIERE: June 18, 1972, New York City Ballet, New York State Theater. Conductor: Robert Craft. (Annual New York City Ballet Gala Benefit.)

CAST: I. Sara Leland, Marnee Morris, Lynda Yourth, Helgi Tomasson, Edward Villella, Robert Weiss; 5 demi-solo women; 5 demi-solo men; 16 women; II. Leland, Villella; III. Entire cast.

NOTE: An ensemble ballet of driving energy, the first and third movements contrasting with a meditative pas de deux in the second movement.

STAGINGS: 1981, Zürich.

374 VIOLIN CONCERTO
(from 1973 called STRAVINSKY VIOLIN CONCERTO)

MUSIC: By Igor Stravinsky (Concerto in D for violin and orchestra, 1931, commissioned by Blair Fairchild).

PRODUCTION: Lighting by Ronald Bates.

PREMIERE: June 18, 1972, New York City Ballet, New York State Theater. Conductor: Robert Irving. Violinist: Joseph Silverstein. (Annual New York City Ballet Gala Benefit.)

CAST: TOCCATA: Karin von Aroldingen, Kay Mazzo, Jean-Pierre Bonnefous, Peter Martins, 8 women, 8 men; ARIA I: von Aroldingen, Bonnefous; ARIA II: Mazzo, Martins; CAPRICCIO: Entire cast.

NOTE: The first movement is in eight parts, each overlapping into the next. Both the second and third movements are pas de deux showing contrasting relationships between the partners. The finale includes references to Russian motifs in the score. Balanchine had previously used this music for the ballet *Balustrade* with scenery and costumes; *Violin Concerto* was performed in practice clothes, without décor.

REVISIONS: 1977, New York City Ballet: entry of first male dancer altered and other changes made for Dance in America telecast; changes retained in stage version.

TELEVISION: 1977 (Dance in America, PBS).

See 192

375 DANSES CONCERTANTES

MUSIC: By Igor Stravinsky (*Danses Concertantes* for chamber orchestra, 1941-42, commissioned by Werner Janssen).

PRODUCTION: Scenery and costumes by Eugene Berman (from the Ballet Russe de Monte Carlo production, 1944), courtesy of the Ballet Foundation. Costumes executed by Barbara Matera.

PREMIERE: June 20, 1972, New York City Ballet, New York State Theater. Conductor: Robert Irving.

CAST: Lynda Yourth, John Clifford, 8 women, 4 men.
MARCHE; PAS D'ACTION; THÈME VARIÉ (4 variations); PAS DE DEUX; MARCHE.

NOTE: Originally presented by the Ballet Russe de Monte Carlo, New York, 1944, with similar choreography.

*See 220**

376 DIVERTIMENTO FROM 'LE BAISER DE LA FÉE'

MUSIC: By Igor Stravinsky (excerpts from *Divertimento*, concert suite, 1934, and the full-length ballet, *Le Baiser de la Fée*, 1928).

PRODUCTION: Costumes by Eugene Berman (from *Roma* [306]). Lighting by Ronald Bates.

PREMIERE: June 21, 1972, New York City Ballet, New York State Theater. Conductor: Robert Irving.

CAST: Patricia McBride, Helgi Tomasson; Bettijane Sills, Carol Sumner, 10 women.

NOTE: Unlike Balanchine's earlier staging of the full score, the *Divertimento* tells no story, although certain sections suggest quest and foreboding.

REVISIONS: 1974, New York City Ballet: New pas de deux (with ensemble) added; two principal dancers bid farewell in elegiac conclusion to music from the score of *Le Baiser de la Fée* that incorporates Tschaikovsky's 'None But the Lonely Heart.'

See 178, 271*

377 SCHERZO À LA RUSSE

MUSIC: By Igor Stravinsky (1925).

PRODUCTION: Costumes by Karinska. Lighting by Ronald Bates.

PREMIERE: June 21, 1972, New York City Ballet, New York State Theater. Conductor: Hugo Fiorato.

CAST: Karin von Aroldingen, Kay Mazzo, 16 women.

NOTE: Reminiscent of Russian women's folk ensembles; performed in nursemaid costumes with aristocratic headdresses.

REVISIONS: 1982, New York City Ballet (Stravinsky Centennial Celebration): Substantially rechoreographed in the same style.

378 DUO CONCERTANT

MUSIC: By Igor Stravinsky (*Duo Concertant* for violin and piano, 1939).

PRODUCTION: Lighting by Ronald Bates.

PREMIERE: June 22, 1972, New York City Ballet, New York State Theater. Pianist: Gordon Boelzner. Violinist: Lamar Alsop. Both instrumentalists on stage.

CAST: Kay Mazzo, Peter Martins.

  I. CANTILENA; II. ECLOGUE I; III. ECLOGUE II; IV. GIGUE; V. DITHYRAMB.

NOTE: The performance of the musicians on stage is integral to the conception of the ballet. Standing at the piano with the musicians, the dancers listen to the first movement. During the next three movements they dance, mirroring the music and each other, and pause several times to rejoin the musicians and to listen. In the final movement, the stage is darkened; within circles of light the dancers enact a love story.

379 PULCINELLA

MUSIC: By Igor Stravinsky (*Pulcinella: Ballet with Song in One Act after Pergolesi*, 1919-20).

CHOREOGRAPHY: By George Balanchine and Jerome Robbins.

PRODUCTION: Scenery and costumes by Eugene Berman. Scenery executed by Nolan Scenery Studios. Lighting by Ronald Bates. Masks and props by Kermit Love.

PREMIERE: June 23, 1972, New York City Ballet with children from the School of American Ballet, New York State Theater. Conductor: Robert Irving.

CAST: *Pulcinella*, Edward Villella; *Girl*, Violette Verdy; *Pulcinella's Father*, Michael Arshansky; *Devil*, Francisco Moncion, Shaun O'Brien; *Beggars*, George Balanchine, Jerome Robbins; *Concubines*, 2 men; *2 Policemen*; *Little Boy*; *6 Musicians*; *Townspeople*, 7 women, 5 men; *Pulcinellas*, Deni Lamont, Robert Weiss, 10 men, 12 children.

NOTE: Balanchine created a libretto of his own, working with Robbins. Beginning with Pulcinella's funeral procession, the ballet depicts his resurrection through a pact with the devil, his continued career of mockery, petty crime and debauchery, his defeat of the devil at a spaghetti feast, and a celebration of his victory by dancing. *Pulcinella* was first choreographed by Léonide Massine in 1920 for Diaghilev's Ballets Russes.

REVISIONS: New York City Ballet: Numerous early revisions.

See 35

380 CHORAL VARIATIONS ON BACH'S 'VOM HIMMEL HOCH'

MUSIC: By Igor Stravinsky (Variations on two treatments of *Vom Himmel Hoch* by Johann Sebastian Bach [from his *Christmas Oratorio*, 1734, and his *Canonic Variations on Vom Himmel Hoch* for organ, 1748] for mixed chorus and orchestra, 1956, dedicated to Robert Craft).

PRODUCTION: Scenery by Rouben Ter-Arutunian. Lighting by Ronald Bates.

PREMIERE: June 25, 1972, New York City Ballet with children from the School of American Ballet, New York State Theater. Conductor: Robert Irving. Chorus: Gregg Smith Singers.

CAST: Karin von Aroldingen, Melissa Hayden, Sara Leland, Violette Verdy, Anthony Blum, Peter Martins, 15 women, 13 men, 12 children.

NOTE: The choral variations are accompanied by danced variations leading to a grand défilé. At the end, the dancers kneel.

381 SYMPHONY OF PSALMS

Music: By Igor Stravinsky (for mixed voices and orchestra, 1930, commissioned by Serge Koussevitsky).

Production: Staged by George Balanchine. Scenery by Rouben Ter-Arutunian.

Premiere: June 25, 1972, New York City Ballet, New York State Theater. Conductor: Robert Craft. Chorus: Gregg Smith Singers.

Note: This work, performed by the Gregg Smith Singers with the dancers assembled on stage behind the chorus, closed the Stravinsky Festival of the New York City Ballet.

1973

382 TSCHAIKOVSKY PIANO CONCERTO NO. 2
(briefly called PIANO CONCERTO NO. 2)

Music: By Peter Ilyitch Tschaikovsky (Piano Concerto No. 2 in G major, Op. 44, 1879, abridged, rewritten and rearranged by Alexander Siloti).

Production: Costumes by Karinska. Lighting by Ronald Bates.

Premiere: January 12, 1973, New York City Ballet, New York State Theater. Conductor: Robert Irving. Pianist: Gordon Boelzner.

Cast: Patricia McBride, Peter Martins; Colleen Neary; Tracy Bennett, Victor Castelli; 2 female demi-soloists; 16 women, 6 men.
 ALLEGRO BRILLANTE–ANDANTE; ANDANTE NON TROPPO; ALLEGRO
 CON FUOCO.

Note: Originally presented by American Ballet Caravan, Rio de Janeiro, 1941, titled *Ballet Imperial*. While the choreography is essentially the same as the Sadler's Wells (Royal Ballet) presentation of 1950, the Imperial Russian décor and tutus of the 1964 New York City Ballet production were replaced in 1973 by simple chiffon dresses and a plain backdrop.

New productions by Balanchine companies: 1979, New York City Ballet: New costumes by Ben Benson.

See 194*, 349

383 FÜRST IGOR (PRINCE IGOR)
Opera in Four Acts and Prologue by Alexander Borodin
ACT II POLOVTSIAN DANCES

CHOREOGRAPHY: Original choreography by Michel Fokine (1909); staged by George Balanchine.

PREMIERE: February 23, 1973, Deutsche Oper, Berlin. Danced by Ballett der Deutschen Oper. Conductor: Gerd Albrecht.

CAST: 4 women, 7 men.

See 104

384 CORTÈGE HONGROIS

MUSIC: By Alexander Glazounov (from *Raymonda*, Op. 57, produced 1898).

PRODUCTION: Scenery and costumes by Rouben Ter-Arutunian. Lighting by Ronald Bates.

PREMIERE: May 17, 1973, New York City Ballet, New York State Theater. Conductor: Robert Irving. (Preview: Annual New York City Ballet Gala Benefit, May 16.)

CAST: Melissa Hayden, Jacques d'Amboise [classical]; Karin von Aroldingen, Jean-Pierre Bonnefous [character]; 16 couples. CZARDAS: von Aroldingen, Bonnefous; PAS DE QUATRE: 4 women; VARIATION I: Colleen Neary; VARIATION II: 4 men; VARIATION III: Merrill Ashley; PAS DE DEUX: Hayden, d'Amboise.

NOTE: Created to honor Melissa Hayden on the occasion of her retirement. A suite of dances alternating classical and character styles, conceived in the tradition of the late works of Petipa. In the apotheosis the entire cast pays homage to the ballerina.

See 18, 233*, 309, 339

385 BEGIN THE BEGUINE

MUSIC: By Cole Porter.

CHOREOGRAPHY: By George Balanchine (uncredited), one of five sections of the ballet *Salute to Cole*, choreographed by Edward Villella.

PRODUCTION: Produced by Hal de Windt. Costumes by Peter Wexler.

PREMIERE: May 31, 1973, Philharmonic Hall, New York. Conductor: André Kostelanetz.

CAST: Patricia McBride, Edward Villella.

NOTE: Performed as part of a New York Philharmonic Promenade concert.

1974

386 VARIATIONS POUR UNE PORTE ET UN SOUPIR

MUSIC: Sonority by Pierre Henry (14 of 25 numbers from *Variations pour une Porte et un Soupir*, first performed 1963).

PRODUCTION: Scenery and costumes by Rouben Ter-Arutunian. Lighting by Ronald Bates.

PREMIERE: February 17, 1974, New York City Ballet, New York State Theater.

CAST: Karin von Aroldingen, John Clifford.

NOTE: The ballet is a set of fourteen variations in pas de deux form, for a female 'Door' and a male 'Sigh.' The dancers' movements are in precise accord with the separate sounds and vibrations that form the score. An integral part of the choreography is an enormous black cape attached to the 'Door,' which in the end envelops the 'Sigh.'

387 COPPÉLIA

MUSIC: By Léo Delibes (*Coppélia, ou la Fille aux Yeux d'Émail*, produced 1870, with excerpts from *Sylvia, ou la Nymphe de Diane*, produced 1876, and *La Source* [*Naïla*], 1866). Book by Charles Nuitter, after E. T. A. Hoffmann's *Der Sandmann* (1815).

CHOREOGRAPHY: Choreography by Alexandra Danilova and George Balanchine after Marius Petipa (1884; revised 1894 by Lev Ivanov and Enrico Cecchetti), with additional choreography by George Balanchine.

PRODUCTION: Scenery and costumes by Rouben Ter-Arutunian. Costumes executed by Karinska and Barbara Matera, Ltd. Lighting by Ronald Bates.

PREMIERE: July 17, 1974, New York City Ballet, Saratoga Performing Arts Center, Saratoga Springs, New York. Conductor: Robert Irving. (First New York State Theater performance, with children from the School of American Ballet, November 20.)

CAST: *Swanilda/Coppélia*, Patricia McBride; *Frantz*, Helgi Tomasson; *Dr. Coppélius*, Shaun O'Brien. ACT I: *The Doll Coppélia*; *Villagers*, 8 couples; *Mayor*, Michael Arshansky; *Swanilda's Friends*, 8 women. ACT II: *Swanilda and Her Friends*; *The Automatons: Astrologer, Juggler, Acrobat, Chinaman.* ACT III: *Burgomaster*; *Villagers, Brides, Grooms,* and *Friends*, 8 women, 6 men; DEDICATION OF THE BELLS: WALTZ OF THE GOLDEN HOURS: Marnee Morris, 24 children; *Dawn*, Merrill Ashley; *Prayer*, Christine Redpath; *Spinner*, Susan Hendl; *Jesterettes*, 4 women; DISCORD AND WAR: Colleen Neary, Robert Weiss, 8 couples; PEACE (pas de deux): McBride, Tomasson; FINALE.

   Act I. A Village Square in Galicia.
   Act II. Dr. Coppélius' Secret Workshop.
   Act III. A Village Wedding and Festival of Bells.

NOTE: Balanchine and Danilova collaborated to reproduce parts of Petipa's choreography for *Coppélia*, which they had learned while students at the Imperial Ballet School; Danilova had later become a leading interpreter of the role of Swanilda. Balanchine created entirely new choreography for Act III, and for the mazurka and czardas in Act I, and made slight revisions in other dances in Act I. Because the leading male role was originally danced by a woman, there is no provision for male variation or supported pas de deux in the score. Using music from *Sylvia*, Balanchine created a male variation for Act I and a complete pas de deux for Act III, in which the male variation is taken from his *Sylvia: Pas de Deux* [273]. The production was partially commissioned by the Saratoga Performing Arts Center.

REVISIONS: 1974, New York City Ballet: Act III costumes altered before first New York performance and new children's costumes designed by Karinska; coda added to Act III PEACE pas de deux.

STAGINGS: 1977, Geneva.

TELEVISION: 1978 (Live from Lincoln Center, PBS).

See 36, 266, 273, 274, 291, 350, 364

388 BORIS GODUNOV
Opera in Three Acts and Ten Scenes by Modest Moussorgsky
ACT II, SCENE 2 POLONAISE

PREMIERE: December 16, 1974, Metropolitan Opera, New York. Danced by Metropolitan Opera Ballet. Conductor: Thomas Schippers.

CAST: Corps de ballet.

See 54, 298

1975

389 SONATINE

MUSIC: By Maurice Ravel (1906).

PRODUCTION: Lighting by Ronald Bates.

PREMIERE: May 15, 1975, New York City Ballet, New York State Theater. Pianist: Madeleine Malraux. (Preview: Annual New York City Ballet Gala Benefit, May 14.)

CAST: Violette Verdy, Jean-Pierre Bonnefous.

NOTE: *Sonatine* was first presented as the opening work of the Ravel Festival of the New York City Ballet (detailed in *Festivals Directed by Balanchine*, page 312), which included the premieres of eight Balanchine works [389-396].

STAGINGS: 1975, Paris; 1976, Geneva.

390 L'ENFANT ET LES SORTILÈGES
Lyric Fantasy in Two Parts

MUSIC: By Maurice Ravel (1920-25). Libretto by Colette (translated by Catherine Wolff).

PRODUCTION: Scenery and costumes by Kermit Love. Supervising Designer: David Mitchell. Lighting by Ronald Bates.

PREMIERE: May 15, 1975, New York City Ballet, New York State Theater. Conductor: Manuel Rosenthal. (Preview: Annual New York City Ballet Gala Benefit, May 14.)

CAST: Each role performed by a singer off stage (six singers) and a dancer on stage. *Child* (sung and danced), Paul Offenkranz; *His Mother*; *Armchair*; *Bergère*; *Clock*; *Tea Pot*; *Chinese Cup*; *Fire*, Marnee Morris; *Cinder*; *3 Shepherdesses*; *3 Shepherds*; *Princess*, Christine Redpath; *Little Math Man*; *10 Numbers*; *Black Cat*, Jean-Pierre Frohlich; *Gray Cat*, Tracy Bennett; *Dragonflies and Moths*, Colleen Neary, 7 women; *Big Frog*; *5 Little Frogs*; *Tree* (sung only); *Squirrels and 2 Trees*, Stephanie Saland, 5 women, 2 men.

OTHER VERSIONS: 1925, Opéra de Monte-Carlo (*L'Enfant et les Sortilèges*, danced by Diaghilev's Ballets Russes). 1946, Ballet Society (*The Spellbound Child* [*L'Enfant et les Sortilèges*]). 1981, for the PBS television series *Dance in America* (*The Spellbound Child / L'Enfant et les Sortilèges*).

See 48*, 235, 416

391 SHÉHÉRAZADE

MUSIC: By Maurice Ravel (*Shéhérazade: Ouverture de Féerie*, 1898).

PRODUCTION: Lighting by Ronald Bates.

PREMIERE: May 22, 1975, New York City Ballet, New York State Theater. Conductor: Robert Irving.

CAST: Kay Mazzo, Edward Villella, 2 couples, 8 women.

392 LE TOMBEAU DE COUPERIN

MUSIC: By Maurice Ravel (four movements orchestrated by the composer from the six-part suite originally written for piano, 1919).

PRODUCTION: Lighting by Ronald Bates.

PREMIERE: May 29, 1975, New York City Ballet, New York State Theater. Conductor: Robert Irving.

CAST: LEFT QUADRILLE: Judith Fugate, Jean-Pierre Frohlich; Wilhelmina Frankfurt, Victor Castelli; Muriel Aasen, Francis Sackett; Susan Hendl, David Richardson; RIGHT QUADRILLE: Marjorie Spohn, Hermes Condé; Delia Peters, Richard Hoskinson; Susan Pilarre, Richard Dryden; Carol Sumner, Laurence Matthews.

PRÉLUDE; FORLANE; MENUET; RIGAUDON.

NOTE: The two quadrilles perform in geometric patterns, often with identical steps and gestures, simultaneous or canonic.

STAGINGS: 1975, Paris; 1976, Geneva; 1977, Dutch National; 1981, Zürich.

393 PAVANE

MUSIC: By Maurice Ravel (*Pavane pour une Infante Défunte* for piano, 1899; orchestral version, 1911).

PRODUCTION: Lighting by Ronald Bates.

PREMIERE: May 29, 1975, New York City Ballet, New York State Theater. Conductor: Robert Irving.

CAST: Patricia McBride.

NOTE: A lament, choreographed for a solo dancer and a piece of chiffon she holds.

394 TZIGANE

MUSIC: By Maurice Ravel (1924).

PRODUCTION: Costumes by Joe Eula and Stanley Simmons (from *Koddly Dances* [Clifford], 1971, uncredited). Lighting by Ronald Bates.

PREMIERE: May 29, 1975, New York City Ballet, New York State Theater. Conductor: Robert Irving. Violinist: Lamar Alsop.

CAST: Suzanne Farrell, Peter Martins, 4 couples.

NOTE: A choreographic fantasy on gypsy dance styles and personality.

STAGINGS: 1975, Paris.

TELEVISION: 1977 (Dance in America, PBS).

395 GASPARD DE LA NUIT

MUSIC: By Maurice Ravel (*Gaspard de la Nuit*, three poems for piano solo, 1908, inspired by poems of the same name by Aloysius Bertrand).

PRODUCTION: Scenery and costumes by Bernard Daydé; execution supervised by David Mitchell. Lighting by Bernard Daydé in association with Ronald Bates.

PREMIERE: May 29, 1975, New York City Ballet, New York State Theater. Pianist: Jerry Zimmerman.

CAST: ONDINE: Colleen Neary, Victor Castelli, 5 women; LE GIBET: Karin von Aroldingen, Nolan T'Sani, 8 women, 3 men; SCARBO: Sara Leland, Robert Weiss, 3 men.

NOTE: Bertrand's Gaspard represents the evils of the night. The ballet's atmosphere is black magic; mirrors figure importantly in each of the three sections, which bear the titles of the poems.

396 RAPSODIE ESPAGNOLE

MUSIC: By Maurice Ravel (1907).

PRODUCTION: Costumes by Michael Avedon. Lighting by Ronald Bates.

PREMIERE: May 29, 1975, New York City Ballet, New York State Theater. Conductor: Robert Irving.

CAST: Karin von Aroldingen, Peter Schaufuss, Nolan T'Sani, 12 couples.
PRÉLUDE DE LA NUIT; MALAGUEÑA; HABAÑERA (pas de deux); FERIA.

397 FAUST

Opera in Five Acts by Charles Gounod
ACT III, SCENE I WALPURGISNACHT BALLET

PREMIERE: June 3, 1975, Théâtre National de l'Opéra, Paris. Danced by Paris Opéra Ballet. Conductor: Michel Plasson.

CAST: Claudette Scouarnec, Sylvie Clavier, Jean-Paul Gravier; Joysane Consoli, Janine Guiton, corps de ballet.

NOTE: In 1980, the WALPURGISNACHT BALLET entered the New York City Ballet repertory as an independent work.

STAGINGS: 1979, Chicago Lyric Opera; 1980, New York City Ballet (WALPURGISNACHT BALLET only).

See 45, 117, 151, 227, 413

398 THE STEADFAST TIN SOLDIER

MUSIC: By Georges Bizet (from *Jeux d'Enfants*, Opp. 22-26, 1871: no. 6, TROMPETTE ET TAMBOUR; no. 3, LA POUPÉE; no. 11, PETIT MARI, PETITE FEMME; no. 12, LE BAL).

PRODUCTION: Scenery and costumes by David Mitchell. Lighting by Ronald Bates.

PREMIERE: July 30, 1975, New York City Ballet, Saratoga Performing Arts Center, Saratoga Springs, New York. Conductor: Robert Irving. (First New York State Theater performance January 22, 1976.)

CAST: Patricia McBride, Peter Schaufuss.

MARCHE; BERCEUSE; DUO; GALOP.

NOTE: Balanchine transformed the Hans Christian Andersen story into a pas de deux recounting the courtship and love between the tin soldier and the paper-doll ballerina. The soldier gives the ballerina his tin heart, but a draft pulls her into the fire in the fireplace and she is consumed. All that remains is the heart, which the soldier, weeping, rescues. The production was commissioned by the Saratoga Performing Arts Center.

STAGINGS: 1981, Zürich.

TELEVISION: 1979 (Dance in America, PBS).

See 310*

399 ORFEO ED EURIDICE

Opera in Two Acts and Five Scenes by Christoph Willibald Gluck
DANCES OF SHEPHERDS AND SHEPHERDESSES; FURIES AND DEMONS;
BLESSED SPIRITS

PREMIERE: November 22, 1975, Chicago Lyric Opera. Danced by
Chicago Lyric Opera Ballet. Conductor: Jean Fournet.

CAST: Corps de ballet.

See 170*, 345, 400

1976

400 CHACONNE

MUSIC: By Christoph Willibald Gluck (ballet music from *Orfeo ed
Euridice*, produced 1762, with music from the Paris production of 1774).

CHOREOGRAPHY: By George Balanchine, staged by Brigitte Thom.

PRODUCTION: Lighting by Ronald Bates.

PREMIERE: January 22, 1976, New York City Ballet, New York State
Theater. Conductor: Robert Irving.

CAST: Suzanne Farrell, Peter Martins; PAS DE TROIS: Renee Estopinal,
Wilhelmina Frankfurt, Jay Jolley; PAS DE DEUX: Susan Hendl, Jean-
Pierre Frohlich; PAS DE CINQ: Elise Flagg; Bonita Borne, Elyse Borne,
Laura Flagg, Nichol Hlinka; PAS DE DEUX: Farrell, Martins; CHACONNE:
Farrell, Martins; Susan Pilarre, Marjorie Spohn, Tracy Bennett, Gerard
Ebitz, corps de ballet.

NOTE: The finale of Gluck's opera is in the form of a dance, rather
than song. This choreography, first performed in the 1963 Hamburg
State Opera production of *Orfeo ed Euridice* [345], was somewhat
altered for presentation as the ballet *Chaconne*, particularly the
sections for Farrell and Martins. Initially danced in practice clothes;
costumes by Karinska were added in the spring of 1976.

REVISIONS: New York City Ballet, spring 1976: Opening ensemble
added to 'The Dance of the Blessed Spirits.'

Stagings: 1978, Paris.

Television: 1978 (excerpts, Dance in America, PBS); 1979 (CBC, Montreal).

See 170*, 345, 399

401 UNION JACK

Music: By Hershy Kay (adapted from traditional British sources as given below, 1976, commissioned by the New York City Ballet).

Production: Scenery and costumes by Rouben Ter-Arutunian, including a drop curtain for Part II from the New York City Opera production of *La Cenerentola* (1953). Scottish costumes by Sheldon M. Kasman of Toronto. Lighting by Ronald Bates.

Premiere: May 13, 1976, New York City Ballet, New York State Theater. Conductor: Robert Irving. (Preview: Annual New York City Ballet Gala Benefit, May 12.)

Cast: i. scottish and canadian guards regiments: ('Keel Row') lennox: Helgi Tomasson, 9 men; dress macleod: Jacques d'Amboise, 9 men. ('Caledonian Hunt's Delight') green montgomerie: Sara Leland, 9 women. ('Dance wi' My Daddy') menzies: Peter Martins, 9 men; dress macdonald: Kay Mazzo, 9 women. ('Regimental Drum Variations') macdonald of sleat: Karin von Aroldingen, 9 women. (Scottish theme from the *Water Music* by George Frederick Handel) r.c.a.f. (royal canadian air force): Suzanne Farrell, 9 women. ('Amazing Grace,' 'A Hundred Pipers') finale: Entire cast. ii. costermonger pas de deux (music-hall songs, ca. 1890-1914: 'The Sunshine of Your Smile,' 'The Night the Floor Fell In,' 'Our Lodger's Such a Naice Young Man,' 'Following in Father's Footsteps,' 'A Tavern in the Town'): *Pearly King*, Jean-Pierre Bonnefous; *Pearly Queen*, Patricia McBride; 2 young girls, donkey. iii. royal navy (traditional hornpipe melodies, 'Rule Britannia'): von Aroldingen, Victor Castelli, Bart Cook; d'Amboise, 8 women, 8 men; Leland, Mazzo, Tomasson; Martins, 8 women, 8 men; wrens (women's royal naval service): Farrell, 8 women; finale: Entire cast.

Note: Created to honor the British heritage of the United States on the occasion of its Bicentennial. Part I is based on Scottish military tattoos and folk-dance forms performed in an open castle square.

Part II is a music-hall pas de deux for the costermonger Pearly King and Queen of London, with two little girls and a donkey, danced before a drop suggesting Pollock's toy theaters. Part III is a series of variations employing hornpipes, sea songs, work chants, jigs, and drill orders of the Royal Navy, in a quay-side setting. For the finale, hand flags signal 'God Save the Queen' in a marine semaphore code as the British Union Jack appears.

REVISIONS: 1976, New York City Ballet: March sections shortened immediately after premiere; second half of GREEN MONTGOMERIE section completely rechoreographed; ending of COSTERMONGER scene redone several times.

402 PAL JOEY
Musical Theater

Balanchine worked with Edward Villella (as Joey) on choreography for 'Bewitched, Bothered and Bewildered' in the 1976 Circle in the Square production of Richard Rodgers and Lorenz Hart's *Pal Joey*. Villella withdrew from the production before the premiere.

403 THE RELUCTANT KING (LE ROI MALGRÉ LUI)
Comic Opera in Three Acts by Emmanuel Chabrier
ACT II FÊTE POLONAISE; DANCE OF THE ROYAL POLISH GUARDS

PREMIERE: November 19, 1976, Juilliard American Opera Center, The Juilliard Theater, New York. Danced by students of the School of American Ballet. Conductor: Manuel Rosenthal.

CAST: Corps de ballet.

See 265

1977

404 THE SLEEPING BEAUTY: AURORA'S SOLO, VISION SCENE

MUSIC: By Peter Ilyitch Tschaikovsky (produced 1890).

CHOREOGRAPHY: After the choreography of Marius Petipa. Choreography for the GARLAND DANCE by Michael Vernon. Choreography for Aurora's solo in the VISION SCENE by George Balanchine.

PRODUCTION: Staged and directed by André Eglevsky. Scenery and costumes by Peter Farmer.

PREMIERE: April 14, 1977, The Eglevsky Ballet, Hofstra University, Hempstead, New York.

CAST: *Princess Aurora*, Patricia McBride; *Prince*, Peter Schaufuss; *Lilac Fairy*, Leslie Peck; corps de ballet.

See 65, 225, 259, 281, 418

405 ÉTUDE FOR PIANO

MUSIC: By Alexander Scriabin (Étude in C-sharp minor, Op. 8, no. 1).

PRODUCTION: Costumes by Christina Giannini.

PREMIERE: June 4, 1977, Spoleto Festival U.S.A., Charleston, South Carolina. Pianist: Boris Bloch. (First New York City Ballet performance June 12, New York State Theater. Pianist: Gordon Boelzner.)

CAST: Patricia McBride, Jean-Pierre Bonnefous.

406 VIENNA WALTZES (briefly called WIENER WALZER)

MUSIC: By Johann Strauss the Younger, Franz Lehár and Richard Strauss (as given below).

PRODUCTION: Scenery by Rouben Ter-Arutunian, executed by Nolan Scenery Studios. Costumes by Karinska. Lighting by Ronald Bates.

PREMIERE: June 23, 1977, New York City Ballet, New York State Theater. Conductor: Robert Irving. (Preview: Annual New York City Ballet Gala Benefit, June 15, with Jean-Pierre Bonnefous in the role later danced by Jorge Donn.)

CAST: TALES FROM THE VIENNA WOODS (J. Strauss, Op. 325, 1868): Karin von Aroldingen, Sean Lavery, 10 couples; VOICES OF SPRING (J. Strauss, Op. 410, 1885): Patricia McBride, Helgi Tomasson, 8 women; EXPLOSION POLKA (J. Strauss, Op. 43, ca. 1848): Sara Leland, Bart Cook, 3 couples; GOLD AND SILVER WALTZ (Lehár, 1905): Kay Mazzo, Peter Martins, 8 couples; FIRST SEQUENCE OF WALTZES FROM 'DER ROSEN-KAVALIER' (R. Strauss, arranged 1944): Suzanne Farrell, Jorge Donn (guest artist); von Aroldingen, Lavery; McBride, Tomasson; Leland, Cook; Mazzo, Martins; entire cast.

NOTE: Each waltz suggests a different mood. The first three take place in the Vienna Woods: a formal dance, wood spirits, a comic polka. The scenery evolves: The trees develop tendrils of décor to form the dancing-room of the 'Merry Widow' (GOLD AND SILVER WALTZ); in the finale, the roots of the trees become the chandeliers of a gala, mirrored ballroom for WALTZES FROM 'DER ROSENKAVALIER.'

REVISIONS: New York City Ballet: GOLD AND SILVER WALTZ changed many times; minor revisions in VOICES OF SPRING.

1978

407 BALLO DELLA REGINA

MUSIC: By Giuseppe Verdi (ballet music from *Don Carlos*, Act III, produced 1867, with some additions from the same score).

PRODUCTION: Costumes by Ben Benson. Lighting by Ronald Bates.

PREMIERE: January 12, 1978, New York City Ballet, New York State Theater. Conductor: Robert Irving. (Preview: Opening Night New York City Ballet Gala Benefit, November 15, 1977.)

CAST: Merrill Ashley, Robert Weiss; Debra Austin, Bonita Borne, Stephanie Saland, Sheryl Ware; 12 women.

NOTE: Using the ballet music from *Don Carlos*, with reference through lighting and costumes to the original tale of a fisherman's search for the perfect pearl, Balanchine created a work for a ballerina and her partner, with solos for four women.

TELEVISION: 1979 (Dance in America, PBS).

408 KAMMERMUSIK NO. 2

MUSIC: By Paul Hindemith (1924).

PRODUCTION: Costumes by Ben Benson. Lighting by Ronald Bates.

PREMIERE: January 26, 1978, New York City Ballet, New York State Theater. Conductor: Robert Irving.

CAST: Karin von Aroldingen, Colleen Neary, Sean Lavery, Adam Lüders; 8 men.

NOTE: In four movements (I.; II.; III. KLEINES POTPOURRI; IV. FINALE), performed without interruption.

409 TRICOLORE

MUSIC: By Georges Auric (1978, commissioned by the New York City Ballet).

CHOREOGRAPHY: Ballet conceived and supervised by George Balanchine. Choreography by Peter Martins, Jean-Pierre Bonnefous and Jerome Robbins.

PRODUCTION: Scenery and costumes by Rouben Ter-Arutunian. Lighting by Ronald Bates.

PREMIERE: May 18, 1978, New York City Ballet, New York State Theater. Conductor: Robert Irving. (Preview: Annual New York City Ballet Gala Benefit, May 17.)

CAST: PAS DE BASQUE (choreographed by Martins): Colleen Neary, Adam Lüders, 4 couples, 8 women, 8 men; PAS DEGAS (choreographed by Bonnefous): Merrill Ashley, Sean Lavery, 2 female demi-soloists, 10 women, 6 men; MARCHE DE LA GARDE RÉPUBLICAINE (choreographed by Robbins): *La Garde Républicaine*, 2 couples, 18 women, 18 men; *Majorettes*, Karin von Aroldingen, 8 women; APOTHEOSIS: *Mademoiselle Marianne*, Nina Fedorova; entire cast.

NOTE: A salute to France in music and dance: With *Stars and Stripes* [318] and *Union Jack* [401], the work completes a trio of ballets projected as an 'Entente Cordiale.' Balanchine chose Auric to compose the score for the occasion; they had first collaborated under Diaghilev in 1924 on *La Pastorale* [62], and again in 1932 on *La Concurrence* [130].

1979

410 LE BOURGEOIS GENTILHOMME

MUSIC: By Richard Strauss (concert suite, ca. 1917). Libretto after Molière.

CHOREOGRAPHY: By George Balanchine and Jerome Robbins. COOKS DANCE by Peter Martins (uncredited). Assistant to the Choreographers: Susan Hendl.

PRODUCTION: Scenery and costumes designed by Rouben Ter-Arutunian. Costumes executed by Karinska. Lighting by Gilbert Hemsley, Jr.

PREMIERE: April 8, 1979, New York City Opera, New York State Theater. Corps de ballet composed of students of the School of American Ballet. Conductor: Cal Stewart Kellogg.

CAST: *Lucile*, Patricia McBride; *M. Jourdain*, Jean-Pierre Bonnefous; *Cléonte*, Rudolf Nureyev; DIVERTISSEMENT: Darla Hoover, Michael Puleo, six women; *Maid*; *6 Lackeys*; *4 Cooks*; *2 Attendants to Cléonte*.

NOTE: Performed with Henry Purcell's opera *Dido and Aeneas*.

REVISIONS: 1980, New York City Ballet: Choreography credited to Balanchine alone; several dancing passages for Cléonte removed, replaced by mime passages for Cléonte and Lucile.

STAGINGS: 1979, Paris; 1980, Zürich.

OTHER VERSIONS: 1932, Ballets Russes de Monte-Carlo. 1944, Ballet Russe de Monte Carlo.

See 131*, 221, 414

411 DIDO AND AENEAS

Opera in a Prologue and Three Acts by Henry Purcell
PANTOMIME

CHOREOGRAPHY: By Peter Martins. Pantomime scenes directed by Frank Corsaro in collaboration with George Balanchine.

PREMIERE: April 8, 1979, New York City Opera, New York State Theater. Danced by students of the School of American Ballet. Conductor: Cal Stewart Kellogg.

CAST: *Attendants to Dido,* 8 girls; *Attendants to Aeneas,* 4 boys; *Witches, Sailors, Animals, Torch Bearers.*

1980

412 BALLADE

MUSIC: By Gabriel Fauré (*Ballade* for piano and orchestra, Op. 19, 1881).

PRODUCTION: Scenery and costumes by Rouben Ter-Arutunian (from *Tricolore,* PAS DEGAS [409]), lighting by Ronald Bates.

PREMIERE: May 8, 1980, New York City Ballet, New York State Theater. Conductor: Robert Irving. Pianist: Gordon Boelzner.

CAST: Merrill Ashley, Ib Andersen, 10 women.

NOTE: The music (celebrated in Proust) is in one movement with three underlying sections; the ballet is a series of pas de deux and solos for a ballerina and her cavalier, accompanied from time to time by the corps of women.

NEW PRODUCTIONS BY BALANCHINE COMPANIES: 1982, New York City Ballet: Performed without décor; costumes by Ben Benson (from *Introduction and Fugue* [J. Duell], 1981), lighting by Ronald Bates.

413 WALPURGISNACHT BALLET

From Gounod's 'Faust'

MUSIC: By Charles Gounod (from *Faust*, produced with ballet music 1869).

CHOREOGRAPHY: By George Balanchine. Staged by Brigitte Thom.

PRODUCTION: Lighting by Ronald Bates.

PREMIERE: May 15, 1980, New York City Ballet, New York State Theater. Conductor: Robert Irving. (Preview: School of American Ballet Gala Benefit, January 24.)

CAST: Suzanne Farrell, Adam Lüders; Heather Watts; Stephanie Saland, Judith Fugate; 20 women.

NOTE: Balanchine's presentation as an independent ballet of the work he originally staged as part of the Paris Opéra production of Gounod's *Faust* [397] in 1975.

See 45, 117, 151, 227, 397

414 LE BOURGEOIS GENTILHOMME

MUSIC: By Richard Strauss (concert suite, ca. 1917). Libretto after Molière.

CHOREOGRAPHY: By George Balanchine. Assistant to the Choreographer: Susan Hendl.

PRODUCTION: Scenery and costumes by Rouben Ter-Arutunian. Lighting by Ronald Bates.

PREMIERE: May 22, 1980, New York City Ballet, New York State Theater. Conductor: Robert Irving.

CAST: *M. Jourdain*, Frank Ohman; *Cléonte*, Peter Martins; *Lucille*, Suzanne Farrell; DIVERTISSEMENT: Heather Watts, Victor Castelli, 6 women; *Maid*; *6 Lackeys*; *4 Cooks*; *2 Assistants to Cléonte*.

NOTE: Originally presented by the New York City Opera, 1979.

OTHER VERSIONS: 1932, Ballets Russes de Monte-Carlo. 1944, Ballet Russe de Monte Carlo.

See 131*, 221, 410*

415 ROBERT SCHUMANN'S 'DAVIDSBÜNDLERTÄNZE'

MUSIC: By Robert Schumann (Op. 6, 1837).

PRODUCTION: Scenery and costumes by Rouben Ter-Arutunian. Lighting by Ronald Bates.

PREMIERE: June 19, 1980, New York City Ballet, New York State Theater. On-stage pianist: Gordon Boelzner. (Preview: Annual New York City Ballet Gala Benefit, June 12.)

CAST: Karin von Aroldingen, Adam Lüders; Suzanne Farrell, Jacques d'Amboise; Heather Watts, Peter Martins; Kay Mazzo, Ib Andersen.

NOTE: Four couples perform the eighteen *Dances of the League of David*, choreographed to Schumann's piano music written to Clara Wieck, who later became his wife. The original bylines expressing Schumann's multiple selves were expunged by him from later editions of the score. Although the dances suggest facets of Schumann and Clara's personalities, the ballet is in essence musical, not biographical.

TELEVISION: 1982 (CBS Cable).

1981

416 THE SPELLBOUND CHILD /
L'ENFANT ET LES SORTILÈGES
Made for Television

MUSIC: By Maurice Ravel (1920-25). Lyric fantasy in two parts based on a poem by Colette (translated by Catherine Wolff).

PRODUCTION: Produced by Emile Ardolino and Judy Kinberg. Conceived for television and with choreography by George Balanchine, in collaboration with Kermit Love. Directed by Emile Ardolino. Design concept, puppets, models, and costumes by Kermit Love. Supervising Designer: David Mitchell. Lighting by Ralph Holmes.

FIRST TELECAST: May 25, 1981, Dance in America, PBS. Danced by New York City Ballet, students from the School of American Ballet, and others. Conductor of New York City Ballet orchestra: Manuel Rosenthal. Singers off-camera.

CAST: *Boy*, Christopher Byars; *Mother*; *Armchair*; *Lady Chair* (2 women); *Clock*; *Teapot*; *Chinese Cup*; *Fire*, Karin von Aroldingen; *5 Shepherds*; *5 Shepherdesses*; *2 Cats*; *Wounded Tree*; *Dragonflies*, 4 women; *Bats*, 2 women, 1 man; *Moths*, 6 women; *2 Frogs*; *2 Owls*; *Toads*, 8 boys.

NOTE: Created for color television, this production used elements of the 1975 staging, and employed special effects, including animation for certain parts of the narrative.

OTHER VERSIONS: 1925, Opéra de Monte-Carlo (*L'Enfant et les Sortilèges*, danced by Diaghilev's Ballets Russes). 1946, Ballet Society (*The Spellbound Child* [*L'Enfant et les Sortilèges*]). 1975, New York City Ballet (*L'Enfant et les Sortilèges*, Ravel Festival).

See 48*, 235, 390

417 MOZARTIANA

MUSIC: By Peter Ilyitch Tschaikovsky (Suite No. 4, *Mozartiana*, Op. 61, 1887; based on Mozart's Gigue in G major [K. 574], Minuet in D major [K. 355], the motet 'Ave, Verum Corpus' [K. 618], and variations on 'Les Hommes Pieusement' from Gluck's comic opera *La Rencontre Imprévue* [K. 455]).

PRODUCTION: Costumes by Rouben Ter-Arutunian.

PREMIERE: June 4, 1981, New York City Ballet with students from the School of American Ballet, New York State Theater. Conductor: Robert Irving. (Annual New York City Ballet Gala Benefit.)

CAST: PREGHIERA: Suzanne Farrell, 4 young girls; GIGUE: Christopher d'Amboise; MENUET: 4 women; THÈME ET VARIATIONS: Farrell, Ib Andersen; FINALE: Entire cast.

NOTE: The ballet is completely different from the work Balanchine created to this music in 1933, and modified thereafter. The order of the first two movements is reversed to begin with the PREGHIERA (based on the motet 'Ave, Verum Corpus'), in which the ballerina dances a prayer, attended by four young girls. The 1981 *Mozartiana* was first presented on the opening night of the Tschaikovsky Festival of the New York City Ballet (detailed in *Festivals Directed by Balanchine*, page 313), which included the premieres of four Balanchine works [417-420]. Throughout the festival and until the end of the New York season on June 28, the scenery was an architectural structure with movable ranks of translucent plastic cylinders by Philip Johnson and John Burgee, in arrangements and with lighting designs by Ronald Bates.

See 134*, 149

418 TEMPO DI VALSE:
GARLAND DANCE from THE SLEEPING BEAUTY

MUSIC: By Peter Ilyitch Tschaikovsky (as given below).

CHOREOGRAPHY: By George Balanchine (two of five parts), Jacques d'Amboise and John Taras.

PRODUCTION: Costumes for GARLAND DANCE by Karinska (from DIAMONDS in *Jewels* [358] and *Chaconne* [400]) and Rouben Ter-Arutunian (from *Coppélia* [387]).

PREMIERE: June 9, 1981, New York City Ballet with students from the School of American Ballet, New York State Theater. Conductor: Robert Irving.

CAST: GARLAND DANCE from *The Sleeping Beauty*, Act I (produced 1890): 25 women, 16 men, 16 young girls.

NOTE: Sixteen couples dance, each couple holding aloft a garland of flowers in the form of an arch; a chain of little girls enters, weaving under the garlands, and is joined by nine older girls. In addition to the GARLAND DANCE, the short works presented under the general title *Tempo di Valse* during the Tschaikovsky Festival (and later in the season) were the WALTZ OF THE FLOWERS from *The Nutcracker* [302] by Balanchine, VALSE-SCHERZO by d'Amboise, and VARIATION VI FROM TRIO IN A MINOR and WALTZ FROM EUGEN ONEGIN, ACT II by Taras.

See 65, 225, 259, 281, 404

419 HUNGARIAN GYPSY AIRS

MUSIC: By Sophie Menter (*Hungarische Zigeuner Weisen*), orchestrated by Peter Ilyitch Tschaikovsky.

PRODUCTION: Costumes by Ben Benson.

PREMIERE: June 13, 1981, New York City Ballet, New York State Theater. Conductor: Robert Irving. Pianist: Richard Moredock.

CAST: Karin von Aroldingen, Adam Lüders; 4 women, 4 men.

420 SYMPHONY NO. 6—PATHÉTIQUE: FOURTH MOVEMENT, ADAGIO LAMENTOSO

MUSIC: By Peter Ilyitch Tschaikovsky (Symphony No. 6 in B minor, Op. 74, 1893 [first movement omitted]).

CHOREOGRAPHY: By George Balanchine (ADAGIO LAMENTOSO) and Jerome Robbins.

PRODUCTION: Costumes for ADAGIO LAMENTOSO by Rouben Ter-Arutunian.

PREMIERE: June 14, 1981, New York City Ballet, New York State Theater. Conductor: Robert Irving.

CAST: FOURTH MOVEMENT, ADAGIO LAMENTOSO: Karin von Aroldingen, Judith Fugate, Stephanie Saland; 16 women; *12 Angels*; group of hooded figures; child.

NOTE: The first movement of the symphony was omitted; the second, ALLEGRO CON GRAZIA, was choreographed by Robbins; the third, ALLEGRO MOLTO VIVACE, was played by the orchestra with curtain lowered. The fourth and final movement was Balanchine's ADAGIO LAMENTOSO: Women mourners dance in grief; angels with tall white wings and hooded figures in purple are followed by a procession of monks who prostrate themselves to form a living cross; a child enters carrying a candle. To the final chords, the child extinguishes the candle. The ADAGIO LAMENTOSO closed the Tschaikovsky Festival of the New York City Ballet.

1982

421 TANGO

MUSIC: By Igor Stravinsky (1940 [1953 instrumentation by Stravinsky]).

PREMIERE: June 10, 1982, New York City Ballet, New York State Theater. Conductor: Robert Irving. (Annual New York City Ballet Gala Benefit.)

CAST: Karin von Aroldingen, Christopher d'Amboise.

NOTE: The dancers perform in vaudeville-style costumes, the woman in abbreviated black lace, the man in Spanish dress. The premiere used Stravinsky's orchestration for jazz ensemble; subsequent performances were danced to the composer's score for solo piano, with the pianist on stage. *Tango* was first presented on the opening night of the Stravinsky Centennial Celebration of the New York City Ballet (detailed in *Festivals Directed by Balanchine*, page 316), which included the premieres of four Balanchine works [421-424]. The décor throughout the Centennial Celebration incorporated the architectural settings created by Johnson/Burgee for the Tschaikovsky Festival of 1981, arranged and lighted by Ronald Bates.

422 NOAH AND THE FLOOD

MUSIC: Dance-drama by Igor Stravinsky (*The Flood*, 1962, written for television). Text chosen and arranged by Robert Craft from *Genesis*, the *Te Deum* and *Sanctus* hymns, and the fifteenth-century York and Chester miracle plays.

CHOREOGRAPHY: Staged by George Balanchine and Jacques d'Amboise.

PRODUCTION: Designed by Rouben Ter-Arutunian (costumes and masks from the 1962 television production [342]; hanging backdrop based on the 1962 designs; some new décor).

PREMIERE: June 11, 1982, New York City Ballet with students from the School of American Ballet, New York State Theater. Conductor:

Robert Craft. Off-stage singers: Members of the New York City Opera chorus; Chorus Master: Lloyd Walser.

CAST: VOICES: *Narrator* (spoken), John Houseman; *Voices of God* (basses), Robert Brubaker, Barry Carl; *Voice of Satan* (tenor), John Lankston. DANCERS: *Adam*, Adam Lüders; *Eve*, Nina Fedorova; *Lucifer*, Bruce Padgett; *Noah*, Francisco Moncion; *Noah's Wife*, Delia Peters; *The Family*, 2 women, 3 men; *Builders of the Ark*, 8 women, 8 men.

NOTE: Balanchine's staged presentation for the Stravinsky Centennial Celebration of the morality play originally conceived for television, reproducing almost exactly the choreographed sections of the original production. THE PROLOGUE and SATAN'S ARIETTA were omitted; the narration, divided among several actors on television, was spoken solely by John Houseman on stage. The décor was based on the designs for television, but the animals, which in the original production had been miniature toys belonging to Balanchine, were replaced by large cut-outs carried in procession by students of the School of American Ballet.

See 342*

423 ÉLÉGIE

MUSIC: By Igor Stravinsky (*Élégie-Elegy* for solo viola, 1944).

PREMIERE: June 13, 1982, New York City Ballet, New York State Theater. On-stage violist: Warren Laffredo.

CAST: Suzanne Farrell.

NOTE: Balanchine first choreographed Stravinsky's *Élégie* as a pas de deux in 1948, and then as a solo in 1966. At the opening and closing of this newly choreographed work the dancer kneels in a circle of light on the darkened stage.

See 245*, 355

424 PERSÉPHONE

MUSIC: By Igor Stravinsky (*Mélodrame* in three scenes for tenor, narrator, mixed chorus, children's choir, and orchestra, commissioned by Ida Rubinstein, 1933). Text by André Gide.

CHOREOGRAPHY: Staged by George Balanchine, John Taras and Vera Zorina.

PRODUCTION: Designed by Kermit Love.

PREMIERE: June 18, 1982, New York City Ballet, New York State Theater. Conductor: Robert Craft. Singers: Members of the New York City Opera chorus; Chorus Master: Lloyd Walser. The American Boychoir prepared by Brad Richmond and Robert Hobbs.

CAST: *Perséphone* (spoken), Vera Zorina; *Eumolpus the Eleusinian Priest* (tenor), Joseph Evans; *Spirit of Perséphone*, Karin von Aroldingen; *Pluto*, Mel Tomlinson; *Mercury*, Gen Horiuchi; *Nymphs*, 9 women; *Shades of the Underworld*, 9 women, 6 men.

NOTE: Presented by Balanchine on the one-hundredth anniversary of the composer's birth as the last ballet of the Stravinsky Centennial Celebration, forty-nine years after its first production, which Stravinsky had hoped Balanchine would choreograph. *Perséphone* was originally presented by Ballets Ida Rubinstein in 1934, choreographed by Kurt Jooss and narrated by Ida Rubinstein. In the Balanchine staging, the costumed chorus is grouped on both sides of the stage, framing the action. Perséphone, abducted by Pluto, dwells in the underworld during Autumn and Winter, but is restored to earth each year to bless mankind in Spring and Summer. Gide's text ends:

> *No spring can ever live again*
> *Unless the seed beneath the ground*
> *Consents to die, and wakens then*
> *To make the future's field abound.*

425 VARIATIONS FOR ORCHESTRA

MUSIC: By Igor Stravinsky (*Variations in Memory of Aldous Huxley*, 1965).

PRODUCTION: Lighting by Ronald Bates.

PREMIERE: July 2, 1982, New York City Ballet, New York State Theater. Conductor: Robert Irving.

CAST: Suzanne Farrell.

NOTE: The premiere of this ballet intended for the Stravinsky Centennial Celebration took place two weeks after its official close. Balanchine had first choreographed a solo for Suzanne Farrell to this music as the final section of his 1966 work for the New York City Ballet, in which the music was played three times. The 1982 work was entirely rechoreographed.

See 353

SOURCE NOTES

Entries in the *Catalogue* have been compiled from printed programs, and information from critical reviews in newspapers, periodicals, and the published works cited in the *Bibliography*. Additional information has been provided by the persons named in the notes that follow. Printed sources are included in the notes only when the information is available from a single source; author, title and page reference are given for books cited in the *Bibliography*, with publisher and date provided for other works.

Principal archives and public collections consulted include the Bibliothèque de l'Arsenal (Collection Rondel), Paris; Bibliothèque et Musée de l'Opéra, Paris; Bibliothèque Ste. Geneviève (Collection Doucet), Paris; Garrick Club, London; Harvard Theatre Collection; Lenin State Library, Moscow; Leningrad State Institute of Theater, Music and Cinematography; Moscow Institute of the History of the Arts; Moscow Theater (Bakrushin) Museum; Museum of the Vaganova Choreographic School, Leningrad; The New York Public Library Dance Collection and Slavonic Division; Opéra de Monte-Carlo Archives; library of the Royal Theater, Copenhagen; Theatre Museum at the Victoria and Albert Museum, London.

1 - 35 Full documentation of Balanchine's activities before he left the Soviet Union in 1924 is not possible. Although printed programs of official performances at the Maryinsky Theater and School in St. Petersburg (later State Theater of Opera and Ballet/Petrograd Theater [Ballet] School, now Kirov Theater and School) exist, none have been found for the performances given by the Young Ballet; a single poster announcing the opening concert is in the Museum of the Vaganova Choreographic School, Leningrad.

Research was carried out in the Soviet Union by Elizabeth Souritz (Moscow: Moscow Institute of the History of the Arts) and Vera Krasovskaya (Leningrad: State Institute of Theater, Music and Cinematography); and by Gunhild Schüller of the Institut für Theaterwissenschaft, University of Vienna, who visited Moscow and Leningrad in 1981. Major printed resources consulted were the newspapers *Krasnaya gazeta* and *Zhizn' iskusstva*, the periodicals *Teatr* and *Teatr i iskusstvo*, and the weekly of the Petrograd/Leningrad Academic Theaters: *Evhenedel'nik petrogradskikh gosudarstvenniykh akademicheskikh teatrov; Evhenedel'nik akademicheskikh teatrov v Leningrade*. Entries 1-35 are based on the research of Souritz, Krasovskaya and Schüller; on interviews conducted with Pëtr Gusev in Leningrad (Poel Karp, 1980), and with Balanchine, Alexandra Danilova and Tamara Geva in New York (Nancy Reynolds and Gunhild Schüller, 1979-81); and on material from publications cited in full in the *Bibliography*: Balanchine's *Complete Stories of the Great Ballets*, Tamara Geva's *Split Seconds*, Mikhail Mikhailov's *My Life in Ballet*, Natalia Roslavleva's *Era of the Russian*

Ballet, Yuri Slonimsky's *Balanchine: The Early Years*, Bernard Taper's *Balanchine: A Biography*, and A. E. Twysden's *Alexandra Danilova*.

Information about the Rhineland tour of the Principal Dancers of the Russian State Ballet (ending with an engagement at the Empire Theatre, London) comes primarily from announcements and reviews in the local press.

36, 37 Grigoriev, *The Diaghilev Ballet*, p. 209; amplified by Balanchine, Alicia Markova, Anton Dolin.

38 Balanchine.

48 Boris Kochno.

50, 51 John Martin, *Ruth Page: An Intimate Biography* (New York: Dekker, 1977), p. 61; corroborated by Balanchine, Ruth Page. Additional music information provided by Balanchine.

53 Revisions information in Hillary Ostlere, 'Rieti and Balanchine,' *Ballet Review* 10:1 (Spring 1982), p. 8.

61 Additional production information in Buckle, *Diaghilev*, p. 466.

64 Revisions information in Macdonald, *Diaghilev Observed*, p. 348. Additional information provided by Boris Kochno, David Vaughan.

65 Alicia Markova.

73, 74 Tamara Geva, Lincoln Kirstein. Although contained in a revue, these pieces were reviewed by the dance critic of the *New York Times*, December 11, 1927.

75 Balanchine, Alicia Markova.

83 Information provided by Keith Money; corroborated by Balanchine.

84 Additional information provided by Alexandra Danilova; additional revisions information provided by Nancy Goldner, Allegra Kent.

85 Additional production information in Macdonald, *Diaghilev Observed*, p. 364.

91 Uncredited choreography acknowledged by Balanchine.

94 Boris Kochno has corrected the general misunderstanding that the book for the ballet is based on a story by Pushkin. The printed program for the premiere performance names the conductor as *l'auteur*, Sergei Prokofiev; this is repeated by Prokofiev in his *Autobiography* (Moscow: Foreign Languages Publishing House, 1959, p. 74), and by Robert Craft in *Stravinsky in Pictures and Documents* (p. 287). Grigoriev (*The Diaghilev Ballet*, p. 278) gives Roger Desormière as conductor, which Balanchine believes to be correct.

95 Additional information provided by Alicia Markova and Anton Dolin, who danced *Moods* together for several years.

97 Boris Kochno.

98 Scenery and costumes credited to Angèles Ortiz in later programs.

100 Additional music information provided by Ulla Poulsen.

105 Ulla Poulsen.

107 Balanchine, Elizabeth Baron [Betty Scorer], Natasha Gregorova Cookson, Alicia Markova, Doris Sonne Toye, and brief reviews in *Era*.

110 Music information provided by Balanchine.

129 Music information provided by Balanchine and Vittorio Rieti; additional information provided by Kathrine Sorley Walker.

131 Note corroborated by Balanchine.

133 Balanchine, Georges Auric, Boris Kochno.

134 Revisions information provided by Balanchine and Patricia Wilde (who performed in the Ballet Russe de Monte Carlo version); additional information provided by Lincoln Kirstein.

135 Balanchine.

136 Boris Kochno.
139 Music information provided by Balanchine.
141 Additional music information provided by Balanchine. Revisions information provided by Balanchine, Ruthanna Boris, Rosemary Dunleavy, Annabelle Lyon, Marie-Jeanne.
142 Additional music information provided by Kay Swift, Morton Gould.
143 Tamara Geva, Marie-Jeanne.
144 Ruthanna Boris.
146 Lincoln Kirstein.
147 Mentioned in the *New York Times*, May 4 and 12, 1935. Additional information provided by William Dollar.
155 Information about scenery provided by Lincoln Kirstein.
157 Information provided by William Dollar, at the suggestion of Gisella Caccialanza.
160 Structure of ballet divertissement clarified by Ruthanna Boris.
164 Music information provided by Balanchine; date verified in Balanchine–Kirstein–A. Everett Austin correspondence, Wadsworth Atheneum, through the assistance of Jill Silverman; additional information provided by Lincoln Kirstein.
165 Structure of ballet clarified by William Dollar.
166 Balanchine.
167 Ruthanna Boris.
172 Balanchine.
178 Additional revisions information provided by Maria Tallchief.
182 Additional information about dance numbers provided by Balanchine.
185 Balanchine.
186 Balanchine.
190 Additional information provided by Katherine Dunham: The collaboration was so complete that it is impossible to be specific about individual contributions.

192 Kathrine Sorley Walker, Lincoln Kirstein.
194 Additional revisions and stagings information provided by Balanchine, Una Kai, Patricia McBride.
202 *New York Times*, June 18, 1982.
205 *Washington Post*, March 1, 6, 7, 1964. Margaret Graham.
206 Edward Bigelow.
212 Gisella Caccialanza.
214 Information provided by Balanchine; corroborated by André Eglevsky.
215 Tanaquil Le Clercq.
216 Balanchine.
218 Additional information about dance numbers provided by Balanchine.
219 Structure of dance numbers clarified by Alexandra Danilova, Maria Tallchief, Frederic Franklin.
220 Balanchine, Nikita Talin.
222 Additional music information provided by Vittorio Rieti.
223 Marie-Jeanne.
224 Balanchine.
225 Additional music information provided by Balanchine, Gordon Boelzner.
226 - 228 Balanchine, Marie-Jeanne, Patricia Wilde.
231 Balanchine, Tanaquil Le Clercq, March of Dimes.
232 Additional music information provided by Vittorio Rieti; additional revisions and stagings information provided by Rosemary Dunleavy, John Taras.
233 Additional information about the conception of the ballet provided by Balanchine, Alexandra Danilova; additional revisions information provided by Nikita Talin, Maria Tallchief; additional stagings information provided by Frederic Franklin, Lew Christensen; structure of *Pas de Dix* clarified by Maria Tallchief.
234 Balanchine.
237 Lew Christensen.

241 Lincoln Kirstein.

243 Betty Cage.

244 John Taras.

246 Nancy Goldner.

247 Balanchine, Maria Tallchief, Marjorie Tallchief, Victoria Simon, André Eglevsky, George Skibine.

249 Fred Danieli.

257 Uncredited movement direction acknowledged by Balanchine.

259 Balanchine, Maria Tallchief.

261 Balanchine, Tanaquil Le Clercq.

262 Balanchine, Maria Tallchief.

264 Additional information about choreography for the Firebird provided by Maria Tallchief.

266 Tanaquil Le Clercq.

267 Additional information about costumes provided by Barbara Horgan, Edward Bigelow.

273 Arlene Croce, David Vaughan.

274 Balanchine, Melissa Hayden.

275 David Vaughan.

285 Additional music information provided by Robert Irving; additional revisions information provided by Merrill Ashley, Arlene Croce, Rosemary Dunleavy, Robert Irving.

290 Balanchine.

291 Balanchine, Tanaquil Le Clercq, Jacques d'Amboise.

294 Information provided by Virginia Brooks, New York Public Library Dance Collection; corroborated by Melissa Hayden.

296 Tanaquil Le Clercq, Jacques d'Amboise.

297 - 299 Tanaquil Le Clercq.

302 Additional music information provided by Balanchine, Gordon Boelzner, Robert Irving; revisions information provided by Balanchine, Rosemary Dunleavy.

305 Tanaquil Le Clercq, Arthur Mitchell.

309 Additional revisions information provided by Arlene Croce.

311 Kirk Browning.

314 Additional music information provided by Balanchine, Robert Irving; additional revisions information provided by Arlene Croce, Rosemary Dunleavy, Suki Schorer.

316 Revisions information provided by Nancy Goldner.

323 Additional music information provided by Vittorio Rieti.

332 Additional music information provided by Gordon Boelzner.

340 Additional music information provided by Gordon Boelzner, Robert Irving.

345 Derivation of the ballet Chaconne and additional revisions information provided by Balanchine.

348 Information about costumes provided by Barbara Horgan.

350 Structure of ballet and its relationship to Sylvia: Pas de Deux [273] and La Source [364] clarified by Arlene Croce, Melissa Hayden, Suki Schorer, Jacques d'Amboise.

351 Additional revisions information provided by Arlene Croce.

358 Additional revisions information provided by Rosemary Dunleavy.

363 Patricia McBride.

367 Alfonso Catá, Karl Reuling.

369 Rosemary Dunleavy.

375 Balanchine.

376 Additional music information provided by Gordon Boelzner; additional revisions information provided by Nancy Goldner, Patricia McBride.

385 Patricia McBride.

387 Additional music information provided by Gordon Boelzner, Robert Irving; additional revisions information provided by Betty Cage, Arlene Croce, Nancy Goldner.

390 Barbara Horgan, Deborah Koolish.

400 Balanchine, Arlene Croce, Nancy Goldner.

402 Information corroborated by Edward Villella.

404 Information corroborated by Patricia McBride.

405 Additional music information provided by Gordon Boelzner, Joseph Wishey.

410 Rosemary Dunleavy.

414 Susan Hendl.

417 Balanchine.

420 Music information provided by Gordon Boelzner.

422 Deborah Koolish, Gordon Boelzner.

423 Gordon Boelzner.

425 Gordon Boelzner.

APPENDIXES

AMERICAN COMPANY ITINERARIES

Producing Company of the School of American Ballet

1934   December 6-8, Hartford, Connecticut: Avery Memorial Theater

American Ballet

1935   February 7-8, Bryn Mawr College: Goodhart Hall
March 1-17, NEW YORK SEASON: Adelphi Theatre
August 10-11, Philadelphia: Robin Hood Dell
August 12, 19, New York: Lewisohn Stadium
September 28, White Plains, New York: Westchester County Center
EASTERN UNITED STATES TOUR
    October 14-15, Greenwich, Connecticut: Greenwich High School
      Auditorium
    October 16, Bridgeport, Connecticut: Central High School
      Auditorium
    October 17, New Haven, Connecticut: Shubert Theatre
    October 18, Allentown, Pennsylvania: Lyric Theatre
    October 19, Princeton, New Jersey: McCarter Theatre
    October 21, Harrisburg, Pennsylvania: Majestic Theatre
    October 22, Scranton, Pennsylvania: Temple Theatre
RESIDENT COMPANY OF THE METROPOLITAN OPERA, NEW YORK, AS
  AMERICAN BALLET ENSEMBLE, December 1935 - April 1938
1936   February 14, Hartford, Connecticut: Avery Memorial Theater

American Ballet Caravan

1941   SOUTH AMERICAN TOUR
    June 25 - July 6, Rio de Janeiro, Brazil: Teatro Municipal
    July 8-11, São Paulo, Brazil: Teatro Municipal
    July 18-30, Buenos Aires, Argentina: Politeama
    August 1-4, Montevideo, Uruguay: Estudio Auditorio del S.O.D.R.E.
    August 6-7, Rosario, Argentina: Teatro Colón
    August 9-10, Córdoba, Argentina: Teatro Rivera Indarte
    August 12-15, Mendoza, Argentina: Teatro Independencia
    August 19-27, Santiago, Chile: Teatro Municipal

August 28, Viña del Mar, Chile
September 10-23, Lima, Peru: Teatro Municipal
September 30 - October 2, Cali, Colombia
October 4-5, Manizales, Colombia
October 7-9, Medellín, Colombia
October 14-21, Bogotá, Colombia: Teatro Colombia
October 31 - November 4, Caracas, Venezuela: Teatro Municipal

Ballet Society

1946 November 20, New York: Central High School of Needle Trades
1947 January 13-14, New York: Hunter College Playhouse
February 18-20, New York: Heckscher Theater (operas, *The Medium, The Telephone*)
March 26, New York: Central High School of Needle Trades
May 18, New York: Ziegfeld Theater
November 12, New York: City Center
November 20, New York: Museum of Modern Art Auditorium (film, Cocteau's *La Belle et la Bête*)
1948 January 22-23, New York: Hunter College Playhouse (opera, *Far Harbour*)
February 9, New York: City Center
March 22, New York: City Center
April 28 - May 1, New York: City Center

New York City Ballet

1948 RESIDENT COMPANY OF THE NEW YORK CITY OPERA, October 1948 - May 1949
October 11 - November 23, NEW YORK SEASON: City Center
1949 January 13-23, NEW YORK SEASON: City Center
November 23 - December 11, NEW YORK SEASON: City Center
1950 February 21 - March 19, NEW YORK SEASON: City Center
ENGLISH TOUR
July 10 - August 19, London: Royal Opera House, Covent Garden
August 28 - September 2, Manchester: Palace Theatre
September 4-9, Liverpool: Empire Theatre
September 11-16, Croydon: Davis Theatre
November 21 - December 10, NEW YORK SEASON: City Center

1951　February 13 - March 11, NEW YORK SEASON: City Center
　　　April 23 - May 6, Chicago: Opera House
　　　June 5-24, NEW YORK SEASON: City Center
　　　September 4-23, NEW YORK SEASON: City Center
　　　November 13 - December 16, NEW YORK SEASON: City Center
1952　February 12 - March 16, NEW YORK SEASON: City Center
　　　EUROPEAN TOUR
　　　　　April 15 - May 8, Barcelona: Gran Teatro del Liceo
　　　　　May 10, Paris: Théâtre National de l'Opéra (Exposition Inter-
　　　　　　nationale des Arts: L'Oeuvre du XXe Siècle; sous les auspices du
　　　　　　Congrès pour la liberté de la culture)
　　　　　May 11-15, Paris: Théâtre des Champs-Élysées (Exposition Inter-
　　　　　　nationale des Arts . . . .)
　　　　　May 18-30, Florence: Teatro Comunale (Maggio Musicale
　　　　　　Fiorentino)
　　　　　June 1-4, Lausanne: Théâtre Municipal (Grandes Fêtes du Juin)
　　　　　June 6-7, Zürich: Stadttheater (Zürcher Juni-Festwochen)
　　　　　June 9-25, Paris: Théâtre des Champs-Élysées
　　　　　June 27 - July 3, The Hague: Gebouw voor Kunsten en
　　　　　　Wetenschappen (Holland Festival)
　　　　　July 7 - August 23, London: Royal Opera House, Covent Garden
　　　　　August 25-30, Edinburgh: Empire Theatre (Edinburgh Festival)
　　　　　September 3, 6, Berlin: Schiller Theater (Berliner Festwochen)
　　　　　September 4-5, 7, Berlin: Städtische Oper (Berliner Festwochen)
　　　November 4 - January 25, 1953, NEW YORK SEASON: City Center
1953　February 12-13, Baltimore: Lyric Theatre
　　　February 14-16, Washington, D. C.: Constitution Hall
　　　May 5 - June 14, NEW YORK SEASON: City Center
　　　WESTERN UNITED STATES TOUR
　　　　　July 2-3, Red Rocks, Colorado: Red Rocks Theater
　　　　　July 6 - August 1, Los Angeles: Greek Theatre
　　　　　August 3-14, San Francisco: War Memorial Opera House
　　　EUROPEAN TOUR
　　　　　September 8-13, Milan: Teatro alla Scala
　　　　　September 18-20, Venice: Teatro La Fenice
　　　　　September 22-27, Milan: Teatro alla Scala
　　　　　September 28-29, Como: Teatro Sociale
　　　　　October 3-11, Naples: Teatro di San Carlo

October 13-16, Rome: Teatro dell'Opera
October 18-20, Florence: Teatro Comunale
October 22-25, Trieste: Teatro Comunale Giuseppe Verdi
October 27-28, Bologna: Teatro Duse
October 30 - November 1, Genoa: Teatro Carlo Felice
November 3-5, Munich: Bayerische Staatsoper, Prinzregenten-
    theater
November 7-8, Stuttgart: Württembergische Staatstheater,
    Stuttgart Staatsoper
November 11-17, Brussels: Théâtre Royale de la Monnaie

1954 January 12 - March 21, NEW YORK SEASON: City Center
UNITED STATES TOUR
    May 26 - June 6, Chicago: Opera House
    June 10-16, Seattle: Orpheum Theatre
    June 19 - July 3, San Francisco: War Memorial Opera House
    July 5 - August 15, Los Angeles: Greek Theatre
August 31 - September 26, NEW YORK SEASON: City Center
November 3 - December 19, NEW YORK SEASON: City Center

1955 February 15 - March 13, NEW YORK SEASON: City Center
EUROPEAN TOUR
    April 9-17, Monte Carlo: Grand Théâtre du Casino de Monte-Carlo
        (Salle Garnier)
    April 20-24, Marseilles: Opéra Municipal
    April 28-30, Lyons: Opéra de Lyon
    May 6-9, Florence: Teatro Comunale (Maggio Musicale Fiorentino)
    May 11-15, Rome: Teatro dell'Opera
    May 18-20, Bordeaux: Grand-Théâtre (Mai Musical de Bordeaux)
    May 2 - June 5, Lisbon: Teatro Nacional de San Carlos
    June 8-14, Paris: Théâtre des Champs-Élysées (Salut à la France)
    June 16-18, Lausanne: Théâtre de Beaulieu
    June 20-22, Zürich: Stadttheater (Zürcher Juni-Festwochen)
    June 24-27, Stuttgart: Württembergische Staatstheater,
        Stuttgart Staatsoper
    June 29 - July 3, Amsterdam: Stadsschouwburg (Holland Festival)
    July 4-8, The Hague: Gebouw voor Kunsten en Wetenschappen
        (Holland Festival)
UNITED STATES TOUR
    July 20 - August 13, Los Angeles: Greek Theatre

August 15-28, San Francisco: War Memorial Opera House
August 30 - September 3, Seattle: Moore Theatre
September 7-18, Chicago: Opera House
November 8 - January 1, 1956, NEW YORK SEASON: City Center
1956 February 28 - March 25, NEW YORK SEASON: City Center
April 3-22, Chicago: Opera House
May 31 - June 1, Stratford, Connecticut: American Shakespeare
Festival Theatre (Mozart Festival)
EUROPEAN TOUR
August 26-30, Salzburg: Festspielhaus (Salzburger Festspiele)
September 1-9, Vienna: Staatsoper
September 12-15, Zürich: Stadttheater
September 18-23, Venice: Teatro La Fenice (Biennale)
September 26-28, Berlin: Titania-Palast (Berliner Festwochen)
September 29, Berlin: Städtische Oper (Berliner Festwochen)
September 30 - October 1, Berlin: Titania-Palast (Berliner
Festwochen)
October 4-7, Munich: Bayerische Staatsoper, Prinzregententheater
October 9-10, Frankfurt: Städtische Oper
October 12-14, Brussels: Théâtre de la Monnaie
October 15, Antwerp: Koninklijke Vlaamse Opera/Théâtre Royal
Flammande
October 17-21, Paris: Théâtre National de l'Opéra
October 23-24, Cologne: Aula der Universität
October 26-31, Copenhagen: Det Kongelige Teater
November 3-11, Stockholm: Operan
December 18 - March 3, 1957, NEW YORK SEASON: City Center
1957 April 23 - May 12, Chicago: Opera House
November 3, Philadelphia: Academy of Music
November 19 - January 19, 1958, NEW YORK SEASON: City Center
1958 January 20-24, Washington, D. C.: Loew's Capitol Theatre
FAR EASTERN TOUR
March 17-30, Tokyo: Shinjuku Koma Theatre
April 1-6, Tokyo: Sankei Hall
April 10-13, Osaka: Festival Hall (Osaka International Festival of
Music, Art and Drama)
April 17 - June 14, Sydney: Empire Theatre
June 16 - August 5, Melbourne: Her Majesty's Theatre

August 8-10, Manila: U. P. [University of the Philippines] Theater

September 2-28, NEW YORK SEASON: City Center

UNITED STATES TOUR

> October 11-12, Lafayette, Indiana: Purdue University, Edward C. Elliott Hall of Music
>
> October 13-15, East Lansing, Michigan: Michigan State University Auditorium
>
> October 16-17, Bloomington, Indiana: Indiana University Auditorium
>
> October 20-22, Washington, D. C.: Loew's Capitol Theatre
>
> October 23-25, Philadelphia: Academy of Music

November 25 - February 1, 1959, NEW YORK SEASON: City Center

1959 January 1, Albany, New York (Governor's Inaugural Ball)

May 12 - June 14, NEW YORK SEASON: City Center

UNITED STATES TOUR

> July 27 - August 8, Los Angeles: Greek Theatre
>
> August 11-16, Ravinia (Ravinia Festival)

August 25 - September 20, NEW YORK SEASON: City Center

October 19-21, Washington, D. C.: Loew's Capitol Theatre

October 22-24, Philadelphia: Academy of Music

December 8 - February 7, 1960, NEW YORK SEASON: City Center

1960 March 29 - April 24, NEW YORK SEASON: City Center

UNITED STATES TOUR

> July 16-20, Bear Mountain, New York (Empire State Music Festival)
>
> July 25 - August 6, Los Angeles: Greek Theatre
>
> August 9-14, Ravinia (Ravinia Festival)

November 8 - January 15, 1961, NEW YORK SEASON: City Center

1961 January 21-22, Baltimore: Lyric Theatre

January 24-26, Washington, D. C.: Loew's Capitol Theatre

March 14 - April 9, NEW YORK SEASON: City Center

UNITED STATES/CANADIAN TOUR

> July 13-19, Bear Mountain, New York: Anthony Wayne Recreation Area (Empire State Music Festival)
>
> July 24-29, Vancouver, British Columbia, Canada: Queen Elizabeth Theatre (Vancouver International Festival)
>
> July 31 - August 2, San Francisco: War Memorial Opera House
>
> August 4-12, Los Angeles: Greek Theatre
>
> August 15-20, Ravinia (Ravinia Festival)

August 29 - September 17, NEW YORK SEASON: City Center

UNITED STATES TOUR

    October 5-8, Cleveland, Ohio: Music Hall-Public Auditorium

    October 10-12, East Lansing, Michigan: Michigan State University Auditorium

    October 13-15, Detroit, Michigan: Masonic Auditorium

    October 17, Corning, New York

    October 19, Farmingdale, Long Island, New York: Farmingdale Senior High School

    October 20-21, Mineola, Long Island, New York: Mineola Theatre

    October 23-25, Raleigh, North Carolina: North Carolina State College, William Neal Reynolds Coliseum

December 5 - February 4, 1962, NEW YORK SEASON: City Center

1962 UPSTATE NEW YORK TOUR

    February 10, Rochester, New York: Eastman Theatre

    February 11, Buffalo, New York: Kleinhans Music Hall

    February 13, Albany, New York: Fabian's Palace Theatre

April 24 - May 13, NEW YORK SEASON: City Center

UNITED STATES TOUR

    July 2-14, Los Angeles: Greek Theatre

    July 16-21, San Francisco: War Memorial Opera House

    July 24 - August 4, Seattle: Seattle World's Fair Opera House

    August 7-12, Ravinia (Ravinia Festival)

EUROPEAN/RUSSIAN TOUR

    September 1-2, Hamburg: Staatsoper

    September 5-8, Berlin: Deutsche Oper

    September 11-15, Zürich: Stadttheater

    September 18-20, Stuttgart: Württembergische Staatstheater

    September 22-23, Cologne: Opernhaus

    September 25-26, Frankfurt: Grosses Haus

    September 29 - October 4, Vienna: Theater an der Wien

    October 9, Moscow: Bolshoi Theater

    October 10-17, Moscow: Palace of Congresses

    October 18, Moscow: Bolshoi Theater

    October 19-25, Moscow: Palace of Congresses

    October 26-28, Moscow: Bolshoi Theater

    October 31 - November 1, Leningrad: Kirov Theater

    November 2-8, Leningrad: Lensoviet Palace of Culture

November 11-18, Kiev: Opera House

November 21-25, Tbilisi: Opera House

November 28 - December 1, Baku

December 14-31, NEW YORK SEASON: City Center

1963 January 18, Washington, D. C.: National Guard Armory (Second Inaugural Anniversary Salute)

March 12 - April 21, NEW YORK SEASON: City Center

UNITED STATES TOUR

    July 27-28, Brookville, Long Island, New York: C. W. Post College, Festival Tent (Long Island Festival of the Arts)

    July 29 - August 4, Washington, D. C.: Carter Barron Amphitheatre

    August 6-11, Ravinia (Ravinia Festival)

August 27 - September 29, NEW YORK SEASON: City Center

December 3 - January 26, 1964, NEW YORK SEASON: City Center

1964 April 24 - May 17, NEW YORK SEASON: New York State Theater

UNITED STATES TOUR

    July 20 - August 1, Washington, D. C.: Carter Barron Amphitheatre

    August 3-8, Ravinia (Ravinia Festival)

    August 10-23, Los Angeles: Greek Theatre

September 22 - November 8, NEW YORK SEASON: New York State Theater

November 10-12, Raleigh, North Carolina: North Carolina State College, William Neal Reynolds Coliseum

December 11 - February 21, 1965, NEW YORK SEASON: New York State Theater

1965 SOUTHWESTERN UNITED STATES TOUR

    February 24-28, Houston, Texas: Music Hall

    March 2, San Antonio, Texas: Municipal Auditorium

    March 3, Austin, Texas: University of Texas, Municipal Auditorium

    March 5-7, Dallas, Texas: State Fair Music Hall

    March 10-11, Bloomington, Indiana: Indiana University Auditorium

    March 13-14, St. Louis, Missouri: Kiel Opera House

    March 15, Urbana, Illinois: University of Illinois, University Assembly Hall

April 20 - June 13, NEW YORK SEASON: New York State Theater

EUROPEAN/MIDDLE-EASTERN TOUR

    June 28 - July 3, Paris: Théâtre National de l'Opéra

    July 8-12, Milan: Teatro alla Scala

July 15-18, Spoleto: Teatro Nuovo (Festival dei due Mondi)

July 21-24, Venice: Teatro La Fenice

July 28 - August 2, Dubrovnik: Terasa Tvrdave Revelin (Dubrovačke Ljetne Igre)

August 5-8, Athens: Herodes Atticus Theater (Athens Festival)

August 11, Jerusalem: Binyenei Ha'ooma (Israel Festival)

August 12-17, Tel Aviv: Fredric R. Mann Auditorium (Israel Festival)

August 20-23, Salzburg: Festspielhaus (Salzburger Festspiele)

August 26-27, Amsterdam: Stadsschouwburg

August 30 - September 11, London: Royal Opera House, Covent Garden

September 23 - October 31, NEW YORK SEASON: New York State Theater

December 24 - January 16, 1966, NEW YORK SEASON: New York State Theater

1966 March 8-10, Philadelphia: Academy of Music

March 12-13, Newark, New Jersey: Symphony Hall

March 29 - May 22, NEW YORK SEASON: New York State Theater

July 8-31, SARATOGA SPRINGS SEASON: Saratoga Performing Arts Center

August 4-14, Washington, D. C.: Carter Barron Amphitheatre

August 16-21, Ravinia (Ravinia Festival)

UNITED STATES/CANADIAN TOUR

September 22-25, Montreal: Place des Arts

October 3-4, East Lansing, Michigan: Michigan State University Auditorium

October 6, Columbus, Ohio: Veterans' Memorial Hall

October 8-9, Cincinnati, Ohio: Music Hall

October 14-15, St. Louis, Missouri: Kiel Opera House

October 18-19, Lafayette, Indiana: Purdue University, Edward C. Elliott Hall of Music

October 21-22, Detroit, Michigan: Masonic Auditorium

October 24-29, Toronto: O'Keefe Centre for the Performing Arts

November 18 - February 5, 1967, NEW YORK SEASON: New York State Theater

1967 March 28 - May 7, NEW YORK SEASON: New York State Theater

May 9-11, Boston: Music Hall

May 13-14, Newark, New Jersey: Symphony Hall

July 2-5, Montreal: Salle Wilfrid-Pelletier, Place des Arts (Expo 67)

July 7-30, SARATOGA SPRINGS SEASON: Saratoga Performing Arts Center

August 3-12, Columbia, Maryland: Merriweather Post Pavilion of Music

August 14-19, Ravinia (Ravinia Festival)

August 28 - September 2, Edinburgh: Empire Theatre (Edinburgh Festival)

October 31 - November 5, Chicago: Auditorium Theatre

November 14 - February 18, 1968, NEW YORK SEASON: New York State Theater

1968 April 23 - June 16, NEW YORK SEASON: New York State Theater

July 4-28, SARATOGA SPRINGS SEASON: Saratoga Performing Arts Center

July 31 - August 4, Columbia, Maryland: Merriweather Post Pavilion of Music

August 12-17, Ravinia (Ravinia Festival)

August 30 - September 1, Cuyahoga Falls, Ohio: Blossom Music Center

November 19 - February 16, 1969, NEW YORK SEASON: New York State Theater

1969 April 22 - June 15, NEW YORK SEASON: New York State Theater

June 20-26, Monte Carlo: Grand Théâtre du Casino de Monte-Carlo (Salle Garnier) (Festival International de Ballets)

July 3-27, SARATOGA SPRINGS SEASON: Saratoga Performing Arts Center

July 30 - August 3, Columbia, Maryland: Merriweather Post Pavilion of Music

August 12-17, Ravinia (Ravinia Festival)

August 21-24, Cuyahoga Falls, Ohio: Blossom Music Center

November 18 - February 15, 1970, NEW YORK SEASON: New York State Theater

1970 May 19 - June 14, NEW YORK SEASON: New York State Theater

July 1-26, SARATOGA SPRINGS SEASON: Saratoga Performing Arts Center

August 4-8, Columbia, Maryland: Merriweather Post Pavilion of Music

August 11-18, Ravinia (Ravinia Festival)

August 20-23, Cuyahoga Falls, Ohio: Blossom Music Center

August 25 - September 6, NEW YORK SEASON: New York State Theater

November 2-7, Toronto: O'Keefe Centre for the Performing Arts

November 17 - February 14, 1971, NEW YORK SEASON: New York State Theater

1971 April 27 - June 27, NEW YORK SEASON: New York State Theater
      July 6-31, SARATOGA SPRINGS SEASON: Saratoga Performing Arts
         Center
      August 9-15, Ravinia (Ravinia Festival)
      August 17-29, NEW YORK SEASON: New York State Theater
      November 16 - February 20, 1972, NEW YORK SEASON: New York State
         Theater

1972 May 2 - July 2, NEW YORK SEASON: New York State Theater
      July 5-29, SARATOGA SPRINGS SEASON: Saratoga Performing Arts Center
      August 11-14, Munich: Bayerische Staatsoper Nationaltheater
         München (Münchner Opernfestspiele)
      August 21-26, Ravinia (Ravinia Festival)
      August 29 - September 3, Vienna, Virginia: Wolf Trap Farm for the
         Performing Arts
      RUSSIAN/POLISH TOUR
         September 21-24, Kiev: Palace of Culture
         September 27 - October 1, Leningrad: Lensoviet Theater
         October 4-8, Tbilisi: New Philharmonic Concert Hall
         October 10-14, Moscow: Palace of Congresses
         October 17-18, Łodz, Poland: Teatr Wielki
         October 20-21, Warsaw: Teatr Wielki
      November 14 - February 18, 1973, NEW YORK SEASON: New York State
         Theater

1973 May 1 - July 1, NEW YORK SEASON: New York State Theater
      July 3-28, SARATOGA SPRINGS SEASON: Saratoga Performing Arts
         Center
      August 13-25, Los Angeles: Greek Theatre
      August 28 - September 2, Vienna, Virginia: Wolf Trap Farm for the
         Performing Arts
      December 12 - February 17, 1974, NEW YORK SEASON: New York
         State Theater

1974 February 19 - March 3, Washington, D. C.: Kennedy Center
      April 30 - June 30, NEW YORK SEASON: New York State Theater
      July 3-27, SARATOGA SPRINGS SEASON: Saratoga Performing Arts Center
      August 12-24, Los Angeles: Greek Theatre
      September 5-8, Philadelphia: Academy of Music
      November 12 - February 16, 1975, NEW YORK SEASON: New York
         State Theater

1975   March 25 - April 6, Washington, D. C.: Kennedy Center
April 29 - June 29, NEW YORK SEASON: New York State Theater
July 9 - August 2, SARATOGA SPRINGS SEASON: Saratoga Performing
    Arts Center
September 3-7, Vienna, Virginia: Wolf Trap Farm for the
    Performing Arts
November 11 - February 15, 1976, NEW YORK SEASON: New York State
    Theater

1976   February 17-29, Washington, D. C.: Kennedy Center
April 27 - June 27, NEW YORK SEASON: New York State Theater
July 14-31, SARATOGA SPRINGS SEASON: Saratoga Performing
    Arts Center
September 22 - October 10, Paris: Théâtre des Champs-Élysées
    (International Festival de Danse de Paris)
November 16 - December 12, NEW YORK SEASON: New York State
    Theater

1977   January 25 - February 20, NEW YORK SEASON: New York State Theater
February 22 - March 13, Washington, D. C.: Kennedy Center
March 16-19, Santo Domingo, Dominican Republic: Teatro Nacional
May 3 - July 3, NEW YORK SEASON: New York State Theater
July 5-30, SARATOGA SPRINGS SEASON: Saratoga Performing Arts Center
November 15 - February 19, 1978, NEW YORK SEASON: New York State
    Theater

1978   February 21 - March 5, Washington, D. C.: Kennedy Center
March 23-25, West Palm Beach, Florida: West Palm Beach Auditorium
    (Palm Beach Festival)
May 2 - July 2, NEW YORK SEASON: New York State Theater
July 5-22, SARATOGA SPRINGS SEASON: Saratoga Performing Arts Center
August 8-13, Copenhagen: Concert Hall, Tivoli Gardens
November 14 - February 18, 1979, NEW YORK SEASON: New York State
    Theater

1979   February 20 - March 4, Washington, D. C.: Kennedy Center
UPSTATE NEW YORK TOUR
    March 16-18, Rochester, New York: Eastman Theatre
    March 22-25, Syracuse, New York: Civic Center
    March 28-31, Buffalo, New York: Shea's Buffalo Theatre
April 18-29, Chicago: Auditorium Theatre
May 1 - July 1, NEW YORK SEASON: New York State Theater

July 3-21, SARATOGA SPRINGS SEASON: Saratoga Performing Arts Center
September 4-22, London: Royal Opera House, Covent Garden
October 2-21, Washington, D. C.: Kennedy Center
November 13 - February 17, 1980, NEW YORK SEASON: New York State Theater

1980 March 11-16, Chicago: Auditorium Theatre
March 21-26, West Palm Beach, Florida: West Palm Beach Auditorium (Palm Beach Festival)
April 29 - June 29, NEW YORK SEASON: New York State Theater
July 8-26, SARATOGA SPRINGS SEASON: Saratoga Performing Arts Center
EUROPEAN TOUR
   August 19-30, Copenhagen: Concert Hall, Tivoli Gardens
   September 2-6, Berlin: Deutsche Oper (Berliner Festwochen)
   September 10-21, Paris: Théâtre des Champs-Élysées (International Festival de Danse de Paris)
October 8-19, Washington, D. C.: Kennedy Center
November 11 - February 15, 1981, NEW YORK SEASON: New York State Theater

1981 March 23-28, West Palm Beach, Florida: West Palm Beach Auditorium (Palm Beach Festival)
April 28 - June 28, NEW YORK SEASON: New York State Theater
July 7-25, SARATOGA SPRINGS SEASON: Saratoga Performing Arts Center
October 7-11, Fort Worth, Texas: Tarrant County Convention Center
October 27 - November 1, Boston: Metropolitan Center
November 17 - February 21, 1982, NEW YORK SEASON: New York State Theater

1982 UPSTATE NEW YORK TOUR
   March 10-14, Rochester, New York: Eastman Theatre
   March 17-21, Syracuse, New York: Crouse-Hinds Concert Theatre
May 4 - July 4, NEW YORK SEASON: New York State Theater

FESTIVALS DIRECTED BY BALANCHINE

Asterisks indicate world premieres. Choreography, costume and scenic design, and lighting credits follow title, with *Catalogue* number for Balanchine works.

STRAVINSKY FESTIVAL, April 27 and 28, 1937
American Ballet, Metropolitan Opera House, New York City

> *Apollon Musagète*, Balanchine/Chaney, 176
> *The Card Party*, Balanchine/Sharaff, 177
> *Le Baiser de la Fée*, Balanchine/Halicka, 178

STRAVINSKY FESTIVAL, June 18-25, 1972
New York City Ballet, New York State Theater

JUNE 18, GALA BENEFIT

> *Fanfare for a New Theater*, Orchestra
> *Greeting Prelude: Happy Birthday*, Orchestra
> *Fireworks*, Orchestra
> *Sonata*, Balanchine, 372
> *Scherzo Fantastique*, Robbins/Bates
> *Symphony in Three Movements*, Balanchine/Bates, 373
> *Violin Concerto*, Balanchine/Bates, 374
> *Firebird*, Balanchine-Robbins/Chagall/Bates, 264

JUNE 20

> *Symphony in E Flat*, Clifford/Simmons/Bates
> *The Cage*, Robbins/Rosenthal/Sobotka
> *Concerto for Piano and Winds*, Taras/Ter-Arutunian/Bates
> *Danses Concertantes*, Balanchine/Berman, 375

JUNE 21

> *Octuor*, Tanner/Bates
> *Serenade in A*, Bolender/Simmons/Bates
> *The Faun and the Shepherdess*, Mezzo-soprano and Orchestra
> *Divertimento from 'Le Baiser de la Fée,'* Balanchine/Berman/Bates, 376
> *Ebony Concerto*, Taras/Bates
> *Scherzo à la Russe*, Balanchine/Karinska/Bates, 377
> *Circus Polka*, Robbins/Bates

JUNE 22

> *Scènes de Ballet*, Taras/Karinska/Bates
> *Duo Concertant*, Balanchine/Bates, 378
> *The Song of the Nightingale*, Taras/Ter-Arutunian/Bates
> *Capriccio for Piano and Orchestra*, Balanchine/Harvey/Karinska/Bates
>   [RUBIES from *Jewels*, 358]

JUNE 23

> *Concerto for Two Solo Pianos*, Tanner/Simmons/Bates
> *Piano-Rag-Music*, Bolender/Simmons/Bates
> *Ode*, Lorca Massine/Bates
> *Dumbarton Oaks*, Robbins/Zipprodt/Bates
> *Pulcinella*, Balanchine–Robbins/Berman/Bates, 379

JUNE 24

> *Apollo*, Balanchine/Bates, 284
> *Orpheus*, Balanchine/Noguchi/Bates, 246
> *Agon*, Balanchine/Bates, 316

JUNE 25

> *Choral Variations on Bach's 'Vom Himmel Hoch,'* Balanchine/
>   Ter-Arutunian/Bates, 380
> *Monumentum pro Gesualdo*, Balanchine/Ter-Arutunian, 334
> *Movements for Piano and Orchestra*, Balanchine/Ter-Arutunian, 344
> *Requiem Canticles*, Robbins/Bates
> *Symphony of Psalms*, Orchestra and Chorus, with dancers assembled
>   on stage, 381

RAVEL FESTIVAL, May 14-31, 1975
New York City Ballet, New York State Theater

MAY 14, GALA BENEFIT

> *Sonatine*, Balanchine/Bates [preview]
> *Concerto in G*, Robbins/Ter-Arutunian/Bates [preview]
> *L'Enfant et les Sortilèges*, Balanchine/Love/Bates [preview]

MAY 15-17

> *Sonatine*, Balanchine/Bates, 389
> *La Valse*, Balanchine/Rosenthal/Karinska, 277
> *L'Enfant et les Sortilèges*, Balanchine/Love/Bates, 390
> *Concerto in G*, Robbins/Ter-Arutunian/Bates

MAY 22-24

Introduction and Allegro for Harp, Robbins/Scaasi/Bates

Shéhérazade, Balanchine/Bates, 391

Alborada del Gracioso, d'Amboise/Braden/Bates

Ma Mère l'Oye, Robbins/Simmons/Bates

Daphnis and Chloe, Taras/Eula/Bates

MAY 29-31

Le Tombeau de Couperin, Balanchine/Bates, 392

Pavane, Balanchine/Bates, 393

Un Barque sur l'Océan, Robbins/Welles/Bates

Tzigane, Balanchine/Eula/Bates, 394

Gaspard de la Nuit, Balanchine/Daydé–Bates, 395

Sarabande and Danse [Debussy, orchestrated by Ravel], d'Amboise/
Braden/Bates

Chansons Madécasses, Robbins/Bates

Rapsodie Espagnole, Balanchine/Avedon/Bates, 396

TSCHAIKOVSKY FESTIVAL, June 4-14, 1981
New York City Ballet, New York State Theater

Throughout the Festival the principal scenery was an architectural
structure with movable ranks of translucent plastic cylinders by Philip
Johnson and John Burgee, in arrangements and with lighting designs by
Ronald Bates.

JUNE 4, GALA BENEFIT

Lisa's aria from *Pique Dame*, Soprano and Orchestra

Lensky's aria from *Eugen Onegin*, Tenor and Orchestra

Duet from *Undine*, Soprano, Tenor and Orchestra

Overture-Fantasy from *Romeo and Juliet*, Orchestra

Mozartiana, Balanchine/Ter-Arutunian, 417

Capriccio Italien, Martins/Ter-Arutunian

Pas de Deux [from Piano Concerto No. 1, 2nd movement], Robbins/
Benson

Tempo di Polacca, Balanchine/Karinska [DIAMONDS Polonaise from
Jewels, 358]

JUNE 5

Capriccio Italien

Pas de Deux [from Piano Concerto No. 1, 2nd movement]

313

Souvenir de Florence, Taras/Ter-Arutunian
Tschaikovsky Piano Concerto No. 2, Balanchine/Karinska, 382

JUNE 6, MATINEE
Capriccio Italien
Pas de Deux [from Piano Concerto No. 1, 2nd movement]
Souvenir de Florence
Tschaikovsky Piano Concerto No. 2

JUNE 6, EVENING
Serenade, Balanchine/Karinska, 254
Concert Fantasy, d'Amboise/Ter-Arutunian
Symphony No. 1, Martins/Benson

JUNE 7, MATINEE
Capriccio Italien
Pas de Deux [from *Swan Lake*, Act III], Balanchine/Karinska, 331
Scherzo Opus 42, d'Amboise/Ter-Arutunian
Concert Fantasy
Symphony No. 1

JUNE 7, EVENING
Swan Lake, Balanchine/Ter-Arutunian, 285
Concert Fantasy
Souvenir de Florence

JUNE 9
Concert Fantasy
Andante Elegiaco, Balanchine/Karinska [DIAMONDS pas de deux from
    Jewels, 358]
Capriccio Italien
Piano Concerto No. 3 [Allegro Brillante], Balanchine/Karinska, 312
Tempo di Valse
    *GARLAND DANCE FROM THE SLEEPING BEAUTY, Balanchine/Ter-
        Arutunian–Karinska, 418
    *VALSE-SCHERZO, d'Amboise/Ter-Arutunian
    WALTZ OF THE FLOWERS FROM THE NUTCRACKER, Balanchine/
        Ter-Arutunian, 302
    *VARIATION VI FROM TRIO IN A MINOR, Taras
    *WALTZ FROM EUGEN ONEGIN, ACT II, Taras/Ter-Arutunian
    The sequence of dances was altered in subsequent performances.

314

JUNE 10

Capriccio Italien
Pas de Deux [from Piano Concerto No. 1, 2nd movement]
Souvenir de Florence
Tempo di Valse

JUNE 11

Divertimento from 'Le Baiser de la Fée' [Stravinsky, based on and
  dedicated to Tschaikovsky], Balanchine/Berman, 376
Inmitten des Balles, Op. 38, no. 3; *Versöhnung*, Op. 25, no. 1; *Lied der
  Mignon: Nur wer die Sehnsucht kennt*, Op. 6, no. 6, Soprano and Piano
Piano Pieces, Robbins/Benson
Tempo di Valse

JUNE 12

Introduction and Fugue [from Suite No. 1 in D major], Duell/Benson
A selection of songs, as performed June 11
Scherzo Opus 42
Piano Pieces
Suite No. 3, Balanchine/Benois, 369

JUNE 13, MATINEE

Divertimento from 'Le Baiser de la Fée'
Hungarian Gypsy Airs [Sophie Menter, orchestrated by
  Tschaikovsky], Balanchine/Benson, 419
Suite No. 2, d'Amboise/Braden
Tempo di Valse

JUNE 13, EVENING

Suite No. 2
Piano Concerto No. 3 [Allegro Brillante]
Andante Elegiaco
Symphony No. 1

JUNE 14, MATINEE

Introduction and Fugue
A selection of songs, as performed June 11 and 12
Scherzo Opus 42
Piano Pieces
Suite No. 3

JUNE 14, EVENING

Souvenir de Florence

ÉLÉGIE from *Suite No. 3*
Andante Elegiaco
Symphony No. 6—Pathétique
   ALLEGRO CON GRAZIA, Robbins/Benson
   ALLEGRO MOLTO VIVACE, Orchestra
   ADAGIO LAMENTOSO, Balanchine/Ter-Arutunian, 420

STRAVINSKY CENTENNIAL CELEBRATION, June 10-18, 1982
New York City Ballet, New York State Theater

The décor throughout the Festival incorporated the architectural setting created by Johnson/Burgee for the Tschaikovsky Festival of 1981, arranged and lighted by Ronald Bates.

JUNE 10, GALA BENEFIT
   Fanfare for Two Trumpets
   Circus Polka, Robbins
   Fireworks, Orchestra
   Tango, Balanchine, 421
   Piano-Rag-Music, Martins/Benson
   Duo Concertant, Balanchine, 378
   Pastorale, d'Amboise/Benson
   Capriccio for Piano and Orchestra, Balanchine/Karinska [RUBIES from *Jewels*, 358]
   Concerto for Piano and Wind Instruments, Taras/Ter-Arutunian
   Symphony in Three Movements, Balanchine, 373

JUNE 11
   Noah and the Flood, Balanchine–d'Amboise/Ter-Arutunian, 422
   Suite from Histoire du Soldat, Martins/Benson
   Eight Easy Pieces, Martins/Benson
   Stravinsky Violin Concerto, Balanchine, 374

JUNE 12, MATINEE
   Noah and the Flood
   Monumentum pro Gesualdo, Balanchine, 334
   Movements for Piano and Orchestra, Balanchine, 344
   Pastorale
   Serenade en La, d'Amboise/Benson
   Symphony in Three Movements

316

JUNE 12, EVENING
>   *Divertimento from 'Le Baiser de la Fée,'* Balanchine/Berman, 376
>   *Scherzo à la Russe,* Balanchine, 377
>   *Norwegian Moods,* Christensen
>   *Concerto for Piano and Wind Instruments*
>   *Agon,* Balanchine, 316

JUNE 13, MATINEE
>   *Circus Polka*
>   *Fireworks,* Orchestra
>   *Monumentum pro Gesualdo*
>   *Movements for Piano and Orchestra*
>   *Piano-Rag-Music*
>   *Élégie,* Balanchine, 423
>   *Tango*
>   *Concerto for Two Solo Pianos,* Martins/Benson
>   *Noah and the Flood*

JUNE 13, EVENING
>   *Noah and the Flood*
>   *Concerto for Piano and Wind Instruments*
>   *The Cage,* Robbins/Sobotka
>   *Agon*

JUNE 15
>   *Divertimento from 'Le Baiser de la Fée'*
>   *The Cage*
>   *Monumentum pro Gesualdo*
>   *Movements for Piano and Orchestra*
>   *Pastorale*
>   *Serenade en La*
>   *Symphony in Three Movements*

JUNE 16
>   *Orpheus,* Balanchine/Noguchi, 246
>   *Four Chamber Works,* Robbins/Miller
>   *Capriccio for Piano and Orchestra*

JUNE 17
>   *Suite from Histoire du Soldat*

317

Four Chamber Works
Divertimento from 'Le Baiser de la Fée'

JUNE 18

Zvezdoliki [*Le Roi des Étoiles*], Orchestra and Chorus
Apollo, Balanchine, 284
*Perséphone, Balanchine–Taras–Zorina/Ter-Arutunian, 424
Symphony in Three Movements

ROLES PERFORMED BY BALANCHINE

Roles are listed chronologically by year of first performance, and alphabetically by title of work within each year. Final parentheses refer to sources other than printed programs, identified in the key which follows the *Roles* listing; published sources with reference to page number precede unpublished. Numbers in brackets refer to *Catalogue* entries.

1915-1917

1916 *La Jota Aragonesa* (Glinka/Fokine); Maryinsky; ROLE UNDETERMINED. First character role. (Balanchine, p. 749; Taper, p. 49)

1917 *Tarantella* (unknown); Alexandrinsky; DUET with Mara Dolinskaya. (*Petrogradskaya gazeta*, January 4, 1917, p. 4)

The Bear [*Medved'*] (Chekhov); St. Petersburg/Petrograd ballet school theater; OLD MAN. (Taper, p. 45; Kisselgoff, *New York Times*, November 10, 1975. Balanchine)

Don Quixote (Minkus/Petipa); Maryinsky; SPANISH BOY (Act I). (Slonimsky, p. 5)

The Fairy Doll (Bayer/Legat); 1) Maryinsky; MARCH OF THE TOY SOLDIERS. (Slonimsky, p. 6). 2) Place undetermined; PAS DE TROIS with O. Barysheva and Nicholas Efimov. Later performed with Lydia Ivanova and Efimov in the Chinese theater at Tsarskoye Selo. (Slonimsky, p. 31)

La Fille du Pharaon (Pugni/Petipa); Maryinsky; MONKEY. First named role in a printed program. (Taper, p. 47)

A Midsummer Night's Dream (Shakespeare/Mendelssohn); Mikhailovsky; BUG. (Balanchine, p. 749; Reynolds, p. 216)

The Nutcracker (Tschaikovsky/Ivanov); Maryinsky; TOY SOLDIER; KING OF MICE; CHILD PRINCE; GRAND DIVERTISSEMENT. (Balanchine, p. 748; Slonimsky, p. 6; Taper, p. 49)

Orfeo ed Euridice (Gluck/Fokine/Meyerhold); Maryinsky; FURY IN HADES. (Balanchine, p. 749; Slonimsky, p. 26. Krasovskaya)

Paquita (Deldevez–Minkus/Petipa); Maryinsky; MAZURKA (Act III). (Slonimsky, p. 5. Balanchine)

Le Pavillon d'Armide (Tcherepnine/Fokine); Maryinsky; JESTER. (Reynolds; Balanchine)

Polovtsian Dances from Prince Igor (Borodin/Fokine); Maryinsky; YOUNG
   BOY. (Slonimsky, p. 6)
Professor Storitsyn (Andreyev); Alexandrinsky; YOUNG STUDENT.
   (Balanchine, p. 749; Kisselgoff, *New York Times*, November 10, 1975)
Raymonda (Glazounov/Petipa); Maryinsky; DANCE OF THE ARAB BOYS
   (Act II). (Slonimsky, p. 5)
The Sleeping Beauty (Tschaikovsky/Petipa); Maryinsky; RETINUE OF
   CARABOSSE (Prologue), PEASANT [GARLAND] WALTZ (Act I), PAS D'ACTION
   (Act I), HOP O' MY THUMB AND THE SEVEN BROTHERS (Act III), A CUPID
   (Act III). Balanchine's first appearance on stage was in a performance
   of *The Sleeping Beauty*. (Balanchine, p. 746; Slonimsky, p. 6)
The Storm or *The Thunderstorm* [*Groza*] (Ostrovsky); St. Petersburg/
   Petrograd ballet school theater; ROLE UNDETERMINED. (Taper, p. 45)
Woe from Wit or *Wit Works Woe* or *The Trouble with Reason* [*Gore ot
   uma*] (Griboyedov); Alexandrinsky and/or St. Petersburg/Petrograd
   ballet school theater; CHATSKY. (Taper, p. 45; Slonimsky, p. 6;
   Kisselgoff, *New York Times*, November 10, 1975)

1918 - October 1924

1919   *Harlequinade* (Drigo/Petipa); Petrograd Theater (Ballet) School
       graduation performance; FRIEND. (Slonimsky, p. 26. Balanchine;
       Schüller)
       Paquita (Deldevez–Minkus/Petipa); Petrograd Theater (Ballet) School
       graduation performance; PAS DE TROIS with Alexandra Danilova and
       Lydia Ivanova. (Balanchine; Schüller)

1920   *The Magic Flute* (Drigo/Ivanov); Petrograd Theater (Ballet) School
       graduation performance; LUKE, with Lydia Ivanova as LISE.
       (Slonimsky, p. 31. Balanchine; Schüller)

1920? *La Nuit* (Rubinstein/Balanchine [1]); Petrograd Theater (Ballet) School;
       DUET with Olga Mungalova. Also performed *La Nuit* while a
       student with Lydia Ivanova, Tamara Geva and Alexandra
       Danilova; with the Young Ballet; in nightclubs in the Soviet Union;
       and on the 1924 tour of the Principal Dancers of the Russian State
       Ballet. (Taper, p. 58. Balanchine; Reynolds; Schüller)

1921   *Chopiniana* [*Les Sylphides*] (Chopin/Fokine); Tavrichesky Garden,
       Petrograd; POET, with Elizaveta Gerdt. Possibly performed in an
       earlier production. (Slonimsky, p. 26. Schüller)

       Le Corsaire (Adam–Drigo–Minkus–Pugni/Petipa); place undetermined;
       ENSEMBLE. (Balanchine)

       Javotte (Saint-Saëns/Mariquita–Gerdt–Chekrygin); Petrograd Theater
       (Ballet) School, for his graduation performance; JEAN, with Nina
       Vdovina as JAVOTTE. (Slonimsky, p. 30. Schüller)

       Lezghinka (music unknown); Petrograd Theater (Ballet) School, for his
       graduation performance; traditional Georgian dance (SOLO) staged
       by Alexander Shiryaev. (*Petrogradskaya pravda*, May 26, 1921, p. 4.
       Balanchine)

       [*Pas de Deux*] (Schubert/Preobrajenska); Petrograd Theater (Ballet)
       School graduation performance; DUET with Nina Stukolkina.
       (Balanchine; Schüller)

       Poème (Fibich/Balanchine [4]); Petrograd Theater (Ballet) School; DUET
       with Alexandra Danilova? (Slonimsky, p. 50; Taper, p. 59)

       Swan Lake (Tschaikovsky/Petipa–Ivanov); Pavlovsk, near Petrograd;
       PRINCE SIEGFRIED, with Elizaveta Gerdt as ODETTE and Soliannikov as
       ROTHBART. Balanchine replaced an injured dancer on a program
       in which he was to have been one of eight HUNTERS. (Balanchine;
       Schüller)

1921? *Firebird* (Stravinsky/Lopukhov); place undetermined; MONSTER DANCE.
       (Balanchine)

1922   *The Nutcracker* (Tschaikovsky/Ivanov); State Theater of Opera and
       Ballet, Petrograd; SOLOIST, BUFFOONS' DANCE (TREPAK). Later
       interpolated into Balanchine's version of *The Nutcracker* [302].
       (Slonimsky, p. 32. Reynolds; Schüller)

       Solveig (Grieg–Asafiev/Petrov), State Theater of Opera and Ballet,
       Petrograd; NOCTURNE (Act I), NORWEGIAN DANCE (Act II); MIME SCENE
       (Act III). (Schüller; Souritz)

       Tarantella (unknown); Red Army charity performance; DUET with
       Olga Preobrajenska. (Taper, p. 59. Balanchine; Reynolds)

       Waltz (unknown/Balanchine [9]); resort at Sestroretsk, near Petrograd;
       DUET with Alexandra Danilova. (Balanchine; Schüller)

Waltz and Adagio (Balanchine/Balanchine [7]); place undetermined; DUET with Alexandra Danilova. (Slonimsky, p. 54. Schüller)

1922?   *Harlequinade* (Drigo/Petipa); Moscow recital; PAS DE TROIS with Tamara Geva and Nicholas Efimov. (Geva, p. 287)

Matelotte or *Sailor's Hornpipe* (Traditional, arranged by Zuev/Balanchine [11]); place undetermined; TRIO for a woman and two men. Performed with Alexandra Danilova and Nicholas Efimov on the 1924 tour of the Principal Dancers of the Russian State Ballet. (Beaumont, p. 220. Reynolds; Schüller)

1922-1923   *Orientalia* (Cui/Balanchine [12]); place undetermined; BLIND OLD BEGGAR, with Nina Mlodzinskaya as YOUNG ORIENTAL DANCER. (Slonimsky, p. 40; Mikhailov, April 1967, p. 6)

1923   *Adagio* (Saint-Saëns [from *Javotte*]/Balanchine [17]); Young Ballet, Alexandrinsky Hall, Duma, Petrograd; JEAN, with Alexandra Danilova as JAVOTTE. (Slonimsky, p. 64. Reynolds; Schüller; Souritz)

Coppélia (Delibes/Petipa–Lopukhov?); State Theater of Opera and Ballet, Petrograd; MAZURKA and CZARDAS (Act I). (Schüller)

Dance Symphony (Beethoven [Symphony No. 4]/Lopukhov); State Theater of Opera and Ballet, Petrograd; ENSEMBLE. (Kirstein, p. 218-19; Slonimsky, p. 42-44. Schüller)

Don Quixote (Minkus/Petipa); State Theater of Opera and Ballet, Petrograd; SEGUIDILLA. (Slonimsky, p. 26. Schüller)

Enigma (Arensky [from *Egyptian Nights*]/Balanchine [25]); place undetermined; DUET with Lydia Ivanova. Later performed with Tamara Geva in the Soviet Union, on the 1924 tour of the Principal Dancers of the Russian State Ballet, and in the 1924 audition for Diaghilev in Paris. (Balanchine; Reynolds; Schüller)

La Fille du Pharaon (Pugni/Petipa); State Theater of Opera and Ballet, Petrograd; KEEPER OF THE PYRAMIDS (later revealed as GENIE), SCÈNE MIMIQUE, GRAND PAS DE CROTALES. (Schüller; Souritz)

La Fille Mal Gardée (Hertel/Petipa–Ivanov); State Theater of Opera and Ballet, Petrograd; DANSE BOHÉMIENNE. (Schüller)

La Halte de Cavalerie (Armsheimer/Petipa); State Theater of Opera and Ballet, Petrograd; HUSSAR. (Schüller)

Internationale (unknown/Petrov); place and role undetermined. (Balanchine; Schüller)

Polovtsian Dances from Prince Igor (Borodin/Fokine); State Theater of
Opera and Ballet, Petrograd; POLOVTSIAN. (Slonimsky, p. 60)

The Sleeping Beauty (Tschaikovsky/Petipa–Lopukhov); State Theater of
Opera and Ballet, Petrograd; MINUET, BLIND MAN'S BUFF (Act II).
(Slonimsky, p. 30. Schüller; Souritz)

Swan Lake (Tschaikovsky/Petipa–Ivanov); State Theater of Opera
and Ballet, Petrograd; VALSE CHAMPÊTRE (Act I). (Slonimsky, p. 30.
Schüller; Souritz)

Tannhäuser (Wagner); State Theater of Opera and Ballet, Petrograd;
YOUTH IN LOVE in the Grotto of Venus. (Slonimsky, p. 30. Schüller)

1923-1924   *Étude* (Scriabin/Balanchine [30]); Young Ballet, place undetermined; DUET with Tamara Geva. Probably performed in the 1924
audition for Diaghilev in Paris; performed on programs of
Diaghilev's Ballets Russes in 1925.

Oriental Dance (Moussorgsky [from *Khovanshchina*]/Balanchine [31]);
Young Ballet, place undetermined; DUET with Tamara Geva.
(Reynolds)

Elegy (Rachmaninoff/Balanchine [32]); Young Ballet, Pavlovsk, near
Petrograd; TRIO with Tamara Geva and Nicholas Efimov.
Possibly performed earlier at another location; performed on the
1924 tour of the Principal Dancers of the Russian State Ballet;
possibly performed in the 1924 audition for Diaghilev in Paris.
(Slonimsky, p. 64. Schüller)

1924, JANUARY-OCTOBER   *La Bayadère* (Minkus/Petipa), State Theater
of Opera and Ballet, Petrograd/Leningrad; FIRE DANCE (Scene 3).
(Slonimsky, p. 26. Schüller)

Le Corsaire (Adam–Drigo–Minkus–Pugni/Petipa); State Theater
of Opera and Ballet, Petrograd/Leningrad; DANCE OF THE CORSAIRS.
(Schüller)

Dutch Dance (Grieg or Lortzing/Balanchine or Petrov or Lopukhov [3]);
Principal Dancers of the Russian State Ballet, Empire Theatre,
London; DUET with Alexandra Danilova. Possibly performed earlier
in the Soviet Union. (Reynolds)

The End of the Fifth Act (variety show); Vol'naia Komediia, Petrograd/
Leningrad; ROLES UNDETERMINED. (Souritz)

Four Seasons (Glazounov/Leontiev); State Theater of Opera and Ballet, Petrograd/Leningrad; BACCHANT (AUTUMN). (Balanchine; Schüller)

Hungarian Gypsy Dance (Brahms/Balanchine [13]); Principal Dancers of the Russian State Ballet, Schwechtasaal, Berlin; DUET with Tamara Geva. (Reynolds)

Invitation to the Dance (Weber/Balanchine [34]); Young Ballet, Pavlovsk?, near Petrograd; TRIO with Alexandra Danilova and Mikhail Mikhailov. Performed on the 1924 tour of the Principal Dancers of the Russian State Ballet. (Mikhailov; Reynolds)

Le Pavillon d'Armide (Tcherepnine/Fokine–Balanchine? [33, NOTE]); State Theater of Opera and Ballet, Petrograd/Leningrad; DUET with Elizaveta Gerdt. (Gusev; Reynolds; Schüller)

Spanish Dance (probably Glazounov [from *Raymonda*]/Balanchine [18]); Young Ballet, Pavlovsk, near Petrograd; DUET with Tamara Geva. (Schüller)

Carnaval (Schumann/Fokine); State Theater of Opera and Ballet, Petrograd/Leningrad; EUSEBIUS, THE POET. (Slonimsky, p. 26. Reynolds)

La Esmeralda (Pugni–Drigo/Petipa); State Theater of Opera and Ballet, Petrograd/Leningrad; BEGGAR. (Slonimsky, p. 30, 33; Taper, p. 68-69)

The Magic Flute (Drigo/Ivanov); State Theater of Opera and Ballet, Petrograd/Leningrad; MARQUIS. Possibly performed earlier. (Balanchine)

Le Pavillon d'Armide (Tcherepnine/Fokine); State Theater of Opera and Ballet, Petrograd/Leningrad; JESTER. Possibly the role first danced in 1915-1917.

Le Rossignol (Stravinsky); State Theater of Opera and Ballet, Petrograd/Leningrad; ROLE UNDETERMINED. (Balanchine; Reynolds)

November 1924 - August 1929, Diaghilev's Ballets Russes

Listings for the years of Balanchine's association with the Ballets Russes are limited to roles identified in programs in the collections of the Theatre Museum of the Victoria and Albert Museum and the library of the Garrick Club in London, the Collection Rondel of the Bibliothèque de l'Arsenal in Paris, the Archives of the Opéra de Monte-Carlo, and in the collection of Nathalie Branitzka, now in the possession of her son, André von Hoyer, of Pittsfield, Massachusetts.

1924 *Aurora's Wedding* (Tschaikovsky [from *The Sleeping Beauty*]/Petipa–
Sergeyev–Nijinska); Coliseum, London; POLONAISE.

Contes Russes (Liadov/Massine); Coliseum, London; FOLK DANCE.

Polovtsian Dances from Prince Igor (Borodin/Fokine); Coliseum, London;
POLOVTSIAN WARRIOR.

Soleil de Nuit (Rimsky-Korsakov/Massine); Coliseum, London;
BUFFOON.

1925 *Aurora's Wedding* (Tschaikovsky [from *The Sleeping Beauty*]/Petipa–
Sergeyev–Nijinska); 1) Opéra de Monte-Carlo; SCÈNE ET DANSE DES
DUCHESSES; probably also FARANDOLE and MAZURKA. 2) Nouvelle Salle
de Musique (Salle Ganne), Monte Carlo; PRINCE CHARMING with Vera
Nemtchinova as PRINCESS AURORA. Also danced this role with
Nemtchinova at the Coliseum, London, and in 1926 with Alexandra
Danilova at the Opéra de Monte-Carlo. 3) Coliseum, London; PAS
DE SEPT of the Maids of Honour and Their Cavaliers.

La Boutique Fantasque (Rossini–Respighi/Massine); Coliseum, London;
KING OF SPADES in the Mazurka.

Carnaval (Schumann/Fokine); 1) Nouvelle Salle de Musique (Salle
Ganne), Monte Carlo; PIERROT. 2) Coliseum, London; VALSE NOBLE.

Le Chant du Rossignol (Stravinsky/Balanchine [52]); Théâtre Gaieté
Lyrique, Paris; MECHANICAL NIGHTINGALE.

Cimarosiana (Cimarosa [from *Le Astuzie Femminili*]/Massine); Opéra
de Monte-Carlo; CONTREDANSE.

Contes Russes (Liadov/Massine); Opéra de Monte-Carlo; DANSES
POPULAIRES.

Les Fâcheux (Auric/Nijinska); Nouvelle Salle de Musique (Salle Ganne),
Monte Carlo; POLICEMAN.

Hérodiade (Massenet/Balanchine [46]); Opéra de Monte-Carlo; ACT III
BALLET.

Narcisse (Tcherepnine/Fokine); Nouvelle Salle de Musique (Salle
Ganne), Monte Carlo; GREEK.

Petrouchka (Stravinsky/Fokine); Coliseum, London; OLD FATHER OF THE
FAIR.

Schéhérazade (Rimsky-Korsakov/Fokine); Opéra de Monte-Carlo;
NEGRO.

Les Tentations de la Bergère (*The Faithful Shepherdess*) (Monteclair–
Casadesus/Nijinska); Opéra de Monte-Carlo; BARON.

Thamar (Balakirev/Fokine); Nouvelle Salle de Musique (Salle Ganne), Monte Carlo; LEZGHINKA.

Le Tricorne (*The Three-Cornered Hat*) (Falla/Massine); 1) Nouvelle Salle de Musique (Salle Ganne), Monte Carlo; ALGUAZIL (POLICEMAN). 2) Coliseum, London; GYPSY.

1926 *Cimarosiana* (Cimarosa [from *Le Astuzie Femminili*]/Massine); His Majesty's Theatre, London; PAS DE SIX, FINALE.

L'Oiseau de Feu (*Firebird*) (Stravinsky/Fokine); Lyceum Theatre, London; KASTCHEI.

Mazurka (Tschaikovsky/Petipa); Soirée Artistique, benefit for Grand Duc André, Monte Carlo?; ROLE UNDETERMINED.

Petrouchka (Stravinsky/Fokine); Opéra de Monte-Carlo; OLD SHOWMAN.

Pulcinella (Stravinsky/Massine); Théâtre Sarah Bernhardt, Paris; FOURBO.

Les Tentations de la Bergère (*The Faithful Shepherdess*) (Monteclair–Casadesus/Nijinska); Opéra de Monte-Carlo; HYMÉNÉE.

Thamar (Balakirev/Fokine); His Majesty's Theatre, London; SERVANT OF THAMAR.

Le Tricorne (*The Three-Cornered Hat*) (Falla/Massine); His Majesty's Theatre, London; GOVERNOR (CORREGIDOR).

The Triumph of Neptune (Berners/Balanchine [64]); Lyceum Theatre, London; SNOWBALL, LEADING HARLEQUIN, BEGGAR.

1926? *Le Chant du Rossignol* (Stravinsky/Balanchine [52]); Opéra de Monte-Carlo; NIGHTINGALE. Balanchine performed the role he had created for Alicia Markova, who was ill, at a command performance for the Princesse Héréditaire of Monaco. (Taper, p. 96-98, 339-40)

1927 *Barabau* (Rieti/Balanchine [53]); Opéra de Monte-Carlo; SERGEANT. (Balanchine)

Cimarosiana (Cimarosa [from *Le Astuzie Femminili*]/Massine); 1) La Scala; PAS DE SEPT. 2) Staatsoper, Vienna; PAS RUSTIQUE with Alexandra Danilova and Serge Lifar.

Turandot (Puccini/Balanchine [68]); Opéra de Monte-Carlo; LES PORCELAINES DE CHINE (Act II).

1928   *Carnaval* (Schumann/Fokine); His Majesty's Theatre, London;
FLORESTAN.

Cléopâtre (Arensky–Taneyev–Rimsky-Korsakov–Glinka–Glazounov/
Fokine); Opéra de Monte-Carlo; CLEOPATRA'S FAVORITE SLAVE,
with Alice Nikitina as the female FAVORITE SLAVE.

Les Noces (Stravinsky/Nijinska); Théâtre Sarah Bernhardt, Paris;
ENSEMBLE.

Romeo and Juliet (Lambert/Nijinska–Balanchine [61]); Opéra de Monte-
Carlo; THE MAESTRO, REHEARSING AS TYBALT.

Soleil de Nuit (Rimsky-Korsakov/Massine); Opéra de Monte-Carlo;
BOLBYL (THE INNOCENT).

1929   *Le Bal* (Rieti/Balanchine [93]); Opéra de Monte-Carlo; SPANISH ENTRANCE,
with Felia Doubrovska and Léon Woizikowsky.

Les Fâcheux (Auric/Massine); Théâtre Sarah Bernhardt, Paris;
LA MONTAGNE (ERASTE'S VALET).

August 1929-1933

1929   *Dark Red Roses: Tartar Ballet, 'Jealousy'* (Moussorgsky [from
Khovanshchina]/Balanchine [97]); TARTAR, with Lydia Lopokova as
HIS WIFE and Anton Dolin as the MINSTREL. (Taper, p. 126)

1930   [*Duet* and *Trio*]. (Liszt/Balanchine [100]); Royal Danish Ballet, Tivoli
Gardens, Copenhagen; DUET with Elna Jørgen-Jensen; TRIO with
Elna Lassen and Ulla Poulsen.

Polovtsian Dances from Prince Igor (*Fyrst Igor*) (Borodin/Fokine–
Balanchine [104]); Royal Danish Ballet, Royal Theater, Copenhagen;
WARRIOR CHIEF.

Le Spectre de la Rose (*Rosendrømmen*) (Weber/Fokine–Balanchine [105]);
Koncert Palæet, Copenhagen; SPIRIT OF THE ROSE, with Ulla Poulsen
as the YOUNG GIRL.

Les Sylphides (Chopin/Fokine); Royal Danish Ballet, Royal Theater,
Copenhagen; POET.

1932   *Cotillon* (Chabrier/Balanchine [129]); Ballets Russes de Monte-Carlo,
Opéra de Monte-Carlo; LA TOILETTE and CHAPEAU sections. In the

preview performance Balanchine danced the role later danced by
David Lichine.

Numéro les Canotiers ('The Waves of the Danube' [a waltz tune popular
in Russia]/Balanchine [133]); Villa Blanche, near Toulon; TRIO with
Mme Georges Auric and Boris Kochno. (Kochno)

1933 *L'Errante* (Schubert/Balanchine [138]); Les Ballets 1933, Savoy Theatre,
London; LEADING MALE DANCER. (Reynolds)

From 1934

1940 *I Was an Adventuress* [191]; ORCHESTRA LEADER, under the stage name
Fortunio Bonanova.

1941 *Divertimento* (Rossini/Balanchine [196]); American Ballet Caravan
South American tour; RAT. (Reynolds, p. 70)

1946 *Resurgence* (Mozart/Balanchine [231]); March of Dimes Benefit,
Waldorf Astoria Hotel, New York; THREAT OF POLIO. (March of
Dimes)

1950 *Mazurka from 'A Life for the Tsar'* (Glinka/Balanchine [272]); New York
City Ballet, City Center of Music and Drama, New York; ENSEMBLE,
partnering Vida Brown.
Prodigal Son (Prokofiev/Balanchine [267]); New York City Ballet, City
Center of Music and Drama, New York; FATHER.

1952 *The Pied Piper* (Copland/Robbins); New York City Ballet, Théâtre des
Champs-Élysées?, Paris; CLARINETIST (mimed). Performed incognito.
(*Dance Magazine*, March 1960, p. 63. Balanchine)

1956 *The Concert* (Chopin/Robbins); New York City Ballet, City Center of
Music and Drama, New York; HUSBAND (mime portions).
(Reynolds, p. 172)

1958 *The Nutcracker* (Tschaikovsky/Balanchine [302]); telecast, Playhouse 90
(CBS); DROSSELMEYER. (*Dance Magazine*, March 1959, p. 15-17)

1965 *Don Quixote* (Nabokov/Balanchine [352]); New York City Ballet, New York State Theater; DON QUIXOTE. Also danced in subsequent years.

1972 *Pulcinella* (Stravinsky/Balanchine–Robbins [379]); New York City Ballet, New York State Theater; BEGGAR.

Published Sources
Full citations are given in the *Bibliography*

George Balanchine. *Complete Stories of the Great Ballets.*
Cyril Beaumont. *The Diaghilev Ballet in London.*
Tamara Geva. *Split Seconds.*
S. L. Grigoriev. *The Diaghilev Ballet, 1909-1929.*
Lincoln Kirstein. *Movement & Metaphor.*
Mikhail Mikhailov. *My Life in Ballet.*
Nancy Reynolds. *Repertory in Review.*
Yuri Slonimsky. *Balanchine: The Early Years.*
Bernard Taper. *Balanchine: A Biography.*

Unpublished Sources

Balanchine. Interviews with Nancy Reynolds, 1980, 1981.
Gusev. Pëtr Gusev, interview with Poel Karp, February 1981.
Kochno. Boris Kochno, interview with Hoyt Rogers and Harvey Simmonds, February 8, 1979.
Krasovskaya. Vera Krasovskaya, letter to Nancy Reynolds, March 13, 1980.
March of Dimes. Letter to Susan Au, March 16, 1981.
Reynolds. Dossier compiled by Nancy Reynolds.
Schüller. Dossier compiled by Gunhild Schüller.
Souritz. Letters from Elizabeth Souritz to Nancy Reynolds and Susan Summer, 1980, 1981.

BIBLIOGRAPHY

This selective bibliography provides an initial list for further study of the work of George Balanchine. Given here are Balanchine's writings, arranged chronologically; principal writings in book form about Balanchine's works and the companies with which he has been associated (including a selection from general guides to ballet), arranged alphabetically by author; and titles of the most important periodicals and newspapers consulted in the preparation of this catalogue. Annotated indexes to pertinent articles in *Era* and *Dancing Times* (London), *Dance Magazine* (New York), and the *New York Times* form part of the archives of the project, and appear in an edited form in *Ballet Review* 11:2, 3 [Spring, Summer 1983]. Among important sources for the study of Balanchine's work not here included are notes and articles in the house and souvenir programs of the companies with which he has been associated, a collection of which is included in the project archives.

I. Writings by Balanchine

BOOKS

Balanchine's Complete Stories of the Great Ballets. Edited by Francis Mason. Garden City, New York: Doubleday, 1954.

Balanchine's New Complete Stories of the Great Ballets. Edited by Francis Mason. Garden City, New York: Doubleday, 1968.

Histoire des mes ballets. Translated by Patrick Thévenon. Paris: Fayard, 1969.
Based on the 1968 *New Complete Stories of the Great Ballets*, but including only ballets choreographed by Balanchine.

101 Stories of the Great Ballets (with Francis Mason). Garden City, New York: Doubleday, 1975.
Intermediary work between the 1968 and 1977 editions of the *Complete Stories of the Great Ballets*; adds fifty-one ballets choreographed between 1968 and 1974.

Balanchine's Complete Stories of the Great Ballets (with Francis Mason). Revised and enlarged edition. Garden City, New York: Doubleday, 1977.

CONTRIBUTIONS TO BOOKS

'Marginal Notes on the Dance.' In *The Dance Has Many Faces*, edited by Walter Sorell. Cleveland/New York: World, 1951, pp. 31-40. Second

edition, revised and expanded, New York: Columbia University
    Press, 1966, pp. 93-102.
Preface to *The Classic Ballet: Basic Technique and Terminology*, by Lincoln
    Kirstein and Muriel Stuart. New York: Knopf, 1952.
Preface to *Labanotation*, by Ann Hutchinson. New York: New Directions,
    1954. Revised and expanded edition, New York: Theatre Arts, 1970.
'Ballet in America.' In *The Book of Knowledge 1955 Annual*, pp. 145-48.
    New York/Toronto: The Grolier Society, 1955.
'The Purpose of Ballet Society' and 'A Summing Up.' In *A Conference
    on Ballet—A National Movement*, pp. 9-12, 58-62. New York: Ballet
    Society, 1960.

ARTICLES

'The Non-Commissioned Officer's Widow, or How A. L. Volinsky
    Whipped Himself.' *Teatr* 13 (25 December 1923), 7.
'Dance Your Way to Health.' *Sunday Chronicle* (London), 7 July 1929.
    Excerpts reprinted in *Dancing Times* n.s. 227 (August 1929), 434-35.
'Les "Ballets 1933."' *Excelsior* (Paris), 4 June 1933.
'Ballet Goes Native.' *Dance* [East Stroudsburg, Pa.] 3:3 (December
    1934), 13.
'Dance Will Assert Its Importance.' *Dance* [East Stroudsburg, Pa.] 6:1
    (April 1939), 10.
'Ballet on Record.' *Listen* 1:4 (February 1941), 6-7.
'Balanchine Defines Dance as Visual Art.' As told to Robert Sabin.
    Musical America 64:5 (25 March 1944), 27.
'The American Dancer.' *Dance News* 4:4 (April 1944), 3, 6.
'Ballet in Films.' *Dance News* 5:4 (December 1944), 8.
'Notes on Choreography.' *Dance Index* 4:2, 3 (February-March 1945),
    20-31.
'The Dance Element in Strawinsky's Music.' In 'Strawinsky in the
    Theatre: A Symposium,' edited by Minna Lederman. *Dance Index*
    6:10, 11, 12 (October-December 1947), 250-56. Reprinted in *Stravinsky
    in the Theatre*, edited by Minna Lederman. New York: Pellegrini &
    Cudahy, 1949, pp. 75-84.
'Diaghileff and His Period.' *Dance News* 15:2 (August 1949), 6.
'Recording the Ballet.' *Dance Observer* 17:9 (November 1950), 132-33.
'Création d'un ballet' [7 October 1931]. *Revue chorégraphique de Paris*
    (May 1952), 9.

'La Peinture et la danse.' *Le Figaro* (Paris), 10-11 May 1952.

'The Met at Work: Directing a Rake.' House program, Metropolitan Opera, New York, 16 February 1953 et seq.

'George Balanchine Writes' [guest columnist, Dorothy Kilgallen's syndicated 'Voice of Broadway']. *Times-Herald* (Olean, New York), 24 June 1954.

'From There I See Patterns . . .' *Greek Theatre Magazine* (Los Angeles) 19-31 July 1954.

'Ivesiana.' *Center* 1:5 (August-September 1954), 5.

'George Platt Lynes.' Souvenir program, New York City Ballet, 1957. Reprinted in *George Platt Lynes: Photographs 1931-1955*, by Jack Woody. Los Angeles: Twelvetrees Press, 1981.

'A Word from George Balanchine.' *Playbill* (New York), 25 November 1957 et seq. Reprinted in *Dance Magazine* 32:1 (January 1958), 34-35.

'At Last: Congress Listens' (with others). *Dance Magazine* 36:2 (February 1962), 34-35.

'Balanchine Talks to Russia about His Artistic Credo.' *Dance News* 41:4 (December 1962), 5. Excerpted from *The Soviet Artist* (Moscow), October 1962.

'Now Everybody Wants to Get Into the Act.' *Life* 58 (11 June 1965), 94A-98, 100, 102.

'From Ballet into Movie: Balanchine Tells How.' *World Journal Tribune* (New York), 16 April 1967.

'La Mauvaise Musique inspire . . .' and 'La Musique de Stravinsky et la danse.' House program, Paris Opéra, 7 April 1978 et seq.

II. Books Relating to Balanchine

Amberg, George. *Ballet in America: The Emergence of an American Art.* New York: Duell, Sloan and Pearce, 1949.

Includes discussions of Balanchine's work in the chapters 'The Ballet Russe III—Americanization,' 'Lincoln Kirstein I—The Foundations,' 'Lincoln Kirstein II—The Performance,' 'The Musical Comedy.'

Anderson, Jack. *The Nutcracker Ballet.* London: Bison, 1979.

Includes a discussion of Balanchine's 1954 New York City Ballet production.

———. *The One and Only: The Ballet Russe de Monte Carlo.* Brooklyn, New York: Dance Horizons, 1981.

Includes information on Balanchine's association with and choreography for the company.

The Ballet Society 1946-1947. New York: Ballet Society, 1947.
Includes general information on Ballet Society; sections on the ballets *The Spellbound Child, The Four Temperaments, Renard,* and *Divertimento,* and on the School of American Ballet.

Barnes, Clive. *Ballet in Britain Since the War.* London: C. A. Watts, 1953.
Chapter titled 'The American Visiting Companies' includes an analysis of Balanchine's work, pp. 75-77.

Baryshnikov, Mikhail. *Baryshnikov at Work: Mikhail Baryshnikov Discusses His Roles.* Edited and introduced by Charles Engell France. With photographs by Martha Swope. New York: Knopf, 1976.
Includes a chapter on *Theme and Variations.*

Beaton, Cecil. *Ballet.* London/New York: Wingate, 1951.
Describes Balanchine's work in Europe in the early 1930s, including *Cotillon,* 'Luna Park' from the 1930 Cochran Revue, *L'Errante,* and dances for Sir Oswald Stoll's variety shows, pp. 41, 48-49, 53-55.

Beaumont, Cyril W. *Complete Book of Ballets.* London: Putnam, 1937/ New York: Grosset and Dunlap, 1938.
Includes descriptions of *The Triumph of Neptune, La Chatte, The Gods Go A-Begging, Le Fils Prodigue,* and *Cotillon,* as well as a brief biography of Balanchine and an excerpt from an interview published in *Dance Journal,* August-October 1931.

———. *Ballets of Today: Being a Second Supplement to the Complete Book of Ballets.* London: Putnam, 1954.
Includes descriptions of *Ballet Imperial, Orpheus* and *Night Shadow.*

———. *The Diaghilev Ballet in London: A Personal Record.* Third edition. London: Adam and Charles Black, 1951.
Includes descriptions of Balanchine's work for Diaghilev.

Buckle, Richard. *Buckle at the Ballet: Selected Criticism.* London: Dance Books / New York: Atheneum, 1980.
Includes reviews of New York City Ballet performances.

———. *Diaghilev.* London: Weidenfeld and Nicolson / New York: Atheneum, 1979.
Includes information on Balanchine's association with the Ballets Russes.

Chujoy, Anatole. *The New York City Ballet.* New York: Knopf, 1953.

Clarke, Mary. *The Sadler's Wells Ballet: A History and an Appreciation.* London: A. and C. Black / New York: Macmillan, 1955.
Includes a description and analysis of Balanchine's 1950 staging of *Ballet Imperial* for the company, pp. 248-50, 254.

Crisp, Clement, and Clarke, Mary. *Making a Ballet*. London: Studio Vista, 1974 / New York: Macmillan, 1975.
Includes Balanchine among the choreographers analyzed and quoted.

Croce, Arlene. *Afterimages*. New York: Knopf, 1977.
————. *Going to the Dance*. New York: Knopf, 1982.
Both include reviews of New York City Ballet performances.

Dance Index 4:2, 3 (February-March 1945): 'George Balanchine.'
Includes 'Notes on Choreography' by George Balanchine, 'Balanchine's Choreography (1930)' by Agnes de Mille, 'A Note on Balanchine's Present Style' by Edwin Denby, 'Ballets by George Balanchine,' 'Musicals with Choreography by George Balanchine,' and 'Motion Pictures with Choreography by George Balanchine'.

Deakin, Irving. *Ballet Profile*. New York: Dodge, 1936.
Chapter titled 'Georgei Melitonovitch Balanchivadze' gives a detailed biography.

Denby, Edwin. *Dancers, Buildings and People in the Streets*. New York: Horizon, 1965.
Includes reviews of New York City Ballet performances; also the articles 'Some Thoughts about Classicism and George Balanchine' and 'Balanchine Choreographing.'
————. *Looking at the Dance*. New York: Horizon, 1949.
Includes reviews of Balanchine's works for the Ballet Russe de Monte Carlo in the 1940s, the Original Ballet Russe (*Balustrade*), and the New Opera Company (*Ballet Imperial*).

Detaille, Georges, and Mulys, Gérard. *Les Ballets de Monte-Carlo 1911-1944*. Paris: Éditions Arc-en-Ciel, 1954.
Includes information about, synopses and photographs of Balanchine ballets performed in Monte Carlo by Diaghilev's Ballets Russes, the Ballets Russes de Monte-Carlo, and Ballets de Monte-Carlo (René Blum).

de Valois, Ninette. *Come Dance with Me: A Memoir, 1898-1956*. London: H. Hamilton / Cleveland/New York: World, 1957.
Describes Balanchine's first days with Diaghilev's Ballets Russes, including his teaching *Marche Funèbre* to the company, pp. 83-84.
————. *Invitation to the Ballet*. London: Bodley Head, 1937 / New York: Oxford University Press, 1938.
Includes brief comments on Balanchine's work for Diaghilev's Ballets Russes and Les Ballets 1933.
————. *Step by Step*. London: W. H. Allen, 1977.
Chapter titled 'Diaghilev' contains a brief description of Balanchine's performance as Grandfather of the Fair in *Petrushka*.

Divoire, Fernand. *Pour la danse*. Paris: Éditions de la Danse, 1935.
Describes works choreographed for Les Ballets 1933, including *Fastes, L'Errante, Les Sept Péchés Capitaux*, pp. 122-24.

Dolin, Anton. *Divertissement*. London: S. Low, Marston, 1931.
Briefly mentions Balanchine and his ballets in a description of the final years of the Diaghilev company, pp. 195, 200-201, 205-6; describes how Dolin, Balanchine and Lydia Lopokova learned of Diaghilev's death during the filming of *Dark Red Roses*, pp. 212-15.

————. *The Sleeping Ballerina: The Story of Olga Spessivtzeva*. London: Frederick Muller, 1966.
Describes her creation of the title role in *La Chatte*, pp. 46-49.

Drew, David (ed.). *The Decca Book of Ballet*. London: Frederick Muller, 1958.
Includes descriptions of many Balanchine ballets.

Duke, Vernon. *Passport to Paris*. Boston: Little, Brown, 1955.
Includes information on Balanchine's years with Diaghilev and on his musical comedy collaborations with Duke.

Franks, A. H. *Twentieth Century Ballet*. London: Burke / New York: Pitman, 1954.
Includes a chapter on Balanchine.

Geva, Tamara. *Split Seconds: A Remembrance*. New York: Harper & Row, 1972.
Describes Balanchine's life and early works in Russia, the tour of the Principal Dancers of the Russian State Ballet, work for Diaghilev's Ballets Russes, arrival in America, first performance of the American Ballet (1935), and the musical comedy *On Your Toes* (1936).

Goldner, Nancy. *The Stravinsky Festival of the New York City Ballet*. New York: Eakins, 1973.

Goldner, Nancy, and Kirstein, Lincoln. *Coppélia: New York City Ballet*. New York: Eakins, 1974.

Goode, Gerald (ed.). *The Book of Ballets: Classic and Modern*. New York: Crown, 1939.
Includes descriptions of *Le Bourgeois Gentilhomme, La Chatte, La Concurrence, Cotillon*, and *Les Dieux Mendiants*.

Grigoriev, Serge Leonidovich. *The Diaghilev Ballet 1909-1929*. Translated and edited by Vera Bowen. London: Constable, 1953. Reprinted, Harmondsworth, Middlesex: Penguin, 1960; Brooklyn, New York: Dance Horizons, 1974.
Includes information on Balanchine's association with the Ballets Russes, 1924-29.

Grigorovich, Yuri (ed.). *Balet entsiklopediĩa (Ballet Encyclopedia)*. Moscow: Sovetskaĩa entsiklopediĩa, 1981.
Includes articles on Balanchine and a number of his associates.

Gruen, John. *Erik Bruhn: Danseur Noble*. New York: Viking, 1979.
Includes a chapter describing Bruhn's season with the New York City Ballet, 1959-60, and discusses his appearances with the company in 1963.

———. *The Private World of Ballet*. New York, Viking, 1975.
Includes an interview with Balanchine (1972), and interviews with a number of his associates, and dancers of the New York City Ballet.

Guest, Ivor. *Le Ballet de l'Opéra de Paris: Trois siècles d'histoire et de tradition*. Translated by Paul Alexandre. Paris: Théâtre National de l'Opéra/Flammarion, 1976.
Includes Balanchine's works choreographed and staged for the company.

Haddakin, Edward [A. V. Coton]. *A Prejudice for Ballet*. London: Methuen, 1938.
Includes descriptions of *Cotillon* and *Aubade*, pp. 73-76, 121.

———. *Writings on Dance, 1938-68*. Selected and edited by Kathrine Sorley Walker and Lilian Haddakin. London: Dance Books, 1975.
Includes reviews of New York City Ballet performances.

Haggin, Bernard H. *Ballet Chronicle*. New York: Horizon, 1970.
Reviews from 1947 to 1970 include discussions of Balanchine's works for Ballet Theatre, Ballet Society, and the New York City Ballet.

———. *Discovering Balanchine*. New York: Horizon, 1981.
Includes biographical material and accounts of personal encounters with Balanchine in a short text accompanied by many photographs.

Hall, Fernau. *An Anatomy of Ballet*. London: A. Melrose, 1953 / New York (titled *World Dance*): A. A. Wyn, 1954.
Chapter titled 'Post-Expressionist Pseudo-Classicism' includes a section on Balanchine and a section on his companies from Les Ballets 1933 to the New York City Ballet. Briefly discusses Balanchine's work for the Ballet Russe de Monte Carlo (1944-46), pp. 416-17.

———. *Modern English Ballet: An Interpretation*. London: Andrew Melrose, 1950.
Discusses Balanchine's work for Diaghilev and his choreographic style, pp. 59, 61-62.

Haskell, Arnold L. *Balletomania: The Story of an Obsession*. London: Gollancz / New York: Simon and Schuster, 1934. Reprinted with

additional material as *Balletomania: Then and Now*, London: Weidenfeld and Nicolson / New York: Knopf, 1977.
Chapter titled 'Four Choreographers' includes a section on Balanchine.

Howard, Ruth Eleanor. *The Story of the American Ballet*. New York:
Ihra, 1936.
Discusses Balanchine's activities in founding the School of American Ballet
and leading up to the formation of the American Ballet, with a history of the
company until its association with the Metropolitan Opera. Provides lists
and brief biographies of dancers; lists of repertory and opera ballets.

Jowitt, Deborah. *Dance Beat: Selected Views and Reviews, 1967-1976*.
New York: Dekker, 1977.
Includes reviews of New York City Ballet performances.

Kameneff, Vladimir. *Russian Ballet through Russian Eyes*. London: Russian
Books and Library, 1936.
Includes brief comments on *La Chatte, Cotillon* and *La Concurrence*, pp. 21-22,
31; description of the first scene of *Apollon Musagète*, p. 33.

Kanin, Garson. *Hollywood*. New York: Viking, 1974.
Includes reminiscences of Balanchine's meetings with Samuel Goldwyn
during the filming of *The Goldwyn Follies*, pp. 108-13.

Kirstein, Lincoln. *Blast at Ballet: A Corrective for the American Audience*.
New York: Lincoln Kirstein, 1938. Reprinted in *Three Pamphlets
Collected*, Brooklyn, New York: Dance Horizons, 1967.
Includes information on Balanchine's early years in America and the activi-
ties of the American Ballet, including its association with the Metropolitan
Opera.

————. *Dance: A Short History of Classic Theatrical Dancing*. New
York: Putnam, 1935. Reprinted, Brooklyn, New York: Dance
Horizons, 1969.
Discusses Balanchine's early life in Russia, his years with Diaghilev's Ballets
Russes, his work for the Royal Danish Ballet and the Ballets Russes de
Monte-Carlo, Les Ballets 1933, and his early work in America, pp. 309-11,
314-24.

————. *Flesh Is Heir: An Historical Romance*. New York: Brewer,
Warren & Putnam, 1932. Reprinted, Carbondale and Edwardsville,
Illinois: Southern Illinois University Press, 1975.
The chapter 'Flesh Was Fair: 1929' includes a description of *Le Fils Prodigue*,
pp. 197-99.

————. 'For John Martin: Entries from an Early Diary.' *Dance
Perspectives* 54 (1973).

Describes Balanchine during the Paris and London seasons of Les Ballets 1933 and the discussions leading to his coming to America.

————. *Movement & Metaphor: Four Centuries of Ballet*. New York: Praeger, 1970.

Includes chapters on *Apollon Musagète, Orpheus* and *Agon*.

————. *The New York City Ballet*. With photographs by George Platt Lynes and Martha Swope. New York: Knopf, 1973.

————. *Thirty Years: Lincoln Kirstein's The New York City Ballet*. New York: Knopf, 1978.

Text of the 1973 publication (without photographs) expanded to cover the period through 1978.

————. *Union Jack: The New York City Ballet*. New York: Eakins, 1977.

Kochno, Boris. *Diaghilev and the Ballets Russes*. New York: Harper & Row, 1970. (*Diaghilev et les Ballets Russes*. Paris: Fayard, 1973.)

Includes discussions of Balanchine's works for the company.

Kochno, Boris, and Luz, Maria. *Le Ballet*. Paris: Hachette, 1954.

Discusses Balanchine's ballets for Diaghilev, pp. 265-81; for the Ballets Russes de Monte-Carlo, pp. 293-98; for Les Ballets 1933, pp. 300-301; and for the Paris Opéra in 1947, pp. 338-39.

Koegler, Horst. *Balanchine und das moderne Ballett*. Velber bei Hannover: Friedrich, 1964.

Krokover, Rosalyn. *The New Borzoi Book of Ballets*. New York: Knopf, 1956.

Includes descriptions of many Balanchine ballets.

Lawrence, Robert. *The Victor Book of Ballets and Ballet Music*. New York: Simon and Schuster, 1950.

Includes descriptions of many Balanchine ballets.

Lawson, Joan. *A History of Ballet and Its Makers*. London: Pitman, 1964.

Includes sections on 'George Balanchine and the Neo-classical Ballet' (covering his work for Diaghilev) and 'George Balanchine and the Neo-classical Ballet in America.'

Levinson, André. *La Danse d'aujourd'hui: Études—Notes—Portraits*. Paris: Éditions Duchartre et Van Buggenhoudt, 1929.

Discusses Balanchine's work for Diaghilev in the chapter 'Grandeur et décadence des "Ballets Russes"'; *Le Chant du Rossignol* and *Apollon Musagète* are also discussed in the chapter 'Stravinsky et la danse théâtrale.'

————. *Les Visages de la danse*. Paris: Éditions Bernard Grasset, 1933.

Includes chapters on 'Derniers ballets de Diaghilew'; '"Les Ballets Nemtchinova" (1928-1930)' (*Aubade*, pp. 62-63); 'Georges Balanchine à

Mogador: Offenbach et Les Ballets Russes d'*Orphée aux Enfers*'; 'Les Ballets Russes de Monte-Carlo (1re saison 1932)' (*Cotillon, La Concurrence, Le Bourgeois Gentilhomme*, pp. 70-76); 'Les Ballets 1933 de Georges Balanchine.'

Lifar, Serge. *Histoire du ballet russe depuis les origines jusqu'à nos jours*. Paris: Éditions Nagel, 1950. (*A History of Russian Ballet from Its Origins to the Present Day*. Translated by Arnold L. Haskell. London: Hutchinson, 1954.)
Discusses Balanchine's work for Diaghilev's Ballets Russes, pp. 265-69, 273-75; and in the 1930s, p. 282 (London edition).

———. *Serge Diaghilev: His Life, His Work, His Legend*. New York: Putnam, 1940. (*Serge de Diaghilew, sa vie, son oeuvre, sa légende*. Monaco: Éditions du Rocher, 1954.)
Includes a section on 'Balanchine as Choreographer'; also discusses roles danced by Lifar in Balanchine ballets.

Lopukhov, Fëdor. *Puti baletmeĭstera* (*Paths of a Ballet Master*). Berlin: Petropolis, 1925.

———. *Shes'desi̅at let v balete: Vospominani̅ia i zapiski baletmeĭstera* (*Sixty Years in Ballet: A Balletmaster's Notes and Memoirs*). Moscow: Iskusstvo, 1966.
Lopukhov's works provide background information on ballet in Russia in the early twentieth century.

Macdonald, Nesta. *Diaghilev Observed by Critics in England and the United States 1911-1929*. Brooklyn, New York: Dance Horizons / London: Dance Books, 1975.
Includes reviews of Balanchine's works for Diaghilev from 1926.

Martin, John. *World Book of Modern Ballet*. Cleveland/New York: World, 1952.
Includes chapters titled 'Balanchine Discovers America' (1933-41) and 'America Discovers Balanchine' (1946-52).

Maynard, Olga. *The American Ballet*. Philadelphia: MacRae Smith, 1959.
Includes sections on 'George Balanchine,' 'Balanchine's American Ballet and Kirstein's Ballet Caravan,' 'Ballet Society,' 'The New York City Ballet,' and 'The School of American Ballet.'

Mazo, Joseph H. *Dance Is a Contact Sport*. New York: Saturday Review Press/Dutton, 1974.
Account of a season (1973) spent with the New York City Ballet.

Merlin, Olivier. *Stravinsky*. Paris: Hachette, 1968.
Includes an interview with Balanchine on *Agon* and the approaching New York City Ballet tour of the Soviet Union (1962).

Michaut, Pierre. *Le Ballet contemporain 1929-1950*. Paris: Librairie Plon, 1950.

Discusses Balanchine's work for Diaghilev, pp. 2-3; the unfinished *Créatures de Prométhée*, pp. 37-41; his work for the Ballets Russes de Monte-Carlo, pp. 66-75; for Les Ballets 1933, pp. 103-8; for the Grand Ballet du Marquis de Cuevas, pp. 341-43; for the Paris Opéra in 1947, pp. 352-59.

Mikhailov, Mikhail. *Zhizn' v balete* (*My Life in Ballet*). Leningrad: Iskusstvo, 1966.

Excerpts from Chapter 2 published as 'My Classmate: Georges Balanchivadze' in *Dance News* 50:3, 4, 5 (March, April, May 1967), 12, 6, 8-9.

Minnelli, Vincente, and Arce, Hector. *I Remember It Well*. Garden City, New York: Doubleday, 1974.

Includes a description of Balanchine's choreography for the 'Words without Music' ballet in the 1936 Ziegfeld Follies, p. 79.

Moore, Lillian. *Artists of the Dance*. New York: Thomas Y. Crowell, 1938. Reprinted, Brooklyn, New York: Dance Horizons, 1969.

Chapter titled 'George Balanchine' gives his biography to 1937.

———. *Echoes of American Ballet*. Edited and introduced by Ivor Guest. Brooklyn, New York: Dance Horizons, 1976.

Chapter titled 'The Metropolitan Opera Ballet, 1883-1951' includes a brief discussion of Balanchine's work for that company.

Nabokov, Nicolas. *Old Friends and New Music*. Boston: Little, Brown, 1951.

Chapter titled 'Ode' includes mentions of Balanchine during his years with Diaghilev's Ballets Russes and briefly describes a rehearsal of *Apollon Musagète*. Chapters titled 'Christmas with Stravinsky' and 'Stravinsky in Hollywood' describe a visit made by the author, Balanchine and Maria Tallchief at the time of the composition of *Orpheus* (1947).

Newman, Barbara. *Striking a Balance: Dancers Talk about Dancing*. Boston: Houghton Mifflin, 1982.

Includes interviews with Felia Doubrovska, Serge Lifar, Lew Christensen, Tanaquil Le Clercq, Desmond Kelly, Jean-Pierre Bonnefous, Peter Martins, Merrill Ashley, and others, with commentary on the performance of roles in the Balanchine repertory.

Nikitina, Alice. *Nikitina, by Herself*. Translated by Baroness Budberg. London: Allan Wingate, 1959.

Includes descriptions of her participation in Balanchine's ballets for Diaghilev's Ballets Russes (*Barabau, La Chatte, Apollon Musagète, Le Bal*), Cochran's 1930 Revue ('Luna Park,' Tschaikovsky pas de deux), and her own 1932 recital in Paris.

Palmer, Winthrop. *Theatrical Dancing in America: The Development of the Ballet from 1900.* Second edition, revised. South Brunswick, New Jersey: A. S. Barnes / London: Thomas Yoseloff, 1978.
Includes sections on 'The Abstract Ballets of George Balanchine after 1945' and 'The Repertoire of New York City Ballet'; chapter on 'Lincoln Kirstein's "American Ballet."'

Payne, Charles, et al. *American Ballet Theatre.* New York: Knopf, 1978.
Includes information on works choreographed by Balanchine for the company.

Propert, Walter Archibald. *The Russian Ballet 1921-1929.* London: Bodley Head, 1931 / New York: Greenberg, 1932.
Includes discussions of Balanchine's works for Diaghilev's Ballets Russes.

Rebling, Eberhard. *Ballett A-Z: Ein Führer durch die Welt des Balletts.* Third edition. Wilhelmshaven: Heinrichsofen's Verlag, 1977.
Includes descriptions of *Agon, The Card Party, The Four Temperaments, Orpheus, Prodigal Son,* and *The Seven Deadly Sins.*

Regner, Otto Friedrich, and Schneiders, Heinz-Ludwig. *Reclams Ballettführer.* Fifth edition, completely revised. Stuttgart: Reclam, 1972.
Includes descriptions of many Balanchine ballets.

Reynolds, Nancy. *Repertory in Review: Forty Years of the New York City Ballet.* New York: Dial, 1977.

Reynolds, Nancy, and Reimer-Torn, Susan. *In Performance: A Companion to the Classics of the Dance.* New York: Harmony, 1980.
Includes a chapter on Balanchine and the ballets *Apollo, Serenade, Concerto Barocco, The Four Temperaments, Pas de Dix, Agon,* and *Star and Stripes.*

Riobó, Julio F., and Cucullu, Carlos. *El Arte del ballet en el Teatro Colón.* Buenos Aires: Corletta & Castro, 1945.
Includes discussions of *Apollon Musagète* and *Concierto de Mozart.*

Robert, Grace. *The Borzoi Book of Ballets.* New York: Knopf, 1946.
Includes descriptions of *Apollon Musagète, Le Baiser de la Fée, Ballet Imperial, Danses Concertantes, Waltz Academy*; also discusses *Prodigal Son.*

Roslavleva, Natalia. *Era of the Russian Ballet.* London: Gollancz / New York: Dutton, 1966.
Provides background information on ballet in the Soviet Union in the 1920s.

Schaïkevitch, André. *Olga Spessivtzeva, magicienne envoutée.* Paris: Librairie les Lettres, 1954.
Includes discussions of *La Chatte,* pp. 87-90; *Les Créatures de Prométhée,* pp. 98-99.

Sharaff, Irene. *Broadway and Hollywood: Costumes Designed by Irene Sharaff.* New York: Van Nostrand Reinhold, 1976.
Includes a description of the 1936 production of *On Your Toes*, pp. 30, 33.

Siegel, Marcia B. *At the Vanishing Point: A Critic Looks at Dance.* New York: Saturday Review Press, 1972.
The section 'Balanchine's America' includes reviews of New York City Ballet performances.

———. *The Shapes of Change: Images of American Dance.* Boston: Houghton Mifflin, 1979.
The chapter 'Neoclassicism I' includes discussions of *Serenade* and *Concerto Barocco*; the chapter 'Balanchine's America' discusses *The Four Temperaments*, *Ivesiana*, *Agon*, and *Episodes*.

———. *Watching the Dance Go By.* Boston: Houghton Mifflin, 1977.
Includes reviews of New York City Ballet performances.

Slonimsky, Yuri. 'Balanchine: The Early Years.' Translated by John Andrews. Edited by Francis Mason. *Ballet Review* 5:3 (1975-76).

Smakov, Gennady. *Baryshnikov: From Russia to the West.* New York: Farrar, Straus & Giroux, 1981.
Includes a chapter titled 'With Balanchine and Robbins.'

Sokolova, Lydia. *Dancing for Diaghilev: The Memoirs of Lydia Sokolova.* Edited by Richard Buckle. London: Murray, 1960 / New York: Macmillan, 1961.
Includes descriptions of ballets choreographed by Balanchine for the Ballets Russes.

Souritz, Elizabeth J. *Khoregraficheskoe iskusstvo dvadtsatykh godov: Tendentsii, razvitiia (Choreographic Art of the Twenties: Tendencies, Developments).* Moscow: Iskusstvo, 1979.
Includes a discussion of Balanchine's work, pp. 64-71.

Stokes, Adrian. *Russian Ballets.* London: Faber & Faber, 1935.
Includes descriptions of *Cotillon* and *La Concurrence*, with an analysis of Balanchine's choreographic style, pp. 184-96.

Stravinsky, Igor. *Chroniques de ma vie.* Paris: De Noël et Steele, 1935. (*Chronicles of My Life.* London: Gollancz, 1936. *An Autobiography.* New York: Simon and Schuster, 1936; reprinted, New York: Norton, 1962.)
Includes a description of the composition of the score and Balanchine's choreography for *Apollon Musagète*, pp. 210-15, 224-27 (New York edition).

———. *Selected Correspondence*, Volume I. Edited and with commentaries by Robert Craft. New York: Knopf, 1982.
Includes 'Correspondence with Lincoln Kirstein, 1946-1966,' pp. 263-95.

Stravinsky, Igor, and Craft, Robert. *Dialogues and a Diary*. Garden City, New York: Doubleday, 1963.
Includes a section on *Apollo*, pp. 16-20, and working notes for Stravinsky's collaboration with Balanchine on *The Flood*, pp. 89-98.

———. *Themes and Episodes*. New York: Knopf, 1966.
Section titled 'Eye Music' discusses Balanchine's *Movements for Piano and Orchestra*; Balanchine's choreography is also discussed in sections on '*Jeu de Cartes*,' '*Danses Concertantes*,' and '*Orpheus*.'

Stravinsky, Vera, and Craft, Robert. *Stravinsky in Pictures and Documents*. New York: Simon and Schuster, 1978.
Includes information on collaborations with Balanchine.

Stravinsky and the Dance: A Survey of Ballet Productions, 1910-1962, in Honor of the Eightieth Birthday of Igor Stravinsky. Catalogue by Selma Jeanne Cohen, with an introduction by Herbert Read. New York: Dance Collection of The New York Public Library, 1962.
Includes ballets choreographed by Balanchine.

Stravinsky and the Theatre: A Catalogue of Decor and Costume Designs for Stage Productions of His Works 1910-1962. New York: Dance Collection of The New York Public Library, 1963.
Includes designs for ballets choreographed by Balanchine.

Swope, Martha. *A Midsummer Night's Dream: The Story of the New York City Ballet's Production Told in Photographs by Martha Swope*. Edited by Nancy Lassalle, with an introduction by Lincoln Kirstein. New York: Dodd, Mead, 1977.

———. *The Nutcracker: The Story of the New York City Ballet's Production Told in Pictures by Martha Swope*. Edited by Nancy Lassalle, with an introduction by Lincoln Kirstein. New York: Dodd, Mead, 1975.

Taper, Bernard. *Balanchine: A Biography*. Revised and updated edition. New York: Macmillan / London: Collier Macmillan, 1974.

Terry, Walter. *Ballet Guide*. New York: Dodd, Mead, 1976.
Includes descriptions of many Balanchine ballets.

———. *I Was There: Selected Dance Reviews and Articles 1936-1976*. Compiled and edited by Andrew Mark Wentink. New York: Dekker, 1978.

344

Includes reviews of Balanchine's works for Ballet Society, the New York City Ballet, the Original Ballet Russe (*Balustrade*), Ballet Theatre, and in musical comedy.

Twysden, Aileen Elizabeth. *Alexandra Danilova*. London: Beaumont, 1945 / New York: Kamin, 1947.
Describes Balanchine and his ballets in the Soviet Union in the 1920s, on tour with the Principal Dancers of the Russian State Ballet, with Diaghilev's Ballets Russes, and with the Ballet Russe de Monte Carlo. Provides an analysis of his choreography and Danilova's influence on it, pp. 86-87. Chapter titled 'Favourite Ballets' includes descriptions of *Les Dieux Mendiants* (*The Gods Go A-Begging*) and *Le Baiser de la Fée*.

Tyler, Parker. *The Divine Comedy of Pavel Tchelitchew: A Biography*. New York: Fleet, 1967.
Includes discussions of Balanchine's *L'Errante* (1933 version), *Magic*, *Orpheus*, *Balustrade*, and *Concerto*, pp. 353-68, 383-84, 385-87, 437, 442.

Vaillat, Léandre. *La Danse à l'Opéra de Paris*. Paris: Amiot-Dumont, 1951.
Includes a discussion of Balanchine's work as guest ballet master at the Opéra in 1947 in chapters titled 'M. Balanchine à l'Opéra,' 'Sérénade,' 'Apollon Musagète,' 'Le Baiser de la Fée,' and 'Le Palais de Cristal.'

Walker, Kathrine Sorley. *De Basil's Ballets Russes*. London: Hutchinson, 1982.
Includes information on Balanchine's work for the de Basil companies.

Ware, Walter. *Ballet Is Magic: A Triple Monograph—Harriet Hoctor, Paul Haakon, Patricia Bowman*. New York: Ihra, 1936.
Includes a description of 'Night Flight' from the Ziegfeld Follies of 1936 in the monograph on Hoctor, pp. 1-3.

Wentink, Andrew Mark. *The Steadfast Tin Soldier: The Story of George Balanchine's New York City Ballet Production, Told in Photographs by Steven Caras*. Brooklyn, New York: Dance Horizons, 1981.

White, Eric Walter. *Stravinsky: The Composer and His Works*. Second edition. Berkeley and Los Angeles: University of California Press, 1979.
Includes discussions of Balanchine's choreography to Stravinsky scores.

Williamson, Audrey. *Ballet of Three Decades*. London: Rockcliff / New York: Macmillan, 1958.
Includes comments on Balanchine's works for the Grand Ballet du Marquis de Cuevas (*La Sonnambula*), New York City Ballet, and Sadler's Wells Ballet (*Ballet Imperial*), pp. 113, 116-20, 170-71.

———. *Ballet Renaissance*. London: Golden Gallery / New York: Transatlantic Arts, 1948.

> Includes comments on Balanchine's works for Ballet Theatre (*Waltz Academy, Apollo*), p. 81.

III. Principal Periodicals and Newspapers Consulted

Dance Magazine (New York)
Dancing Times (London)
Era (London)
Evhenedel'nik akademicheskikh teatrov (Petrograd/Leningrad)
Krasnaya gazeta (Leningrad)
New York Herald Tribune
New York Times
Teatr (Leningrad)
Teatr i iskusstvo (Petrograd)
Theatre Arts (New York)
Variety (New York)
Zhizn' iskusstva (St. Petersburg/Petrograd)

INDEXES

Numbers refer to Catalogue entries

TITLES BY CATEGORY

KEY TO COMPANIES
STAGING BALANCHINE WORKS

United States

Alabama (State of Alabama Ballet)

American Ballet (1935-38; resident Metropolitan Opera company as American
Ballet Ensemble; see also New York City Ballet)

American Ballet Caravan (see also New York City Ballet)

American Ballet Ensemble (1935-38; see also New York City Ballet)

American Ballet Theatre (see also Ballet Theatre)

American Concert Ballet

American Festival Ballet Company (Idaho)

American Shakespeare Festival (Connecticut)

Arizona Ballet Theatre (disbanded)

Atlanta Ballet (until 1968 known as Atlanta Civic Ballet)

Augusta Ballet (Georgia)

Ballet Borealis (Minnesota; now called Andahazy Ballet Company)

Ballet International (de Cuevas company, 1944-45; see also *Other Countries*:
de Cuevas)

Ballet la Jeunesse (Los Angeles)

Ballet Metropolitan (Ohio)

Ballet of Los Angeles (1964-67; also called Western Ballet)

Ballet Oklahoma

Ballet Russe de Monte Carlo (1938-62; in North America from 1939)

Ballet Russe Highlights (Massine company, 1945-47)

Ballet Society (1946-48; see also New York City Ballet)

Ballet Theatre (in 1957 became American Ballet Theatre)

Ballet West (see also Utah Civic Ballet)

Baltimore Ballet (see also Maryland Ballet)

Berkshire Ballet (Massachusetts)

Bernhard Ballet (Connecticut)

Boston Ballet (see also New England Civic Ballet)

Chicago Ballet

Chicago City Ballet (see also Chicago Lyric Opera Ballet)

Chicago Lyric Opera

Chicago Lyric Opera Ballet (in 1980 separated from Chicago Lyric Opera to
form Chicago City Ballet)

Cincinnati Ballet Company

City Center Light Opera (New York City, 1954-68)

New York City Ballet (see also American Ballet, American Ballet Caravan,
     American Ballet Ensemble, Ballet Society, Producing Company of the
     School of American Ballet)
New York City Opera (City Center Opera, 1943-66; New York City Opera,
     from 1966)
New York Dance Theatre
Newburgh Ballet (New York)
North Carolina Dance Theatre
Nureyev and Friends
Ohio Ballet
Oklahoma City Ballet
Pacific Northwest Dance Theatre (Seattle, Washington; in 1980 became Pacific
     Northwest Ballet)
Pennsylvania Ballet
Pittsburgh Ballet Theatre
Prince George's Ballet (Maryland; disbanded)
Princeton Ballet (New Jersey)
Producing Company of the School of American Ballet (1934; see also New
     York City Ballet)
Richmond Ballet (Virginia)
Ringling Brothers and Barnum & Bailey Circus
San Diego Ballet
San Francisco Ballet
San Francisco Civic Light Opera
San Juan (Ballets de San Juan, Puerto Rico)
Second International Dance Festival (Second North American International
     Dance Festival of Stars, Chicago, 1978)
Stars of American Ballet (disbanded)
Syracuse Ballet Theatre (disbanded)
Toledo Ballet (Ohio)
Tulsa Ballet Theatre
U. S. Terpsichore (New York City)
Utah Civic Ballet (in 1967 became Ballet West)
Washington Ballet (Washington, D. C.)
Wisconsin Ballet

Other Countries

Alberta Ballet Company (Canada)
Anton Dolin with Anna Ludmila and Company (1929)
Australian Ballet

Florence (Teatro Comunale [Ballet])
Frankfurt (Ballett der Städtischen Bühnen)
Geneva (Grand Théâtre de Genève [Ballet])
Geneva (Grand Théâtre de Genève [Opera])
Gothenburg (Stora Teaterns Balett, Sweden)
Grand Ballet Classique de France
Les Grands Ballets Canadiens (Montreal)
Hamburg (Ballett der Hamburgischen Staatsoper)
Hamburg (Hamburgische Staatsoper)
Hungary (State Opera Ballet, Magyar Allami Operahaz)
Iran (Iranian National Ballet; disbanded)
Israel Ballet (also known as Israel Classical Ballet)
Kirov Ballet (Leningrad; see also State Theater of Opera and Ballet)
La Plata (Teatro Argentino [Ballet])
London Festival Ballet
Maly Opera Theater (Petrograd)
Matsuyama Ballet Company (Japan)
Mexico (Ballet Clásico de Mexico, renamed Compañía Nacional de Danza)
Mexico (Ópera Nacional, Palacio de Bellas Artes)
Monte Carlo (Opéra de Monte-Carlo)
Monte Carlo (Théâtre de Monte-Carlo)
Munich (Ballett der Bayerischen Staatsoper)
Naples (Teatro San Carlo [Ballet])
National Ballet of Canada (Toronto)
Netherlands Ballet (Het Nederlands Ballet; in 1961 merged with Amsterdam
    Ballet to form Dutch National Ballet)
New Zealand Ballet
Norway (Den Norske Opera [Ballet])
Noverre Ballet (Stuttgart, 1971-73)
Original Ballet Russe (see also Ballets Russes de Monte-Carlo)
Palermo (Teatro Massimo [Ballet])
Paris (Théâtre National de l'Opéra)
Paris (Théâtre National de l'Opéra [Ballet])
Pavlova Company (1913-31)
Petrograd Drama Theater
Philippines (Cultural Center of the Philippines Dance Company; now also
    called Ballet Philippines)
Principal Dancers of the Russian State Ballet (1924)
Reggio Emilia (A.T.E.R., Associazione Teatri Emilia-Romagna [Ballet])
Rio de Janeiro (Teatro Municipal [Ballet])
Rome Opera Ballet (Teatro dell'Opera di Roma [Ballet])

GENERAL INDEX

Catalogue entry titles appear in small capitals

Moussorgsky, Modest, 31, 43, 54, 97, 208, 218, 298, 388

Mouveau, 96

MOVEMENTS FOR PIANO AND ORCHESTRA (Stravinsky), 334, 344

Moxzer, Jieno, 190

Moylan, Mary Ellen, 203, 206, 220, 221, 236, 238, 239

Mozart, Wolfgang Amadeus, 81, 134, 149, 157, 164, 181, 205, 231, 241, 251, 253, 274, 286, 311, 313, 314, 417

Mozart Festival, see American Shakespeare Festival Mozart Festival

MOZARTIANA (Tschaikovsky), 134, 149, 286, 417

Mravinsky, Evgeny, 8

Muelle, Jules, see La Maison Jules Muelle

Mullowny, Kathryn, 141, 142, 144, 145, 153, 154, 160, 165, 173, 174, 178

Mungalova, Olga, 1, 7, 8, 16, 19, 29

Munich (Ballett der Bayerischen Staatsoper), 84, 141, 195, 236, 240, 288, 314

Muratore, Lucien, 109

EL MURCIÉLAGO (J. Strauss II), see THE BAT

Murray, Honey, 217

Murray, Wynn, 175, 183, 201

MUSIC AND DANCE, 274

Music at Work, 203

A MUSICAL JOKE (Mozart), 313

Musil, Karl, 367

Musser, Tharon, 319, 325, 326

Muszely, Melitta, 341

Muti, Nuccy, 299

Nabokov, Nicolas, 139, 352

Naples (Teatro San Carlo [Ballet]), 194

Nathan, H. & L., Ltd., see H. & L. Nathan, Ltd.

National Academy Ballet (Illinois), 309

National Ballet (Washington, D. C.), 94, 141, 195, 232, 233, 236, 273

National Ballet of Canada (Toronto), 141, 195, 236

National Ballet of Illinois, see National Academy Ballet

National Broadcasting Company, see NBC

National Orchestral Society, 230, 241, 245, 274

National Theater Company, see Belgrade (National Theater Company, Balet Narodno Pozorište)

Het Nationale Ballet, Amsterdam, see Dutch National Ballet

NATIVE DANCERS (Rieti), 323

Nault, Fernand, 242, 259

NBC (National Broadcasting Company), 84, 195, 232, 236, 247, 264, 273, 282, 285, 288, 291, 294, 302, 311, 312, 315, 316, 318, 324, 331, 333, 347, 351, 358, 359, 361, 368

NBC Opera Theatre, 311

Neary, Colleen, 382, 384, 387, 390, 395, 408, 409

Neary, Patricia, 339, 349, 352, 358, 367

Het Nederlands Ballet, see Netherlands Ballet

Negro Debutante Ball, 296

Neher, Caspar Rudolph, 136

Nellemose, Kirsten, 103

Nemtchinova, Vera, 41, 44, 98

Netherlands, 269

Netherlands Ballet, 141, 195, 232, 236; see also Dutch National Ballet

Neu, Thea, 319

New Amsterdam News, 296

New Group, see Royal Ballet Touring company

New England Civic Ballet, 288, 309; see also Boston Ballet

New Jersey Ballet (West Orange), 247, 318, 331, 333, 366

New Opera Company (New York City), 194, 206-211, 216

New York City Ballet, 48, 84, 94, 107, 129, 132, 134, 136, 141, 170, 177, 178,

397

ACKNOWLEDGMENTS

The preparation and publication of *Choreography by George Balanchine* has been made possible by grants from Gillian Attfield, Ballet Society, Mr. and Mrs. Sid R. Bass, the Doll Foundation, the Eakins Press Foundation, the Ford Foundation, the Lassalle Fund, Earle I. Mack, the National Endowment for the Arts, Mr. and Mrs. Henry Paschen, Frances Schreuder, and the Wallace Fund.

From its beginning the project has been considered a collaborative effort. Mr. Balanchine's personal participation has been vital. Special thanks are due Barbara Horgan and Edward Bigelow of the New York City Ballet. Mrs. Mark Schorer made available the results of research toward a biography of Balanchine, and has served as valued consultant. Important assistance has been given by the following (and often in the case of persons with institutional associations, their staffs): Barbara J. Allen (Consulate General of the United States of America, Leningrad), Jacques d'Amboise, Peter Anastos, Leda Anchutina, Sergio Mascareñas del Angel (Instituto Nacional de Bellas Artes, Mexico City), Bene Arnold, Karin von Aroldingen, Dame Sonia Arova, Erik Aschengreen, Suzanne Aubert (Grand Théâtre de Genève), Daniel Aubry (Archives, Opéra de Monte-Carlo), Georges Auric, Irina Baronova, Ann Barzel, Nicole Beauséjour (RM Productions, Munich), Marika Besobrasova, Gordon Boelzner, Todd Bolender, Ruthanna Boris, Vida Brown, Kirk Browning, Richard Buckle, Gage Bush, Miguel Cabrera, Alfonso Catá, Yvonne Chouteau, Lew Christensen, Marie-Françoise Christout (Bibliothèque de l'Arsenal, Paris), Mary Clarke, Heinz Clauss, John Clifford, Selma Jeanne Cohen, Roberta Cooper (American Shakespeare Festival, Stratford, Connecticut), Mari Cornell, Fred Danieli, David Daniels, Alexandra Danilova, Karen Davidov, Kensington Davison, Roxanna Deane (Martin Luther King Memorial Library, Washington, D.C.), Carole Deschamps, Fernand Detaille, Deutsche Oper am Rhein (Berlin), Charles Dickson, Anton Dolin, William Dollar, Felia Doubrovska, Paul Draper, Lucille Duncan (Center for Inter-American Relations, New York), Katherine Dunham, Rosemary Dunleavy,

Marina Eglevsky, Richard Englund, Antonio José Faró, Olga Ferri, Enzo Valenti Ferro (Teatro Colón, Buenos Aires), Charles France, Frederic Franklin, Julia Gade, Beth Genné, Tamara Geva, Nancy Goldner, Solange Golovine, Edward Gorey, Susan Gould, Margaret Graham, Natasha Gregorova, Robert Greskovic, Nicolas Grimaldi (National Association for Regional Ballet), Ivor Guest, Pëtr Gusev, Marianna Hallar (Library of the Royal Theater, Copenhagen), Carolyn Harden (Theatre Museum, London), Camille Hardy, Russell Hartley (San Francisco Archives for the Performing Arts), Henley Haslam, Baird Hastings, Melissa Hayden, Susan Hendl, Laurie Horn, Marian Horosko, Olga and André von Hoyer, Merle Hubbard, Heinrich Huesmann (Theatermuseum, Munich), David Huntley (Boosey & Hawkes, Inc.), Robert Irving, George Jackson, Jillana, Robert Joffrey, Clark Jones, Martine Kahane (Bibliothèque et Musée de l'Opéra, Paris), Una Kai, Poel Karp, Tibor Katona (Orchestre National de Monte-Carlo), Allegra Kent, William P. Kiehl (United States International Communications Agency), Lincoln Kirstein, Anna Kisselgoff, Boris Kochno, Horst Koegler, Gabriella Komleva, Bernard L. Koten, Svend Kragh-Jacobsen, Nadia Lacoste (Centre de Presse, Principauté de Monaco), Moscelyne Larkin, Niels Bjørn Larsen, Juan Ubaldo Lavanga, George Laws, Tanaquil Le Clercq, Sara Leland, Tatiana Leskova, Library of Congress Newspaper Annex, Rolf Liebermann, Michael Lland, Lady Lousada, Conrad Ludlow, Pamela Lumsden (Library of the Garrick Club, London), Annabelle Lyon, Shona Dunlop MacTavish, Patricia McBride, Don McDonagh, Martha Mahard (Harvard Theatre Collection), John E. Malmstad (Department of Slavic Languages, Columbia University), Raymond Mander and Joseph Mitchenson (Mander and Mitchenson Collection, London), Giora Manor, Marie-Jeanne, Dame Alicia Markova, Francis Mason, Carlos Heria Massardo (Teatro Municipal, Santiago, Chile), Larry Miller, Arthur Mitchell, Yvonne Mounsey, John Mueller (Dance Film Archives, University of Rochester), Betty June Myers, Colleen Neary, Patricia Neary, Vera Nemtchinova, Barbara Newman, Jack L. Noordhorn (Columbia University Libraries), Frank Ohman, Arbie Orenstein, Genevieve Oswald (The New York Public Library Dance Collection), Ruth Page, Susan Pilarre, Freda Pitt, Richard Ploch

(Library of the Dance Notation Bureau, New York), Nina Popova,
Ulla Poulsen, Ali Pourfarrokh, Denise Prézeau (Canadian Broadcasting
Corporation), Børge Ralov, Dame Marie Rambert, Jack Reed,
Janet Reed, Susan Reimer-Torn, Karl Reuling, Rupert Rhymes
(London Coliseum), Vittorio Rieti, Claire Robilant (Library, London
School of Contemporary Dance), Raúl Roger, Francis Rosset (Société
des Bains de Mer, Monte Carlo), Francia Russell, Richard Temple
Savage (Music Library, Royal Opera House, London), Jorgen Schiott,
Suki Schorer, Betty Scorer, Joysanne Sidimus, Jill Silverman, Victoria
Simon, George Skibine, Boris Skidelsky (Royal Opera House
Archives, London), David R. Smith (Walt Disney Archives, Burbank,
California), Arkadi Sokolow (Leningrad State Institute of Theater,
Music and Cinematography), Zachary Solov, Doris Sonne, Marco
Sorgetti, Mary Stuart (Slavic and East European Department,
University of Illinois at Urbana-Champaign), Mark E. Swartz (Harvard
Theatre Collection), Kay Swift, Nikita Talin, Maria Tallchief, Marjorie
Tallchief, John Taras, Alberto Testa, Brigitte Thom, Giampiero Tintori
(Museo Teatrale, La Scala, Milan), Roy Tobias, Rojelio Tristam (Argentine
Consulate, New York), Alexander Trubizin, Hilda Soto U (Archivo
Municipal de Ballet, Santiago, Chile), Dame Ninette de Valois, David
Vaughan, Violette Verdy, Celida Parera Villalon, Edward Villella,
Lynn Visson, Kathrine Sorley Walker, Barbara Weisberger, Andrew
Mark Wentink, Joachim Wenzel (Hamburgische Staatsoper), Elaine
Whitelaw (March of Dimes, White Plains, New York), Patricia Wilde,
Roland John Wiley (School of Music, University of Michigan),
E. Virginia Williams, Joseph Wishey, Sarah Woodcock (Theatre
Museum, London), Rochelle Zide-Booth, Vera Zorina, and the
artistic directors, administrators and archivists who assisted in
establishing the record of stagings. The final quatrain of Gide's
Perséphone has been translated by Richard Wilbur.

The manuscript of this *Catalogue* was read with essential corrective
attention by Edward Bigelow, Gordon Boelzner, Betty Cage, Lew
Christensen, Arlene Croce, Rosemary Dunleavy, Nancy Goldner,
Barbara Horgan, Robert Irving, Lincoln Kirstein, Anna Kisselgoff, Boris
Kochno, Deborah Koolish, Tanaquil Le Clercq, John Martin, Francis
Mason, Ruth Schorer, John Taras, David Vaughan, and Henry Wisneski.

Printed from Monotype Dante by letterpress
at the Stamperia Valdonega in Verona, Italy.
First edition 2000 copies
JANUARY 1983